Metagrammar

Erik Camayd-Freixas

Metagrammar

Critical Thinking and Problem Solving in the Age of Artificial Intelligence

palgrave
macmillan

Erik Camayd-Freixas
Department of Modern Languages
Florida International University
Miami, FL, USA

ISBN 978-3-031-92336-4 ISBN 978-3-031-92337-1 (eBook)
https://doi.org/10.1007/978-3-031-92337-1

Cover credit: Serg Myshkovsky/GettyImages

This Palgrave Macmillan imprint is published by the registered company Springer Nature Switzerland AG
The registered company address is: Gewerbestrasse 11, 6330 Cham, Switzerland

In the beginning was the word.

John 1:1

To Joy

Preface

What if there were a method, a model of reasoning that could power our thoughts and actions in our personal and professional life? That is exactly what this book is about. Metagrammar is a new practical way of critical thinking based on my theory that grammar contains a complete blueprint for the way we experience the world, our *reading* and understanding of natural and social processes, as well as all the solutions, behaviours and designs with which we *write* our imprint on the world. This book explains the theory of metagrammar in an accessible language, how to harness, develop and apply it to personal concerns, different fields, current affairs and pressing social problems in an age when judgement is clouded by disinformation, and human agency is being replaced by the functions of machine learning, artificial intelligence and other emerging technologies.

Grammar applies only as far as the sentence. Period. Everything beyond the sentence is *beyond* grammar, that is, it belongs to the domain of *meta*-grammar, a form of organisation modelled on the grammar of the natural languages that we speak. When people talk about the 'logic' of different things, they in fact mean their metagrammar. This applies to all fields of human endeavour, from our everyday life decisions, negotiations, plans and goals to complex systems design and problem solving. It is the science behind how things work, something like the DNA or organising principle behind human thought and action. The realisation that these are organised grammatically is a new viewpoint that has far-reaching implications. It changes the way people think. All knowledge, story, purpose and reasoning, even consciousness itself, are mediated by language. Metagrammar (in contrast to the debunked notion of a chimerical 'grammar of grammars') is simply the practical transposition of grammatical functions beyond language to our interaction with the world. It is not singular but multiple. Everything that functions has a particular metagrammar that can be optimised. This new theory and method of reasoning revises present knowledge about critical thinking and problem solving, opens new avenues of inquiry in linguistics, education, cognitive psychology, science, technology and engineering, and has the potential to change current paradigms about the acquisition of knowledge.

The first part of this book provides evidence from cognitive science, linguistics, genre theory and narratology to analyse the interdependence between human language and thought. This sets the stage for a critical contrast with the metagrammar of computer languages and artificial intelligence. The second and third parts apply metagrammar as a method of critical thinking and problem solving to human behaviour, personal goals, social processes and technical systems, culminating with a critical look at the control of technology, human-centred solutions and translational science.

Miami, FL, USA Erik Camayd-Freixas

Contents

About the Author

Erik Camayd-Freixas is Professor of Modern Languages at Florida International University. He studied cognitive science at Tufts University with Daniel Dennett and semiotics with Umberto Eco at Harvard University, where he received a PhD in Romance Languages and Literatures. He has published nine books and numerous articles on literary and social theory and has received several academic and human rights awards for his application of metagrammar to textual analysis and social policy. He has practised as a forensic linguist and communications analyst in litigation support, testified before Congress and contributed briefs to the Senate Judiciary Committee and the U.S. Supreme Court. A researcher, practitioner and trainer of simultaneous interpretation, he has interpreted for fifteen heads of state, including U.S. presidents and popes Benedict and Francis. His interests include cognitive linguistics, narrative and genre theory, intellectual history, philosophy of language and artificial intelligence. Beyond academia, he is a family man, vintage auto mechanic and sailor.

List of Figures

Part I

Aspects of the Theory of Metagrammar

1

Origins and Destinations

Introduction

Natural language grammar is the most sophisticated problem-solving system that humans will ever devise. It is the product of the collective genius of humanity across many generations; so sophisticated that it enables us to represent, describe and narrate anything that we could possibly experience or imagine, thanks to a finite set of grammatical patterns or functional structures. At the same time, it is so elegantly simple and intuitive that children can absorb it and learn to speak grammatically with ease from an early age even before formal schooling.

We absorb or infer grammar since childhood from our everyday language use, and we internalise it to the point that it becomes second nature when we speak. As a result, we fail to notice that everything we think and do has a grammatical structure behind it. It starts with variations of a simple schema: subject-verb-object (SVO) plus modifiers (adjectives to describe nouns and adverbs to modulate verbs), and then it moves on to more complex structures, because grammar is a system made up of systems (verbal, nominal and prepositional systems, among others). We also fail to notice that putting words together grammatically is a problem-solving process. We have become so good at it that we just

E. Camayd-Freixas, *Metagrammar*, https://doi.org/10.1007/978-3-031-92337-1_1

put together pat phrases (syntactic structures) and substitute different words into them to create different meanings. Where we fail most critically is in noticing that those same grammatical functions to which we are oblivious are effectually *transferred* to our interactions with our environment. Our grammatical system already contains a blueprint for all the critical thinking and problem-solving functions we could ever need. Metagrammatical thinking, in turn, focuses on the *transfer of skills from grammar to all other functions between the self and the world*, whether verbal or non-verbal, including those which are beyond language.

This view of language as a problem-solving system is obvious to translators, but everyone can so perceive it with minimal explanation. Those with whom I have discussed my theory now instinctually 'see' the metagrammar of things with a critical eye. They also apply it to their own plans and actions. People do not act logically or even psychologically. We think, act and understand grammatically. Metagrammatical critique is equally intuitive. Just like we are taken aback when we hear ungrammatical speech, so do we recoil when we see antisocial behaviour, bad manners or ethical breaches, because ethics, manners and social behaviour each have its commonly accepted norms and conventions, that is, its metagrammar. We can then analyse what went wrong in their functional steps. This way of thinking creates a critical awareness of our purposeful and goal-oriented actions and evaluates the functional effectiveness of everything around us.

Few things are more edifying than watching others (and us) make good and bad decisions, act properly or not, with accompanying results and consequences. We often apply the wrong *know-how*, the wrong metagrammar, to our actions and decisions. A modus operandi that works for one thing may not work for another. It is a crucial mistake to transfer a familiar way of doing things from one context to another, where it does not quite fit. Metagrammar proposes a more systematic approach: starting afresh from the new set of goals, to then work out a set of solutions tailored to the new situation. Grammatical awareness and metagrammatical reasoning then allow us to properly transfer fitting functional patterns from other areas of our knowledge base. This applies broadly to multidisciplinary contexts. By the same token, no one can be an expert in such a wide range of fields. I can only hope that others will take up this inquiry, apply it to their own specialities and, where applicable, mend my errors and straighten my torts. Still, beyond my fields of semiotics, narrative theory and cognitive linguistics, I have amassed a diverse practical toolbox along the way, the product of curiosity, experience, introspection, research, dialogue and reasoning.

Antecedents

This book has been brewing for some decades, but it is now that it has become urgent, with the rise of viral disinformation, the subversion of truth and disintegration of trust, as well as the benefits and threats of artificial intelligence. The decline of grammar and foreign language education in the United States has reached a new low over several decades, resulting in a noticeable deficit in critical thinking among college students, professionals in different fields, individuals engaged in public discourse, let alone the general population.

At a less crucial time, when I was a graduate student at Harvard, I came across a few books that came to inspire this one. First was *The Monkey Grammarian* (1981 [1974]), by poet laureate Octavio Paz. Hanuman, the Monkey Grammarian, is a Hindu-Buddhist deity reputed as an innovator who can always find a solution out of any difficult situation and is considered a grammarian who straddles nature and culture—the animal, human and divine realms.

> Hanuman smiles with pleasure at the analogy that has just occurred to him: calligraphy and vegetation, a grove of trees and writing, reading and a path. Following a path: reading a stretch of ground, deciphering a fragment of world [...] the difference between human writing and divine consists in the fact that the number of signs of the former is limited, whereas that of the latter is infinite; hence the universe is a meaningless text, one which even the gods find illegible. The critique of the universe (and that of the gods) is called grammar. (p. 47)

Next was *Grammatical Man* (1982) by Jeremy Campbell. It suggests that homo sapiens is rather a *homo grammaticus*. I read into it the realisation that all human thought and action are organised grammatically just like the language that gives them form and conveyance. Campbell's book, however, deals not with language, grammar or linguistics, but with science and technology, pursuing a general theory of information. It centres around Shannon's Theorem (1948) about reducing noise to clarify signals in information channels. It relates noise to entropy, the second law of thermodynamics about the concentration and dissipation of heat; then to chemistry, the concentration and dispersion of molecules. It applies to the orderly 'grammar' of DNA as an information system, to the 'coding' of language and evolution, to the algorithms of cybernetics, to the architecture of microchip circuitry and ultimately to the evolving organisation of society—all of it a 'grammar', which Campbell calls 'a mirror of the mind' (p. 170).

Campbell intuits the intimate relationship between language and engineering; between the orderly patterns of nature which we 'read' and the artificial systems that we 'write'. However, he offers no insight into linguistics or the nature of language. In the coming chapters, I will take issue with the reduction of language to information and the tendency to understand language in terms of technology, when it should be the other way around. Ultimately, when Campbell talks about patterns in science and technology, he is unwittingly talking not about grammar but about metagrammar.

The relationship between sentence grammar and all forms of organisation *beyond the sentence* (metagrammar) is both direct and metaphorical. Language compositions beyond the sentence are grouped together into *genres*. In addition to literary genres such as epic, tragedy, lyric, novel, short story, essay and the like, linguistic genres also include personal and business letters and reports, diaries, journalistic articles, historical and ethnographic accounts, political speeches, legal writings and trials, scientific papers and all other modes of discourse. The key is that *extralinguistic modes of organisation also form genres.*

Modes of organisation are either *written* (man-made, artificial, designed) or *read* (experienced, conceptualised). *Written metagrammars* include machines, organisational charts, game and traffic rules, computer codes, circuit and database architectures, mathematical logic, systems of laws, the scientific method and all manners of protocols. *Read metagrammars* are functional representations of biological and physiological systems, organisms and ecosystems, migration patterns, fluid dynamics, electromagnetic patterns, historical events, individual and social behaviour, market forces and all other dynamic patterns. In *semiotics* or the study of systems of signs, all such representations of reality which unfold in time are considered *narratives*, whether they are expressed through language, images, shapes, formulas, algorithms or a combination thereof. They are narratives because all representations of designs and conceptualisation of phenomena are ultimately made up of subject-verb-object sequences or *SVO chains*.

Systems of a similar kind can be grouped into *genres*. The main model of genre is *narrative*, the description of action, which applies to any sequence of events, to anything that unfolds in time and can therefore be narrated. The grammars of different languages, as well as the metagrammars of different phenomena and fields, relate to each other in a web of *family resemblances* (Wittgenstein, 1953). That is, members of a genre, like members of an extended family, may share some features, forming a network of resemblances. They do not necessarily share the same set of core features or *common denominators*. Under resemblance, linguistic and extralinguistic genres can and should be studied together, compared, contrasted and categorised—this being the general mission of metagrammar as an incipient field of study.

All such systems mirror sentence grammar, but their constitutive elements, which in natural grammar would be articles, nouns, verbs, adjectives, adverbs, prepositions, conjunctions, etc., are similar in *function* but different in name and kind. Extralinguistic systems such as those considered by both Paz and Campbell, in nature, science, medicine, engineering and technology, as well as history, psychology, sociology, politics, economics and indeed any branch of organised knowledge (academic fields are in fact genres), also have their metagrammar, worthy of comparative study and crosspollination for enhancing innovation, problem solving and creative critical thinking.

This brings me to another of those inspiring books, Douglas Hofstadter's Pulitzer-winning *Gödel, Escher, Bach: An Eternal Golden Braid*

(1980), whose cover also bears the caption: 'A Metaphorical Fugue on Minds and Machines in the Spirit of Lewis Carroll'. The book is arranged as a series of open dialogues alluding to the double-helix structure of DNA and in keeping with Gödel's Incompleteness Theorem, a demonstration that no ruleset or system is ever complete and self-contained but is instead open-ended. The book's recurring analogy is based on the canons and fugues of Johan Sebastian Bach, relating music to mathematics and logic and to the recursive geometry of M. C. Escher's paradoxical drawings. A translator conversant in English, French and German, Hofstadter is keenly aware of the properties of natural language and their analogical application to extralinguistic fields. In his later meditations, he argues for a fundamental shift in viewpoint: 'every concept we have is nothing but a tightly packaged bundle of analogies, [...] all we do when we think is to move fluidly from one analogy-bundle to another, [...] such concept-to-concept leaps are themselves made via analogical connection' (2001, pp. 499–500). We will return to these topics, since a central line of inquiry that occupies me here is precisely the relationship between natural language and human intelligence, on the one side, and so-called computer languages and artificial intelligence on the other.

Regarding narrative genres, I would mention one more book for now, a true eye opener, Russian formalist Vladimir Propp's *Morphology of the Folktale* (1968 [1928]). Propp identifies 31 *narrative functions* that serve to structure and move the plot forward. Most importantly, he also identifies seven different *character functions* he calls *dramatis personae*, which may be fulfilled by different agents at different times. Variations of these functions apply not only to stories but also to movies and other plots, including courtroom trials, as well as extraliterary processes and even machines. Notice that these character functions are *modelled after the parts of speech in sentence grammar*. Nouns, articles, pronouns, adjectives, verbs, adverbs and prepositions each have a function in the sentence, and yet we can substitute different words for each function to create different meanings. In Propp's narrative theory, the parts of speech become the *dramatis personae* or, in fact, the elements and factors of any system or machine.

In terms of organisational structures, the *dramatis personae* are job positions with their functions (job descriptions) that may be occupied by different persons. The same applies to the functional parts of a machine: they form sequences (sentences or syntax strings) that accomplish specific results in stages, and the sequences are arranged systematically to form a whole narrative text. In this fashion, individuals and particular elements may change, but their functions remain stable. Variations of Propp's functional analysis can be applied to any narrative or process: news events, history, government actions, policy implementation, as well as engineered processes and systems. In fact, what Propp calls 'morphology' (the formal study of words) is really metagrammar (the functional study of narratives).

Visions of Dystopia

Fast-forward a few decades and I now find myself asking students, 'Which is the most complex system that humanity will ever develop?' I get answers ranging from astrophysics to genomic editing to artificial intelligence, some utopian, some dystopian. Occasionally, a student puts forth the correct answer: *Language!* Most people take language for granted. Language professionals do not. They know that language is a precision instrument, a weapon, a double-edged sword and so much more. Wittgenstein puts it clearly:

> Think of the tools in a toolbox: there is a hammer, pliers, a saw, a screw-driver, a rule, a glue pot, glue, nails and screws. The functions of words are as diverse as the functions of these objects. (And in both cases, there are similarities.) Of course, what confuses us is the uniform appearance of words when we hear them spoken or meet them in script and print. For their *application* is not presented to us clearly. [...] It is like looking into the cabin of a locomotive. We see handles all looking more or less alike. [...] But one is the handle of a crank which can be moved continuously (it regulates the opening of a valve); another is the handle of a switch, which has only two effective positions, it is either off or on; a third is the handle of a brake-lever, the harder one pulls on it, the harder it brakes; a fourth, the handle of a pump: it has an effect only so long as it is moved to and fro. (1958 [1953], § 11-12)

Lexicologists in their dictionaries prefer to speak not in terms of the meaning of words, which is changing and can have different shades for different people at different times, but rather they use the precise term *acceptation*, the sense in which the *usage* of a word is accepted by a community of speakers. Nevertheless, mass media, propaganda and advertising can manipulate and distort usage against the grain of critical thinking. Thus, one of the tasks ahead in later chapters is deconstructing the metagrammar of propaganda and disinformation.

The issues of metagrammar, critical thinking and problem solving have acquired a growing sense of urgency with the rise of viral propaganda, disinformation and recent advances in machine learning and artificial intelligence. The problems posed by communication weapons and information wars became acutely evident in the United States starting with the campaign for the 2016 Presidential Elections. Mass and social media were weaponised by actors both foreign and domestic, generating viral propaganda, fake news, and disinformation campaigns via social media, websites, blogs and podcasts, troll farms, fake accounts, bots and algorithmic amplification, echoed by mainstream media and resulting in absurd conspiracy theories and the legitimation of cult-like radical groups that culminated in the Capitol Insurrection of 6 January 2021. It showed how easily the masses, the media and public opinion can be influenced and manipulated. Disinformation apps have become more widely available since then (Klepper & Swenson, 2023). The Presidential Elections of 2024 were a litmus test for any lessons learned. Social engineering and datamining have become hot topics in political science and information security. Political parties and public opinion became increasingly polarised. The anti-mask and anti-vaccine movement that resulted in a failed response to the COVID-19 pandemic was another case in point. The Internet and other sources of information have become highly polluted with info trash. There has been a massive erosion of the all-important institution of TRUST in society; spectacle has taken the place of evidence, truth and critical thinking, while democracy has been gravely undermined by extremist opposition to consensus and practical solutions.

Information weapons, augmented by artificial intelligence, have become increasingly powerful, amplifying deepfakes, voice cloning and all manners of digital forgery. On 2 December 2014, physicist Stephen Hawking told the BBC: 'The development of full artificial intelligence could spell the end of the human race' (Cellan-Jones, 2014). In early 2015, the first Open Letter on Artificial Intelligence was presented at the inaugural conference of the Future of Life Institute in Puerto Rico, calling for research on safe and controllable AI. Hawking and tech magnate Elon Musk, both on the institute's board, along with 150 experts from Cambridge, Oxford, Harvard, MIT, Google, Amazon, IBM and other institutions, signed the letter on 12 January (Future of Life Institute, 2015). Today, large language models (LLMs) based on Artificial Recurrent Neural Networks (ARNNs) also called 'transformers' are 'trained' by feeding them vast corpora of text and other assets from which they machine-learn, through a process called grammar induction or grammatical inference, the formal 'grammar' (read metagrammar) of any dataset. LLM (meta)grammar is a series of *rewrite rules* or *rules of production* that allow it to mimic 'natural language generation' (NLG) through a combination of artificial intelligence and computational linguistics based, in part, on statistical probability of occurrence and mechanical error reduction. The resulting system belongs to the narrative genre termed *generative AI*, which includes LLMs like ChatGPT, released on 14 March 2023 by OpenAI. A year later, on 13 May 2024, they released the more advanced *multimodal* GPT-4o (Generative Pre-trained Transformer 4). Multimodal means that GPT-4o can be 'trained' (loaded) with any combination of images, videos and sounds, as well as text. The company website claims that its product can 'reason', approaching artificial general intelligence (AGI) at a superhuman level (OpenAI, 2024). These LLMs can interact conversationally with the user, mimicking natural language, with advanced *information retrieval* (IR) well beyond human capabilities. They are a powerful research tool but also a double-edged sword.

On 22 March 2023, 'Pause Giant AI Experiments: An Open Letter' was posted and endorsed by Elon Musk, Steve Wozkiak, co-founder of Apple, and over a thousand other tech leaders in industry and academia. The letter calls for a moratorium on the training of AI systems more powerful than GPT-4.

> AI systems with human-competitive intelligence can pose profound risks to society and humanity. [...] As stated in the Asilomar AI Principles, '*Advanced AI could represent a profound change in the history of life on Earth and should be planned for and managed with commensurate care and resources*'. Unfortunately, this level of planning and management is not happening, even though recent months have seen AI labs locked in an out-of-control race to develop and deploy ever more powerful digital minds that no one not even their creators can understand, predict or reliably control [...] *Should* we let machines flood our information channels with propaganda and untruth? [...] *Should* we risk loss of control of our civilization? (Future of Life Institute, 2023)

Days later, U.S. President Joe Biden issued a warning that just like pharmaceuticals and other businesses, 'Tech companies have a responsibility to make sure their products are safe before making them public [and] address the potential risks to our society, to our economy, to our national security' (Miller, 2023). While typically laws are too slow to catch up with technological development, as has been the case with the Internet, these remarks suggest that product liability litigation is one way of deterring from irresponsible deployment. Soon after, purportedly afraid of their own creations, the CEOs of Microsoft and OpenAI testified before Congress, begging for urgent legislation that would regulate AI. However, company insiders warn in an open letter that 'AI companies have strong financial incentives to avoid effective oversight' (Kelly, 2024). The risks 'range from the further entrenchment of existing inequalities to manipulation and misinformation, to the loss of control of autonomous AI systems potentially resulting in human extinction' (Right to Warn, 2024).

Once the cat is out of the bag, it is to be expected that anonymous hackers and international actors beyond the reach of legal jurisdictions could hijack advanced AI. Present harms include 'algorithmic bias, disinformation, democratic erosion and labor displacement', and we 'stand on the brink of even larger-scale risks from increasingly powerful systems: early reports indicate that GPT-4 can be jailbroken to generate bomb-making instructions, and that AI intended for drug discovery can be repurposed to design tens of thousands of lethal chemical weapons in just hours' (Future of Life Institute, 2023). Autonomous systems, which act without human intervention, are perhaps the biggest threat. 'Artificial Intelligence (AI) technology has reached a point where the deployment of such systems is—practically if not legally—feasible within years, not decades, and the stakes are high: autonomous weapons have been described as the third revolution in warfare, after gunpowder and nuclear arms' (Future of Life Institute, 2016). Some like drone swarm and counter-drone military technology are currently under development, but when it comes to cyber threats their invisibility and decentralisation make them much harder to neutralise. This brings us to the present conundrum: does it take AI to control AI, and can tech companies police themselves?

The human-centred managing of AI and other systems requires a problem-solving metagrammar akin to the new field of translational science. As we take a closer look into these matters, it is vital to gain an understanding of the mechanisms by which they affect individuals and society.

Conclusion

Grammar is the internalised model for organising our perception and experience, as well as our thoughts, designs and behaviour. It is a blueprint for critical thinking and problem solving. We unwittingly transfer skills from language grammar to our interaction with the world. This interaction is bidirectional: we 'read' (structure and understand) the world grammatically and we 'write' (think, act and design) upon it. Many studies have used grammar as a metaphor to explain different kinds of systems and mechanisms. However, strictly speaking, grammar operates only as far as the sentence. All forms of organisation beyond the sentence are grammarlike, modelled on and informed by grammar, but being beyond the sentence, they are beyond grammar proper. That is, all systems beyond the sentence have a metagrammar.

Even the most complex metagrammars are simpler than natural language grammar, because they enact only some grammatical structures but never the whole language system. Whether written or read, the systemic metagrammars of different fields of knowledge can be compared and studied together for crosspollination, innovation and optimisation. Metagrammars exhibiting common denominators or a network of family resemblances can be grouped into *genres*. Grammar and metagrammars are not static structures. They unfold in time. Similarly, the genre most applicable to all dynamic systems is *narrative*. Everything that unfolds in time is subject to narration. This makes comparative grammar and narrative theory essential tools for the analysis of processes in the natural and social sciences, communications and humanities. This book takes the first steps in this direction. Much interdisciplinary work remains to be done. The centre of gravity for such work is the emerging field of translational science, which seeks to translate scientific, technological and theoretical advances into human-centred solutions.

Metagrammatical analysis provides a method of critical reasoning aimed, on the one hand, at enhancing the efficiency of processes and, on the other, at critiquing the application of the wrong metagrammar where it does not belong, as well as the interaction of conflicting metagrammars, particularly technological, financial, legal, social and behavioural. In this regard, the latter part of this book is concerned with the humanisation of emerging technologies in the age of artificial intelligence.

References

Campbell, J. (1982). *Grammatical Man: Information, Entropy, Language, and Life*. Simon & Schuster.

Cellan-Jones, R. (2014, 2 December). Stephen Hawking warns artificial intelligence could end mankind. *BBC News*. Retrieved from https://www.bbc.com/news/technology-30290540

Future of Life Institute (2015-on). Open Letters. Retrieved from https://futureoflife.org/fli-open-letters

Hofstadter, D. R. (1980). *Gödel, Escher, Bach: An Eternal Golden Braid*. Vintage.

Hofstadter, D. R. (2001). Epilogue: Analogy as the core of cognition. In D. Gentner, K. Holyoak & B. Kokinov (Eds.), *The Analogical Mind: Perspectives from Cognitive Science*. MIT Press, pp. 499–538.

Kelly, S. M. (2024, 4 June). OpenAI insiders' open letter warns of 'serious risks' and calls for whistleblower protections. *CNN*. Retrieved from https://www.cnn.com/2024/06/04/tech/openai-insiders-letter/index.html
Klepper, D., & Swenson, A. (2023, 14 May). AI-generated disinformation poses threat of misleading voters in 2024 election. *PBS News Hour*. Retrieved from https://www.pbs.org/newshour/politics/ai-generated-disinformation-poses-threat-of-misleading-voters-in-2024-election
Miller, Z. (2023, 4 April). Biden says tech companies must ensure AI products are safe for individuals, national security. *PBS News Hour*. Retrieved from https://www.pbs.org/newshour/politics/biden-says-tech-companies-must-ensure-ai-products-are-safe-for-individuals-national-security
OpenAI. (2024, 13 May). Hello GPT-4o. Retrieved from https://openai.com/index/hello-gpt-4o
Paz, O. (1981 [1974]). *The Monkey Grammarian*. Translated by H. Lane. Arcade Publishing.
Propp, V. (1968 [1928]). *Morphology of the Folktale*. Translated by L. Scott. University of Texas Press.
Right to Warn. (2024, 4 June). *Right to Warn about Advanced Artificial Intelligence*. Retrieved from https://righttowarn.ai
Shannon, C. E. (1948, July, October). A mathematical theory of communication. *The Bell System Technical Journal, 27*, 379–423, 623–656. Retrieved from https://people.math.harvard.edu/~ctm/home/text/others/shannon/entropy/entropy.pdf
Wittgenstein, L. (1958 [1953]). *Philosophical Investigations* (3rd ed.). Translated by G. E. M. Anscombe. Macmillan.

2

Language vs. Thought

Introduction

Nowadays I often ask my students to conduct a little experiment. Here is the challenge. See if you can think without words even for ten seconds. They go into a blank stare like a deer in the headlights, some eyes roll back and not three seconds go by when they start moving their heads from side to side, with that faint smile of defeat. I don't blame them. I cannot either. I turn off the headlights as they seem to wake up from a hypnotic stupor. 'Okay, you can use your words now', and they start reporting what they experienced. 'I started with some mental images but didn't get very far'. 'It's like saying, don't think of a monkey. The words pop up anyway'. 'Thinking without words is the same as putting your mind on blank. That is not thinking at all'.

The relation between language and thought is a fascinating phenomenon. Mental imagery and sensory memory, particularly auditory and visual memory, do play a role in thought, but they appear as flashes, fleeting snapshots or video clips and are soon reinforced or replaced by verbal descriptors called *propositions*. These flashes of thought alone fade too quickly to be able to form a sustained chain of abstract

E. Camayd-Freixas, *Metagrammar*, https://doi.org/10.1007/978-3-031-92337-1_2

reasoning unless they are accompanied by language. Ferdinand de Saussure (1959 [1916]) establishes that *linguistic signs* (words) are composed of an inseparable mix of a concept and a sound-image, as for example, the sound 'horse' and the idea of a horse. He contends that without the help of signs we would not be able to make a clear distinction between any two ideas: 'Without language, though is a vague, uncharted nebula. There are no pre-existing ideas, and nothing is distinct before the appearance of language' (p. 122). Abstract concepts can also be visualised. Emotional concepts, in addition, bring back memories of feelings. But it is the words (sound/images) and our sharp auditory memory of them what allows us to put thoughts together into a sustained chain of discourse, what we call *discursive reasoning*, the ability to think through a problem step by step until a viable conclusion can be drawn. Words can do this precisely because they are functionally arranged into a grammar. *Without grammar and syntax there is no sustained reasoning.*

Short-Term Memory and Animal Minds

Some animals are said to possess the rudiments of 'language', based primarily on their ability to produce purposeful sounds and gestures. Benveniste (1966) denies them this possibility since human languages are made up of a reduced number of meaningless phonemes or sound units that are combined systematically to produce a considerable number of meaningful linguistic *signs* (words), whereas animal *signals* cannot be broken down into smaller constituents (pp. 56–62). Animals emit and react to sight, sound, smell, organic chemicals, vibration, magnetic fields and other sense impressions beyond human perception. But do these *signals* have a grammar? The answer, for similar reasons, is no. Grammar is a system for combining smaller units into larger structures that convey complex meaning. Still, animals exhibit orderly and purposeful behaviour patterns, although these signals are not articulated very far into a string of syntax. Do these behaviour patterns have at least a metagrammar? They do, because *metagrammar is always much simpler than grammar*. Ultimately as well, their metagrammar is in the eye of the (human) beholder, in the patterns that we 'read' and project onto animal behaviour.

Higher animals are conscious, but can they reason? I believe they do at some level, because their behaviour is much more complex and articulated than their 'language'. They exhibit structured behaviour which can be 'read' as meaningful by humans. Let us do away with all black-box concepts like 'instinct', which are stoppers of metagrammar and critical thinking because they purport not to be further analysable. Instead, we could say that some animal behaviour is *physiologically predetermined*, like eating to relieve hunger pangs. Yet much animal behaviour is learned metagrammar from parents and peers, and most of all from their own experience. Metagrammar always tends towards greater economy and efficiency, to the point where certain ways of doing are improved, polished and mastered, becoming institutionalised, often even codified into formulas, recipes and laws.

John Searle (2002) gives a nuanced philosophical account in his chapter on 'Animal Minds' (pp. 61–76). Higher primates, marine mammals and many land mammals, particularly if they are social or domesticated, are the best candidates, but humans are a quantum leap ahead. Based on cognitive science, my own theory about the metagrammar of reasoning is that to be able to joggle a few concepts at a time, long enough to organise them into a grammar, you need an expanded short-term memory (STM) capacity, also known as working memory. This enables us to think. STM stimulates long-term memory (LTM) of past experiences which come to reinforce and flesh out our thoughts. Research shows that we can normally hold 7 ± 2 items in our STM (Miller, 1956). Grammar, however, allows us to organise loose items 'chunking' them into full phrases and sentences, such that these larger units can become a single item, thereby maximising STM capacity. Visualisation and other memory aids also play a role. Moreover, we can let even larger units be the items, such as talking points, arguments, as well as entire topics and stories, bolstering STM efficiency.

When we reconstruct arguments, topics and stories from memory, we typically find the words as we go along like we do in a spontaneous conversation and, thanks to grammar, we build the words into phrases and the phrases into sentences; and, thanks to metagrammar (beyond the sentence), we can organise the sentences into arguments and plots to reconstruct the entire representation of facts and events.

Back to our animal friends, in order to have an expanded STM we need an increased attention span and for this we need our senses to be somewhat muted, much less sensitive than the keen senses of other animals. Otherwise, we would be overwhelmed with inputs and hopelessly distracted and unfocused. Senses are essential for memory and thought, but there is a point of diminishing returns where sensory inputs overwhelm our working memory and focus. I will return to this point regarding the overwhelming bombardment of prompts and sensory inputs that omnichannel media rains upon us, distracting our focus, interrupting our thoughts and redirecting our actions.

The Chicken or the Egg

To say that grammatical language is the product of brain development and evolution is to beg the question, to comingle the result and the cause. An heir of the British empiricists' influence on the French Enlightenment, Saussure held that external experience and socialisation 'teach' the brain the fundamentals of language and grammar. He is an *externalist*. Noam Chomsky, on the other hand, is a modern proponent of the *internalist* position, which posits an innate predisposition for grammatical language—a sort of 'language instinct' (Pinker, 1994). This is the premise of his well-known hypotheses of 'deep structure' and 'universal grammar' (Chomsky, 1965, 1968, 1984, 2000). However, neuroscience does not support the internalist position. Besides, the basic grammatical structure, subject-verb-object (SVO—regardless the order), can be explained by experience alone: when humans first observed a thing out in the world (subject) initiate a movement (verb) that affected another thing (object). In terms of the slow process of evolution, however, it is most likely a case of mutual influence, a dialectics, with *language and brain developing in tandem.*

Another way to see it is to question of what came first, language or thought. It stands to reason that there first must have been a thought to which a sound was attached thus making up a word. Yet, a single word does not a language make, grammar does. And so, the question remains, did grammar (SVO as experienced out in the world) organise thought, or was it the other way around? It might be helpful to turn to the paradox of the chicken and the egg. Once upon a time, there were non-chickens that laid eggs. With each generation, there were minute changes in the hatchlings, until one day a bird hatched that could truly be called a bona fide chicken. Therefore, the egg whence it cometh was first! The problem is that the dividing line for when the bird became a chicken is always arbitrary. Anyone can argue that there was once a non-chicken that grew up to be a chicken that laid the first chicken egg. Hence it is better to say that egg and chicken, thought and language, developed in tandem.

Aside from this fun exercise in metagrammatical reasoning, I am not interested in speculating on the remote origins of language or deciding on the externalist/internalist debate. What interests me as an educator is what happens in childhood. Newborns are unable to focus and are overwhelmed by unfiltered, uncategorised stimuli, with hunger and discomfort often taking over to produce unintentional crying. It is difficult to argue that they can 'think' at this stage, but language comes immediately from the mother, and they soon figure out that crying brings about food and comfort. Exposure to language helps in brain development. Letting aside the elusive (and I would say irrelevant) question of origins, all of us are born into a world where *language already exists*. In real everyday life, language comes first and moulds our thoughts. It comes to us from our parents, peers, TV, school and other sources. It comes already with order and grammar (SVO), which we correlate and verify with our experience of things and movements in the world. We acquire and internalise grammar by usage, not rules, by seeing its effective patterns meaningfully repeated; and we hone it through trial and error by venturing to say things and be corrected. Eventually, if we are lucky, we study grammar at school and learn it as a *system*. We learn to read, which exposes us to new and increasingly sophisticated grammatical patterns, concepts and vocabulary, which allows us to think in new ways and terms. We expand not only our vocabulary and concepts but also our grammatical and syntactic repertoire, enabling us to find better, more efficient and elegant solutions to the problem of expressing ourselves and persuading others. As we gain *experience of the world*, we continue to correlate and verify linguistic patterns against it. We clarify our thoughts by putting them into words, including our thoughts on how things work. We understand ourselves and the world better. All along, there is a constant *correlation of patterns* and a *transfer of skills* from grammar to metagrammar, that is, *from grammatical language to our interaction with the world outside.*

If we are even luckier, we get exposed to a second language and perhaps to a third. In the words of Stanford linguist and computer scientist Dan Jurafsky, 'Understanding why and how languages differ tells us about the range of what is human' (Shashkevich, 2019). Exposure to different languages gives us the opportunity to internalise *comparative grammar*. Each language uses different strategies (word-concepts and grammatical-syntactic-morphological structures) to represent similar meanings. The fact that these are problem-solving strategies becomes very evident in the practice of translation. Finding equivalent word-concepts, rearranging the syntax or word order, transposing or transforming parts of speech (verbs, nouns, adjectives, participles) into one another, modulating cultural connotations and usage and other translational techniques are all part of what translators refer to as finding a *solution.* This mental training increases the repertoire of *solution patterns* and induces great morphosyntactic flexibility for problem solving and innovation—the proverbial 'thinking outside the box'—not just in language but in metagrammar, the repertoire of patterns for 'how things work'.

Further, the realisation that my way is not the only right way is the foundation of critical thinking, beginning with the simple acceptance that the letter 'a' is pronounced 'ei' in my language but 'ah' in another language. At first, second-language learners react with great resistance to the differences in convention, pronunciation, usage and grammar required by the new language. They cling to what they know and insist on using literal translations even for idiomatic expressions, and on imposing their first-language grammar and syntax on the second language, where it does not belong, producing very awkward results. For instance, 'To me hurts the arms' is the literal translation of '*Me duele el brazo*' where Spanish grammar is forced on English. Through a process of (self-) correction, language learners eventually come to accept the new way and understand it. In short, it opens their minds. When this happens, they feel that the new language 'makes sense' and understand its 'logic' (meaning its systemic grammar). For the first time, they feel like 'citizens of the world'. Thereafter, language learning increases exponentially. By the same token, once you learn a second language, you learn how to learn, and it becomes easier to learn additional languages, because you have mastered comparative grammar and turned resistance into acceptance and flexibility.

Linguistic Relativity

The idea that language and thought are interdependent is referred to as *linguistic relativity*, also known by the misnomer 'Sapir-Whorf hypothesis', developed since the 1930s (Vygotsky, 1934; Whorf, 1956; Lakoff, 1987; Lucy, 1992; Boroditsky, 2003). It is a misnomer because, among other reasons, this view has existed since antiquity and has continued to be developed in significant ways to the present day. Various ancient Greek philosophers, sophists and Latin rhetoricians maintained that language helps to mould and develop thought. An heir to this classical tradition, Erasmus of Rotterdam (1974 [1525]), the father of modern philology and seminal translator of the New Testament from Greek into Latin, maintained that language is the 'master' (that is, the teacher) of thought and not the other way around; and that things are intelligible only through words, 'by the sounds we attach to them' (vol. 24, p. 666). Humboldt, Herder and the Romantics considered language to be the carrier of the 'spirit' (worldview, idiosyncrasy) of each nation. The early formulations of linguistic relativity in the 1930s garnered considerable attention until the 1960s, when behaviourists accused them of vagueness and lack of observable scientific evidence, by speculating about mental phenomena via dubious introspection (Skinner, 1957). In time, the purported 'objectivity' of behaviourism became suspect as a partial view of reality. Chomsky (1959) opposed Skinner's radical empiricism and behaviourism and took the first steps towards a cognitive linguistics. Reasoned introspection made a comeback, given that it could be consistently verified by other minds: 'objectivity' gave way to *intersubjectivity* (Habermas, 1987).

Linguistic relativity, on the other hand, continued to face opposition from internalists like Chomsky and Pinker (1994) who favoured 'universal grammar' and the *computational theory of mind* (Fodor, 1975). There is evidence that babies do exhibit some level of language-independent thinking before they develop speech. Whether this is innate, developed from experience with objects, or independent from early language exposure and interaction with parents, remains a matter of debate. Chomsky (1993) argues that communication takes place thanks to a 'shared public language, consisting of shared signs' and a 'public shared meaning' (p. 21). 'Sign, sense and referent are external entities, outside the mind/brain' (p. 17). This exemplifies the internalist perspective. Yet developments in cognitive science and sociolinguistics since the 1970s have provided the missing scientific evidence for linguistic relativity. The emerging field of cognitive linguistics is a case in point (Lakoff & Johnson, 1980; Croft & Cruse, 2004; Evans, 2019). It includes the study of cognitive grammar, which has developed since 1976 (Langacker, 2008). There are, in short, two main competing perspectives in cognitive linguistics: Noam Chomsky's emphasis on structure and internalism versus George Lakoff's emphasis on meaning and linguistic relativity. In *Linguistics Wars* (2021), R. A. Harris traces the ongoing arguments and development of evidence in favour of each of these divergent theories. From an intermediate position, dual-coding theory holds that mental images as much as language structures are operant in thought (Paivio, 1986). Yet none of these various positions negates the relationship between grammar and metagrammar or the fact that language development (and education via language) leads to the development of thinking skills. Even opponents of linguistic relativity adhere to the Language of Thought Hypothesis (LOTH) in the form of a 'mentalese' that precedes natural language in the thinking process (Fodor, 1975; Pinker, 1994). In the end, no one, it seems, can fully escape the language metaphor in describing thought.

Aneta Pavlenko goes a step further in *The Bilingual Mind and what it tells us about language and thought* (2014). She draws from a century of linguistic and cognitive research to show that the relationship between language and thought is direct and not merely metaphorical. Simply put, *language construes experience and organises thought*. Our flux of indistinct sense impressions is linguistically categorised the moment we name them. Naming separates the part from the whole and defines it in terms of other names (words) related to it by categories or semantic fields. The name thus becomes a word-concept, a linguistic sign marked by an inseparable sound-image unit. Similarly, number, time, space and dimensions are symbolic systems of relationships. Verbs construe and categorise the cognition of motion events, 'reprogramming' the mind. We construe our very identity in relation to the narrative storyline of our autobiographical memory, which is language dependent and linked to our inner speech. Bilinguals store memories of different parts and episodes of their lives in the language in which they occurred and then experience a 'tension between the language of the memories and the language of the telling' (p. 188). Each language provides different interpretive frames. Bilinguals are thus immersed in a constant inner debate between languages, grammars, cultures, traditions, memories and ways of thinking. This inner perspectivism facilitates the development of critical intersubjectivity, while the internalised engagement with comparative grammar augments the flexible structural models for problem solving.

Conclusion

The nature vs. nurture debate in psychology continues in psycholinguistics as the opposition between internalists, who believe in an innate capacity from grammatical language, and externalists, who consider language a socially acquired skill. Neither denies the grammarlike organisation of thought and behaviour. However, metagrammar rejects all black-box concepts as analysis stoppers, including an'innate language instinct' and a 'universal grammar'. The basic grammatical structure subject-verb-object (SVO) is already given in our perception of external events, making trivial any appeal to inborn characteristics. Grammar construes experience as meaning and organises thought and behaviour into goals composed of the SVO chains of discursive reasoning. This is a key aspect of the theory of metagrammar, because it implies a correlation and a constant transfer of skills between language (grammar) and the world (metagrammar).

The perspective that language moulds thought is well established in philology. In this sense, grammar is the problem-solving system for generating meaning (thought). It is the conceptual model of metagrammar, the problem-solving system for understanding how things work and designing things that work. Grammar always favours the shortest, wittiest, most economical and elegant solutions for conveying meaning in context. Similarly, metagrammar always tends toward the most efficient and effective solutions for representing and acting upon the world. Both can be developed by training, experience and tricks-of-the-trade apprenticeship, leading to mastery of technique.

We internalise grammar from daily use, but this is an inefficient way limited to language exposure, which may include faulty constructions. A more effective way is through the formal study of grammar as a complete system. Exposure to other languages enhances our command of vocabulary and syntax, broadening our repertoire of solutions and our flexibility for 'thinking outside the box'. Bilingualism from language exposure helps but is not a substitute for the formal study of comparative grammar and contrastive syntax, which deepens our understanding of the problem-solving flexibilities of grammar. Grammatical proficiency translates into metagrammatical aptitude for critical understanding and problem solving in all areas of the real world. The same applies to comparative metagrammar to the extent that conceptual patterns and practical solutions in one area can be transferred and adapted to a new context. In cases when they cannot be transferred, contrastive (meta)syntax can still serve to critique and troubleshoot one system in contrast to another.

References

Benveniste, É. (1966). *Problèmes de linguistique générale*. Paris: Gallimard. *Problems in General Linguistics*. Translated by M. Meeks. University of Miami Press, 1971.

Boroditsky, L. (2003). 'Linguistic Relativity' in *Encyclopedia of Cognitive Science*. Wiley.

Chomsky, N. (1959). A review of B. F. Skinner's *Verbal Behavior*. *Language, 35*(1), 26–58.

Chomsky, N. (1965). *Aspects of the Theory of Syntax*. MIT Press.

Chomsky, N. (1968). *Language and Mind*. Harcourt Brace Jovanovich.

Chomsky, N. (1984). *Modular Approaches to the Study of the Mind*. San Diego University Press.

Chomsky, N. (1993). *Language and Thought*. Moyer Bell.

Chomsky, N. (1997). *Media Control: The Spectacular Achievements of Propaganda* (2nd ed.). Seven Stories Press.

Chomsky, N. (2000). *New Horizons in the Study of Language and Mind*. Cambridge University Press.

Croft, W., & Allan Cruse, D. (2004). *Cognitive Linguistics*. Cambridge University Press.

Erasmus, D. (1974 [1525]). *De Lingua* in *Collected Works of Erasmus, 24*. University of Toronto Press.

Evans, V. (2019). *Cognitive Linguistics: A Complete Guide* (2nd ed.). Edinburgh University Press.

Fodor, J. A. (1979). *The Language of Thought*. Harvard University Press.

Habermas, J. (1987). *The Philosophical Discourse of Modernity*. MIT Press.

Harris, R. A. (2021). *The Linguistics Wars: Chomsky, Lakoff and the Battle over Deep Structure* (2nd ed.). Oxford University Press.

Lakoff, G. (1987). *Women, Fire and Dangerous Things: What Categories Reveal about the Mind*. The University of Chicago Press.

Lakoff, G., & Johnson, M. (2003 [1980]). *Metaphors We Live By*. The University of Chicago Press.

Langacker, R. W. (2008). *Cognitive Grammar: A Basic Introduction*. Oxford University Press.

Lucy, J. A. (1992). *Grammatical Categories and Cognition: A Case Study of the Linguistic Relativity Hypothesis*. Cambridge University Press.

Miller, G. A. (1956). The magical number seven, plus or minus two: some limits on our capacity for processing information. *Psychological Review, 63*, 81–97.
Paivio, A. (1986). *Mental Representations: A Dual Coding Approach*. Oxford University Press.
Pavlenko, A. (2014). *The Bilingual Mind and What it Tells Us About Language and Thought*. Cambridge University Press.
Pinker, S. (1994). *The Language Instinct: How the Mind Creates Language*. William Morrow & Company.
Saussure, F. de (1959 [1916]). *Course in General Linguistics*. In C. Bally & A. Sechehaye (Eds.). Translated by W. Baskin. The Philosophical Society.
Searle, J. R. (2002). *Consciousness and Language*. Cambridge University Press.
Shashkevich, A. (2019, 22 August). The power of language: how words shape people, culture. *Stanford News*. Retrieved from https://news.stanford.edu/2019/08/22/the-power-of-language-how-words-shape-people-culture
Skinner, B. F. (1992 [1957]). *Verbal Behavior*. Copley Publishing Group.
Vygotsky, L. (1962 [1934]). *Thought and Language*. MIT Press.
Whorf, B. (2012 [1956]). In J. B. Carroll et al. (Eds.), *Language, Thought and Reality: Selected Writings of Benjamin Lee Whorf*. MIT Press.

3

Communication vs. Representation

Introduction

If we take, for instance, advertising, it can hardly be disputed that language affects thought and behaviour. We say that false advertising and other forms of persuasive discourse 'misrepresent' reality. Language, as we shall see, is a representational system. Connotation and evocation play a role in affecting perception. In a study of witness testimony, two groups of people who saw the same car accident were asked two differently worded versions of the same question. The first group was asked, 'About how fast were the cars going when they made *contact* with each other?' The second group was asked, 'About how fast were the cars going when they *smashed* into each other?' The latter group gave higher estimates of speed, and some subjects even reported seeing broken glass where in fact there was none (Loftus & Palmer, 1974).

The spirit is an invention of the body,
The body, an invention of the world,
The world, an invention of the spirit.
—Octavio Paz (1971 [1967], p. 193)

E. Camayd-Freixas, *Metagrammar*, https://doi.org/10.1007/978-3-031-92337-1_3

This is all within the same language, but what happens when different languages use different expressions with different cultural evocations? In American English, if we say, 'I live on a ranch', the picture represented is that of an affluent, fenced-in property of sizable acreage, with a stately home, cattle and horses. But in Mexican Spanish, '*Vivo en un rancho*' can mean 'I live in a shack with dirt floor'. Classifications and boundaries are often language dependent (Lakoff, 1987). Inuit has several words for different varieties of snow. Hopi has different grammatical and conceptual structures for representing time. Zuni classifies green and blue under the same word and its speakers have difficulty distinguishing shades within that spectrum. Indigenous languages and precolonial cultures tend to represent geographical space as irradiating from a centre of power, but with no defined limits or boundaries—the opposite of the modern state's conception of property and territory as delimited by fixed borders, fences and walls (Camayd-Freixas, 2002). Languages that have grammatical gender classify nouns, adjectives, articles and pronouns as male, female or neuter, and their speakers perceive and describe objects in terms consistent with their gender. Halliday (2014) observes that 'the fact that these differ from one language to another is a reminder that categories are in fact construed in language' (p. 30). Grammatical gender exemplifies the multifunctionality of words. Gender agreement can link an *antecedent* noun to distant adjectives and pronouns, which then assume the deictic function of 'the former' and 'the latter'—resulting in a more efficient and elegant solution.

All these examples define language as representation, not as communication. We will see the difference soon enough. As discussed in Chapter 2, Ferdinand de Saussure (1959 [1916]), the father of modern linguistics and semiotics, conceived of words as *linguistic signs* made up of a sound-image representing a concept, with alphabetic or phonetic writing in turn representing sounds. This suggests that at the most basic level, language is representation. In the case of pictographic and ideographic writing systems, such as Mayan or Chinese, the glyphs and characters make a visual or conceptual representation of images and ideas that are immediately perceived as speech. On closer inspection, they are also logo-syllabic, containing representations of syllable sounds that inflect the visual symbols grammatically to indicate person, number, gender, case, tense, aspect or mood. Metaphors, analogies and other figures of speech are perhaps the most representational features of language.

Simply put, speakers represent their mental images with words. In so doing, they 'paint' a mental picture for their listeners, who recompose their own similar images, based on a common language, context and cultural conventions; that is, in Searle's terms, 'a shared human background' and 'a system of representation' (2002, pp. 152–153). The popular phrase that probes for understanding, '*Are you picking up what I'm putting down?*', captures the gist of this process very efficiently by means of a brief visual metaphor.

Mental Pictures

Let us now refine the representational process by considering the complexity of what we metaphorically call a 'mental picture'. Philosopher of mind Daniel Dennett, in his classic *Consciousness Explained* (1991), gives a very nuanced account of what our mental images really are. British empiricists Locke and Hume considered that the human mind starts off as a tabula rasa, a clean slate. It then receives sense impressions by experiencing the world. These sense impressions form simple primary ideas in the mind and these simple ideas are then associated by contiguity (things that appear together) and similarity (or contrast) to make complex ideas. But Dennett observes that this is not so straight forward. Sensations come from all five senses and three domains: (1) experiences from the external world, including our own bodily sensations; (2) experiences from the internal world, 'such as fantasy images, the inner sight and sounds of daydreaming and talking to yourself, recollections, bright ideas and sudden hunches; and (3) experiences of emotions, ranging from [...] joy, hatred, embarrassment, lust, astonishment, to [...] pride, anxiety, regret' and many others (p. 45).

Our taste buds are sensitive only to sweet, sour, salty and bitter, with our sense of smell providing all the other nuances of taste. Our senses of touch and movement are aided by 'almost unnoticed clicking and scraping sounds' that accompany the texture, consistency, vibration and heat conductivity of objects. Our hearing, particularly of speech, is heavily influenced by meaning, memory and expectations. All these factors correlate with our sense of sight, activating many different areas of the brain, such that perception and its interpretation are 'the products of an elaborate process of integration of information from a variety of sources' (p. 47). This corresponds with the metaphorical *mixture of senses*: the colour of sounds, tasting with our nose, seeing with our fingers, feeling our emotions—which Symbolist poets and cognitive scientists call *synaesthesia*.

'When we perceive speech, we are aware of more than just the identities and grammatical categories of the words [...] a distinctive British voice [...] *hear* his smile [...] a sense that laughter was behind the words [...] the rise and fall of intonation, but also the rasps and wheezes and lisps, to say nothing of the whine of peevishness, the tremolo of fear, the flatness of depression'. All these nuances make for 'different auditory flavours' (p. 51).

Dennett further challenges our naïve view of mental images as 'pictures-in-the-head'. We take our field of vision to be uniformly detailed and focused from the centre to the outer edges, whereas only the centre is focused and everything around it is a blur. '[O]ur eyes, unlike television cameras, are not steadily trained on the world but dart about [up to five times per second] in an incessant and largely unnoticed game of visual tag with the items of potential interest. [...] [T]he *contents* of visual experience, are in a format unlike any other mode of representation, neither pictures nor movies nor sentences nor maps nor scale models nor diagrams. [...] Mental imagery comes in all modalities, not just vision' (pp. 54–58).

I would add a few reflections. Our mental images are not 'pictures' directly, but indirect memories or 'ghost' fragments. Our mind can remember past smells, tastes, sounds, pictures and the 'feel' of both, objects and emotions. Memory, therefore, plays a key role in that process of reconstitution and integration of multiple stimuli, as well as in the impression that our field of vision is uniformly sharp and seamless. The constant darting of the eyes across the visual field is an instance of what cognitive psychologists call *attention fluctuation*. Our eyes additionally vibrate imperceptibly from side to side. Experiments in cognition have shown that if we attach contact lenses with mini cameras to our eyes such that they move in tandem and the same fixed picture is projected onto the same areas of our retinas, the neural axons get depleted from firing electrochemical transmitters over and over for the same stimuli, causing us after a while to go temporarily blind. Attention fluctuation has the opposite effect: it keeps us alert—an adaptation to danger, choices and problem solving that makes for an obvious evolutionary advantage.

Significantly, when we focus our attention, propositions immediately come to mind in the form of mental words, like 'talking to ourselves', except that these mental words and sentences are often extremely fast and abbreviated sound fragments ('mentalese'), making propositional thought many times faster than actual speech. If we need to express our thoughts or consider them more carefully, we can reconstruct and spell out the entire wording, sentence, topic or story. Otherwise, we keep thinking in flash mode, which is a controlled mixture of fragmentary sense-sound-and-image memories. This combination of inner language and memory gives definition to our vague thoughts and interprets or assigns meaning to our mosaic of sensory stimuli. Attention fluctuation applies to our memories, thoughts and intentions such that we appear to be engaged in a constant internal brainstorming.

Dennett proposes a clever Multiple Drafts model of consciousness, in which the constant integration and interpretation of stimuli is akin to a continuous 'editing process'. He warns against 'the tempting mistake of supposing that there must be a single narrative (the "final" or "published" draft, you might say) that is canonical—that is the *actual* stream of consciousness of the subject' (p. 113). Dennett refers to the incessant flow of inner speech and images. However, once you verbalise a composite draft to another person, you have in fact chosen, organised and published a set narrative, which you hope will evoke similar mental images in your interlocutor. You may try to modify it with later speech, but in any case, you can never take it back or unsay it. Hence the adage, 'You are the master of what you keep and a slave to what you say'.

Mind or Matter

Finally, Dennett sets out to refute Descartes' dualism, the old notion that brain and mind are two separate things. He considers dualism to be passé and materialism to be the prevailing wisdom. In other words, the mind is the brain, and someday neuroscience may be able to explain mental events (thoughts) in purely physical terms.

My own view is that no matter how much neuroscience approaches an explanation, there will always be a quantum leap between physical processes and abstract thought. Further, it seems that we do not think only with the brain but with the entire body and all its senses in the context of our environment, history and culture. From Adam Smith's *The Theory of Moral Sentiments* (2018 [1759]) to the modern Attribution Theory of Emotions in psychology, the evidence is that we first experience physical arousal in the form of a feeling 'at the pit of the stomach', increased heartrate and perspiration, pupil dilation, changes in breathing patterns and galvanic skin conductivity; and then, we use cues from the environment to interpret and *name* our reaction as love, fear, anger, indignation, anxiety, etc. One emotion can indeed be reinterpreted and renamed as another if cues from the environment change in the presence of residual arousal. This may seem as a purely physical explanation, but the point is that when we interpret and name our physical state, we use propositions, language, in short, we *create a narrative.*

This is not a concession to dualism, but the realisation of the physicality of language (breathing, vocalisation, articulation), which nevertheless enables us to produce abstract meaning by arranging sound-images or word-concepts into grammatical patterns. This reveals that the old mind–body paradox is owed to an error in metagrammatical reasoning. To wit, physiology and thought have both been looked at from the outside, as grammatical objects. The perspective of the grammatical subject has been missing until now. As soon as it is supplied, it becomes evident that physiology produces language, and language produces thought, in an SVO chain. That is, *language is the cog, the missing link at the centre of the millenary debate among the philosophies of idealism, dualism and materialism.* Look no further: language is the hinge between physiology and thought. It is both physical and abstract, sound and image, all at once. Like a photon, which exhibits characteristics of both particle and wave, language lies at the relativity threshold between matter and energy. And to think that the solution to the old mind-matter problem has always been there, literally under our noses!

Communication Is for Gadgets

Regardless of how complex and metaphorical the concept of 'mental images' may be, the view of language as representation has a basis in Saussure, Chomsky, Fodor, Lakoff and other linguists and is the common ground of otherwise opposing theories. Then, how come the popular conception of language as communication?

From the Latin *communis* ('common'), the term has become synonymous with the transmission of information, owing to the so-called Communication Revolution, which we might say started when Samuel Morse patented the telegraph in 1837. Shortly after, thousands of miles of cable linked the eastern United States, exponentially faster, cheaper and more reliably than transportation or travel. The first transatlantic cable was laid in 1848, facilitating industry, finance, news and personal telegrams. Communication became centralised, and coverage remained unevenly distributed. Telegrams fostered a truncated language not unlike today's texting. Experiments in voice telegraphy eventually led to the telephone, while wireless telegraphy led to the radio, with the world's first commercial broadcasting station, Pittsburgh's KDKA, starting transmission in 1920. Then came television, computers, satellites, cellular phones and the Internet.

Communication became synonymous with the means or medium for sending and receiving 'information'. Nevertheless, information is nothing but meaningless bits of data until they are interpreted by humans, that is, *reconfigured into meaningful representation.* In a strict sense, communication and information are for gadgets. Humans *represent* to each other via language, and language does not send information packets but representation packets. The anthropomorphism of gadgets and the tendency to describe and theorise about human functions in terms of gadgetry are commercially driven aspects of *techno-mythology* perpetuated by insidious advertising and promotion—another instance of language affecting perception and thought, here in a negative sense, creating a *false conscience*.

The prestige of technology as synonymous with science and modernity led to the use of electronic communication systems as a *metaphor* for the (human) use of natural language. The communication of *information* took the place of the representation of ideas. The turning point was Claude Shannon's 'A Mathematical Theory of Communication' (1948), which launched information theory. At Bell Telephone Laboratories, Shannon was working with telegraphy, telephony and early television, particularly with statistical methods of modulation to reduce transmission noise and clarify the signal. Chapter 14 examines his theory in detail and its crucial role in the development of the computer and artificial intelligence. Suffice it to note for now that the machine concept of *information* is divorced from that of human meaning: 'Frequently messages have *meaning* [...] These semantic aspects of communication are irrelevant to the engineering problem'—which Shannon schematises in Fig. 3.1.

By the 1970s, the followers of Saussure's structuralism, particularly Roman Jakobson, had developed a rigid concept of language that they applied even to literary texts. It was loosely based on Shannon's theory of communication. Structuralist literary theory, led by Roland Barthes,

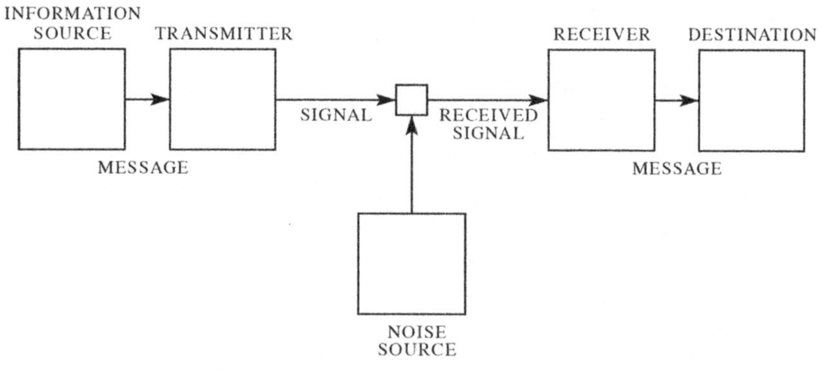

Fig. 3.1 Schematic diagram of a general communication system (Shannon,1948, pp. 1–2)

went as far as to reduce the literary experience to Jakobson's 'communicative framework' represented by a simplistic diagram, which began on the left with a box labelled 'Sender' (the author), an arrow to another box labelled 'Message' (the literary text), another arrow to another box labelled 'Receiver' (the reader) and a bubble that engulfed them all, labelled 'Context'. It was a strictly linear process of 'encoding' and 'decoding' via a 'channel' designed to give linguistics a scientific veneer borrowed from emerging electronic technologies. Semiotics, an otherwise valid aspect of structuralism, was a partner in crime as it studies not only language but all 'systems of signs' as constituting a 'text' and resembling a 'language'. It bears pointing out that the organisation of any other system of signs beside natural language (say, the system of traffic signs) is not a grammar, which stops with the sentence, but a metagrammar, which emulates sentence structure.

The result of the insidious technological metaphor is the *substitution* of linguistics by 'information theory'; of narration and description by 'information'; and of representation by 'communication'. The advantage is that, contrary to representation, which is qualitative, information can be measured, reduced to mathematical formulas and eventually digitised for computation. The danger is the growing fallacy of the anthropomorphic machine, the delusion that computers can be made to our image and likeness and the concomitant *reduction of human value* to computable measurements, which has come to dominate the assessment of all aspects of human behaviour (especially at school and at work) in the form of metrics with formulas that calculate the benefit for *organisations*, but not for human individuals or their happiness.

Language is representation and humans represent to each other. Computers will *never* be able to do this, to represent or understand *meaning*, to form mental images, let alone to feel, think, learn or be, in any way, 'intelligent'.

Conclusion

From the most basic level, the linguistic sign is a word-concept unit, a combination of a physical sound that *represents* a mental image tied to *meaning*. Language is the physical representation of meaning. Arranging word-concepts into grammatical patterns generates a flow of meaning that ultimately makes for a discursive narrative. This narrative represents the thoughts, ideas and images of the speaker, which the listener is to mentally reconstruct and interpret in corresponding fashion. The language process is entirely symbolic and representational. Metaphorically, words are like actors on a theatre stage.

However, the electronic communications age has self-servingly promoted a machine-like image of representational language as a communication circuit, with a sender encoding a message, transmitting it as information bits through a channel, and a receiver decoding it based on a shared code. The theatre model with figures representing meaning on a stage is hereby reduced to a telegraph sending dots and dashes in Morse Code down a wire. At the other end, the receiver—a human telegrapher—decodes the beeps that represent letters, but as soon as he takes down full words and sentences, he is inescapably working with a written *representation* of sounds that represent meaning. Linguistics, cognitive science and, of course, computer science have been complicit in promoting this false analogy. In the end, grammar is a complex and exhaustive system for creating meaning, whereas machines can never handle meaning. They can only handle codes, whose meaning is always supplied by humans.

There is nothing trivial about this distinction. The machine model leads to a very different set of values and social policies, whose goal is the profit-driven replacement of human labour. Moreover, true technological development is better served by pursuing a highly sophisticated rather than a simplified model. Natural language grammar is that highly sophisticated model, the internalised source of all metagrammars, whether they handle meaning in the social sphere or just codes in the field of technology. The closer a metagrammar or system follows the multi-functionality of natural grammar, the more efficient, sophisticated and capable.

References

Camayd-Freixas, E. (2002). Enunciating space, locating identity: Garcilaso de la Vega's *Comentarios reales de los Incas*. In A. Santa & M. Meléndez (Eds.), *Mapping Colonial Spanish America: Places and Common Places of Identity, Culture and Experience*. Bucknell University Press, pp. 102–120.

Chomsky, N. (1957). *Syntactic Structures*. Mouton.

Dennett, D. (1991). *Consciousness Explained*. Little, Brown & Co.

Halliday, M. A. K. (2014). *Introduction to Functional Grammar* (4th ed.). Revised by C. Matthiessen. Routledge.

Lakoff, G. (1987). *Women, Fire and Dangerous Things: What Categories Reveal about the Mind*. The University of Chicago Press.

Loftus, E. F., & Palmer, J. C. (1974). Reconstruction of automobile destruction: an example of the interaction between language and memory. *Journal of Verbal Learning and Verbal Behavior, 13*(5), 585–589.

Paz, O. (1971 [1967]). *Blanco*. Translated by C. Tomlinson & G. Aroul. *Configurations*. New Directions.

Saussure, F. de. (1959 [1916]). *Course in General Linguistics*. C. Bally & A. Sechehaye (Eds). Translated by W. Baskin. The Philosophical Society.

Searle, J. R. (2002). *Consciousness and Language*. Cambridge University Press.

Shannon, C. E. (1948, July-October). A mathematical theory of communication. *The Bell System Technical Journal, 27*, 379–423, 623–656. Retrieved from https://people.math.harvard.edu/~ctm/home/text/others/shannon/entropy/entropy.pdf

Smith, A. (2018 [1759]). *The Theory of Moral Sentiments: To which is added, a Dissertation on the Origin of Language*. Franklin Classics.

References

4

Language vs. Notation

Introduction

A few years ago, I was invited to deliver a keynote speech on ethics to a consortium of seven colleges in the American Midwest. My topic was precisely this, understanding key aspects of language to deconstruct Internet propaganda and rescue our critical thinking. I struggled to find an image for the first slide of my PowerPoint presentation that could illustrate language as a mechanism. I canvased O'Reilly's *Graph Databases* (Robinson et al., 2015) and other visualisation manuals but could not find anything remotely suitable or complex enough to represent language. My first problem in representing language as a machinery is that language is *multidimensional*. Words have denotation (what they name), connotation (what they imply) and evocation (the memories and emotions they recall in individuals and communities). If it does not have all three, it is not a language. My next problem is that language is *multifunctional*. Each word in a sentence not only has the function of conveying these three dimensions of meaning, but also serves diverse grammatical functions, including part of speech (noun, verb, etc.), position in the syntax and relation with other words, all of which play a pivotal role in sentence structure and meaning. The different dimensions

E. Camayd-Freixas, *Metagrammar*, https://doi.org/10.1007/978-3-031-92337-1_4

and functions are all part of a shared context, which also includes the situation of the speech act as well as the sociocultural history of speaker and audience.

In the end, I settled for representing language as a complicated set of gears of a machinery, each gear with a sequential function; and then copying that set of gears three times as shadows of each other, to signify the different dimensions of denotation, connotation and evocation. Then I ran into a further problem: gears and machines are linear in function, whereas language is not so limited. Word order or syntax can be changed around without affecting the meaning, much like in math the order of the factors does not affect the product. More importantly, words, even though they appear in sequence, cross-reference each other in non-linear recursive fashion to create a gestalt of coherent grammar and full meaning: the *phrase*. The basic unit of full meaning is the phrase, not the individual words.

Various conclusions are to be drawn from this. First, connotation and evocation make language polysemic, having rich multiple meanings and of course the potential for ambiguity and manipulation. Separating its denotation or direct meaning from its connotations and evocations is an important preliminary step for critical thinking. Second, language cannot be represented mechanically, because it is non-linear, multi-dimensional, multifunctional, polysemic, as well as context-dependent and culture-bound. It is organic and fluid, not mechanical. Systems of signs that do not have these basic characteristics are not languages but, if anything, *metagrammatical simulations of language*. For example, the numbers, variables and symbols of mathematics have only quantitative denotation but no qualitative meaning, connotation or emotional content of their own. Therefore, math is not a language but a *notation.* Yet it is part of language because it can be sounded out, narrated and assigned meaning.

The multifunctionality of each word in natural human language presents an important lesson for machine and systems design. The more its different parts serve multiple functions and, in general, the more it models natural language, the higher its efficiency and synergy, its redundancy and reliability, and the more capable and sophisticated the machine.

Sound is another essential part of language. Cognitive science research shows that language is processed aurally, 'through the ear' so to speak. When we think or read quietly, we sound out the words mentally, even in partial or abbreviated form ('mentalese'), in order to fully understand them. This process of talking to ourselves, called *subvocalisation*, is accompanied by minute movements of the larynx and vibrations of the vocal cords. Even sign language and lip reading are accompanied at least partially by subvocalisation. Similar parts of the brain are activated by deaf signers and hearing speakers alike. Congenitally deaf people, who have never heard speech, can still perceive vibrations, emit sounds, subvocalise them and remember them. They also report hearing mental 'voices' called auditory voice hallucinations (AVH). It is not clear how much of their thought process is image-based or to what extent it uses subvocal reinforcement.

Our hominid ancestors 'spoke' for thousands of years before developing writing, evolution playing a part in this development. Writing systems may be pictographic, ideographic, or phonetic, but they all work in support of memory and speech (Derrida, 1976). Saussure argued convincingly that words are composed of a sound and the mental image it evokes. Each language has a different word or sound assigned to each image, mostly arbitrarily by use and habit until it became a generalised social convention accepted by the community of speakers. Writing or the graphic representation of speech is not language itself but merely a notation, a translation of sounds into visual prompts, tactile in the case of Braille.

Logic vs. Truth

No reasonable person, I believe, would argue that the Morse Code is a language. It is in fact a notation of alphabetic writing, which is in turn a notation of speech. The phonetic alphabet is a notation of phonemes or speech sounds. The complexity of the system is not a factor. The secret codes of cryptography are still notations regardless of the complexity of the encryption. The set of numbers, variables and symbols of mathematical notation represents operations. The so-called formal 'languages' of logic, math, linguistics and computer science are really translations of everyday ambiguous language into a code, a *notation* without ambiguity.

Formal logic is also referred to as mathematical logic, and both notation systems, one numerical and the other alphabetic, are similarly arranged into formulas and theorems. Logic translation, also called natural language formalisation, entails converting a sentence in natural language into the symbols of a logic formula. It bears noting that all formalisation reduces to a notation that eliminates ambiguity, resulting in an impoverishment of language. At the other end of the spectrum there is poetry, an enrichment of language in terms of aesthetics, imagery and plurality of meaning. Formalisation is metonymical: it works strictly by contiguity of symbols. Poetry is, in addition, metaphorical: it works also by similarity and contrast. In the formalisation process, however, the meaning of words is abstracted into variables that can represent any number of other words. That is, meaning is abstracted and then discarded, replaced by symbolic variables (*tokens* in computer science). As a result, formal logic can determine the validity of an argument, but not its truth, which is tied to meaning.

Take a perfectly logical example: 'all S = F, W = S, therefore W = F', meaning 'All Sea animals are Fish. Whales are Sea animals. Therefore, Whales are Fish'. The argument is formally valid but semantically untrue because whales are mammals, not fish. By the same token, logic translations cannot capture connotation, irony, sarcasm, evocation, emphasis, tone, style, figures of speech or any of the emotional or stylistic content of natural language. Neither can algorithms. Regardless their complexity, algorithms are also a linear notation, a binary tree for a set of sequential commands or operations. Their composition by addition and accumulation, sequentially piled one after another with some redundancy, gives only the illusion of complexity, but they are rudimentary compared to the multifunctional and multidimensional grammar of natural human languages.

Formal logic, despite admittedly being a mathematical notation, has borrowed for itself the concepts of natural language, such as *formal* 'language, grammar and syntax', as well as 'alphabet' for its set of symbols and 'letter' for its individual symbols. Computer science has followed suit. This is purely a matter of analogy and convenience of reference, but it is not literally true. Formalised text, by any other name, is a notation, a glorified Morse Code. I do not mean to trivialise or devalue the immense usefulness of formalisation, which among other things provides a link between linguistics and computer science.

Noam Chomsky is a key figure in formal linguistics. His early seminal work, *Syntactic Structures* (1957), is 'an attempt to construct a formalised general theory of linguistic structure' and 'develop a *transformational* model'. The goal is to construct a formalised 'grammar' that can be viewed as 'a device of some sort' (i.e., a machine) to generate sentences that closely approach natural language. *Rules of transformation* would then be applied to syntactic structures in order to generate grammatical sentences. He would call his method *transformational-generative grammar*. His grammar, however, would be 'independent of meaning'—that is, abstracted into a notation with formulas and transformational theorems. A basic subject-verb-object sentence such as 'The man caught a fish' is abstracted into NP_1-VP-NP_2 (noun phrase 1 + verb phrase + noun phrase 2). It is clearly a notation. Nevertheless, Chomsky begins *Syntactic Structures* with the following definition: 'From now on I will consider a *language* to be a set of sentences constructed out of a finite set of elements [...] Similarly, the set of "sentences" of some formalised system of mathematics can be considered a language' (pp. 11–13). Like in the example above, Chomsky's arbitrary definition is formally valid but semantically untrue, because its premise (all notations are languages) is false. Algebra is a notation; therefore, algebra is a language. But clearly, a whale is not a fish, and a string of symbols is not a 'sentence'!

I will return to Chomsky later, but for now I would like to highlight a few important points. It is significant that Chomsky (1957) was working during the development of the modern programmable computer, first proposed by Alan Turing (1936), with workable models being built by IBM in the 1950s. Chomsky's insistence on formalising a natural language (English) into a standard notation independent of meaning, and the sheer frequency with which he uses the word 'device' or 'machine' as a hypothetical sentence generator, shows that he is fundamentally working on the concept of a language program for the up-and-coming computer. Not only was he on the cutting edge of technology, but he was in fact ahead of his time. His transformational-generative grammar

(TGG) was indeed a blueprint for today's 'generative pre-trained transformer' (GPT). The attentive critical reader may already suspect that Chomsky's systematic 'rules of transformation' are no longer a grammar but a metagrammar. His formal system, once made independent of meaning, is no longer a language but an abstract notation. In his above quote ('the set of "sentences" of some formalised system of mathematics can be considered a language'), he places mathematical 'sentences' in quotations to indicate that it is merely a metaphor, but with a sleight of hand he subsequently normalises the use of the term *language*, without quotations, to refer to mathematical notation, as though its meaning was literally true and not figurative—another case of bait-and-switch to derail critical thinking.

What a Difference a Word Makes

Here is the main point in this discussion: computer codes are literally notations and only figuratively speaking, *languages*. Since the term 'computer language' is already broadly accepted, there is no sense in trying to change it, so long as we are cognisant of its purely metaphorical rather than literal meaning. There is nothing trivial about this distinction. Innumerable fallacies owe their existence to the habit of mind of carelessly (and often willingly) taking figurative speech literally. The following is a true story.

At a meeting of the university faculty senate, concerned with a motion to eliminate the 'foreign' language requirement, particularly for STEM disciplines (science, technology, engineering and math), an argument in favour was that students would be better served by learning computer 'languages' instead. I was dumbfounded to see how little most people and even PhDs in other fields understand about the true nature and fundamental usefulness of languages. They think languages are only good for 'communicating' with other people, travelling, asking for directions, ordering at a French restaurant or asking 'Où sont les toilettes?' They might even think that they wasted their time studying French when they discover that toilets in Europe are marked W.C.—Water Closet. The global expansion of English propelled by technology and the mass media is leading Americans to abandon other languages, thinking that they can make do with English alone. Second-language requirements and bilingual education are under attack in schools and universities across the United States. The accessibility of machine translation on your phone is leading people around the world to adopt a similar single-language attitude, neglecting even the study of English, formerly thought of as necessary to 'get ahead'. Significantly, many of my colleagues at the faculty senate meeting thought that computer 'languages' are actual languages, rather than notations or *codes* based, not on language, but on Boolean algebra. To the 26 characters in the English alphabet (50 if you include punctuation marks), Boolean algebra only has two, 0 and 1. To the thousands of operations that natural language grammar brings to bear on those 26 characters, Boolean algebra only has three: *and*, *or* and *not*. Concurrently with our faculty senate meeting, a bill was being pushed through the state legislature to substitute second-language requirements in public schools with computer coding, a mechanical skill (like typing in the age of dictation and speech recognition) doomed to become obsolete with the advent of new notations and technologies and the rise of user interfaces—beginning with Windows and HTML, which made DOS coding obsolete, and ending with GPT or LLM platforms, which can do the coding for us.

The brief arguments that many of us were able to adduce in favour of languages and their core importance for the development of critical thinking and problem-solving skills were not enough to convey such a complex rationale in a few seconds, within the short attention span of a meeting debate. A simple meme—the phrase 'computer language'—was enough to undo decades of data, empirical research and argumentation. Also weighing against us was an unspoken secondary reason: funding criteria are now tied to metrics, with student enrolment as a main consideration. The financial competition among departments and disciplines is another symptom of *applying the wrong metagrammar where it does not belong*. Capitalism constantly applies the metagrammar of business to all kinds of areas where returns on investment are intangible and qualitative values are at stake, in this case higher education. The resulting impoverishment in educational quality has a severe impact on the intellectual development of students and the future of society.

We lost the vote 21 to 17 and the second-language requirement was eliminated. On my way out, an elder statesman came to me and said: 'When I was in college, I was allowed to substitute my language requirement with Fortran'. That is, the obsolete FORTRAN 77, limited to numerical computation and one of almost 9,000 computer scripts for different applications—a veritable Tower of Babel. Developed by IBM in 1955 and updated numerous times, Fortran remains a binary command-based notation, as opposed to more versatile ones like HTML, JavaScript or Python, which seek to approach the structure of natural speech. 'And how is that working out for you?'—I thought to myself but did not say it, because I learned as a child to quietly observe and learn from the mistakes of others. Whereas computer coding notations (which the tech industry passes off as 'languages') are rigid and have versions with limited shelf-life before falling into obsolescence, millions of people will continue to speak their living, communal and evolving natural languages just like they have for centuries.

Unfortunately, in the United States and elsewhere, bilingual and second-language education are under attack, often out of ideological or political motivations based on populist nativism, prejudice and near-sighted anti-immigrant agendas. Starting in academic year 2023–2024, some public colleges and universities became keen on closing their world languages departments as non-essential (Bauman, 2023; Walkowitz, 2023). The pretext is billed as 'sustainable business models for higher education' (Hartocollis, 2023). Such is the sales pitch of the consulting firm RPK Group, part of 'an unholy alliance of far-right ideology and mercenary venture capitalists' (Weatherby, 2023, p. A22). This marketing start-up misappropriates the concept of 'sustainability' from the fields of environment and development, to give targeted cuts the façade of a greenish agenda. Their premise is based on the fallacy that the relationship between society and education, or among departments in a university, is a zero-sum game. Education is a qualitative investment, not a quantifiable return, but quality and synergy play no part in their equation. Not surprisingly, there is not one single PhD in their organisation, and very few of their 'higher-education consultants' even have a master's degree, albeit in *unrelated fields*. Their pitch is to the overgrown managerial class who syphon resources away from teaching.

The co-opting of education by politicians and ideologues only leads to censorship and indoctrination, while the wrongful application of business metagrammar, especially under the myth of 'sustainable finance', sacrifices foundational studies in favour of vocational, market-ready skills. Without a liberal arts foundation, higher education grows into a crooked and hollow tree.

Conclusion

Traditionally, linguists have granted language two dimensions of meaning: *denotation* (what it literally names) and *connotation* (what it figuratively implies). Following functional metagrammar, I have added a third functional dimension: *evocation*, given the role of both individual and communal memory for the determination of meaning through usage, within a shared geographical space, social history, generation and culture. This makes language analysable from all relevant perspectives. Critical thinking and unbiased problem solving require recognising and managing connotations and evocations without distorting the purely denotative or literal function of language. Albeit, neutral, unambiguous, literal natural language still has an irreducible *meaning*, without which it would be merely a notation.

Technological culture, however, seeks to formalise language by setting aside its meaning and quality and reducing it to formulas, amenable to quantification and computation. The problem arises when the notation is falsely enthroned as a 'language' using the same metaphorical and figurative speech that science and logic purport to avoid. The proponents typically begin by placing human qualities in quotation marks indicating their figurative application to machines, to later normalise their usage and consummate their deceit by supressing the quotations. This replaces quality with quantity and reduces any proposition of value to arbitrary metrics designed to exercise institutional power over individuals. The manoeuvre applies machine or business metagrammar beyond its legitimate scope, squarely where it does not belong. The application of a wrong metagrammar results in a distortion in the structure of institutions, organisations, government, society, personality, as well as the prevailing system of values and beliefs. Once ingrained, the distortion becomes fixed, institutionalised and difficult to modify.

References

Bauman, D. (2023, 11 August). Why is West Virginia U. making sweeping cuts? *The Chronicle of Higher Education*. Retrieved from https://www.chronicle.com/article/why-is-west-virginia-u-making-sweeping-cuts.

Chomsky, N. (1957). *Syntactic Structures*. Mouton.

Derrida, J. (1976). *Of Grammatology*. Translated by G. C. Spivak. The Johns Hopkins University Press.

Hartocollis, A. (2023, 19 August). Slashing its budget, West Virginia asks what is essential. *The New York Times*, Section A, Page 14. Retrieved from https://www.nytimes.com/2023/08/18/us/west-virginia-university-budget-cuts-deficit.html.

Robinson, I., Webber, J., & Eifrem, E. (2015). *Graph Databases* (2nd ed.). O'Reilly Media Inc.

Turing, A. M. (1936, 12 November). On computable numbers, with an application to the Entscheidungsproblem. *Proceedings of the London Mathematical Society*. Retrieved from https://www.cs.virginia.edu/~robins/Turing_Paper_1936.pdf

Walkowitz, R. L. (2023, 19 September). Gutting language departments would be a disaster. *The Chronicle of Higher Education*. Retrieved from https://www.chronicle.com/article/gutting-language-departments-would-be-a-disaster

Weatherby, L. (2023, 20 August). What just happened at West Virginia University should worry all of us. *The New York Times*, Opinion, Section A, Page 22. Retrieved from https://www.nytimes.com/2023/08/20/opinion/west-virginia-university-cuts.html

5

Grammar and Cognitive Function

Introduction

Is there such a thing as grammatical intelligence? In *The War Against Grammar* (2003), Classics professor David Mulroy quotes the reaction of a colleague, English composition professor Karen Heise upon reading her first student essays: 'What I saw horrified me: sentence fragments, gross spelling errors, punctuation misuse, *jumbled thinking*, and even sometimes no thinking at all'. Her college students 'couldn't communicate in complete sentences, *much less logical paragraphs*' (p. 13; *my italics*). This sense of grammatical decline accompanying a decline in clear thinking is a familiar experience for educators. Conversely, teachers commonly notice that 'smart' students write well and learn better. Writing well entails constructing cogent, complex and varied grammatical sentences, but this ability extends beyond the sentence to the organisation of ideas, evidence and critical argumentation.

That is, grammatical ability extends to reasoning. Learning better, on the other hand, is related to reading comprehension, the mirror image of writing well, characterised by grammatical understanding and critical relation of ideas. Professor Mulroy tested reading comprehension by asking students to paraphrase the first sentence of the U.S. Declaration

E. Camayd-Freixas, *Metagrammar*, https://doi.org/10.1007/978-3-031-92337-1_5

of Independence, whose literal meaning is: when historical circumstances lead a people to become independent, they have a duty to explain why.

> When in the course of human events, it becomes necessary for one people to dissolve the political bands which have connected them with another, and to assume among the powers of the earth, the separate and equal station to which the Laws of Nature and Nature's God entitle them, a decent respect to the opinions of mankind requires that they should declare the causes which impel them to the separation.

Mulroy reports that most students missed the point, and some were downright misguided, with answers like, '…as a group of people everyone is equal, but when it comes to the laws of nature, only the strong will survive' or 'Cut your earthly bonds and wear the mantle of Nature and God' (pp. 17–19). This was not due to a lack of vocabulary but to poor grammatical understanding of a complex sentence, starting with an inability to identify its subject and main verb. Instead of grasping the literal meaning, students filled the gap in comprehension with their own personal ideologies and beliefs. Mulroy titles this section of *The War Against Grammar* (2003) 'Why Did We Revert to Tribalism?'.

In the case of both reading and writing, grammatical ability extends beyond the sentence to the organisation of thought, and therefore to tasks that go beyond language itself and are associated with general intelligence. Mulroy sees in the above responses 'a kind of higher illiteracy' in which even students who can express themselves adequately 'lack the tools' of 'grammatical analysis' (p. 19). In this chapter, we will review evidence that grammatical literacy translates into metagrammatical skills and how these are enhanced by training.

Grammar Acquisition

We all infer grammar from our daily language use, but some individuals develop this ability on their own to a high degree, even without formal grammatical training. Before we jump to the non-explanation that this is a 'natural' ability or that grammatical understanding is somehow the 'black-box' product of 'innate' intelligence, we must consider the evident opposite, that school-independent proficiency is due to the quality and variety of language exposure, from early childhood to young adulthood. Schooling can then be added to the equation. One way to enhance these skills is of course to study grammar, not as a set of constricting rules, but rather as a complete *system* of enabling functions. Without formal study, spontaneous development is usually slow and limited. Taught in the context of metagrammar, as a source of practical reasoning with concrete applications to everyday life, grammar should become a meaningful and relevant subject in primary, secondary and higher education. The more we understand grammar, the better equipped our toolbox for problem solving, critical thinking and innovation.

Unfortunately, grammar is taught less and less in schools at all levels, even though it has been the foundation of the liberal arts since Greco-Roman times. Most people simply get by with the unreasoned grammar they infer from common usage, often unaware of their own ungrammatical constructions. This in turn is reflected in diminished critical-thinking and problem-solving skills. Mulroy traces this 'war against grammar' to a tendentious push towards 'scientific' (quantitative) linguistics and away from traditional (qualitative) grammar and rhetoric, a push that culminated in the 1950s. Its epitome, Mulroy points out, is Charles Fries' influential *The Structure of English* (1952), whose very first page 'compares the new scientific attitude toward languages to Harvey's work on the circulation of blood and traditional grammar to the practice of bleeding' (p. 5). Followers of this 'anti-grammar' trend helped to bring about a sharp decline in formal grammar instruction. Significantly, this was accompanied by a decline in national standardised SAT (Scholastic Aptitude Test) scores. 'The average verbal score dropped over 50 points, from 478 in 1963 to the 420 s in the seventies. The quantitative score fell from 502 to 466 in 1980'. In 1996, SAT scores had to be artificially 'recentred' to bring their average back to about 500 (p. 10).

The best training method for improving reasoning skills, beyond studying formal grammar, is to study comparative grammar of two or more languages, particularly if they are very different. Traditionally, this was best accomplished by studying Classics: Latin and, to a lesser extent, ancient Greek. Yet enrolment in Classics declined as well. Mulroy noticed that students were having difficulties in Classics due to a lack of knowledge of English grammar and basic grammatical concepts and terminology. They ended up avoiding Classics courses as a result. The problem was generalised to the modern languages. 'In 1965, 16.5% of college credits were earned in foreign language courses. This figure fell to 7.8% in 1977' (p. 11). In fact, the figure fell as low as 7.3% in 1980 and, after reaching a high of 9.1% in 2006, it has again fallen sharply to an all-time low of 6.5% in 2021 (Lusin et al., 2023). This secular decline coincides with the rise of the digital age, from calculators to computers to the Internet, which supports widespread quantification. Another sharp decline after 2010 coincides with a national push to promote STEM (science, technology, engineering and math) and a corresponding cut in Title VI federal funding of foreign language programs in higher education. Politics also played a role, particularly in the U.S. House of Representatives, which controls the purse. In public secondary schools (grades 9–12), the United States saw a gradual increase in foreign language study from 20.9% of students in 1948 to 43.6% in 2000 (U.S. Department of Education, 2002). College enrolments stayed flat, however, suggesting a shift to lower-level high school courses. This post-World War II surge in high school language enrolment appears to reflect the increased awareness of foreign cultures, communications, travel, globalisation and immigration, but the effect did not last: K-12 foreign language enrolment has again fallen sharply to 19.66% in 2015 (American Councils for International Education, 2017). In comparison, median foreign language enrolment in Europe reaches 92% (Devlin, 2018).

On the one hand, the anti-grammar movement led to native language deficiencies, which made foreign language study more challenging and less attractive. On the other hand, starting with Charles Fries' 'aural-oral' method, second-language teaching methodology also moved away from grammar in favour of communicative, conversational and task-based approaches. Translation exercises, which promote grammar, syntax and usage abilities, were especially demonised as retarding verbal fluency. A quick path to fluency, errors and all, has become the quantifiable evidence of 'successful' language learning. The gradual qualitative development of reasoning skills through mastery of grammar is ignored, because it can only be measured via expensive longitudinal studies that make variables difficult to isolate. Despite the decline in its formal study, we still infer grammar from language use. The process of grammatical inference is greatly enhanced when we contrast the grammar of our native language with that of a second language. As a result, foreign language study remains the best way to acquire grammatical literacy and develop critical reasoning skills.

Evidence considered later in this chapter shows that comparative grammar expands our problem-solving toolbox and our syntactic flexibility for innovation and 'thinking outside the box'. It breaks away from our functional fixedness on a single grammar and makes thinking more nuanced, open and accepting of differences. Studies show a direct correlation between command of comparative grammar and general intelligence. The latest neuroscience research further documents the benefits of bilingualism for childhood development, adult cortical activity in problem solving and elderly preservation of cognitive function.

Comparative Grammar

> 'Languages throw light on each other: one language can, after all, see itself only in the light of another language' –(M. Bakhtin, 1981, p. 12)

According to linguistic typology, subject-verb-object or SVO languages (e.g., John loves Mary) are the prevailing convention for 42% of world languages, including most Western languages; whereas 45% are subject-object-verb or SOV (John Mary loves) including many Eastern languages, only 12% start with the verb and fewer than one per cent start with the object. However, the syntax of most languages is flexible enough to grammatically allow for almost any combination of the three. In some languages, adjectives and partitive genitives are placed after the noun (blades *of* grass); in others, before the noun (of wood the boat) with occasional flexibility (the wooden boat). In terms of modifier phrases, some use prepositions while others use postpositions. English is changing from pre to post (This is the book about which I told you > This is the book I told you about). Suffice it to say that each language has different ways of saying the same thing, but *different* languages find remarkably different systemic *solutions* to achieve the same result.

This is where comparative grammar truly becomes mind expanding, giving us a much larger repertoire of syntactic patterns and functional structures and a heightened flexibility for seeing new paths to problem solving. In addition, it frees us from our functional fixedness on the structures of our native language and opens our minds to the fact that other languages have different but equally valid ways of expression, this being the foundation of critical thinking, but also of tolerance and appreciation for diversity, given that languages are inseparable from cultures. Being bilingual implies being bicultural. The earlier in life this occurs, the better, but it is never too late. You do not have to become fluent in a second language to apprehend the systemic structural differences. All you need is an understanding and acceptance of comparative grammar.

The comparison of the verbal, nominal and prepositional systems is particularly illuminating. These grammatical systems are further discussed in Chapter 6 next. Here, some general examples should suffice to illustrate the point.

In Romance languages like Spanish, conjugations (changing the verb endings) can indicate person, tense, aspect and mood, with occasional use of helping verbs. English uses a simpler system of helping verbs to achieve the conjugational function, and moods are simplified, with the subjunctive fast becoming archaic. This makes English easier to learn, facilitating its diffusion. It also makes English syntax more rigid, having to compensate for it with a more extensive vocabulary and complex pronunciation; for instance, Spanish has five vowel sounds while English has fourteen. A recent strategy to shorten English syntax is the transposition of parts of speech, frowned upon by English teachers, particularly turning nouns into verbs (she 'medalled' at the Olympics and 'authored' a book). Simplification of the verbal system obscures or eliminates conjugation, a lack remedied by foreign language study. Significantly, *conjugation is the conceptual model for all non-verbal distributive systems*, physical, biological, mechanical, electronic or digital, whether the recipients are of the same or different kinds—this being a prime example of grammar modelling metagrammatical systems.

While conjugations apply to verbs, declensions apply to nouns by changing their ending to specify different syntactic functions. There must be agreement in the gender, number and case of *nominals* (nouns, articles, pronouns and adjectives). In a sense, conjugation by person is to verbs, what declension by case is to nouns. Latin, for example, has a typical set of cases, comprised of nominative, vocative, genitive, accusative, dative and ablative, with different endings for each case. Many languages besides Latin have declensions, for example, Greek, German, Slavic, Finnish, Semitic, Turkic, Quechua, as well as some African and other language families.

Historically, classical Latin had both conjugations and declensions, which made it very complex, but as the Roman Empire expanded using foreign mercenaries into regions that had different substrate languages, these new speakers simplified the language by adding Latin prepositions (*ad*, *ex*, etc.) instead of declensions. The Romance languages that followed kept the conjugational system inherited from Latin, but replaced declension with a prepositional system, which was simpler but also unstable, as prepositions were added, changed or disused. Old English had a moderate declension system, but it has been so simplified in Modern English that nouns and adjectives have no case declension to speak of and only pronouns have some. In addition, the prepositional system has been further simplified by using collocation (word order) instead of some prepositions to indicate case; for example, *John* (nominative) *gave Mary* (dative) *flowers* (accusative) in lieu of 'John gave flowers *to* Mary' (nominative-accusative-dative). Lacking more complex conjugation and declension systems, English speakers find it more difficult to learn languages that do have them.

The price of simplicity and monolingualism in general is having a limited toolbox for finding varied and complex expressive solutions, a limited knowledge of grammar and a limited control of syntax. Hence the importance of comparative grammar, especially between dissimilar languages. Bilingualism by itself is not optimal without the formal study of contrastive syntax and comparative grammar. Grammatical reasoning is the basis for metagrammatical reasoning.

Human Intelligence

Educators may readily notice that grammatical understanding and command correlate with general academic aptitude, some would say with 'intelligence', although I prefer to call it metagrammatical flexibility. I am not so sure that intelligence can truly be measured and will not defend that position. In the early days of the construct 'intelligence quotient' (IQ), psychometrics was employed pseudo-scientifically by eugenicists, racists and sexists. Today, we know that the supposed measures of intelligence have proven to be consistent across sexes, races and cultures. I am cognisant as well of biologist Stephen Jay Gould's critique in *The Mismeasure of Man* (1996). There are qualitative aspects that evade measurement, such as creativity, discipline and perseverance, which brings to mind Michelangelo's famous quote, 'Genius is infinite patience'. Proponents of the concepts of 'emotional' and 'social' intelligence, among others, posit the existence of different kinds of intellectual abilities. After these caveats, let us review some of the evidence.

English psychologist and statistician Charles Spearman, in his famous article on 'General Intelligence' (1904), published an experimental result which has been replicated countless times, that those who do well in one type of intelligence task also do well in the others. That is, the results of different types of cognitive tests correlate with each other and with the total result of the entire battery of tests. This led Spearman to posit a single 'general intelligence factor' he called 'the *g* factor'. He devised a new statistical formula to measure this correlation, Spearman's rank correlation coefficient, used in factor analysis, to arrive at the *g* factor (another 'black box'), a single intelligence capability of unknown nature, supposedly at work in all types of tests. Spearman's *g* even correlates with non-verbal cognitive tests, such as visualisation and spatial manipulation tests that focus on abstract reasoning. This may be due to mental imagery and sensory tasks being inseparable from verbal propositions and grammarlike operations. Nevertheless, the *g* factor is simply a mathematical construct, a statistical coefficient. Modern neuroscientists contend that this measurement corresponds, not to a single, central mental ability, but rather to a group of cognitive skills that involve different parts of the brain. This is consistent with the development and transfer of multifunctional (meta)grammatical skills.

The predictive validity of *g* has a strong correlation with scholastic achievement, as *g* relates to the ability to learn new material and understand new concepts and meanings (Jensen, 1998, p. 270). This validity diminishes gradually for predicting job placement, job performance and income, as other factors come into play. Yet, it is in scholastic achievement that Spearman's results are most interesting. His research on English-speaking students across 'the four branches of school studies' (Classics, French, English and Math) reveals that the level of performance which correlates most strongly with general intelligence (*g*) is in the study of Classics, Latin and Greek (0.96), followed by French (0.88), English (0.80) and Math (0.75), this hierarchy being constant (Spearman, 274–276). This suggests that comparative grammar has a very high correlation with general intelligence. Similarly, Wechsler (1958) found that the highest correlation (0.83) with his Adult Intelligence Scale (WAIS) was in the score for vocabulary. For a comprehensive account of intelligence tests and theories, see Hunt (2018).

The Bilingual Edge

Further evidence is found in studies of bilingualism, starting with Peal & Lambert's 'The Relation of Bilingualism to Intelligence' (1962). They tested 10-year-old students from six French schools in Montreal, including groups of French monolinguals and French–English bilinguals. The subjects were administered verbal and non-verbal intelligence tests, as well as measures of attitudes towards the English and French communities. The study found that bilinguals performed significantly better than monolinguals on both verbal and non-verbal intelligence tests. Factor analysis on the data suggested that the 'structures of intellect' vary between the two groups. Bilinguals have a more developed 'language asset' that increases their capacity for concept formation and gives them greater 'mental flexibility' as they appear to have 'a more diversified set of mental abilities'. The researchers also quote a Welsh study on the importance of bilingual education: 'the teaching of Welsh along with English does what the efficient study of any two languages must do: it frees the mind from the tyranny of words', such that it can focus on meaning and concepts, unrestricted by a single language (pp. 1–5). Peal & Lambert further found that bilingual and bicultural experience fostered greater acceptance of the second-language community and less resistance to the second language (pp. 19–22).

Current studies of bilingualism often include a cognitive neuroscience perspective. The all-important factors of attention span and control were tested in groups of English monolinguals and Korean-English bilinguals, controlling for first and second-language proficiency, exposure and age of acquisition. In a non-verbal pitch discrimination test, subjects were asked to count infrequent tones while their EEG was recorded to detect neural correlates of 'sustained attention'. The research found that bilinguals had greater sustained attention than monolinguals at all ages of acquisition, especially at an early age (Chung-Fat-Yim et al., 2023). In turn, early bilingualism leads to enhanced foreign language learning in secondary school (Nguyen & Winsler, 2021). Chung-Fat-Yim and colleagues additionally determined that high exposure to their native language was also significant, with both bilinguals and monolinguals performing better than their lower-exposure counterparts. The study concluded that both bilingualism and higher language exposure shaped neural processes for sustained attention and control, with implications for perception and learning.

Cognitive neuroscientist Ellen Bialystok (1999, 2015) sets aside the question of intelligence and focuses instead on the uncontroverted concept of *executive function*, in which bilinguals consistently outperform monolinguals. Located in the prefrontal cortex, executive function allows the brain to access particular regions or memories. It has two components that are central to problem solving: *monitoring* (for patterns, options, relevant items, errors) and *inhibition* (suppression of irrelevant data, interference and erroneous responses, to narrow down the options). There is growing evidence that executive function in bilinguals is more efficient and accurate, as they constantly adjust proactive (monitoring) and reactive (inhibition) cognitive control to achieve efficient performance (Morales et al., 2013). In the bilingual mind, both languages are coactivated, requiring constant selection (monitoring and inhibition).

Bilinguals employ both global and local control mechanisms to manage coactivated languages that compete for selection (Seo & Prat, 2023). Executive function is closely related to memory. Grant et al. (2023) found that individuals were more accurate in eliminating false memories and disinformation when using their foreign language, this being evidence that a foreign language increases the use of memory monitoring, which in turn supports critical thinking. The benefits of bilingualism for memory, cognitive function and linguistic performance are present across the lifespan, fending off cognitive decline, contributing to cognitive reserves and mental acuity in old age and retarding by four years the onset of symptoms in those suffering from dementia (Bialystok et al., 2007, 2014).

In addition to the EEG and the availability of the CAT scan since the late 1970s, many researchers currently use more recent fMRI technology (functional magnetic resonance imaging) to map brain activity and the flow of oxygenated blood in real time in response to language and cognitive tasks. The prevailing wisdom is that bilingualism entails constant *conflict resolution* in linguistic and cognitive processes, opening new pathways of brain activity that increase neuroplasticity (Costa, 2021; Costa et al., 2008).

Polyanskaya et al. (2022) further found a bilingual advantage in 'metacognitive performance' (tracking one's own cognitive performance) in linguistic tasks, including self-monitoring for error reduction. This bilingual advantage increases with the simultaneous acquisition and use of 'typologically different languages' (that is, languages with syntactically different conjugational and declensional-prepositional systems) leading to the development of *diverse processing strategies* and enhanced metacognition, including *greater grammatical awareness*. Numerous studies since the 1970s define metacognition as 'the ability to monitor and regulate one's own cognitive processes and behaviour' via two important components: 'knowledge about cognition and regulation of cognition, which in turn affords regulation of behaviour' (p. 2706).

Bilingual code switching in real time, or toggling back and forth between languages, has been found to involve resolving among conflicting linguistic representations and modulating the deployment of additional processes of cognitive control, thereby increasing conflict adaptation moment by moment and assisting in subsequent conflict resolution (Adler et al., 2020). Cognition involves a modulated balance between automaticity and cognitive control. Research has shown that language control in professional translation differs from that of other bilingual activities. Professional translators, bilinguals and monolinguals performed a memory search task to test how automaticity is acquired through consistent practice. Monolinguals showed higher levels of automaticity after extensive practice in the learning phase of the task but paid a cognitive price when the task and its learning condition changed. On the contrary, professional translators and bilinguals, in that order, carried out the task in a more controlled fashion in the initial learning stage and were less affected by a switch in the learning condition. They continued to exert control over the memory search despite practice. The ability to maintain control was considered the result of professional translation and bilingual everyday practice (Togato et al., 2022). In every case, practice and experience enhance the development of skills.

Conclusion

After centuries of being the cornerstone of education, the study of grammar declined with the rise of electronic media, starting with commercial television in the 1950s. The study of Classics would be practically abandoned. The emphasis on conversational methods of second-language teaching reflects a tendency to combine education with entertainment. Student recruitment and retention became the economic imperative. Effortless fluency and role-playing won over the concentration required for grammatical reasoning. Meanwhile, grammar teaching was reduced to tedious repetition and rote memorisation. School had to be fun, and grammar was anything but. Business metagrammar, imposed on education, has led to viewing students and parents as clients who wish for immediate results and gratification. Still to this day, grammar is seen as a superfluous discipline too far removed from marketable skills and immediate job placement after graduation. Science and technology attract lucrative government and industry subsidies, while companies seek to spend less in on-the-job training, expecting to hire industry-ready graduates. These and other reasons revolve around the failure to see grammar as a foundational skill, a place reserved for mathematics.

Nevertheless, studies since the early twentieth century have established that grammatical skills can be developed particularly through comparative language study and general language exposure, which correlate with academic achievement, general intelligence and intercultural understanding, fostering a more flexible and diversified set of mental abilities. The latest neuroscience research points to the importance of comparative grammar and bilingualism for the development of neuroplasticity, executive function and higher cognitive skills, including sustained attention and control, error and disinformation detection, regulation of cognitive processes and behaviour, monitoring memory, options and solutions, efficient inhibition of irrelevant data and important aspects of problem solving, including conflict resolution.

Incidentally, inhibition of irrelevant data to focus on promising leads is a uniquely efficient trait of human intelligence. Computers on the contrary run through all available possibilities no matter how meaningless and absurd. Current large language models (LLMs) attempt to replicate this metagrammar by categorising data and prioritising associated categories in which to conduct non-strategic exhaustive search.

References

Adler, R. M., Valdés Kroff, J. R., & Novick, J. M. (2020). Does integrating a code-switch during comprehension engage cognitive control? *Journal of Experimental Psychology: Learning, Memory and Cognition, 46*(4), 741–759. Retrieved from https://doi.org/10.1037/xlm0000755

American Councils for International Education. (2017, June). *The National K-12 Foreign Language Enrollment Survey Report*. Retrieved from https://www.americancouncils.org/sites/default/files/FLE-report-June17.pdf

Bakhtin, M. M. (1981). *The Dialogic Imagination.* Translated by C. Emerson & M. Holquist. University of Texas Press.

Bialystok, E. (1999). Cognitive complexity and attentional control in the bilingual mind. *Child Development, 70*, 636–644.

Bialystok, E. (2015). Bilingualism and the development of executive function: the role of attention. *Child Development Perspectives, 9*(2), 117–121.

Bialystok, E., Craik, F. I. M., & Freedman, M. (2007). Bilingualism as a protection against the onset of symptoms of dementia. *Neuropsychologia, 45*, 459–464.

Bialystok, E., Poarch, G., Luo, L., & Craik, F. I. M. (2014). Effects of bilingualism and aging on executive function and working memory. *Psychology and Aging, 29*, 696–705.

Chung-Fat-Yim, A., Bobb, S. C., Hoshino, N., & Marian, V. (2023, July 10). Bilingualism alters the neural correlates of sustained attention. *Translational Issues in Psychological Science*. American Psychological Association. Advance online publication. Retrieved from https://doi.org/10.1037/tps0000373

Costa, A. (2021). *The Bilingual Brain: And What It Tells Us about the Science of Language*. Penguin.

Costa, A., Hernández, M., & Sebastián-Gallés, N. (2008). Bilingualism aids conflict resolution: evidence from the ANT task. *Cognition, 106*, 59–86.

Devlin, K. (2018). Most European students are learning a foreign language in school while Americans lag. *Pew Research Center, 6 August*. Retrieved from https://www.pewresearch.org/short-reads/2018/08/06

Fries, C. C. (1952). *The Structure of English*. Harcourt, Brace & World.

Gould, S. J. (1996). *The Mismeasure of Man* (2nd ed.). Norton.

Grant, L. H., Pan, A. Y., Huang, Y., Gallo, D. A., & Keysar, B. (2023). Foreign language reduces false memories by increasing memory monitoring. *Journal of Experimental Psychology, 152*(7), 1967–1977. Retrieved from https://doi.org/10.1037/xge0001378

Hunt, E. (2018). *Human Intelligence*. Cambridge University Press.

Jensen, A. R. (1998). *The* g *Factor: The Science of Mental Ability*. Praeger.

Lusin, N., Peterson, T., Sulewski, C., & Zafer, R. (2023). Enrollments in languages other than English in US institutions of higher education, Fall 2021. *Modern Language Association*. Retrieved from https://www.mla.org/content/download/191324/file/Enrollments-in-Languages-Other-Than-English-in-US-Institutions-of-Higher-Education-Fall-2021.pdf

Morales, J., Gómez-Ariaza, C. J., & Bajo, M. T. (2013). Dual mechanisms of cognitive control in bilinguals and monolinguals. *Journal of Cognitive Psychology, 25*(5), 531–546.

Mulroy, D. (2003). *The War Against Grammar*. Boynton/Cook Publishers.

Nguyen, V. H., & Winsler, A. (2021). Early bilingualism predicts enhanced later foreign language learning in secondary school. *Developmental*

Psychology, 57(11), 1926–1942. Retrieved from https://doi.org/10.1037/dev0001248

Peal, E., & Lambert, W. E. (1962). The relation of bilingualism to intelligence. *Psychological Monographs: General and Applied, 76*(27), 1–23. Retrieved from https://doi.org/10.1037/h0093840

Polyanskaya, L., Manrique, H. M., Marín, A., García-Palacios, A., & Ordin, M. (2022). Typological differences influence the bilingual advantage in metacognitive processing. *Journal of Experimental Psychology: General, 151*(11), 2706–2719. Retrieved from https://doi.org/10.1037/xge0001225

Seo, R., & Prat, C. S. (2023). Investigating local and global control mechanisms in bilingual grammatical processing. *Journal of Experimental Psychology: Learning, Memory and Cognition.* Advance online publication. Retrieved from https://doi.org/10.1037/xlm0001251

Spearman, C. (1904). General intelligence objectively determined and measured. *The American Journal of Psychology, 15*(2) (April), 201–292.

Togato, G., Macizo, P., & Bajo, T. (2022). Automaticity and cognitive control in bilingual and translation expertise. *Canadian Journal of Experimental Psychology, 76*(1), 29–43. Retrieved from https://doi.org/10.1037/cep0000268

U.S. Department of Education, National Center for Education Statistics, Common Core of Data (2002). *State Nonfiscal Survey of Public Elementary/Secondary Education, 1982 through 2000.* Retrieved from https://nces.ed.gov/programs/digest/d09/tables/dt09_056.asp

Wechsler, D. (1958). *The Measurement and Appraisal of Adult Intelligence* (4th ed.). Williams & Witkins.

6

From Grammar to Metagrammar

Introduction

There is no postponing it. I have to get technical about grammar. Why do people hate it so? I would venture two main reasons based on the way it has traditionally been taught. First, students and critical thinkers alike rebel against the rigid imposition of rules, known as *normative* or *prescriptive* grammar, the idea that the right way is this, and what you are doing is wrong. This has long been superseded by *descriptive* grammar, which simply describes how people speak in different communities, without passing judgement. Second, grammar is almost always taught as unrelated to everyday life, except for learning how to write and speak 'correctly'—something that can be inferred from fun interactive activities and practice without racking our brain. I do not remember being told ever in school that *grammar teaches you how to think*. I would have paid more attention!

Grammar is not a set of restrictive rules but rather a system of enabling functions that we constantly transfer to our daily interaction with the world. It is time to illustrate some of the many structures through which it moulds our thoughts and actions, that is, the many links between grammar and metagrammar. This chapter first considers *sentence rule*

E. Camayd-Freixas, *Metagrammar*, https://doi.org/10.1007/978-3-031-92337-1_6

grammar, that is, grammar seen from the outside. Then it moves on to *systemic functional grammar*, which is grammar seen from the inside. My aim here is threefold: (1) to open a window into the complex functions of natural grammar and the rich repertoire of operations it offers for understanding similar patterns in nature, society and ourselves; (2) to highlight the core functional structures which organise grammar into a cogent system that serves as an aspirational model for the design and comprehension of other systems *beyond* grammar, in any field of human endeavour; and (3) to highlight the elegant simplicity of grammar, which models the logic and function (the metagrammar) of other systems much simpler than language. Our language is a complete map for exploration, understanding and creation. It is a vast toolbox ready for us to transfer to and from the world outside.

Diacritics

Let us begin by noticing that grammar is a *diacritical* system. Many languages have diacritical marks, including different types of accents, tildes, apostrophes and others, to distinguish or differentiate among letters, words, pronunciations and meanings. Spanish uses the diacritical accent to differentiate words and parts of speech. For example, *este* (this) is a demonstrative adjective, whereas *éste* (he or this one) is a pronoun; *solo* means 'alone' (an adjective) while *sólo* means 'only' (an adverb). Words are also diacritical. English uses 'to lay' as a transitive verb that takes an object to complete its meaning ('to lay down *the book*') versus 'to lie down' which is intransitive; 'fewer' is for things you can count ('fewer items') while 'less' is for things you cannot ('less water'). Verb tenses differentiate among moments in time. In short, every single grammatical structure expresses a difference. *Logical differentiation is the most basic function of grammar and the very foundation of critical thinking*.

Grammar proper applies only within the sentence. All patterns beyond the sentence belong to metagrammar. Patterns also are differentiated diacritically, even as they exhibit family resemblances forming a genre. Thus, grammar and metagrammar articulate the basic complementary functions of thinking: apprehension and construction of *similarity* and *difference*. Both systems, and all others, are based on constituent elements (nouns) and their functions (verbs) arranged into (meta)grammatical sequences (narratives).

It is easy to see the relationship between grammar and metagrammar as an analogy or metaphor. However, there is also a direct (metonymical) relationship between functional grammar (language engineering) and all forms of organisation beyond the sentence in such fields as systems theory or engineering design. Mathematics is the means of measurement and logical verification, but the means of conceptualisation and organisation is grammatical in nature. Every system, method, mechanism, program, ruleset, organisation or protocol has its metagrammar—vaguely called its 'logic' in popular parlance, an equivocal term. Logic is to math what grammar is to language. Logic is simply the transcription of everyday ambiguous language into a *notation* without ambiguity. In contrast to such vague terms as the 'logic' of something which obscure the inner workings of things, metagrammar can be critically read and analysed, broken down into steps or constituent parts, in order to evaluate the internal efficacy of any process.

Metagrammar is a method of reasoning much more complex than simple cause and effect because it mirrors the complete grammatical system of natural languages. It has two basic applications: 'reading' and 'writing'—both of which are grammatically structured. On the side of perception and cognition, we 'read' (linguistically construe) our experience of the world, including pattern recognition, analysis, synthesis, interpretation and *understanding*—that is, finding matching relationships and categorising new experiences in terms of the previous knowledge they activate in long-term memory. On the production side, we 'write' our imprint on the world, including *behaviour* and *design*, which in turn we critically 'read'—that is, self-experience, evaluate, adapt, correct, proofread and redeploy.

Differential and Distributive Functions

Grammar, and by extension metagrammar, has two main systems: nominal and verbal, configured differently in different languages. Some languages, like Latin and the Romance languages, *inflect* or change the endings of nominals (articles, nouns, pronouns and adjectives) to indicate gender (feminine, masculine, neuter) and number (singular, plural). Latin also inflects nominals to differentiate according to *case*. The cases include *nominative* (to name the subject), *vocative* (to address, call or question), *genitive* (to indicate possession or belongingness), *accusative* (for the direct object that receives the action of the verb), *dative* (for the indirect object to whom something is given) and *ablative* (to separate phrases from the main verb, making nominals to stand alone, unaffected by the other five cases). Notice that these six cases are *exhaustive* in the sense that they cover all the logical possibilities in the use of nominals as are needed for all sentence constructions and the complete expression of meaning. In other words, cases are *systematic*. The inflection of nominals according to case is called *declension*, resulting in a declensional system. In this way, the same noun stem with different endings works to express distinctions of gender, number and case. Most importantly, *the case system is the conceptual model for all differential systems.*

Declensional systems, however, can be quite complicated. Latin has five different modes of declension depending on whether a noun is feminine, masculine or neuter, as well as other irregular variations in endings or stems. Each of these five declensions is further divided into singular and plural forms. That is, the nominal system is composed of two operations: differential and distributive. The case system is differential, distinguishing among six nominal cases, but then these six cases are distributed among the different genders (feminine, masculine, neuter) and numbers (singular, plural) in an *ars combinatoria*—a logical method described by Leibniz (1646–1716) based on Ramon Llull (1232–1316) which forms the basis for combinatorial mathematics used in design, music and the arts. Leibniz's notation for differentiation and integration accounts for independent and dependent variables in infinitesimal and differential calculus.

In Latin, the end result of this *ars combinatoria* yields six cases, times five declensions, times singular and plural for a total of *sixty* different endings for nouns and their related pronouns and adjectives, which must agree in gender, number and case. It is important to note that, like all human languages, Latin developed organically and historically, and that grammar is really a theory that came after to describe the language that already existed and to give it consistency, particularly in writing, such that the language would not vary so fast that different generations would no longer understand each other. Equally important is to note that native speakers of classical Latin in ancient Rome were able to learn their complex language entirely by ear, by acoustic memory, and not by grammatical rules, which came later. All languages are initially learned this way. They are 'logical' in that their *differentials* are necessary and sufficient, and readily 'make sense' to listeners and speakers. This natural process of language acquisition is called grammar induction or grammatical inference.

Languages change and develop historically. Pronunciation and vocabulary are the quickest to vary because they are discrete rather than systematic. Grammar changes slowly because it is a *system* in which any change extends across the entire language; but it does change, giving rise to the field of historical grammar. When the ancient Romans, using foreign mercenaries, expanded their empire to lands with different pre-existing (substrate) languages, their complicated 60-part declension system was replaced by a simpler *prepositional system* (using *of* for genitive, *to* for accusative, *for* for dative, etc.) to distinguish among cases. Eventually, this gave rise to the different Romance languages, which replaced declensions with prepositions.

English developed in a similar way from its own sources when Jutes, Angles and Saxons migrated from the regions of today's Germany, Denmark, Holland and Belgium into Britain between the fifth and seventh centuries. They came in contact with the Celtic substrate and the Latin adstrate of Romano-Britons, Britons, Picts and Gaels, and later with French after the Norman Conquest of 1066. Greek and Latin spread in the fifteenth century during the early Renaissance from monastic and ecclesiastical sources. The stabilisation of Modern English after 1500 is owed in great part to the invention of the printing press and the Tyndale Bible, first printed in Early Modern English circa 1535. English was originally a West Germanic language, related to German and Dutch. Like Modern German, it was originally a *synthetic* language; that is, heavily inflected like Latin, synthesising or *joining* gender, number, case and verbal conjugations into single word stems with different endings. Modern Dutch no longer inflects nominals for case. This was a recent change, whereas English early on became an *analytic* language, that is, mostly uninflected, analytic because it *separated* prepositions and helping verbs from their formerly inflected nouns and verbs. It substituted case declensions with a prepositional system, eliminated most verb conjugations, did away with gender for nouns and number for articles and adjectives ('*the big* boys'; '*the tall* girls')—this being unique among European languages. These analytic features have made English more precise and efficient to learn and disseminate.

Initially, the prepositional system was unstable, with a hesitant or ambiguous use of prepositions, but gradually their use (functions) became clearly differentiated and precise. Considering that there are only six cases and so many more prepositions, it is easy to see that the prepositional system is not only simpler, but also much more specific and accurate, eliminating the frequent ambiguities and difficulties of the numerous word endings. Moreover, articles were added to reinforce the gender and number of nouns, but also to distinguish precisely between the specific and the general by using definite and indefinite articles (*the* vs. *a*). This development is an instance of the tendency for grammar (and metagrammar) to *become more precise and efficient over time*. Even though prepositions took the place of case declension, they still indicate all the different cases by using a different set of systemic *solutions*. Prepositions may obscure the cases, but the cases are still there, as present as ever. We just need to be cognisant of the different case functions of prepositions.

The verbal system is also inflected. Verbs have *tense* (degrees of past, present and future), *aspect* (perfect, progressive or imperfect, the action concluded, ongoing or not) and *mood* (indicative, imperative, subjunctive). Other moods that languages inflect or *grammaticalise* include, conditional, exhortative (urging), dubitative (doubting), optative (wishing), hypothetical and potential. Tense, aspect and mood form an *exhaustive* differential system, enabling all possible aspects of action in any linear system, including machines. In addition, the different verbal forms are conjugated (distributed and combined) for the first, second and third person (*I*, *you*, *s/he*) singular and plural. Some languages have additional forms of respect with degrees of formality for addressing different persons (e.g., the Spanish *tú* vs. *usted*). Verb forms that are not conjugated include infinitives, progressives, participles and gerunds. Like nouns and cases, many languages inflect verb endings for conjugations resulting in a complicated system with many combinations. English simplifies conjugation by using helping verbs (variations of *to have*) instead of inflection. This may obscure the conjugational system, but conjugations are still there in every language. Furthermore, *the conjugational system is the conceptual model for all distributive systems*.

An example is the internal combustion engine, in which the *distributor* sends a spark to each cylinder precisely when the piston reaches maximum compression at top dead centre, igniting the fuel and air mixture, which is also distributed through the manifold and intake valves that open at precise intervals. There must be *agreement* between spark and fuel via synchronised timing (tense), duration (aspect) and ratio (mood). We use linguistic differential and distributional (integrative) operations to conceptualise phenomena and to design systems and processes. The differential function works by similarity and contrast, and the distributional or combinatorial function works by contiguity. Further, the solutions in each case are either more synthetic (joined by inflections) or more analytic (separated into particles: prepositions and helping verbs). Analysis and synthesis are of course basic operations of thought. They form a *matrix* with differentiation and combination, constituting a method of reasoning transferred from grammar to metagrammar, from our internalised language system to our interactions with the world.

Systemic Functional Grammar

It is time to discern between the *description* of language use (rule grammar) and the way language works internally aside from how it is described (functional grammar). Saussure distinguishes between *langue* (the functional *language system*) and *parole* (speech or language use, even if written). Functional language is the internalised intuitive system that we all have in the back of our minds, from which we unconsciously draw to produce effortless grammatical speech. Speech is the outer, observable enactment of language (see *speech act theory* in Chapter 7 next). It follows that what linguists describe as grammar is the observation of the regularities of speech as enacted by a community of speakers. This *external* perspective appears as a set of restrictive rules (with occasional exceptions such as irregular verbs). Rule grammar has traditionally been used to teach languages—with unpopular results. Functional grammar, in contrast, is a view of language from *within* in terms of what it *can* do and *how*.

We initially learn our first language, not by keeping track of rules but by internalising its usable functions. We say, 'Aha! I can use this turn of phrase to get *x*'. We try it, and we are rewarded by people understanding and often giving us what we want. We learn through positive reinforcement and conditioned response to internalise the functions of different linguistic *patterns*, as opposed to the rules of construction used by machines and computers. The solutions (problem solving) embedded in this internalised functional grammar are what we unwittingly transfer to our interaction with the world; that is, from functional grammar to functional metagrammar. We do this intuitively.

True, there is no way to talk about this internalised language system without describing it using speech and traditional grammatical terms. Notwithstanding this limitation, the point is to add a different and complementary perspective: looking at the language system as a source, from within, and not only from its outward limits and results as enacted in speech. The object of metagrammar is to *learn to apply the functions of language consciously and strategically* beyond the sentence, as opposed to mindlessly: not as a way of speaking but as a *mode of reasoning*. Systemic functional grammar (SFG), then, is a special form of description that focuses, not on rules, but on how different *linguomental* structures (see Chapter 7) work to produce specific and meaningful results.

M. A. K. Halliday, the main proponent of SFG, distinguishes language as human, verbal and natural, 'as opposed to *designed semiotics* like mathematics and computer languages; [...] verbal as opposed to music, dance and other languages of art. Of course, all these other systems share certain features with language […] *but none of them incorporates all*' (p. 20, *my italics*). That is, all other systems are simpler than language. It follows that metagrammar is always simpler than grammar. Halliday's *Introduction to Functional Grammar* (2014) and other notable works like Croft's *Morphosyntax* (2022) offer an extensive menu from which to select the operations and functions that are most relevant to specific systems. In this book, I consider several examples and applications, but it must be emphasised that the bulk of this work remains to be done, as well as that of comparing different genres of metagrammar and synthesising more general principles.

Halliday first highlights a central feature: the *compositional* structure of language, 'known as "constituency": larger units of language consist of smaller ones' (p. 5). He identifies three types of constituencies, each one organised by rank: the sounding system or *phonological constituency*, the writing system or *graphological constituency* and the conceptual system or *lexicogrammatical constituency*. This latter linguo-conceptual system is the most relevant. Its field is technically called *lexicogrammar* because it includes morphology, word and concept formation, and their categorisation, in addition to grammar and syntax. Halliday plainly calls it 'grammar' for short, since grammar does include all the constituents smaller than the sentence, right down to letters, syllables and phonemes. In this sense, 'grammar' is also short for *systemic functional grammar* (SFG), the functional model behind metagrammar.

In the ranks of the phonological constituency, consonants and vowels make up phonemes, forming syllables and rhythmic units called feet, which flow into melodic units called lines, articulated by wording and phrasing. In the case of lyrics, the verses may rhyme, form stanzas and, from there, all subgenres of poetry, deriving from the three grammatical persons, as in the typology devised by Wolfgang Kayser (1954). Popular songs have a simple metagrammar with syntactic variations of such constituents as intro, verse, pre and post chorus, refrain, interlude, solo, bridge, coda and outro. Music itself has a more complex metagrammar than just popular song composition, given its many combinations of constituents, from small (notes, half notes, quarter notes, rests) to medium (scales, chords, rhythm, tempo, melody, harmony) to large (rhapsodies, sonatas, symphonies) to styles (baroque, romantic, avant-garde, modern) and genres (classical, rock, jazz), not to mention fusions. An eloquent illustration of the relation of functional language to music is Judy Tarling's *The Weapons of Rhetoric: A Guide for Musicians and Audiences* (2004).

The graphological constituency reveals writing to be a notational translation of speech and to have its own metagrammar derived from phonology: 'As writing systems evolved, they gradually came to model the constituent hierarchy of spoken language, by developing a rank scale of their own. Thus, in modern English writing, we have [...] four ranks: the sentence (beginning with a capital letter and ending with a major punctuation mark [...]), sub-sentence (bounded by some intermediate punctuation mark: colon, semicolon or comma; or dash), word (bounded by spaces) and letter. [...] There is at least one rank above the sentence, namely the paragraph' (pp. 6–7). The metagrammar of the paragraph typically begins with a single main topic, followed by discussion and conclusion, with sentences and paragraphs linked by antecedents and referents. An element of one paragraph may become the main topic of the next, forming a weave of discourse called *text*.

Whereas sub-sentence and sentence are orthographic units of writing, their grammatical counterparts are the clause and the clause complex. The five ranks of the lexicogrammatical constituency are: clause complex (sentence); clause (sub-sentence); word complex (sub-clause, phrase or word group); word and morpheme. As always, each rank is made up of one or more units of the rank next below. Units of every rank may also be grouped together into complexes, the most common being the word complex, such as article-noun-adjective, up to a full phrase. The phrase is the basic translatable unit, the smallest unit of complete, unambiguous meaning. Adjuncts—conjunctions and prepositions—establish relations of meaning acting as a hinge or clause nexus linking clauses together grammatically to form a sentence or clause complex. Prepositions serve to group together two types of word complexes: either an adjectival phrase modifying a noun or an adverbial phrase modulating a verb. Grammar provides great syntactical flexibility to change the order of words in a phrase, phrases in a clause and clauses in a sentence. Syntax also allows for rank shifts, whereby a unit may be embedded to function inside the structure of another unit of the same or higher rank. However, improper composition and careless changes in syntax can also produce ambiguities and errors, and even break down the meaning. Thus, the main function of syntax (and meta-syntax) is relational, but it also has a key secondary function: disambiguation or error reduction.

Each constituent may have several functions. Sentences and clauses have the following: *expounding* (explaining, categorising), *reporting* (inventorying, surveying, chronicling), *recreating* (narrating, dramatising), *sharing* (values, experiences), *doing* (directing, collaborating), *enabling* (instructing, regulating), *recommending* (promoting, advising) and *exploring* (reviewing, arguing). These combine with different contexts and topics to yield different message patterns (Halliday, p. 37). Further down the hierarchy, a word may have three functions, *nominal* (noun, adjective), *verbal* (verb, preposition) and *adverbial* (adverb, conjunction). Each of these has further ramifications, particularly the adverbs. Halliday lists 28 functions for connective and modal adjuncts; for instance, *corrective* ('rather'), *dismissive* ('in any case'), *verificative* ('in fact'), *variative* ('instead'), *comparative* ('likewise'), *causal* ('therefore'), *conditional* ('in that case'), *probability* ('perhaps'), *typicality* ('generally'), *admission* ('to be honest'), *validation* ('strictly speaking'), *presumption* ('apparently') and fourteen others (pp. 84–109).

The basic architecture of systemic functional grammar and metagrammar has four dimensions: (1) *Constituency* or compositional structure with smaller units building up the larger ones; (2) *Classification* by types of functions, wherein the class of an item indicates its potential range of (meta)grammatical functions; (3) *Hierarchy* by levels or ranks of complexity and importance; and (4) *Organisation* by different forms of order or concatenation, such as contiguous sequence, syntax, rules, cause and effect, similarity and contrast, logic and chronology, in addition to order by classification and hierarchy. These four facets combine with three general principles: *exhaustiveness*—'everything in the wording has some function at every rank'; *hierarchy*—'an element of any given rank is constructed out of elements of the rank next below'; and *discreteness*—'each structural unit has clearly defined boundaries' (pp. 74–84). These features work together synergistically, such that every system is always more than the sum of its parts. All constituents have a common denominator in that they are arranged according to their functions. They each have their *roles* in the production of meaningful results. Like in Frank Lloyd Wright's principle of architectural design, *form follows function.*

SFG supports my concepts of multifunctionality and multidimensionality in natural language. The Subject of a sentence has three basic functions: Grammatical Subject (that of which something is said or predicated), Actor or Logical Subject (doer of the action) and Theme or Psychological Subject (that which is the concern of the message). The three roles of Subject, Actor and Theme may be played by the same noun or by different nouns, depending on the syntax. This is analogous to Propp's morphology of narrative where the same function may be played by different characters depending on the place in the storyline. Halliday gives the following grammatical examples:

> *the duke gave my aunt this teapot* (*duke* plays all three roles, Subject, Actor and Theme)
> *my aunt was given this teapot by the duke* (*aunt* Subject; *teapot* Theme; *duke* Actor)
> *this teapot my aunt was given by the duke* (*teapot* Subject; *aunt* Theme; *duke* Actor).

This notion of three Subject functions has been handed down in grammatical theory since the nineteenth century. There are thus three lines of meaning in every clause (pp. 76–84).

Halliday further identifies three higher-order *metafunctions*, which operate simultaneously and constitute the fundamental utility of language in benefit of mankind: (1) to construe—organise and represent—our experience of reality (*ideational metafunction*); (2) to enact our social relations sharing experiences and values through dialogue (*interpersonal metafunction*); and (3) to hold these two together, connecting words grammatically in multiple ways to produce a flow of understandable discourse endowed with cohesion and continuity (*textual metafunction*) (pp. 30–31, 83, 361). Metafunctions are considered a property of systems. They justify the development of systems insofar as their demonstrable *purpose* and *expected results* are to produce human-centred solutions. As such, the analysis of metafunctions is central to translational science, as discussed in Chapter 16.

Grammar is grounded on the textual metafunction, the third line of meaning which enables the construction of text. Halliday considers it an instrument, 'a network of systems, or interrelated set of options for making meaning' (p. 15). Beyond sentence grammar, metagrammars are conceptual models to explain or construct functional relationships in much simpler designed systems. All such systems have roots in natural language but ignore most of its richness, modelling only some of its functions. As such, metagrammar contributes in significant ways to systems theory.

The textual metafunction, to the extent that it can be separated from meaning, can be reduced to the basic subject-verb-object (SVO) structure, as in 'John loves Mary'. We can then flesh out this basic structure by adding modifiers, adjectives and adverbs to describe the nouns and verbs. Adjectives are equivalent to the properties of materials and components in a designed system, while adverbs are equivalent to the characteristics or modes of its operations (verbs). When a single word is not enough to describe a noun or verb, we use in its place a prepositional phrase, which may be adjectival or adverbial. We can add an indirect object, turning SVO into (S + adjectival phrase) + (V + adverbial phrase) + (O + adjectival phrase) + (I –indirect object phrase), as in:

The driver in the red car (Subject Phrase)
[article (*The*) + noun (*driver*) + preposition (*in*) + adjectival phrase (*the red car*)]
inadvertently flashed (Verbal Phrase)
[adverb (*inadvertently*) + verb (*flashed*)]
the bright lights (Direct Object Phrase)
[article (*the*) + adjective (*bright*) + noun (*lights*)]
onto incoming traffic (Indirect Object Phrase)
[preposition (*onto*) + adjective (*incoming*) + noun (*traffic*)].

This is the basic compositional structure. Of course, additional modifiers can be added, the syntax may allow for order variations without affecting the result, and full clauses may be joined together by linking words (adjuncts). *SVO is the basis for all narratives*, for constructing and understanding texts. Hoffmann's *Construction Grammar* (2022) fleshes out SVO by offering a detailed and accessible review of language as a *repertoire* of construction patterns that integrate form, function and meaning.

Notice how language constructions resemble engineering. Every word in a sentence is an *articulation point* like an elbow that can turn 360 degrees and change the line of meaning in any direction. All phrases, clauses and sentences have that same capability. Note also that in terms of semiotics and metagrammar *a machine is a text*. Here is a simple example of language engineering (a manufacturing line and distribution chain logistics) which illustrates the principle that *function (or purpose) is the first iteration of meaning*:

> *Workers pour premeasured containers of prepared ingredients into a heated 60-gallon drum as a mixing pallet comes down for a set time and speed, in preparation for a suction nuzzle to pick up a metered amount of batter and extrude it into six moulds that slide and lift off the conveyor, as cookies come out the other end*. You may start another sentence or continue with this one: (*and then*) *Workers at the final station discard the broken cookies and place the good ones in packages that are sealed by heat-welding and hand-placed into cartons to be palletised ready for shipping.*

At this point, you may begin another sentence or paragraph describing the logistics of shipping through the refrigerated chain, with forklifts loading the pallets into trucks to bring them to regional distribution hubs, transport them to local warehouses, distribute them to a supermarket in your neighbourhood, to be labelled, scanned and hand-placed in the appropriate shelf for sale (the more expensive and profitable at eye level, the lesser ones down below). Finally, a customer puts one package in a shopping cart, goes through the register, pays and drives it home, cooks a beautiful dinner and serves you the cookies for dessert. Enjoy!

Conclusion

The history of languages shows paradigm shifts where grammar becomes more efficient and accurate over time. The same is true for individual development. Grammar is an exhaustive, necessary and sufficient system for generating any desired meaning. Its operations are the same as those of thought and reasoning, including analysis, synthesis, differentiation, categorisation, distribution, logic, and composition by combination of constituent parts. It construes our experience and idea of the world, and it structures the way in which we put our thoughts and intentions into purposeful action. Like other things, grammar can be seen from the outside, that is, from its external physical manifestation as writing and speech; or it can be seen from the inside, the inner functions of language for generating meaning. The external view describes and conceives of grammar as a set of rules, as opposed to internal functions. The same relation applies to metagrammar.

Rule grammar is an external view which sets deterministic limits to what you can do with language. Correspondingly, rule metagrammar sets limits on comprehension and design. An example of rule metagrammar is computer algorithms and machine mechanics that are supposed to consistently produce the same exact result for every command or operation, because their value resides in outcome *reliability* with every repetition. Otherwise, they are considered broken or in error. The opposite obtains from hand tools, craftsmanship, cuisine, thought and behaviour—in short, the human factor. Creators are free to adapt, adjust, improvise, experiment and innovate on the fly. They never bake the same cake twice. In contrast, so-called artificial 'intelligence', based on machine 'learning', attempts to mimic human real-time adaptation through *simulation cycles* based on trial and error: (1) measuring output against a target outcome; (2) inputting the measured difference as error feedback; (3) adjusting and redeploying an error-corrected output; and repeating again and again for successive error reduction in what I will later call an *addiction triangle*. Each cycle, however, is limited by the available dataset and by the ruleset determined or defined by the algorithm. Even if part of the cycle is randomised, the machine is still not free, but instead loses its reliability for achieving a definite outcome or goal. When machines are considered 'intelligent', it is only because the human subject has projected onto them an inner life, a view from the inside. This is a fundamental error because machines have no inner life. They are constructed from the outside and conceived only from the inside of the human linguomental function.

Systemic functional grammar (SFG) shifts the perspective, from the external view of rule-based sentence grammar to an internal view of language (*langue*) that, instead of limits, considers *sets of options* based on the possibilities of the different grammatical functions to achieve a desired effect. Therefore, the functional view of metagrammar provides for greater flexibility and innovation by focusing on capabilities instead of limiting rules.

This gives us a clear understanding of the fundamental relationship between grammar and metagrammar. Humans function based on options, not rules. Such is the 'grammar' of thought and behaviour. Human *inventions*, on the contrary, be they machines and designs, or conceptual models and patterns that we 'read' into nature, are inescapably *rule-based*, having *no interiority*. Ultimately, both machines and conceptual models for understanding the world are designed, rule-based metagrammars. To conceive them, improve them or perfect them, we go back to the 'drawing board'—our internal, *option-based* functional grammar which is always the aspirational model for all our designs. However, these designs, the concrete products of our thoughts, are always based on rules external to them. It would seem that *thinking*, the discursive decision-making process for what is true or not, what to do or not, is fundamentally a negotiated reduction of our internal options to external rules. That is, *metagrammar is ultimately a rule-based reduction of option-based grammar*.

Metagrammatical reasoning, then, suggests that human affairs—in psychology, social sciences, history and humanities—are best thought of in terms of option-based internal functional grammar. However, machines, constructs, compositions and designs are best thought of in terms of rule-based external sentence grammar.

References

Croft, W. (2022). *Morphosyntax: Constructions of the World's Languages.* Cambridge University Press.

Halliday, M. A. K. (2014). *Introduction to Functional Grammar* (4th ed.) Revised by C. Matthiessen. Routledge.

Hoffmann, T. (2022). *Construction Grammar: The Structure of English.* Cambridge University Press.

Kayser, W. (1954). *Interpretación y análisis de la obra literaria.* Translated by M. A. Mouton & V. García Yerba. Gredos.

Tarling, J. (2004). *The Weapons of Rhetoric: A Guide for Musicians and Audiences.* Corda Music.

7

From Language to the World

Introduction

There are several ways in which language is linked to our understanding of and agency on the world. These different ways may not be evident and may require some linguistic explanation and demonstration. This is quite an important issue because it regards the links between grammar and metagrammar. These links are not merely metaphorical or analogical. They are also direct, contiguous or metonymical. British empiricist David Hume (1748) maintained that there are no innate ideas, that all knowledge derives from experience. In this, he opposed René Descartes (2001 [1637]), yet followed him in other respects, particularly in Hume's conception of human understanding. Hume posited that thinking works by association of ideas; simple ideas are associated to form ever more complex ideas; and ideas are associated in our mind and memory according to two principles: *contiguity* (they appear next to each other) and *similarity* (or contrast). We can see Descartes' influence as soon as we place these two principles on the upper right quadrant of the Cartesian coordinate plane. The horizontal *x* axis is sequential and *contiguous* like chronology or the 'line of time'. The vertical *y* axis represents repetition of traits by *similarity* (or contrast) in the timeless dimension of space.

E. Camayd-Freixas, *Metagrammar*, https://doi.org/10.1007/978-3-031-92337-1_7

Hume's principles of contiguity and similarity have had great transcendence in modern linguistics, particularly in structuralism. Ferdinand de Saussure viewed language in terms of these same two principles. On the horizontal linear axis of contiguity, he placed speech (*parole*); on the vertical axis of similarity, he placed the language system (*langue*). The same applies, respectively, to Saussure's *diachronic* and *synchronic* aspects of language, as well as to his concepts of sequential *syntagma* and relational *paradigma* (from the Greek for 'pattern'). Contiguity and similarity, sequence and pattern, the temporal and the spatial, experience and memory, which for Hume are *aspects of thought*, are for Saussure and his followers, *aspects of language*.

Roland Barthes' 'Introduction to the Structural Analysis of Narratives' (1978) places the storyline on the horizontal axis of time, segmenting it into *narrative sequences*, akin to a segment of text. On the vertical axis, the French structuralist places the different motifs or *indices* that recur in different narrative sequences. These indices are grouped together by similarity into sets A, B, C, D… which relate to each other thematically, forming a meaningful pattern (paradigm). Finally, the patterned relationship among these different groups of motifs gives us the overarching theme or fundamental meaning of the work as a whole. Along the same lines, Roman Jakobson (1956) found in his study of aphasia that patients with loss of language function due to brain injury tended to be deficient in expressions of either contiguity (concrete, literal language) or similarity (abstract, figurative language). He could well have put this in terms of a horizontal and a vertical axis but preferred instead to express it as a continuum between two opposite poles of language: *metonymy*, which works by contiguity (e.g., 'saddle' for horse), and *metaphor*, which works by similarity (e.g., 'get back on the saddle').

It is in this sense that I note that the links between grammar and metagrammar are *both* direct (metonymical) and analogical (metaphorical). Remember that the basic arrangement of sentence grammar, metonymical subject-verb-object plus modifiers, is directly transposed back and forth from language to the world. By the same token, Vladimir Propp's morphology of narrative takes the parts of speech from sentence grammar and applies them directly beyond the sentence to narrative sequences and plots—except that now the parts of speech have become his dramatis personae or character roles. That is, when he likens the *functions* of the parts of speech to those of the characters in a metonymical storyline, he also is making an analogy or metaphor, this time based on functional grammar. Thus, the literal and the figurative, metonymy and metaphor, contiguity and similarity are not wholly separate but complementary aspects of language and thought. Indeed, it could be said that speech (parole) and sentence grammar, which are linear (discursive), tend towards the metonymic pole, while thought and functional grammar, which are recursive (non-linear), tend towards the metaphoric pole. Yet both belong to one and the same continuum.

Embodiment and Cognitive Grammar

In *Metonymy and Metaphor in Grammar* (2009), Panther et al. establish from the perspective of cognitive and functional grammar that figuration or meaning (semantics) and context (pragmatics) motivate grammatical structure, which cannot be determined by rules alone. In other words, grammar is as much meaning-based as it is rule-based. Conceptual metaphor and conceptual metonymy are *embodied*: rooted in bodily experience and interaction with the environment. Numerous experiments show that mental image schemata such as the 'container schema' (metonymy–spatial relations–morphology) and the 'path schema' (metaphor–time narrative–syntax) are experientially grounded and form the basis for numerous conceptual formations. Among the external conceptual-pragmatic factors that influence grammatical structure, Panther et al. enumerate information structure, propositional content, metaphor, metonymy, argument structure and event order (pp. 3–4). This perspective contrasts with the internalist position of a rule-based, meaning-independent formal generative grammar which constitutes the premise of computational linguistics.

Sentence grammar and functional grammar are not the only approaches to describing language. A different perspective is afforded by cognitive grammar (CG), a subfield of cognitive linguistics, which is particularly relevant to this discussion because it considers language and thought as interdependent (Langacker, 2000). Starting in the 1970s,

Halliday's systemic functional grammar (SFG) advanced what was then a radical claim: that language *construes* our experience of the world. Ronald Langacker mirrored this perspective in his pioneering concept of CG by observing that grammar itself has meaning as its structures are construed by experience. 'Not only is it meaningful, it also reflects our experience of moving, perceiving and acting on the world. At the core of grammatical meanings are mental operations inherent in these elemental components of moment-to-moment living' (Langacker, 2008, pp. 4–5).

In this view, *grammatical constructions* or the categorisation and organisation of linguistic units are an inseparable union of form and meaning, 'signifier' and 'signified' in Saussure's terms, except that here meaning attaches not only to single words but to syntactic structures as well. Halliday's SFG and Langacker's CG are in fact complementary. Their emphasis on meaning stands in opposition to Chomsky's transformational-generative grammar (TGG), in which abstracted syntactic structures are completely stripped of meaning and formalised into what I earlier called a *notation*, free from ambiguities and amenable to computer manipulation. I fully agree that grammatical constructions embody meaning, but in my view this meaning attaches not to form but to function. From this perspective, the projection of meaning applies to all systems of signs, whether verbal or not, including machines. This is the significance of the principle that *function (purpose) is the first iteration of meaning*—functional meaning as distinct from verbal, social or rhetorical meaning. In this sense, metagrammar, as a functional system, even in its most abstract non-verbal forms, conveys elemental meaning, since its functions embody those of natural grammar, which in turn embody the functions of experience and thought, often for a conscious purpose or reason.

Linguomental Categories

Cognitive linguistics research emerging from the Russian Federation focuses on *linguomental* categories as inseparable units of language and thought (Bychkov et al., 2019; Chernikova et al., 2020; Karimova,

2017; Solodilova & Zakharova, 2020). 'It is the linguomental categories that reflect the closest connection between thinking and language' (Chernikova et al., 2020, p. 3). This aspect of cognitive grammar derives from semiotics. Saussure famously described the signifier and the signified as though printed on either side of a same sheet of paper and thus impossible to separate.

The study of linguomental categories comes directly from the semiotics of Émile Benveniste in his essay 'Categories of Thought and Categories of Language' (1966). Benveniste takes issue with the commonplace notion that language and thought are two separate things, and that the function of language is simply to convey the 'contents' of thought. Content, he argues, acquires form only when it is enunciated. It cannot be dissociated from language, nor can it transcend it (pp. 63–64).

The question is whether we can find aspects of thought that owe nothing to language. We can certainly describe language in its own terms through grammar. But if we could define thought by traits exclusive to it, we would see how it conforms to language and how they relate to each other. Here is where the concept of *categories* becomes central. Whereas thought can freely specify its categories and institute new ones, linguistic categories—the attributes of the collective language system that each speaker inherits—cannot be modified at the discretion of any individual. Thought, in addition, may attempt to pose 'universal' categories that would apply to all languages, whereas linguistic categories always belong to a particular language. This, however, does not mean that thought should have any primacy over language. Instead of universals and generalities, Benveniste argues that a valid and concrete comparison would have to be made within a single language.

Aristotle's book, *Categories* (2012 [347 BCE]), lends itself perfectly for such an analysis. In Chapter IV, Aristotle posits all the categories of predicates that can be asserted about a being, ten in total. Benveniste analyses them linguistically going back to their Greek etymology and presents side by side the utterance and the question it illustrates: (1) Substance ('what?'—any noun, a man, a horse); (2) *Quant*-ity ('how many'); (3) *Qual*-ity ('which?' or 'being how?'); (4) Relation ('compared to what?'—half, large, master); (5) Place ('where?'); (6) Time ('when?'); (7) Position ('in what posture?'—lying, sitting, standing); (8) Condition ('having what?'); (9) Acting ('doing what?'); and (10) Affection, that is, being affected, acted upon or changed by another noun ('to whom?'—passive voice). These are indeed grammatical aspects of the nominal and verbal systems. Substance is simply a noun. Quant*ity* and qual*ity* are two adjectives closely related in Greek morphology. Relation is a basic trait of Greek adjectives: to provide a comparison. Place and time (somewhere and sometime) share the same root in Greek, which forms several other adverbs and expressions of location in time and space. The order and grouping of Aristotle's categories are neither casual nor logical but corresponding instead to specifically Greek morphosyntax. The first six refer to nominal forms, and the latter four to verbal categories, with the last two reflecting the active and passive constructions of verb phrases.

Benveniste concludes 'that those distinctions are rather categories of language, and that in fact Aristotle, reasoning in an absolute manner, simply reencounters certain fundamental categories of the language in which he thinks. [...] It seems to us that those predicates correspond not at all to attributes discovered in things, but to a classification that emanates from the language itself' (pp. 66–67; my translation). In sum, 'No type of language can in and of itself either favour or impede the activity of the mind. The flight of thought is more closely tied to human abilities, the general conditions of the culture, the organisation of society, than the nature of a particular language. Yet the possibility of thought is tied to the language faculty, for language is a structure informed by signification, and to think is to manipulate its signs' (p. 74; my translation). Such is the meaning and nature of *linguomental* categories.

Linguomental categorisation is in fact a cognitive function that allows us to streamline and systematise our knowledge of the world. It is an integral part of learning, especially important for science and education. Categorisation entails generalisation and assignment of linguomental concepts to certain classes that reflect the cumulative social experiences of a culture and historical period, resulting in the construction of an *imago mundi*, a mental model of the world.

Linguomental categories are objectified in the active or current vocabulary of a society during different generations. Some of these word-concepts acquire particular social relevance in different cultural moments as reflected by their currency and frequency of use. These have been termed *actualemes* due to their actuality. Thus, the linguomental analysis of *actualemes* becomes an important tool of social semiotics (Chernikova et al., 2020, pp. 1–7).

> For example, in Soviet times, the concepts of *Soviets, socialism, communism, the Komsomol, pioneers, equality, collectivism, the five-year plan* and many others were among the actualemes. Their lexical representations [...] were actively used in official and unofficial discourses. Currently, these mental and linguistic signs have lost their former social significance. The focus of attention of modern Russian society is already on other actualemes—*capitalism, the market, individualism, success, money, comfort* and others. Consequently, the lexical units that embody them, *capitalism, capitalist, market*, etc. are actively used in Russian speech. (p. 5)

Linguo-cultural analysis also sheds light on the relationship among social groups, issues of national identity, international relations, intercultural integration and communication (Khakimjanovna, 2020). Dialectology teaches us that every language has regional variations by country, province, city, neighbourhood and even street. Families have their own folklore, linguomental frequencies and particular turns of phrase, while individuals have their own idiosyncratic way of speaking, their own idiolect. This method opens a path to the study of *linguomental personality* (Notina et al., 2020).

Speech Act Theory

Language not only construes our experience but also acts upon the world via what we tell ourselves and others. Construing our experience means the way we explain our perceptions to ourselves and assign them a meaning, a category and a value. This is a major part of what we call thinking. Since these self-explanations of perceptions depend on the lexicogrammar we use, the deeper and more nuanced our knowledge of grammar and vocabulary, the more accurate and complete our explanations and thinking will tend to be.

Other things being equal, accuracy and completeness should contribute to how 'objective' our interpretation of experience may be. Admittedly, such 'objectivity' is affected by many other complex factors: whether we are concerned with ourselves, with others, with the planet; and in general, by our attitudes, biases, prejudices, stereotypes, linguo-mental categories and our entire belief and value system. It is evident that our belief and value system is greatly influenced by other people and our conformity to them. Here is where critical thinking comes into play. In later chapters, I will return to critical thinking as *a quest for selfless objectivity*, but for now I shall be content to point out what is perhaps less evident: that our belief and value system is the aggregate product of all our grammar-bound explanations of perceptions. This aggregate makes up the source and background for how our *speech acts* (speech as a form of behaviour) actively affect the world through what we ask of ourselves and others. In a word, *the deeper our knowledge of lexicogrammar, the more effective our speech acts.*

Speech Act Theory was first formulated by J. L. Austin (1962) following precursors like Bühler (1990 [1934]) and Wittgenstein (1958 [1953]) and followed, among others, by Jakobson (1963), Searle (1969, 1979) and Halliday (1978). Previously, language was typically accorded a passive role, such as describing, declaring or stating facts, which may be true or false. Austin looked instead at the active uses of language, such as commands, requests, questions and others, which may be successful or not, effective to different degrees, as opposed to true or false. This first type of utterances which declare facts or give information is the most common within the general category of *locutionary acts*, which include the performance of any utterance. This declarative use of language, however, is deceivingly passive, given that our statements of fact affect other people's worldview as well as our own and help mould the belief and value system of individuals, societies and cultures. While all speech is a form of behaviour and action, certain types of utterances are specifically performative. If a locutionary act includes a command, a request, a question or implies an overt act, it has a direct metonymic effect upon the world and becomes an *illocutionary act*—the category that most interests J. L. Austin and the most relevant to Speech Act Theory. Then, the effect that a speech act has on the hearer, such as convincing, persuading, recruiting, surprising, misleading or a host of other possibilities, is called a *perlocutionary act* (Austin, 1962, pp. 108–109). A further category of speech acts which describe the speech itself (e.g., 'this is a contradiction'; 'we are speaking in circles'; etc.) is that of *metalocutionary acts* or speaking about speech.

Illocutionary acts are, nevertheless, the specific object of Speech Act Theory, which could just as well be called 'illocutionary act theory'. Austin tentatively classifies such performative utterances into: *verdictives*, to issue a verdict, to rate, rank, estimate, diagnose, grade, appraise, classify, analyse; *exercitives*, to exercise powers, rights or influence, to appoint, vote, order, urge, advise, warn; *commissives*, to commit oneself to something, to promise, espouse, support, bet; *behavitives*, to enact social behaviours, to apologise, congratulate, commend, condole, curse, challenge; and *expositives*, to fit into an argument or conversation, to reply, argue, concede, illustrate, assume (Austin, 1962, pp. 150–163).

There are many marginal or overlapping cases of illocutionary acts that resist precise classification. There are even cases in which the speech is also the overt act itself; for example, '*I do*' in reply to a marriage ceremony is in itself to marry; in reply to a courtroom testimony is in itself to solemnly swear. Beyond this, speech acts may be indirect or implied, such as '*Is there any salt?*' for 'Please pass me the salt'. Verdictives may be fair or not, informed, subjective, impartial, biased or tendentious; exercitives may be successful or not, warranted or not, effective or merely honorary and symbolic; commissives and behavitives may be sincere or not, ironic or literal, or merely polite or rhetorical; and expositives may be constructive or not, agreeable or argumentative, factual or hypothetical, or even exploratory as in the role of the devil's advocate. There are in short various *degrees of fit* among the illocutionary act, the speaker's intention and the hearer's interpretation. There are also various degrees of *illocutionary force*.

John Searle (1979) refines this classification based on differences among illocutionary acts that Austin left unresolved, particularly differences of purpose or *illocutionary point*. It bears noting that all such *diacritic* analyses based on *difference*, consciously or not, re-enact the basic conceptual model of differential systems, discussed in Chapter 6, implicit in natural grammar as the declension or differential inflection of nominals by case, number and gender. A key difference is what Searle calls *direction of fit* by which certain types of illocutionary acts intend for *the words to fit the world*, while others mean for *the world to fit the words*. He provides the following alternative taxonomy. *Assertives* commit the speaker to something being the case, in varying degrees of belief. They intend for the words to fit the world (assertions, statements, claims, hypotheses, theories). These can be assessed along a dimension that includes true or false. *Directives* are attempts by the speaker to get the hearer to do something. They intend for the world to fit the words (ask, order, command, request, beg, plead, suggest, invite) and can be assessed in terms of their success or effectiveness. *Commissives* commit the speaker in varying degrees to some future course of action, aiming for the world to fit the words (intend, promise, pledge, vow) and can be assessed based on their degree of fulfilment. *Expressives* express a psychological state (thank, congratulate, apologise, condole, deplore). They presuppose an even fit between the words and the world and can be assessed by their sincerity. *Declarations* (baptising, marrying, contracting, graduating, hiring, firing, resigning, promoting) create a new situation in which successful performance guarantees that the words correspond to the world (pp. 1–17).

Searle devotes considerable space to 'indirect speech acts' (pp. 30–57) and to 'metaphor' (pp. 76–116) seeking to systematise speech acts and their various conditions. He also attempts to reduce these to a notation. For example, in '! *W* (*H* does *A*) ↑', the exclamation mark indicates that the speech act is a strong *Directive*: the speaker *W*ants the *H*earer to do a certain *A*ction, the up arrow indicates that the direction of fit is world-to-words, and the *W* denotes that the 'sincerity condition' is want or wish. Meanwhile, '*C I* (*S* does *A*) ↓' denotes a *Commissive* wherein the 'sincerity condition' is *I*ntention, and the 'propositional content' is that the *S*peaker commits to some future Action, meaning for the words to fit the world, as signified by the down arrow (pp. 13–14).

This attempt at formalisation resembles Chomsky's 'generative grammar' (1957) based on 'rules of transformation' in that it aims towards a formalised logical 'language' (a *notational metagrammar*) as an interface to enable human–computer interaction (HCI). Searle (1969) lays the groundwork for relating speech acts to 'regulative rules' (such as the rules of traffic) and 'constitutive rules' (such as the rules of a game), based in part on Wittgenstein's concept of 'language-games'. The importance of formalised rules is of course that they can be expressed and implemented as an algorithm. However, the marginal and overlapping cases of speech acts, their degrees of belief, commitment and sincerity, their indirect, ironic, oblique or metaphorical reference and all other instances in which the speaker does not mean exactly and literally the same thing that the speech act expresses make speech acts highly resistant to formalisation. Just like Chomsky's generative grammar had to be radically simplified by making it independent of meaning, so would speech act formalisation reduce illocutionary richness and nuance to a simplified notation capable of only rudimentary interactions between humans and machines. Searle's 'direction of fit' is one such simplification.

Still, speech act models of human–computer 'conversation' have been applied with relative success within limited parameters, such as simplified stereotypical conversations between the computer and the clinical staff, based on declarative script-like structures (Morelli et al., 1991). Similar protocols for classification and information retrieval that mimic human conversation have become quite common in the form of customer service chatbots.

The advent of ChatGPT in 2023 and the development of computer modelling and simulation via artificial intelligence mark a paradigm shift away from speech act models, based instead on Bayesian statistics (Thomas Bayes, c. 1701–1761). The metagrammar of Bayesian statistics and probability consists in: (A) a known measurement of a previous state, such as the normal distribution or 'bell curve'; (B) the introduction of a change; and (C) the measurement of the posterior state in relation to the previous one, as a way of calculating the reasonable expectation or degree of belief in future events or results. When this is matched with a Recurrent Artificial Neural Network (RANN) that repeatedly backpropagates an input, distributing it through several layers of factor modulators, and then feeds forward weight-corrected and error-reduced results that in turn become measured inputs, coupled with a computer capable of trillions of calculations per second, the result is a still mechanical but significantly more accurate simulation of natural human language than Chomsky's or Searle's notational metagrammars.

Semiotics

We live daily in a world of signs. A bed invites us to lie down, a chair to sit, a door to pass through. They are meaningful signs because their very function is the first iteration of meaning. We get in our car, and we are presented with a steering wheel, brake and accelerator pedals, shifter, visors, mirrors, seatbelts, buttons and gauges with labels, numbers and icons. We get on the road, and we find it full of signals, lines, signs, traffic lights, etc. We go into a building, and we are guided through hallways, signs, elevators and doorways. The same when we return home and when we interact with our electronic devices. All these elements are arranged systematically, by design. There is certainly a logic to them, efficiency and ergonomics. They have a grammarlike arrangement, a metagrammar. Semiotics, as the study of systems of signs, of all kinds of signs, begins with the study of language as a model for all other semiotic systems beyond sentence grammar. As such, semiotics provides the most comprehensive link between grammar and metagrammar.

Going a step further, we can easily move from verbal to visual semiotics and to a multisensorial or multimodal combination of signs. We can move from a word-concept to a more general sign-concept, if we consider the following. We already know that a word or linguistic sign combines a sound-image with a mental concept. The signifier 'horse' is a sound-image that we automatically associate with 'horse'—not exactly as a visual image but as a mental concept. This mental concept is a fluid melange of impressions from all our senses, together with a synthesis of memory flashes and linguomental propositions or descriptions. In the words of philosopher Daniel Dennett (discussed in Chapter 2), 'Mental imagery comes in all modalities, not just vision' (1991, p. 58). Further, our mental imagery of a 'horse' is constantly changing as we recall recent and older memories of horses. Thus, the verbal sign is a sound-image that triggers mental imagery. Non-verbal signifiers, on the other hand, may come from any of our senses, a smell, a touch, a stomach ache, the sound of rain, a sight, a mixture thereof. We learn to attach an inseparable meaning or signified to these sense impressions in the form of memory images.

Aside from sounds, we are most aware of visual signs. As we have seen, the sight of a bed or a tool, even before we verbalise it, immediately suggests its use, its function. A succession of sights is organised in our mind as strings of signs (like sentences) with a certain order or syntax, a metagrammar that we infer in the same way that we infer grammar from common language use. That is, visual metagrammar follows the same patterns and structures as language grammar. This is what happens, for example, when we drive a car intuitively following the ergonomics of the vehicle and the rules of the road as though in autopilot. Behaviourists would call such visual signs 'cues' which activate memory. They would argue that visual cues instantly provoke a conditioned reflex or response, like the proverbial Pavlovian dog, without the intervention of language. They call it a 'conditioned' reflex because in the past the same sign or cue has come accompanied by a positive or negative reinforcement, by a reward or a punishment, in such a way that we have learned to instantly associate both things, resulting in a trigger-response mechanism. Following the same principle, however, the sound-image of a word instantly provokes mental imagery. We cannot help it. It is a learned conditioned reflex, and our reward is the grasping of meaning. Few things are more mentally rewarding than understanding meaning (the Aha! experience).

The grammarlike organisation of non-verbal signs has been intuited by many authors in many ways. A simple Internet search of the rubric 'grammar of' reveals a wide variety of applications. We just need to substitute 'grammar' in quotations with metagrammar plain and simple. Initially, the approach was conceptual and scientific: Samuel Kent, *The Grammar of Heraldry* (1724); John Robinson, *A Grammar of History* (1814); David Blair, *A Grammar of Chemistry* (1819); James Edward Smith, *Grammar of Botany* (1820); Goldsmith's *Grammar of Geometry* (1832); Peter Parley, *A Grammar of Modern Geography* (1853); David Graham, *The Grammar of Philosophy: A Study of Scientific Method* (1908); continued by Karl Pearson, *The Grammar of Science* (1943).

Soon this conceptual approach modelled on language grammar turned its attention to the visual arts. A classic in the history of design by Owen Jones, *The Grammar of Ornament* (1855, with several editions up to 2006), analyses ornamental patterns in different materials and world styles, from prehistoric to Egyptian, Assyrian, Persian, Greek, Roman, Byzantine, Arabian, Turkish, Indian, Chinese, Celtic, Medieval, Renaissance, Elizabethan, Italian, all the way to the 'leaves and flowers of nature'. There followed Charles Blanc, *The Grammar of Painting and Engraving* (1873). William Goodyear's *The Grammar of the Lotus* (1891, 2012) about the meaning of the lotus motif in the ornamentation of several ancient cultures was among the many followers. George Field's *The Grammar of Colouring* had five posthumous editions by 1896. The tradition was consolidated with a book by Sir Charles Holmes, Director of the National Gallery, *A Grammar of the Arts* (1932). This continues in contemporary visual media: David Desmond, *The Grammar of Television Production* (1974); Michael Langford, *Advanced Photography: A Grammar of Techniques* (1980); Christopher Bowen, *Grammar of the Edit*, fifth edition (2023) and *Grammar of the Shot*, fifth edition (2023) about film and video production.

Manual arts are a good example of the fact that *metagrammar tends toward mastery*. Carol Braider's *The Grammar of Cooking* (1974) and Massimo Montanari's chapter 'The Grammar of Food' in *Medieval Tastes* (2012) also underscore this point. An expert manual, or a recipe from a chef, will not contain all the knacks, tricks, jigs or 'trade secrets' that a master has learned from all-important apprenticeship, experimentation and experience. The same applies to a master mechanic, carpenter or brick layer. The practice of metagrammar brings technique ever closer to perfection, but there will always remain an intangible realm of *tacit knowledge*, discussed in Chapter 16, which resists mechanisation.

The same intuition of grammar moved from visual design to all aspects of human thought and behaviour, from Chapman Cohen's *A Grammar of Freethought* (1921) to Bernard Susser's *The Grammar of Modern Ideology* (1988). Regarding the functioning of society, we can cite Edward Deering Mansfield, *The Political Grammar of the United* States (1833); John Horgan, *The Complete Grammar of Anarchy* (1918) about Irish home rule; Harold Laski, *A Grammar of Politics* (1929); Edwin Mims, *A Grammar of Democracy* (1941); Binkley & Moos, *A Grammar of American Government* (1949); Haridas Muzumdar, *The Grammar of Sociology* (1966); Paolo Virno, *A Grammar of the Multitude* (2004); Clare Hemmings, *The Political Grammar of Feminist Theory*

(2011); George Fletcher, *The Grammar of Criminal Law* (2019), among others. In psychology and moral philosophy, we have G. T. Wrench, *The Grammar of Life* (1908); Ivan Buni's book of stories, *Grammar of Love* (1935); Otto Von Mering, *A Grammar of Human Values* (1961); David Cooper, *The Grammar of Living* (1974) on modern psychiatry; David Foulkes, *The Grammar of Dreams* (1978); Gabriel Moran, *A Grammar of Responsibility* (1996); Stephen Clingman, *The Grammar of Identity* (2013); Malin Fors, *A Grammar of Power in Psychotherapy* (2018); Casartelli et al., *The Grammar of Thinking* (2023).

Kenneth Burke's *A Grammar of Motives* (1945) extends the scope from sentence structure to narrative theory. This is further exemplified among many others by Lawrence Sargent Hall, *A Grammar of Literary Criticism* (1965) and Gerald Prince, *A Grammar of Stories* (1974). Often the concept of 'rhetoric' is used in lieu of 'grammar' but with a similar meaning, as in Wayne Booth's *The Rhetoric of Fiction* (1961). Narrative theory and the analysis of plots has been a fertile ground for metagrammar since Vladimir Propp's *Morphology of the Folktale* (1968 [1928]). We have already seen that plots and narratives extend well beyond literature, to all aspects of human life, as well as to all dynamic systems and non-verbal semiotics, which can be analysed in a similar manner.

Another term, beside grammar and rhetoric, frequently used as a synonym for metagrammar is *system*. There is a milestone book of applied semiotics by structuralist literary critic and eminent semiologist Roland Barthes, *The Fashion System* (1983 [1967]). Based on Saussure's principle that the semiologic 'overflows' the purely linguistic, Barthes embarks on a structural analysis of the 'grammar' and 'rhetoric' of women's clothing as described by fashion magazines. Fashion, like language, is an interplay of elements and functions that produces signification. Some of these functional elements are the fit to the parts of the body where items are worn, the dress code for different occasions, the seasons and the changing vogue. Barthes' method is truly revolutionary, starting with the observation that there are three structures in any fashion item: technological, iconic and verbal. 'The technological structure appears as a mother tongue [Saussure's *langue*] of which the real garments derived from it are only instances of "speech" [*parole*]. The two other structures (iconic and verbal) are also languages, but [...] these are derived languages, "translated" from the mother tongue' (p. 5). When Barthes undertook this project in the mid-1960s, 'linguistics was not yet the model it has since become in the eyes of some investigators [...] semiology was still an entirely prospective discipline' (p. ix). After Barthes' book, semiotic methods have been continuously refined.

This brings us to the metagrammar of contemporary science and technology, essayed in: P. R. Dubhashi, *Grammar of Planning* (1983); J. Lambek's 'Grammar as Mathematics' in the *Canadian Mathematics Bulletin* (1989); Edward Stevens, *The Grammar of the Machine* (1995); Leland Wilkinson, *The Grammar of Graphics* (1999); Bengtsson et al., *A Grammar of Organizing* (2007); Tsubaki et al., *The Grammar of Technology Development* (2008) about digital engineering; Bill Barton, *The Language of Mathematics* (2008); Christopher Timpson, 'The Language of Teleportation' (2008) in quantum mechanics; 'The language and grammar of mathematics' in *The Princeton Companion to Mathematics* (2014); Gorsch and Kiparsky, 'The Grammar of Elements' in *American Scientist* (2019); and Manotosh Kumar Mitra, *Grammar of Mathematics* (2020).

Books modelling grammar tend to adopt an established traditional format, which includes a history of the know-how, accompanied by the different elements (constituents) used in the field. For example, Emily Cole's *The Grammar of Architecture* (2002) traces the history of architectural practice in ancient cultures up to Western Neoclassicism. It then draws a catalogue of architectural elements: domes, columns, towers, arches and arcades, doorways, windows, pediments and gables, roofs, vaulting and stairways—the *dramatis personae* of architectural design. These elements *correspond to the parts of speech in sentence grammar*.

Similarly, Tim Newark's *The Grammar of Warfare* (2009) traces the evolution of warfare around the world from ancient times to the American Civil War in 1865. He reviews the technology and tactics *dictated by the type of weapon* at each step of the way, appending a catalogue of arms and armour, from swords, lances, clubs, axes and bows to siege machines, artillery and firearms, culminating with the Colt revolver. An alarming update is Paul Scharre's *Four Battlegrounds* (2023), referring to land, sea, air and space, including cyberspace. Scharre documents how state-of-the-art warfare technology has far outpaced human tactics and control at a global scale, with robotics directed by advanced AI, fearsome autonomous weapon systems and 'battlefield singularity' on the horizon, whereby drone swarms and all other weaponry are interconnected and centrally orchestrated with superhuman speed and accuracy. My hope is that future warfare turn to war games, conducted by computer simulation, without any loss of life.

Conclusion

For centuries, authors have intuitively used the concept of *grammar* to explain the systematic operations of widely different fields, from arts and human sciences to natural sciences, mathematics and technology.

This book began by clarifying that these are instead *metagrammars*—this being no trivial label, given the following realisations: (a) all metagrammars have the same generic model in natural language grammar; (b) grammar is inseparable from the articulation of thought, critique, conceptualisation and design, making metagrammar a method of reasoning; (c) the metagrammars of different fields are comparable for purposes of crosspollination, innovation and problem solving; (d) this allows for metagrammars to be grouped into *systems of genres* based on common denominators and family resemblances; (e) through comparison and grouping, metagrammar can develop into a systematic field of study; (f) educationally, grammar and metagrammar prove to be foundational subjects at all levels of schooling; (g) the metagrammar of all dynamic systems is expressed as a *narrative*, analysable in terms of its constituent actors, qualities and modes of operation for design and critique, troubleshooting and optimisation.

These last two chapters considered different interfaces between grammar and metagrammar, language and the world, which have led so many authors to intuit the 'grammar' of the most diverse fields. These interfaces include: (a) the external view of 'rule' or *sentence grammar*, with its parts of speech, SVO structure, conjugational, declensional and prepositional systems; (b) *functional grammar*, an internal view of language as a multifunctional set of options for generating meaning and serving the higher purpose ideational, interpersonal and textual metafunctions; (c) *cognitive grammar*, with its linguomental categories and operations, linking linguistic analysis to psychology, social sciences, cultural studies, generational worldviews, identities and personality; (d) *speech act theory*, which considers utterances as language actions that affect the world in different ways; and (e) *semiotics*, which posits language as a system of signs and the conceptual model for all other verbal and non-verbal systems. The metagrammars of different systems are in fact simplified projections of our internalised grammatical system, much like speech and narratives (*parole*) are snippets of the general language system (*langue*).

These different approaches or 'interfaces' between language and reality can be combined in metagrammatical analysis. Here is an important example that appears repeatedly in technology and society: Searle's concept of *direction of fit* in speech act theory, which states that utterances have one of two aims, to have the words fit the world (hypotheses, theories) or the world fit the words (policies and laws). If sentence and cognitive grammars are added to the analysis, in particular the concepts of the literal and the implied, the results can be paradoxical. Science and technology are a literal instance of aiming for the words to fit the world, but as soon as that aim is realised, the direct implication is the exact opposite, the enactment of policy, the directive to follow science and implement technology, for the world to fit the words. We may call this self-fulfilling prophecy based on a circular quantification fallacy, the *science-policy paradox*. We will reencounter it in Chapter 13 about the critique of 'techno-mythology', as the conflicted basis for artificial general intelligence.

References

Aristotle. (2012 [347 BCE]). *The Organon: The Works of Aristotle on Logic* (pp. 1–33). Translated by R. B. Jones, E. & E. M. Edgehill. CreateSpace. Retrieved from https://www.rbjones.com/rbjpub/philos/classics/aristotl/obook_draft.pdf

Austin, J. L. (1962). *How to Do Things with Words*. Harvard University Press.
Barthes, R. (1978). Introduction to the structural analysis of narratives. *Image, Music, Text* (pp. 79–124). Translated by S. Heath. Hill and Wang.
Barthes, R. (1983 [1967]). *The Fashion System*. Translated by M. Ward & R. Howard. Hill and Wang.
Benveniste, É. (1966). *Problèmes de linguistique générale*. Gallimard. *Problems in general linguistics*. Translated by M. Meeks. University of Miami Press, 1971.
Bühler, K. (1990 [1934]). *The Theory of Language: The Representational Function of Language (Sprachtheorie)*. Translated by D. Goodwin. John Benjamins.
Bychkov, D., Gainanova, D., & Umadkereeva, I. (2019). Linguo-cognitive mechanism of representation of 'horde topos' in historical discourse. In D. Bataev et al. (Eds.) *Social and Cultural Transformations in the Context of Modern Globalism, 76*, 561–568. EPSBS. Retrieved from https://doi.org/10.15405/epsbs.2019.12.04.76
Chernikova, N., Sidorova, I., & Fedotov, A. (2020). Linguomental category of relevance and the technology of its study in the organization of scientific and educational activities. *E3S Web of Conferences, 210*, 18048. Retrieved from https://doi.org/10.1051/e3sconf/202021018048
Chomsky, N. (1957). *Syntactic Structures*. Mouton.
Dennett, D. (1991). *Consciousness Explained*. Little, Brown & Co.
Descartes, R. (2001 [1637]). *Discourse on Method, Optics, Geometry, and Meteorology*. Translated by P. J. Olscamp. Hackett.
Halliday, M. A. K. (1978). *Language as Social Semiotic: The Social Interpretation of Language and Meaning*. University Park Press.
Halliday, M. A. K. (2014). *Introduction to Functional Grammar* (4th ed.). Revised by C. Matthiessen. Routledge.
Hume, D. (1748). *Philosophical Essays concerning Human Understanding*. A. Millar.
Jakobson, R. (1956). Aphasia as a linguistic problem; The metaphoric and metonymic poles. Jakobson, R. & Halle, M., *Fundamentals of Language* (pp. 55–82). Mouton.
Jakobson, R. (1963). *Essais de linguistique genérale*. Minuit.
Karimova, V. (2017). Language ethics: linguo-psychology and psycholinguistics. *Psychology and Behavioral Sciences, 6*(2), 16–20. Retrieved from https://www.sciencepublishinggroup.com/article/10.11648/j.pbs.20170602.11
Khakimjanovna, E. M. (2020). Linguocultural study of national mental relations. *International Journal of Research and Development, 5*(6). Retrieved

from https://eprajournals.com/jpanel/upload/1122pm_73.EPRA%20JOURNALS-4712.pdf
Langacker, R. W. (2000). *Grammar and Conceptualization*. Mouton de Gruyter.
Langacker, R. W. (2008). *Cognitive Grammar: A Basic Introduction*. Oxford University Press.
Morelli, R. A., Bronzino, J. D., & Goethe, J. W. (1991). A computational speech act model of human-computer conversations. In *Proceedings of the 1991 IEEE Seventeenth Annual Northeast Bioengineering Conference* (pp. 263–264). Retrieved from https://ieeexplore.ieee.org/document/154675
Notina, E. A., Bykova, I. A., & Radić, N. (2020). Communicative space of translation through the prism of translator's linguo-mental personality. In *Innovation in Language Learning: International Conference*. Retrieved from https://conference.pixel-online.net/files/ict4ll/ed0013/FP/3262-TRN4875-FP-ICT4LL13.pdf
Panther, K. U., Thornburg, L. L., & Barcelona, A. (Eds.) (2009). *Metonymy and Metaphor in Grammar*. John Benjamins.
Propp, V. (1968 [1928]). *Morphology of the Folktale*. Translated by L. Scott. University of Texas Press.
Saussure, F. D. (1959 [1916]). *Course in General Linguistics*. Edited by C. Bally & A. Sechehaye. Translated W. Baskin. The Philosophical Society.
Searle, J. R. (1969). *Speech Acts: An Essay in the Philosophy of Language*. Cambridge University Press.
Searle, J. R. (1979). *Expression and Meaning: Studies in the Theory of Speech Acts*. Cambridge University Press.
Solodilova, I. A., & Tatyana V. Z. (2020). Linguo-cognitive approach in foreign language teaching. In A. Pavlova (Ed.), *Philological Readings, 83*, 627–634. EPSBS. Retrieved from https://doi.org/10.15405/epsbs.2020.04.02.73
Wittgenstein, L. (1958 [1953]). *Philosophical Investigations* (3rd ed.). Translated by G. E. M. Anscombe. Macmillan.

8

Genres of Narrative

Introduction

Anthropologist Clifford Geertz in *The Interpretation of Cultures* (1973) discovered that the ethnographic accounts of early anthropology formed a certain genre made up, like all genres, of certain *conventions* that vitiated the accounts. The viewpoint was that of modern Western man, as the yardstick to appraise 'primitive' cultures, comparing them against supposed 'universal' traits. Since then, Geertz and social scientists in general have used the tools of literary theory and criticism to analyse narratives, events and social behaviour. Something similar happened with Hayden White's *Metahistory* (1973) and *Tropics of Discourse* (1978) as well as Michel de Certeau's *The Practice of Everyday Life* (1984 [1974]) and *The Writing of History* (1988 [1975]). Historiography too is a narrative genre with its tropes, conventions and viewpoint, typically the top-down view of the structures of power, as in 'the victors write the history', with the occasional view from the bottom, as in Howard Zinn's *A People's History of the United States* (1980). Scientific papers also form a genre with its constituent parts (abstract, review of the literature, hypothesis, methodology following the scientific method, statistical results and their interpretation). Idem as to the journalistic genre with

E. Camayd-Freixas, *Metagrammar*, https://doi.org/10.1007/978-3-031-92337-1_8

its Five Ws (who-what-where-when-why) sometimes supplemented by *with*, *how* and *how much*. All specific discourses, narratives and texts are defined in relation to the genre they resemble. This includes the many genres of everyday life. Weddings and courtroom trials, for instance, occur in a timeline of narrative discourse, forming a text. They too—from law to accounting—have their conventions, their protocols, their form of organisation, in short, their generally accepted metagrammar of principles and practice.

Metagrammar and Literary Genre

It is not surprising that the first use of the term 'metagrammar' is related to the structure of literary genres and individual works. The pioneering usage belongs to Earl R. Wasserman (1953) in his analysis of Keats' master poem, 'Ode on a Grecian Urn':

> It is a poem about things: an urn, pipes, trees, lovers, a priest, a town; and poetic images have a grammar of their own that is contained in their dramatic actions. For this *meta-grammar* of poetic imagery, this grammar that transcends verbal grammar, *we have no technical terms* and hence *no formalised methods of analysis*; and yet we must read an imagistic poem with *the same analytical frame of mind that we adopt towards a prose sentence* [...] Does the drama of the last two stanzas enact an independent clause or *a dependent clause in the sentence that the entire poem enacts*? (pp. 14, 47; *my italics*)

Wasserman's 'interlacing patterns' are those of meaning and form, which correspond respectively to the representational and textual metafunctions in Halliday's systemic functional grammar (SFG), discussed in Chapter 6. Wasserman's reading of poetic images is influenced by what Wolfgang Köhler (1947) called a *gestalt*, a holistic form, pattern or configuration. However, when Wasserman enumerates the images, he returns to the verbal. He turns the images into parts of speech, or *dramatis personae* that enact a story, as in Vladimir Propp's *Morphology of the Folktal* (1968 [1928]). Wasserman proposes a 'drama' of images, transposing from the poetic genre to narrative drama, that is, turning description into narrative representation. Significantly, the masters of modern drama, Shakespeare and Lope de Vega, dramatised folk stories, legends and historical events, laying the foundation for today's narrative film (Camayd-Freixas, 2015). Ultimately, any functional sequence of actions resolves into a *narrative genre*.

However, Wasserman's concept of a 'syntax of images' earned him a scathing review by the great philologist and polemicist Leo Spitzer, in 'Ode on a Grecian Urn, or Content vs. Metagrammar' (1955). Spitzer, whose fields are stylistics and etymology, cannot conceive of a narrative of images as relevant 'to our descriptive techniques' (p. 204). He claims that the poem is basically the description of an urn, belonging to the genre of *ekphrasis*, or the poetic verbal reproduction of a pictorial or sculptural work of art. Semiotics, however, and notably art history and criticism do see drama and narrative in images. Yet Spitzer denies imagery any dynamism or sequence, resulting in a static description devoid of narration. No wonder he was 'unable to recognise the cogency [...] of any "imagistic grammar" (or metagrammar or syntax). The use of these metaphors for a sequence of images is obviously meant to imply a rigor traditionally associated with those grammatical terms' (p. 223). Discounting Spitzer's idiosyncrasies, recalled by Hatzfeld (1961, p. 57) in his eulogy about the master's 'invincible sarcasm' and habit of turning his critiques into a praise of his own method, the rigorous Spitzer zeroes in on Wasserman's own admission that 'we have no technical terms' or 'formalised methods of analysis' for 'this meta-grammar of poetic imagery' (Wasserman, 1953, p. 14).

After Wasserman's vague but pioneering definition and Spitzer's rebuttal, the term 'metagrammar' falls into disuse, eclipsed by more established terms in linguistics and literary criticism, such as discourse and textual analysis or 'text grammar vs. sentence grammar' (van Dijk, 1972). It is worth noting that Wikipedia has no entry for 'metagrammar' (yet). Other searches yield isolated hits marred by nonsense definitions like 'the grammar of grammars'—there being no such thing. Chomsky's concept of 'universal grammar', limited to the sentence, is an abstract hypothetical construct that already has a name. So does 'discussion about grammar', properly referred to as grammatical theory. Another isolated claim might be that 'metagrammar' is some esoteric aspect of the 'syntax' of computer 'languages' (which instead are *notations* of Boolean algebra). It is hardly the first time that computer terms are illegitimately borrowed from linguistics, except that in this case, metagrammar is not even a term currently accepted by either linguistics or computer science.

Text Grammars

Teun van Dijk (1972) conducts the first systematic analysis of a possible metagrammar, albeit under the hypothetical name of 'text grammars' (T-grammars), as opposed to the existing sentence grammars (S-grammars). He seeks to extend the domain of grammar beyond the sentence, to any connected discourse, that is, to 'all types of texts', even though he admits that T-grammars 'do not yet exist' (p. 1). This admission, which echoes Wasserman's ('we have no formalised methods of analysis'), is the same lack that I confronted when I embarked on this book and that remains its subject of exploration.

All along, I have suggested several links or interfaces whereby grammatical functions apply beyond the sentence and even beyond language to the metagrammars of both verbal and non-verbal semiotic systems. Given that such interfaces come from different although complementary approaches to grammar, the idea of a unitary rule-based metagrammar is wholly misguided. Such comprehensive metagrammar would be as complex and multilayered as grammar itself. That is, it already exists and is called grammar. 'Metagrammar' in the singular is a field of study, a generic term. Concretely, only particular 'metagrammars' (plural) exist for different systems, and they are always partial and simplified reflections of grammar. Only the grammars of natural languages are comprehensive and exhaustive in that they provide all the flexible options to produce any desired meaning.

Van Dijk limits his scope to verbal texts for a more direct application of sentence grammars. Even though he predictably fails in formulating a ruleset, he does provide a useful menu of transposable functions and linguistic features of S-grammars that directly apply to T-grammars. First, there must be *cohesion* and *sequence* within and among the sentences of any text. Speakers have the capacity to disambiguate sentences from context, *redundancy* or by rearranging the syntax. They also do this for texts based on context, situation and intersentential relations. S-grammars have recursive capacity, *left-recursive* (flashback), *right-recursive* (foreshadowing) and *self-embedding* (digression) which apply to T-grammars as well. In semantic recursiveness, both, sentences and texts, have *presupposition*, *entailment* and *embedded* clauses, which can be dependent or independent from the main action. In a text, they can create logical sequences. Pronominalisation (using a pronoun in place of an antecedent noun) applies more to a sequence of sentences in a text than to an isolated sentence. Conjunctions and adverbs, which operate inside the sentence, also have correlative functions in the construction and inflection of texts. Deixis or indexicality (pointing or referring to a context) pertains to the use of words, phrases or text that derive their meaning from context by referring to time, space and person. Deictics include personal, possessive and demonstrative pronouns (this, those) as well as spatial adverbs (here, there), temporal markers (tomorrow, verb tenses) and many other indexes that interconnect sentence and text.

Teun van Dijk's *Some Aspects of Text Grammars* is an excellent resource for many different types of grammatical operations that apply to metagrammar. Its drawback is that it follows linguistic structuralism too closely and particularly Chomsky's generative grammar, based on syntactic structures and 'rewrite rules' without regard to meaning. As expected, this approach remains limited and quite abstract. Van Dijk's exhaustive attempt to describe sentences and texts at all levels of grammar results in exceedingly complicated formulas to describe rather simple sentences and texts. Following Chomsky's concepts of 'surface' and 'deep' structures, van Dijk reduces texts to these same two descriptive dimensions, whereas a text in fact lends itself to multiple semantic levels of reading and interpretation. Finally, the consideration of 'all types of texts' without classifying them into *genres* results in vague generalities and grammatical micro-details. It is not the grammar of all texts but the grammar of text *genres* that constitutes the object of metagrammar.

Hendricks (1974) notes a growing interest among linguists to go beyond the sentence. He cites Gleason (1964, p. 278) about the need 'for an upward extension of the scope of grammar' by applying 'the grammatical methods used in describing sentence structure', and Himes (1964, p. 23) about the need to bridge the gap between linguistic and cultural analysis through 'the patterning' of texts and cultural behaviour (Hendricks, 1974, p. 11). Hendricks begins a systematic examination of the different approaches of linguistic theory to the structural analysis of texts. The concept of intersentence concordance based on the connection between articles, pronouns and antecedent nouns is considered trivial for stylistics or the analysis of literary texts, with the exception of Halliday's broader concept of 'grammatical cohesion'—followed as well by Teun van Dijk—which stipulates that all deictics build textual cohesion 'only when referring back to preceding sentences, not when pointing forward to a modifier or qualifier' (Halliday, 2014, p. 15). There is however grammatical prediction, especially in analytic languages; such is the case of the Spanish pronoun *le* (…*a*) which announces an upcoming indirect object (*le* + verb + object + *a* + indirect object). Hendricks also cites Sayce (1957, pp. 128–130) on 'the expansion of linguistic patterns of the sentence into the structural patterns of the work' but considers his proposal to be rather metaphorical. 'For example, descriptions of time and setting correspond to the adverbial and adjectival clauses, and transitions are the equivalent of conjunctions […] the hero of a novel may be regarded as the 'noun subject'; the plot, the 'verb'; and the external world and other characters, the 'object' or 'complement'' (Hendricks, 1974, p. 16).

Narrative Theory

A step further is to consider these relations among sentences in a systemic sense, as in Lévi-Strauss, 'The Structural Analysis of Myth' (1955). As opposed to the tactical relations in previous methods based on contiguous sentences, Lévi-Strauss takes sentences at remote intervals of the storyline and groups them together by meaning into classes. Accordingly, the analysis of the Oedipus myth results in four classes of sentences with common elements of symmetrical meaning: 'overrating of blood relationships; underrating of blood relationships; denial of autochthonous origin of man; persistence of autochthonous origin of man' (Hendricks, 1974, p. 17). A similar method is deployed by Roland Barthes in 'Introduction to the Structural Analysis of Narratives' (1978) based on Saussure's axes of discourse: *syntagmatic* (contiguous) and *paradigmatic* (patterned). To review, empiricists held that ideas are associated by *contiguity* (including cause and effect) and *similarity* or contrast. Saussure's syntagmatic (linear) and paradigmatic (associative) axes place discourse and text on the Cartesian plane. The horizontal x axis marks the linear, sequential or contiguous aspect of language along a timeline or storyline, while the vertical y axis marks sporadic points or indexes by recursive similarity or contrast. Roland Barthes divides the storyline (x) into 'narrative sequences' (the equivalent of sentences or theatre scenes). He then marks the recurrence (y) of different elements or motifs called *indices* that appear in different sequences, and groups them together into paradigms, like Lévi-Strauss. Finally, the relationship among the different paradigms gives the main theme or interpretation of the narrative. Therefore, Barthes effectively uses both, sequential and recursive analysis. The Cartesian axes thus establish a referential grid that aids in the description of any narrative, process or event, whether verbal, mechanical or statistical.

Back to Hendricks, after considering different types of approaches to extending grammar beyond the sentence, he draws a dividing line between linguistic description and critical interpretation and places Vladimir Propp's *Morphology of the Folktale* just beyond that line (Hendricks, 1974, pp. 37–41, 95–105). In Propp, Hendricks finds no one-to-one correspondence between the structural units of language and those of narrative plot; consequently, 'linguistics has not been extended, but on the contrary abandoned' (p. 40). Instead of grammatical units, Propp uses characters as the chess pieces of the narrative. However, they are not individual characters, but rather types defined by their function or role in advancing the plot to its resolution. He calls them *dramatis personae*, recalling that *persona* was the actors' *mask* in ancient Greek theatre. Just like different actors could stand in behind the same mask at different times, different characters at times may assume the function of a particular dramatis persona. Nevertheless, I will argue against Hendricks that Propp's dramatis personae are in fact inspired on grammatical parts of speech.

After analysing scores of Russian folktales and looking for common denominators, Propp defines seven types of dramatic personae: (1) the *villain* who creates struggles for the hero; (2) the *dispatcher* who sends the hero off on his quest; (3) the *helper* who aids in the hero's quest; (4) the *princess* or *prize* that the hero must attain; (5) the *donor* who gives the hero some special or magical object; (6) the *hero* who reacts to the dispatcher and donor, overcomes the villain and marries the princess; and (7) the *false hero* who tries to steal the show, take credit for the hero's deeds and get away with the prize. This is akin to Halliday's concept of the subject as Actor, an agent that may fulfil various functions depending on the syntax or the order of events.

Now, if you have already started to think in terms of metagrammar, you might surmise that these *actors* or *agents* can be the cogs of any machine, system, process or event, that is, of any *narrative*. They are the actors of geopolitics, organisational structures, supply chains, manufacturing, etc. For example, in manufacturing, the hero is the raw material; the villain breakage, contamination, friction, etc. (you define it); the dispatcher might be the supplier; the helper might be a lubricant, water, Teflon or some other material; the donor might be an investor or simply a special additive; the princess the finished product; and the false hero the competition. The key behind metagrammar is the recognition of a *structured process with interchangeable parts*, not unlike Chomsky's syntactic structures. The difference is that Chomsky *rewrites* structures according to rigid rules, whereas metagrammar deals with *reading* fluid processes, where any rules of transformation are different in each case. It deals with narrative flow along the *x* axis of a text, wherein the cogs are not the things in themselves but their *function*, as in Propp's dramatis personae or Halliday's systemic functional grammar.

Structure, as a static snapshot, obscures function. When put in motion, structure fades and becomes dynamic process. Together, structure and process conceptually form a functional *system*. Propp identifies 31 different functions that are specific to folktales and other adventure plots, including: absence, interdiction, violation, reconnaissance, delivery, trickery, complicity, villainy, mediation, counteraction, departure, donation, reaction, receipt of donation, guidance, struggle, branding (the hero receives a distinctive epic mark), victory, resolutions, return, pursuit, rescue, disguise, deceit, test, solution, recognition, exposure, transfiguration, punishment of the villain and final reunion or wedding. Not all functions need to be present in every story, but the sequential order is maintained throughout the actions and reactions of the plot, like in any linear system or machine. To see how effective and simple its application is, let us turn to Bakhtin's metagrammatical synopsis of the typical plot of the Greek and Byzantine novels of adventure:

> There is a boy and a girl of *marriageable* age. Their lineage is *unknown, mysterious*. They are remarkable for their *exceptional beauty*. They are also exceptionally *chaste*. They meet each other *unexpectedly*, usually during some festive *holiday*. A *sudden* and *instantaneous* passion flares up between them that is as irresistible as fate, like an incurable disease. However, the marriage cannot take place straightway. They are confronted with obstacles that *retard* and delay their union. The lovers are *parted*, they seek one another, find one another; again, they lose each other, again they find each other. There are the usual obstacles and adventures of the lovers [...] The novel ends happily with the lovers united in marriage. (Bakhtin, 1981, pp. 87–88, italics in the original)

You may recognise this metagrammatical pattern in many of today's movies and shows. The same is true about the structures of epic and tragedy, so carefully delineated in Aristotle's *Poetics*. Modern commentators have simplified their schemas. For example, the structure of epic is characterised by a starting point marked by the coming of age and departure from the mother to embark on the horizontal timeline of adventure. Then, due to a tragic flaw or great betrayal, the epic hero falls to the very bottom of darkness, where he rescues a spark of truth that launches him into the ascending line of redemption, past the original line of adventure and onto the heights of glory. Take for instance the life of any epic hero or great historical figure, the prime example being the life, passion, death, resurrection and apotheosis of Jesus Christ. The epic hero embodies the positive values of the nation in a Manichean world debated between good and evil. The motif of the *journey* is central to the narrative timeline. Tragedy, for its part, presents a conflicted hero, like Hamlet, torn between two ideals, which also tear apart the soul of the spectator—as

Hegel so dramatically put it. Unable to serve two masters and fulfil two different fates, the hero falls, moving us to pity, but at the same time affording us a lesson, a deeper and more nuanced understanding of life. Again, you may recognise this metagrammar in today's fictional plots, as well as in real-life personal, historical and current events.

The three methods of narratology thus far discussed, those of Propp, Lévi-Strauss and Barthes, offer a complementary contrast. Propp focuses on a contiguous sequence of functions, a chain of events that takes place along the horizontal time axis (x). What makes his method groundbreaking is that it is one of genre analysis (the folktale), going beyond sentence grammar to the metagrammar of *genre* as it applies to any individual narrative text, mechanical process or real-life event. Lévi-Strauss also focuses on the structure of a genre (myth) but seeks its meaning by grouping together sentences from different parts of the narrative that have a similar theme. He works on the vertical or paradigmatic (y) axis of similarity, which is the axis of space. Barthes, finally, combines these methods, using both a series of narrative sequences along a timeline (x) and the recurrence of different motifs (indices) of greater or lesser intensity grouped into themes up and down the vertical (y) axis. Taken together, these groups of indices point us to the overarching theme or *purpose* of the text. However, he applies this generically to all narratives regardless of genre. For this reason, the result may lose some specificity as it stays at a general level. There can be no such thing as a 'general theory of texts' or a 'general theory of information'. Practical metagrammar pursues the best of both worlds: a description of both, sequential functions (x) and higher purpose metafunctions (y), but applied to specific genres. Beyond that, there is comparative (intergeneric) metagrammar.

Genre Theory

The practical reason for classifying works into genres is the expectation that the study of one be facilitated by the study of others of its kind (Wellek & Warren, 1977, p. 227). Works belong to the same genre if there are *numerous* others that share a similar metagrammar. It is easy to find commonalities between any two works or among a handful of works. This may not be enough to constitute a genre. While there is no rule of thumb, in statistics the 'magic' number is $n = 30$ to obtain a 95% level of confidence that the sample is representative of the general population. Tzvetan Todorov in *Genres in Discourse* (1990) defines *genre* simply as a 'type of discourse' or a 'class of texts' and holds *discourse* and *text* to be synonymous (p. 1–20). This synonymy is highly significant from the point of view of semiotics and metagrammar. I shall therefore insert synonyms in brackets and italics throughout the following discussion.

Earlier it was established that language is a system of signs [*semiotic system*], but there are countless other non-linguistic semiotic systems, from math to traffic signals to computer programs, all which model natural language grammar while going beyond sentence grammar. It was also established that all semiotic systems produce *text*. In fact, that is all they produce. A system itself is a text and when set in motion, all its products and by-products are also subsidiary texts. A system or text in motion, by virtue of its temporality, is an instance of the *narrative* genre, whose discourse does incorporate description [*modifiers*] but only as a function of the unfolding narrative. Systems and texts are all analysed in terms of their components [*constituents*] and their organisation [*syntax*]. The analysis and description of all systems and texts is called metagrammar.

It may seem at first sight that Todorov, a semiotician, is timid about limiting his analysis of genres to discourse without venturing beyond language. This is only because he is mainly concerned with discussing discursive and literary genres, but he is cognisant that these are a model for non-linguistic genres as well. He does not venture beyond because it is too early for it to be accepted by the community of critics. He is barely establishing the state of the art in genre theory while the concept of metagrammar does not yet exist. However, he does hint to the extension of genre theory to non-linguistic systems:

> [T]here is no reason to limit the notion of genre to literature alone [...] Hence the opposition between literature and nonliterature gives way to a typology of discourses [*texts*] [...] A coherent field of study [*metagrammar*], for the time being parcelled out among semanticists and literary critics, sociolinguists and ethnolinguists, philosophers of language

> and psychologists, thus demands imperiously to be recognised; in it, poetics will give way to the theory of discourse [*texts*] and to the analysis of its genres. [...] Where do genres come from? [...] The question of origin that I would like to raise, however, is not historical but systematic in nature [...] [W]hat presides over the birth of a genre [...]? More precisely, is there such a thing in *language* (*since we are dealing here with genres within discourse*) as forms which [...] may foreshadow genres? [...] [T]he view chosen by the observer reconfigures and redefines the object [and] one tends to forget that the linguist has the viewpoint. (pp. 10–16, *my italics*)

If we substitute the linguist's viewpoint with that of the metagrammarian, we might be so bold as to move beyond language in the analysis and application of genres and texts. While the use of the term *text* beyond language, as a 'weaving' of strands of signs and meaning, is a relatively new, century-old, commonplace of semiotics and semiotic systems, there is nothing new about the use of the term *genre* to refer to classes of any number of things beyond language and literature.

Now we may be better prepared to look at Todorov's insightful points about the properties of genres, while inserting metagrammatical synonyms next to their literary cognates:

- Where do genres come from? Quite simply from other genres. A new genre is always the transformation of an earlier one, or of several: by inversion, by displacement, by combination. [It] is a system in constant transformation. [....] [G]enres arise from the codification of discursive [*textual*] properties. But such codifications are only a static construction for a limited horizon. (pp. 15, 20)
- While innovative works push against the boundaries of their genre, incorporate hybrid elements of different genres and may even claim (falsely so) not to belong to any genre, 'genre' as such has not disappeared; the genres-of-the-past have simply been replaced by others [...] The fact that a work 'disobeys' its genre does not mean that the genre does not exist [...] quite the contrary [...] the transgression requires a law—precisely the one that is to be violated. We might go even further and observe that the norm becomes visible—comes into existence—owing only to its transgressions. (p. 14)

- In a given society, the recurrence of certain discursive [*textual*] properties is institutionalised, and individual texts are produced and perceived in relation to the norm constituted by that codification. A genre, whether literary or not, is nothing other than the codification of discursive [*textual*] properties. (pp. 17–18)
- [T]he choice a society makes among all the possible codifications of discourse [*texts*] determines what is called its *system of genres*. (p. 10)
- It is because genres exist as an institution that they function as 'horizons of expectation' for readers [*users*] and as 'models of writing' [*design*] for authors [*designers*]. [...] [A]uthors [*designers*] write [*design*] in function of (which does not mean in agreement with) the existing generic system. (p. 18)
- Genres communicate indirectly with the society where they are operative through their institutionalization. (p. 19)

Literature is indeed a system of genres, with all its transgressions and displacements (Guillén, 1971). So too may a society be regarded as a system of genres and, at the same time, as a part of other larger systems. However, there is no such thing as a 'genre of genres' just like there is no such thing as a '(meta)grammar of (meta)grammars' because these are *principles of organisation,* and a 'principle of a principle' would be sheer nonsense. A genre is rather like a core, a kernel, a seed, and there can literally be no such thing as a 'seed of seeds'. In contrast, everywhere we look, there are systems made up of smaller discrete systems, rather like fractal roots. It is in this sense that we can speak of systems of genres.

Conclusion

A simple example may clarify the usage of these terms. Societies have many interrelated systems. Take for instance the transportation *system,* which is composed of several *genres* of design: bicycle, motorcycle, car, truck, roadway, train, subway, railway, boat, airplane, airport design and so on. Now take the *genres* of car and airplane design. Each of these genres has its metagrammar of interrelated *systems,* akin to the nominal, verbal, prepositional and other systems of natural language, except that here we are talking about electronic, electromechanical, hydraulic, fuel, ventilation, safety systems and others. Thus, different cars can be compared to learn more about and improve the *genre* of car design, and the latter may be fruitfully compared to airplane design for improving aerodynamics and the different constituent systems or subsystems just mentioned. Each of these (sub)systems in turn also has its metagrammar which can be compared to others for improving, say, the *genre* of hydraulic design and develop more effective materials.

As in language, a system's constituents, of any rank, may be multifunctional; a lubricant for instance reduces friction, moderates temperature and prevents oxidation. In general, the more multifunctionality in the constituents of a system—that is, the more it resembles language—the more efficient the design. Ultimately, the transportation system serves the higher-order metafunction of conveying passengers reliably, safely and comfortably from point A to point B. I shall leave further description to the specialists. Yet, you do not need to be a specialist to realise that comparing the disparate genres of boat and roadway design may not be as fruitful.

By the same token, trying to figure out the metagrammar of an entire society, if it were even possible, does not appear very promising. Todorov warns of 'our inability to discover a common denominator for all "literary" productions (unless it is language use)' (p. 10). We face the same inability regarding society, or any other heterogeneous system made up of countless different genres and subsystems. Nevertheless, Todorov observes, 'each type of discourse usually labelled literary has non-literary "relatives"' (p. 11). Thus, metagrammar is best applied to discrete genres, systems and texts that respond, not to a single common denominator, but to Wittgenstein's concept of *family resemblances*—some have similar noses, others it is the ears, eyes, hair or build. Such is the case for texts of the same genre and systems of the same family. In any event, the establishment of text resemblance is a matter of comparative metagrammar, just like comparative grammar illuminates the similarities and contrasts among different languages.

A final word may be said about Barthes' narrative sequences. When a character enters a theatre stage, that is the beginning of a new scene, of a new narrative sequence. The same applies when a dramatis persona enters a story in text, in film or on screen. In electronics, a narrative sequence is called a circuit; in machinery, a cycle; in algorithms, a syntax string; in logic, a proposition; in mathematics, a formula; in music, a movement. *Sequence* is a fundamental characteristic of language and, by extension, of metagrammar. Even Nvidia's 2024 Blackwell super-chip, and for that matter quantum computing, are not simultaneous but multi-sequential in their processing. *Recursiveness* is also fundamental to language. Moreover, phrases in a sentence and sentences in a text are modular. These are then the intrinsic qualities of language that we transpose to all other systems: *constituency*, *sequence*, *cohesion*, *left* and *right recursiveness*, *embeddedness*, *redundancy* and *modularity*. It is with good reason that D. Y. Tenen reminds us in *Literary Theory for Robots* (2024) that artificial intelligence has its origins in language: 'I am here to tell you that machines have been getting smarter in this way for centuries, long before computers, advancing on far more arcane grounds, like rhetoric, linguistics, hermeneutics, literary theory, semiotics and philology' (p. 2).

References

Aristotle (2013 [c. 335 BCE]). *Poetics.* Translated by A. Kenny. Oxford University Press.

Bakhtin, M. M. (1981). *The Dialogic Imagination.* Translated by C. Emerson & M. Holquist. University of Texas Press.

Barthes, Roland (1978). Introduction to the structural analysis of narratives. *Image—Music—Text* (pp. 79–124). Translated by S. Heath. Hill & Wang.

Camayd-Freixas, E. (2015). From epic to picaresque: the colonial origins of the Latin American novel. In J. A. Garrido Ardila (Ed.), *The Picaresque Novel in Western Literature* (pp. 224–246). Cambridge University Press.

De Certeau, M. (1984 [1974]). *The Practice of Everyday Life.* Translated by S. Rendall. University of California Press.

De Certeau, M. (1988 [1975]). *The Writing of History.* Translated by T. Conley. Columbia University Press.

van Dijk, T. A. (1972). *Some Aspects of Text Grammars. A Study in Theoretical Linguistics and Poetics.* Mouton.

Geertz, C. (1973). *The Interpretation of Cultures.* Basic Books.

Gleason, H. A. (1964). What grammar? *Harvard Educational Review, 34*(2), 267–281.
Guillén, C. (1971). *Literature as System: Essays toward the Theory of Literary History*. Princeton University Press.
Halliday, M. A. K. (2014). *Introduction to Functional Grammar* (4th ed.). Revised by C. Matthiessen. Routledge.
Hatzfeld, H. (1961). Necrology: Leo Spitzer (1887–1960). *Hispanic Review, 29*(1) (January), 54–57.
Hendricks, W. O. (1974). *Essays on Semiolinguistics and Verbal Art*. Mouton.
Himes, D. (1964). Directions in (ethno-)linguistic theory. *American Anthropologist, 66*(3), 6–56.
Köhler, W. (1947). *Gestalt Psychology*. Mentor Books.
Lévi-Strauss, C. (1955). The structural analysis of myths. *Journal of American Folklore, 78*, 428–444.
Propp, V. (1968 [1928]). *Morphology of the Folktale*. Translated by L. Scott. University of Texas Press.
Sayce, R. A. (1957). Literature and language. *Essays in Criticism, 7*, 119–133.
Spitzer, L. (1955). 'Ode on a Grecian Urn', or content vs. metagrammar. *Comparative Literature, 7*(3), 203–225.
Tenen, D. Y. (2024). *Literary Theory for Robots: How Computers Learned to Write*. Norton.
Todorov, T. (1990 [1978]). *Genres in Discourse*. Translated by C. Porter. Cambridge University Press.
Wasserman, E. R. (1953). *The Finer Tone: Keats' Major Poems*. The Johns Hopkins University Press.
Wellek, R., & Warren, A. (1977). *Theory of Literature*. Harcourt Brace Jovanovich.
White, H. (1973). *Metahistory: The Historical Imagination in Nineteenth-Century Europe*. Johns Hopkins University Press.
White, H. (1978). *Tropics of Discourse: Essays in Cultural Criticism*. Johns Hopkins University Press.

Part II

Metagrammar and Critical Thinking

9

Of Tropes and Traps

Introduction

Some of the greatest and most calamitous mistakes, both in personal lives and in society, stem from taking tropes (figurative language) literally. In the previous chapter, we considered the transportation system. Indeed, society could well be viewed as a set of interrelated systems (financial, educational, healthcare and many others). Our need to *simplify our cognitive life* (so as not to be overwhelmed by information and sensory stimuli) soon brings about the temptation to conceptualise society as an organism, say the human body, with its various interrelated systems (nervous, circulatory, skeletomuscular, lymphatic, endocrine, digestive, reproductive, etc.). We may even be tempted to look for a one-to-one correspondence between the different bodily and societal systems (e.g., circulatory and transportation, although the latter does not bleed!). It is worth noting that extending the 'body politic' metaphor into a chain makes it a narrative. Specifically, an extended metaphor is called an *allegory*, a rhetorical figure that we readily associate with a flight of fantasy.

E. Camayd-Freixas, *Metagrammar*, https://doi.org/10.1007/978-3-031-92337-1_9

The concrete historical result here is an entire *ideology* called 'social organicism', which has benign roots in Plato and Aristotle, who nevertheless were smart enough not to carry the false analogy any further. They knew that human organisms die, suffer pain and anguish, have dreams, children and hope; whereas societies heartlessly adapt and, instead of dying, are transformed into a new version of business-as-usual. Fast-forward to the nineteenth century, passing through the prisms of Comte's positivism and Darwin's evolutionism. Now the innocuous little metaphor of the 'social organism' becomes weaponised into a hideous ideology that promotes countless atrocities and ethnic cleansing. One paradigmatic figure was Herbert Spencer (1851), who coined the phrase 'survival of the fittest' and bequeathed us his pseudoscientific and racist ideology of Social Darwinism, by which 'natural law' would provide for imperialism and the strong to 'exterminate' the brute and weak sections of mankind, thereby working out the 'perfect happiness' of society. Some of its corollaries are eugenics, Nazism and the Holocaust. Some of these brutal and nefarious ideologies are alive and well today.

Every metaphor, every analogy, fits only partially and brushes under the rug its ill-fitting falsehoods. The metaphorical comparison acts like a tendentious adjective that taints one concept with the attributes of another. It can humanise or, as in this case, dehumanise. Metaphors, analogies, similes, comparisons and homologies are loaded weapons. The tainted comparison implicit in a metaphor or meme is less severe than that of an entire metaphorical chain or system (allegory). A systematic violence often lies behind a superficial likeness in service of an agenda or ideology. I emphasise *systematic* because each system has a metagrammar. The deeper error, the core of the violence, precisely resides in metaphorically applying, or rather forcing, *the wrong metagrammar where it does not belong*. In Spencer's case, it is applying the metagrammar of biological evolution to social development, which has its own non-biological factors and processes.

The key principle here for critical thinking and metagrammatical reasoning is that, notwithstanding external, superficial similarities, *every comparison between any two systems is false and fraudulent if each system has a different metagrammar or inner working*. This equally applies to organic, mechanistic and other metaphors, including all comparisons between artificial notations or designed semiotics and natural language, between computer programs and human intelligence. Comparisons are essential for understanding, and yet they are always partly true and partly false. Some are harmless and useful, while others are dangerous. Their critical difference is detected at the level of their divergent metagrammars. Like any system, metagrammars can be projected to determine the future state of the system and even to predict its consequences. Critically, *metagrammatical prediction* evaluates divergent systems by projecting them comparatively onto a harmless-dangerous continuum.

Metonymy and Metaphor

Metonymy (contiguity) and metaphor (similarity) are the two main categories of figurative speech, but there are in fact some 282 different rhetorical figures or tropes that inflect meaning in different ways. Under the column of metaphor, for instance, there is euphemism, or its opposite, dysphemism. Like rhymes, tropes are clever; and when words fit together cleverly, it is like they belong; they give the false impression of truth. The following is metonymy at work. The infamous 1995 murder trial of O. J. Simpson dubbed 'the trial of the century' hinged on a little rhyme. A careless prosecutor had Simpson try in open court a bloody glove found at the scene and it seemed too small for the defendant's hands. The defence chanted to the jury, 'If the gloves don't fit, you must acquit!'—and presto, reasonable doubt. Yet, no one *reasoned* that the gloves were not in their original condition. They had been bloody and wet from exposure to the elements and now they were dry, stiff and markedly shrunken, because that is what leather does. No one considered murder for hire either. In fact, when Simpson died in 2024, a witness came forward asserting that the football star had hired mobsters to murder his wife. Still, at the trial, no prosecutorial explanation would suffice, because the rhyme had become a meme, and *a meme is worth a thousand arguments*. Rhyme overcame reason.

Linguist Roman Jakobson (1960) is a key figure who developed the semiotics of Ferdinand de Saussure and Charles Sanders Peirce and was greatly influential in structuralism. He defined six functions of linguistic communication: (1) Referential (involving a shared context); (2) Aesthetic or Poetic (elaborating the message); (3) Emotive (expressing the sender); (4) Conative (moving or persuading the receiver); (5) Phatic (reinforcing the channel); and (6) Metalingual (reinforcing the shared code). Functions 2, 3 and 4 are particularly human and dependent on rhetorical operations and figures of speech. Jakobson also carried out studies of aphasia (loss of language function due to brain injury), identifying two polar types, which impinged not only on speech patterns but also on the grammatical system. These two types are: aphasia as a *similarity* disorder and as a *contiguity* disorder. These, we recall, are the same two operations that Hume and the empiricists claimed to be at play in the association of ideas. Jakobson, however, saw these as *operational features of language*, not thought. This suggests that Hume et al. were wrong in considering ideas and thought as independent of language. Similarity and contiguity are properties of functional grammar, without which there is no concatenation of ideas. For Jakobson, these are best defined as 'the metaphoric and metonymic poles' of language. 'The varieties of aphasia are numerous and diverse, but they all oscillate between the two polar types just described' (1956, p. 76). The implication is that ideas, once they are named, become word-concepts; only then can they be associated and combined by means of linguistic operations within a complete grammatical system. Similarly, the fact that different areas of the brain may be involved in these two types of aphasic disorders does not mean that the brain is 'pre-wired' for similarity (metaphor) and contiguity (metonymy), but rather, that the constant use of language reinforces certain neural pathways leading to the relative specialisation of different areas of the brain.

Jakobson developed these concepts of metonymy and metaphor to an unprecedented level, linking them to the two basic operations of language: Selection (metaphor/similarity) and Combination (metonymy/contiguity). In combination, linguistic units serve as a context for smaller constituents and find their own context in larger linguistic units (cf. Halliday, 2014). The combination of letters into phonemes and phonemes into words is a contexture already established by the code of each language, leaving the speaker little to no freedom of choice. The combination of words into sentences offers much greater freedom, bound only by usage, grammar and syntax; and the combination of a series of sentences into discourse offers even greater freedom, bound only by the metagrammars of purpose, function and genre. Thus, 'combination and contexture are two faces of the same operation' (Jakobson, 1956, p. 60). In contexture-deficient aphasia, the syntactical rules organising words are lost, resulting in agrammatism, whereby the sentence degenerates into a 'word heap' (p. 71). On the other hand, 'selection between alternatives implies the possibility of substituting one for the other, equivalent to the former in one respect and different from it in another. Actually, selection and substitution are two faces of the same operation' (p. 60). In similarity-deficient aphasia, patients have trouble with word choice and substitution, opting for generic words like 'thing' or for items in their immediate view. While they grasp the literal meaning of words, they fail to apprehend their metaphorical or connotational character (p. 69). Further, metonymy is more closely related to prose, metaphor to poetry; metonymy to experience, metaphor to abstract thought; metonymy to grammar, metaphor to metagrammar. However, this does not mean that the relation between grammar and metagrammar is only metaphorical. Both metaphor and metonymy, selection and combination of linguistic units, are equally essential to the normal production and understanding of grammatical language. Both metonymy and metaphor are involved in grammar and metagrammar. Moreover, there are numerous specific grammatical and rhetorical *operations* that literally and directly apply to metagrammar. The relationship between grammar and metagrammar is less along the lines of similarity/substitution and much more along the lines of *derivation.* Metagrammar is derived from grammar.

A popular book by Lakoff and Johnson, *Metaphors We Live By* (1980), emphasises the crucial and ubiquitous role of metaphor in our everyday language, concepts and behaviour. George Lakoff (1987) is a main proponent of the Conceptual Metaphor Theory and the 'embodied mind'. Simply put, he believes that our physical, sensory-motor experience is the source of thought, and that thought is in many ways a metaphor of our bodily experience of space (up and down, left and right, in and out, front and back, cause and effect, etc.) to which we assign certain conventional meanings and connotations (e.g., up is good and down is bad). Thus, our conceptual system is metaphorical in nature, and this is verified by our constant use of metaphorical language. However, this experience-thought-language order is quite the opposite of Halliday's (and my) contention that *language construes experience*. Further, I have argued that, regardless of the chicken and the egg, language, at least in adults, is inseparable from thought (and that is why it *construes*—that is to say, names, categorises, organises and makes sense of—experience). I bring back here the challenge I issue my students to 'think without words' even for ten seconds. I also bring back Saussure's definition of the linguistic sign as being an inseparable dyad of sound (language) and image (thought). To my mind, when Lakoff and Johnson use our everyday metaphorical language as evidence that concepts (without words) have a metaphorical structure, they are putting the cart before the horse and engaging in circular thinking.

Differences aside, *Metaphors We Live By* does make many powerful observations about how metaphor and figurative language impact not only the way we think, but also the way we act. 'Since metaphorical expressions in our language are tied to metaphorical concepts in a systematic way, we can use metaphorical linguistic expressions to study the nature of metaphorical concepts and to gain an understanding of the metaphorical nature of our activities' (p. 7). This makes for some points of contact between 'metaphorical structure' and metagrammar. However, in the theory of metagrammar the systematicity that extends from language to thought to action is not based on a single metaphorical comparison between any two items, but on the complete grammatical system being projected beyond the sentence. Rhetorical *operations*—including metaphor, metonymy and 280 other tropes—are indeed part of the grammatical system. Systemic functional grammar works by the selection/substitution of different word-concepts and their insertion into one of a finite combination set of syntactic structures (cf. Chomsky, 1957). The standard combination unit is the *translatable phrase*, that is, a phrase that has a complete unambiguous meaning and can thus be translated without equivocation. The words plugged into the syntactic structure must fit in terms of grammar (contiguity/metonymy) and meaning (similarity/metaphor). And of course, 'If the words don't fit, you can't admit!'.

Some of the main examples of metaphors proposed by Lakoff and Johnson include, 'ARGUMENT IS WAR' and 'TIME IS MONEY'. For each one, they point out several expressions used in English to enact these metaphors. For instance, we talk about 'winning, attacking, defending, shooting down' an argument or use other similar substitutions that correlate with war. However, we also use these 'war' conventions in most other forms of competition that involve strategy, from sports to chess. In 'time is money', we talk about 'spending, costing, wasting, investing, budgeting, borrowing' time or use other similar substitutions that correlate with money. The authors omit the fact that we use these same verbs to talk about 'energy' and other kinds of measurable quantities that are 'spent'. These examples are more consistent with Jakobson's metaphoric pole of language than with metaphor as a rhetorical figure. As a figure of speech, metaphor is composed of a *vehicle* (the substitution and combination of words) and a *tenor* (a suggested meaning). The rhetorical metaphor works predominantly with nouns, rather than verbs, typically using something concrete as an analogy for something more abstract, as in the case of 'the court of public opinion'. In this case, the falsehood is that public opinion is not regimented by the impartial rules of evidence and the rational metagrammar of a court of law. On the contrary, the metagrammar of public opinion (discussed in Chapters 10 and 11 next) is the same as that of propaganda and mass media manipulation. This metaphor in fact makes the claim that public opinion is above, more valid and trustworthy than a court of law. Lakoff and Johnson warn that metaphor misrepresents the object by 'highlighting some aspects of it and hiding others' (61).

They also admit that such metaphors as 'argument is war' and 'time is money' are in fact culturally dependent conventions of the English language. The fact that there are other languages and cultures that do not use these same comparisons is evidence of their linguistic, rather than conceptual, origin. It bears pointing out with Saussure that when we talk about *convention*, we are talking about language, not thought. Language is indeed a social convention. This raises a much deeper question. Considering the almost systematic frequency with which certain conventions like the 'war' metaphor and the 'money' metaphor are used in different contexts within the Anglo-American tradition, it is worth considering whether they are linguomental categories belonging to larger ideological systems. The frequency of the 'war' metaphor, including the 'war on drugs' and the 'war on terror' in addition to earlier and further examples, denotes contiguity to a warring nation, as is the case with empires, which are constantly engaged in war to extend their territory or *influence* and to defend their *interests* beyond their territory. It remits to the ideology and metagrammar of Empire. The 'money' metaphor, in turn, belongs to a larger or more complex *systemic* metaphor, namely the Market, which of course belongs to the ideology and metagrammar of Capitalism. Academics, for instance, speak about the 'market of ideas', and indeed the 'market' and 'corporate' models are not just metaphorically but directly applied to most other social systems where they do not belong, from healthcare to education to law enforcement to the media. It must be emphasised that the metagrammar of ideology, whether socialist, capitalist or otherwise, is ever-present in societies, from children's stories and cartoons to movies and every other communication medium. Plainly speaking, there is no society free of indoctrination.

Metonymy, as a figure of speech, is the use of a word-concept in place of another that is contiguous to it or appears together. A common instance is naming an attribute in place of the thing itself, as in 'out of the blue' for sky. Another type is synecdoche, or a part for the whole, as in 'we have boots on the ground' or 'eyes onsite' as well as other substitutions like 'the Crown', 'the White House' or 'the Kremlin'. Like metaphor, metonymy involves a substitution and can therefore inflect meaning, express a value judgement and result in another case of bait-and-switch. It is constantly used in advertising to create a narrative in which a product or person repeatedly appears next to a favourable symbol or situation until they 'become' synonymous. Take for instance the national flag constantly appearing behind a politician or the joyous music and vignettes always employed in television ads for medications that may have horrible side effects. Metonymy can in fact be visual and multisensorial as much as verbal, but in every case, its contiguity or sequential aspect serves to create a *narrative*.

Gestalts in Grammar and Metagrammar

Lakoff and Johnson make the following distinction: 'Metaphor is principally a way of conceiving one thing in terms of another and its primary function is understanding. Metonymy, on the other hand, has primarily a referential function, that is, it allows us to use one entity to *stand for* another' (p. 36). They offer an interesting case of metonymy in the sequence of cause and effect. They break down the simple action of moving an object into twelve cognitive steps and assumptions, from intention to planning to viability, motor control, execution, perception, etc., which would constitute the metagrammar of cause and effect (p. 70). Agents, however, do not analyse a simple movement in such detail. To my mind, the agent just enacts the simple grammatical operation, subject-verb-object. Given their working hypothesis that experience makes thought and thought makes language, Lakoff and Johnson argue that all twelve steps are already implicit in an *experiential gestalt* that contains them. They expand this interesting concept citing Eleanor Rosch (1977) on human categorisation to suggest that people categorise objects, say birds, 'in terms of prototypes and family resemblances' based on their experiential gestalts (p. 71). Fair enough, but experience itself is a narrative inseparable from language. Further, we also have language gestalts, indeed *grammar gestalts* by which we pre-cognise long grammatical patterns and structures during Gestalt Language Processing (Peters, 1980; Prizant, 1982). That is why we do not have to prepare entire sentences before we begin to speak; we simply follow a lexicogrammar gestalt and find the words as we go along. Whether experience or language comes first is a moot issue, because experience, narrative and any other symbolic sequence beyond the sentence can be perceived or produced by means of a *metagrammar gestalt* based on the projection of internalised grammatical patterns.

The concept of gestalt, an organisation or pattern perceived to be more than the sum of its parts, belongs to the theory of perception and a broad area of cognitive research on *pattern recognition*. Gestalt perception is the opposite of the analytical process. Patterns may be visual/symbolic or auditory/verbal, often in combination. Their recognition is fundamental for the development of language, writing, categorisation, understanding and the formulation of thoughts and behaviour. Gestalt apprehension is uniquely human, although many animals can recognise patterns with limited apprehension of meaning, but computers cannot.

Programmers in the 1980s falsely claimed to have devised an algorithm for 'gestalt pattern matching', but computers work in sequential operations and cannot really detect or process a gestalt without breaking it down into computable numbers. What programmers devised is now called '*string*-matching algorithms', variations of which are used in search engines, face 'recognition' and biometric software, GPTs and other artificial 'intelligence' applications. Clearly, true intelligence and (re)cognition are not sequential operations. Nevertheless, anthropomorphism in the fields of robotics and computer science have pursued the illusion of human-like machines through the trope of *personification*, representing a thing or an abstraction as a person. Its complement is the *mechanistic metaphor* 'human information processing' viewed as a sort of sequential computation opposite to what humans truly do: representation of meaning. This false assimilation to digital computing nevertheless allowed cognitive science to analyse and measure perception, attention, cognition and memory as sequential strings. It also allowed computer science to mimic these 'mechanised' cognitive processes. This kind of conceptualisation by analogy has great practical value not only for science and technology but also for our everyday functioning. However, its value is only practical and relative to specific purposes. Analogy and metaphor highlight comparison and hide contrast, whereas critical thinking focuses on contrast and the limits of comparison. The danger is when we take comparison, which is by definition *relative,* and we overgeneralise it or make it absolute. 'Oh, we would never do that'—we might tell ourselves—but the normalisation of the comparison via constant repetition becomes ingrained in our belief system, such that we go around basing our decisions and value judgements on it, without a second thought. Lakoff and Johnson illustrate this process by citing another of those metaphors *we live by*: 'THE MIND IS A MACHINE'.

It is wise at this point to establish a distinction among metaphor, analogy and homology, noting their descending order in density of meaning. *Homology* is the abstract similarity between two structures, sequences or processes. It is most independent of meaning in the case of mathematical modelling. In biology, a homology of physiological structures indicates a common ancestry, but that is where the meaning stops. *Analogy* is much richer. It is a mode of reasoning in terms of *relational* patterns of meaning, such as 'arm is to body as limb is to tree' but it can reach much higher levels of complexity. In case-based reasoning, a complex relational pattern, situation or problem (the case) is analysed and compared to similar cases or *analogues* retrieved from long-term memory and adapted in order to derive solutions (Riesbeck & Schank, 1989). The analogue process can be partially mimicked or digitally assisted by AI, especially when dealing with a large number of quantifiable factors, while string-matching algorithms can *mimic* pattern recognition or *abduction*. Gentner et al. (2001) recognise the analytical aspect of analogical thinking, marked by mapping a familiar analogue to a target analogue, identifying systematic similarities and 'aligning the corresponding parts of each analogue' (p. 9). Indeed, we say we 'understand' something when we find a satisfactory correspondence between a new case and a familiar pattern in memory. We can then categorise the new by its family resemblance to one or more prototypes from our previous knowledge and experience. *Metaphor*, in contrast, is holistic rather than analytical. Its meaning is dense, often multiple and nuanced. It resists dissection and reduction, because metaphor points to prototypical similarity between two gestalts. Analogy is frequently used in argumentation to illustrate a point, giving rise to the counterargument that X is a 'false analogy'; yet no one would ever argue that Y is a 'false metaphor' because figurative language already implies a falsehood that seeks to represent a truth. Analogy can be easily stated in literal language; it is in fact a literal comparison, whereas metaphor is figurative by definition and is commonly used for enacting an aesthetic intent and describing emotions and abstractions that literal language cannot fully capture.

Mediating Metaphors, Translating Ideology

I started this chapter decrying the mistakes and dangers of taking figurative language literally, including the consequences of thinking and acting as though society was literally an organism. Reducing a metaphor to an analogy involves the same literalisation and embodies the same dangers. Yet, that is exactly what many cognitive and computer scientists as well as computational linguists purport to do (Cf. Gentner et al., 2001, 'Metaphor Is Like Analogy', pp. 199–253). Their examples of metaphor—'my job is a jail', 'his eyes were burning coals', and others—lose their emotional and human content when the metaphoric whole is reduced to a relational analogy via structure-mapping theory. Regarding the dangers, the oxymoron 'artificial intelligence' is a case in point. It dehumanises and devalues human intelligence, portending that people can and will be profitably replaced by machines, along with the social unrest this entails. Scientists and many linguists are out of their depth when it comes to metaphor, which is the province of rhetoric, poetics and literary theory. An extended metaphor becomes a narrative, not a mapped analogy but an ideological allegory.

Narratologist Wayne Booth (1983 [1961]) establishes the distinction between 'showing' and 'telling' as narrative modes, while Scholes and Kellogg (2006, [1966]) highlight the difference between *representation* and *illustration* as modes of resemblance between art and life. Illustration is limited to a particular point or 'an aspect of general resemblance' (p. 86). Like analogy and 'telling', it is more literal. In Jakobson's terms, analogy aligns with the metonymical pole of language. Conversely, 'showing' and representation are holistic and metaphorical. By the same token, Lakoff and Johnson insist that, as the basis for metaphor, '*experiential gestalts are multidimensional structured wholes*': 'In the "argument is war" metaphor, […] [w]e experience a conversation as an argument when the "war" gestalt fits our perception and actions in the conversation' (p. 81; italics in the original). In this sense, the 'war' gestalt is the vehicle of the metaphor and 'argument' is the tenor.

Given the far-reaching role of metaphor in mediating representation and understanding, I prefer to call these experiential gestalts *mediating metaphors* because they act as the basis for our conceptualisations. *Metaphorical mediation is an important part of the theory of metagrammar. Deconstructing mediating metaphors* (like war, organism, market, machine, game and many others) *is an important part of the metagrammar of critical thinking*. However, mediating metaphors are not usually explicit. Most often they lie hidden as the foundational assumption of arguments, beliefs, narratives, ideologies, explanations, philosophies and theories; in short, *discourses*. Analytical operations such as Derrida's 'deconstruction' or Foucault's 'archaeology of knowledge' pursue this kind of regression, a sort of reverse engineering of discourses, to expose their generative assumptions and binarism. To say that discourses are built upon mediating metaphors speaks to the relativity of beliefs and the behaviours they promote.

Conclusion

By way of illustration, I was once engaged in conversation for several hours with a theologian, not a 'war' argument but more like a joint exploration. We agreed on the premise that the nature of the Devine, like the ultimate nature of things, is unknowable and for many even unnameable. As Lao-Tzu (1993 [c. 500 BCE]) put it, 'The tao that can be told is not the eternal Tao' (Verse 1). Things that cannot be known directly or completely require a *mediating metaphor*. I proceeded to question the anthropomorphic mediation in the conception of God espoused by the three great monotheistic religions of the Western Hemisphere: God as the Father. And, as a Taoist enthusiast, I proposed the validity of the cosmological mediation: God as Nature, a cosmic 'It' that engulfs us, as opposed to a person who judges us. After many twists and turns (God permits suffering, but only so we may know happiness, etc.), we had to agree that ultimately, like all metaphors, both mediations are basically arbitrary ways of looking at it, two sides of the same coin flipped in the air. I even recalled the many times I perfectly 'translated' the parables and mysteries of the Catholic Mass into my own cosmological belief system. It was the same thing in different words. Then the theologian said, 'But what is there more natural for people than to relate to God as a person?'

I had to agree, but still the other version made more sense to me. The theologian said that it was perfectly fine, but 'as long as they are equivalent', he made me promise to give the 'Father' version a chance. I agreed, but as long as I can continue to translate Him.

Now, here is the point. Each conception, each mediating metaphor, leads to a different course of action and behaviour, in this case both good. But not all mediating metaphors yield favourable results or translate into good deeds. Some are downright dangerous and self-serving.

References

Booth, W. (1983 [1961]). Distance and point-of-view: an essay in classification. *The Rhetoric of Fiction*. The University of Chicago Press, Chapter VI.

Chomsky, N. (1957). *Syntactic Structures*. Mouton.

Gentner, D., Holyoak, K., & Kokinov, B. (Eds.) (2001). *The Analogical Mind: Perspectives from Cognitive Science*. MIT Press.

Halliday, M. A. K. (2014). *Introduction to Functional Grammar* (4th ed.). Revised by C. Matthiessen. Routledge.

Jakobson, R. (1956). Aphasia as a linguistic problem; The metaphoric and metonymic poles. In R. Jakobson & M. Halle, *Fundamentals of Language* (pp. 55–82). Mouton.

Jakobson, R. (1960). Linguistics and poetics. In T. A. Sebeok (Ed.), *Style in Language* (pp. 350–377). MIT Press.

Lakoff, G. (1987). *Women, Fire and Dangerous Things: What Categories Reveal about the Mind*. The University of Chicago Press.

Lakoff, G., & Johnson, J. (2003 [1980]). *Metaphors We Live By*. The University of Chicago Press.

Lao-Tzu. (1993 [c. 500 BCE]). *Tao Te Ching*. Translated by S. Addiss & S. Lombardo.. Hackett.

Peters, A. (1980). The units of language acquisition. *Working Papers in Linguistics, 12*, 1–72 (University of Hawaii).

Prizant, B. M. (1982). Gestalt processing and gestalt language in autism. *Topics in Language Disorders, 3*, 16–23.

Riesbeck, C. K., & Schank, R. C. (1989). *Inside Case-Based Reasoning*. Lawrence Erlbaum Associates.

Rosch, E. (1977). Human categorization. In N. Warren (Ed.), *Advances in Cross-Cultural Psychology, 1*. Academic Press.

Scholes, R., & Kellogg, R. (2006 [1966]). *The Nature of Narrative*. Oxford University Press.

Spencer, H. (1851). *Social Statics, or The Conditions Essential to Human Happiness Specified and the First of Them Developed*. John Chapman.

10

Perspective and Critical Thinking

Introduction

There are competing definitions of critical thinking, typically too general and abstract, from careful thinking toward a goal to conceptualising, analysing, synthesising, evaluating and applying available data, observation, experience, reflection, reasoning, arguments and communication, to arrive at an informed judgement or conclusion, by means of rational, sceptical and unbiased consideration, setting aside all feelings and personal interests. But the question is how. If you ask experts in different fields, their answers will usually depend on the discipline, such as the scientific method, the generally accepted accounting principles (GAAP) or the rules of evidence in law. These are all valid and useful guidelines, but they are not sufficient, because in addition to faulty reasoning there are inherent biases in every point of view.

This chapter will take a three-prong approach to the 'how' of critical thinking. First, we will consider the valid methods of reasoning: *induction* and statistics, *deduction* and logic, *abduction* and insight, and I am proposing a fourth, perhaps hybrid mode: metagrammatical reasoning or *metaduction*, based on grammatical congruency. Second, we will consider different types of *fallacies* or forms of faulty reasoning to be avoided

E. Camayd-Freixas, *Metagrammar*, https://doi.org/10.1007/978-3-031-92337-1_10

because they lead to invalid conclusions and errors. Finally, we will consider the effect of observer viewpoints or *perspective* and how it influences the relative perception of truth.

Four Types of Reasoning

Inductive reasoning has a variety of subsidiary methods. A classic example is: *If the future resembles the past*, and water has always boiled at 100 degrees centigrade, we can reasonably infer that under the same conditions (such as pressure and purity) it will continue to do so. Induction is empirical, based on experience, experiments and tests. It starts with an *observation* (experience) followed by detecting a *pattern* and finally projecting the pattern into a *prediction*. It does not offer positive proof but rather reasonable probability. The more consistent the observation and pattern, the stronger the inference or prediction.

This is where statistics comes into play. *Statistical induction* can go from observation to *generalisation* (pattern), from a sample to the general population or from a population pattern to the probability that a certain individual will exhibit the same trait. Humans have an average temperature of 98.6 degrees Fahrenheit. If we check random individuals, there is a high probability that their temperature will not be far from that, but there is near-zero probability that a living person will have a temperature over 120 degrees. A weaker, less scientific prediction or generalisation dispenses with statistics, based instead on anecdotal evidence. It is called *anecdotal induction*. Inferences can also be drawn by *causal induction*; we observe an effect and look back for its probable causes (e.g., if we go out, the ground is wet and there are no obvious sources of water, we can bet that it rained). *Differential induction* is inference by a process of elimination, such as differential diagnosis in medicine, where the doctor orders tests to rule out other causes. Finally, there is *analogical induction*, whereby the observation of shared elements among different things may be used to argue that they also share an additional related element.

Deductive reasoning is more straight forward than induction, because it relates to mathematical logic (if A = B and B = C then A = C). A deduction or logical inference may be valid yet untrue (unsound). That is, if any of its premises is false, the conclusion will also be false, even if the argument is formally valid. In an earlier chapter, we saw an example of such an argument, valid in form but false in meaning: 'All sea animals are fish' (false premise); 'A whale is a sea animal' (true); 'therefore a whale is a fish' (false conclusion). This means that logic can only account for the validity of an argument but not for its truth. Similarly, a mathematical equation may be correct, but this does not mean that what it stands for is true. For example, $1 + 1 = 2$ but I plus my wife had a child and now we are three. The question is whether the mathematical formula is a valid and sound representation of the reality to which it refers.

Each type of reasoning forms a binary tree with its special terminology. A deductive argument may be *valid* or *invalid*. If valid, it may still be *unsound* if any of its premises are false, or it may be *sound* if, in addition to being valid, all its premises are true. However, if its form is invalid, the deduction is automatically unsound.

An inductive argument on the other hand is based on probability, not absolute proof, and such probability may be *weak* or *strong*. If its premises make its conclusion likely, the argument is strong. Otherwise, it is weak even if its premises are true. However, if strong, an inductive argument is *cogent* if its premises are true or *uncogent* if they are not (see Hurley, 2023).

A metagrammatical (or *metaductive*) argument is either a conceptual explanation of phenomena or a plan of action or design, say of a building or machine. It requires a new terminology. The argument may be *grammatical* or *ungrammatical* in form. If grammatical, it may still be *congruent* if it uses fitting parts (nouns) with fitting properties (adjectives), fitting movements (verbs) with the right modulation, fast-slow, hard-soft, hot–cold, etc. (adverbs), and the right articulation, linkage or transition (adjuncts). If the usage is not fitting, the argument is *incongruent*. However, if ungrammatical, it is automatically incongruent. The following chart illustrates these terminology trees (Fig. 10.1).

Metagrammatical reasoning or *metaduction* may be considered an instance of analogical induction, based on the analogy between grammar and metagrammar. However, this relationship is also direct and not only analogical, making metagrammar a hybrid of induction and deduction. Formal systems like mathematics or *formal logic* are abstract because

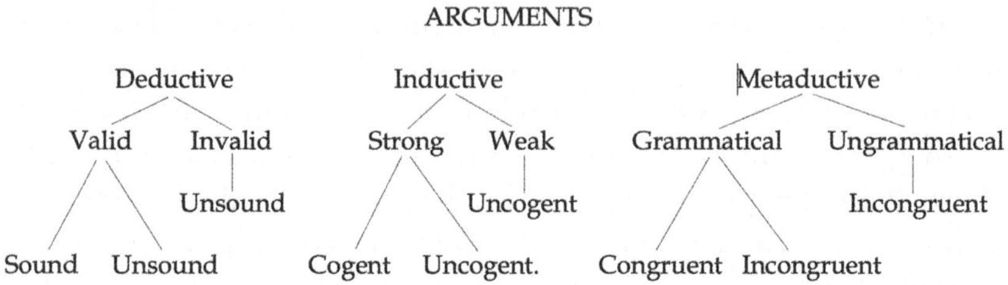

Fig. 10.1 Binary terminology trees for deduction, induction and metaduction

they use numbers and symbols that can represent different things. When formal symbols are given a meaning, then we enter the province of *propositional logic*, also called *sentential logic*. For instance, 'If you have a stock of material and you use some up, you will have a smaller stock'. Both abstract and meaningful arguments have a set of logical functions, that is, a metagrammar called *rules of transformation*, composed of *rules of inference* and *rules of replacement*. However, the difference with regard to induction and deduction is that in metagrammatical reasoning the rules of transformation also include the *functions of grammar* itself as discussed in Chapter 6.

Cognitive psychology seeks to explain the mental processes that take place in deductive reasoning. As expected, people are more successful in the deduction of concrete cases than abstract ones. They are more successful in propositional logic involving positive conditional arguments or *modus ponens* (If *P* then *Q*; *P* therefore *Q*) than negative ones or *modus tollens* (If *P* then *Q*; not *Q* therefore not *P*). There are three cognitive theories which we encountered in Chapter 2 on 'Language vs. Thought'. *Mental logic theory* considers reasoning to be language dependent or propositional. *Mental model theory* argues that it involves non-verbal mental images, spatial or visual schemata and gestalts. *Dual process theory* holds that both cognitive processes are at work in deductive reasoning. As in Chapter 2, my conclusion is that language and thought are naturally inseparable, and therefore these are artificial distinctions, because mental images are turned into propositional language the moment we start thinking or talking to ourselves about them.

Abductive reasoning, defined by Charles Sanders Peirce, has something to say about this verbalisation of images. Peirce writes:

> I see an azalea in full bloom. No, no! I do not see that; though that is the only way I can describe what I see. That is a proposition, a sentence, a fact; but what I perceive is [...] but only an image, which I make intelligible in part by means of a statement of fact. This statement is abstract; but what I see is concrete. I perform an abduction when I so much as express in a sentence anything I see. [...] Not the smallest advance can be made in knowledge beyond the stage of vacant staring, without making an abduction at every step. (Peirce, 1935, 6.461)

In Peirce's semiotics, any sign that we perceive and cognise, even a mental image, triggers an instant abduction, a possible explanation or hypothesis of what it is. This can be a single item or a gestalt pattern. If we see a set of five black dots, one on each corner and one in the centre, we may explain it as a *noun* based on our previous knowledge of the number five in a pair of dice or a chip of dominoes. The pattern of dots becomes a gestalt, a unitary sign, just like the number 5 or a letter pattern forming a word. A traffic light's red, yellow or green we instantly explain as a *verb*, prompting us to take different actions, stop, prepare to stop or proceed with caution. Thus, we use abduction constantly in everyday life, most often without thinking. Behaviourists may call it a conditioned response, but all mental images are semantically explained through language by abduction.

Abductive reasoning, however, can be a complex and deliberate method that involves observing a particular state of the world or a surprising phenomenon and drawing a practical explanation or *abducing* a pragmatic hypothesis. In terms of its terminology tree, the hypothetical abduction must be *plausible* if there is no reason to discard it and should be capable of empirical *verification* by some test or experiment. Otherwise, it may be *implausible*. Another term for abduction is *retroduction*, a sort of reverse engineering that goes back from a piece of evidence to its hypothetical explanation. It is obviously used in science and criminology but also in daily life. The best explanation is one that is *simple*. A plausible abduction may be *elegant* (simple) or *inelegant* (tortuous and convoluted). Elegant abduction makes use of Occam's razor, which 'shaves off' all needless factors in a theory, based on the logic that the more items an explanation depends on, the more the chances that one will be false or fail to work, thus rendering the entire theory implausible. The simplest solution is always the most plausible and the least risky. Occam's razor is a refutation of conspiracy theories, which depend on the absurd idea that many people can carry out some devious scheme in complete secrecy and without detection. The more entities involved, the more absurd. Abductive reasoning, then, is both a form of critical thinking and a technique for problem solving. It illustrates the close connection between these two crucial human abilities. It is also the first step in the process of discovery.

The Metagrammar of Discovery

The basic premise of the theory of metagrammar is that we all possess an *internalised grammar* that automatically guides our interactions with the world. We have inferred its functional patterns since childhood from repeated language use, and now its functions (not rules) are ingrained. The proof that internalised grammar exists lies in *spontaneous speech*, the fact that we do not have to plan sentences, phrases or even words, nor consider any rules before we start speaking. From this internalised functional grammar, we simply abduce metagrammatical functions to understand and act in the world. This process explains away the black-box concepts of instinct, sudden inspiration, insight, innate and implicit or tacit knowledge, which were supposed not to be further analysable.

Habermas (1979) makes a critique of Chomsky that brings to light converging and contrasting concepts. For Chomsky, rule-based linguistic grammar derives from a universal *mental grammar* which is *innate* as opposed to internalised from experience. Accordingly, Chomsky proposes 'a theory of intuitive understanding' or 'intuitive *rule consciousness*' as the system of rules that permits 'the metalinguistic use of one's own ordinary language' (pp. 35–38). Any such metalinguistic use is in fact a metagrammar.

The innate theory contrasts with Ryle (1945) and his differentiation of *knowing how* vs *knowing that*:

> performance itself possesses a certain style, method or *modus operandi*. [It] is not to do two things, one 'in our head' and the other perhaps in the outside world; it is to do one thing in a certain manner. […] Knowledge-how is a concept logically prior to the concept of knowledge-that. […] In short, the propositional acknowledgement of rules, reasons or principles is not the parent of the intelligent application of them; it is a stepchild of that application. (pp. 3–9)

In Ryle's view, mental grammar is a know-how internalised from the experience of doing. Further, it is the origin of intelligence, reasoning and all knowledge of facts. Sciences 'transform a practically mastered pre-theoretical knowledge (know-how) of competent subjects into an objective and explicit knowledge (know-that)' (Habermas, p. 35). Ryle, however, also considers this internalised know-how to be based on rules or principles, whereas metagrammar, following Halliday's systemic functional grammar, considers mental grammar to be based instead on *functions* proven effective by experience.

Meanwhile, Habermas draws from speech act theory to develop his own theory of communicative action, which proposes a linguistic view of social theory as the basis for human action and understanding. Yet, this linguistic view is not based on grammar at all but on 'universal pragmatics': the necessary conditions for reaching social understanding through communicative acts, in conflict, competition, strategy and other interactions. It means social understanding, not individual or cognitive understanding. It is closer to Halliday's third metafunction of language (enacting social interactions) than to grammar. In contrast, the relationship between internalised grammar and social theory is mediated by the application of grammar beyond the sentence as the metagrammar of narrative.

C. S. Peirce held that humans have a unique 'instinct' for abducing new ideas, realisations and plausible hypotheses directly without explanation or trial and error. New ideas cannot originate from deduction or induction, but only from abduction. It is a heuristic approach to problem solving and decision-making used constantly in everyday life, when we make practical decisions 'on instinct' based on incomplete information or assumptions that cannot be immediately verified. Otherwise, we would be utterly paralysed and overwhelmed. Heuristics and abduction ease our cognitive load. In this sense, abduction would be a sort of mental shortcut, an insight that constitutes the first step in what Peirce called 'the logic of discovery'. It starts with the **abduction** of a hypothesis from a set of observations. The hypothesis is then verified through critical **deduction** to see if it follows a ruleset or makes logical sense in terms of necessity and cause and effect. Of course, the insight of logical necessity is itself an abduction. Finally, the coherent hypothesis is submitted to testing and experimentation by **induction**. The logic of discovery is in fact a metagrammar. Peirce sees the trivium of **grammar**, **logic** and **rhetoric**, or method, as the three perspectives on abduction (Paavola, 2004). Interestingly, the first step is precisely *grammar abduction*, followed by logical deduction and the rhetoric or narrative method for expressing the process, the results, their interpretation and implications. This suggests that discovery begins with the abduction of a grammar gestalt. Vitello and Salvi (2023) review recent behavioural and neuroscientific evidence in support of the Gestalt theory of insight problem solving, before which the prevailing view recognised only trial-and-error learning.

This aspect of abductive reasoning is uniquely human and impossible to replicate by a machine: the ability to instantly discard, without further thought, all patently irrelevant or implausible explanations, and zero-in directly, with maximum economy and efficiency, on one or a few that plausibly fit the evidence. Abduction draws from human *tacit knowledge*, discussed in Chapter 16. Computers will never be able to do this because they are incapable of true reasoning. They are unable to discard absurd possibilities by abduction. Instead, they must consider and eliminate every single option one by one until they finally hit on a plausible answer. They create the illusion of intuitive abduction simply because of the machine's processing speed to carry out millions of mechanical step-by-step binary operations per second. Computer programs attempt to mimic this human ability by grouping possible explanations or solutions into relevant *domains*, but the process of eliminating solutions within each domain always remains linear trial and error. Artificial intelligence refines and speeds up this process via *error reduction*, adjusting the numerical weight of variables by running information in millions of backpropagation and feedforward cycles filtered through layers of artificial neural networks.

But here is the key. Humans perform abduction millions of times per day, effortlessly, instantly and with infinite efficiency. Imagine AI machines confronted with Peirce's azalea or everything else they 'saw', even feelings or ideas for which there is no template. In some cases, they would have to discount infinite other possibilities and get stuck in an endless loop, defeated by incomputable numbers. They are limited to finite close environments and their human-derived training data. This alone makes artificial general intelligence (AGI) unsound, uncogent, incongruent and implausible like a conspiracy theory dependent on infinite factors. Moreover, as Peirce points out, abduction can posit new concepts, coin new terms and is a constant source of new ideas, innovations and creative thinking. Machines only 'process' or manipulate information sourced from and interpreted by humans. Calculators do not actually add, subtract, multiply or divide. They simply follow mindless mechanical or coded operations.

Computers, however, are an invaluable tool, because they swiftly perform vast quantities of operations, many of them repetitive and tedious, too cumbersome and lengthy to perform by hand. They avoid human errors in calculation and can keep track of multiple variables. They are extremely good at handling the mechanical aspects of abduction, which have been formalised into computer-friendly *conditional if–then formulas*, as in the following examples. If the set of *preconditions* ***P*** entails → the set of *observations* ***O*** according to logical theory or domain *rule* ***R***, then ***P*** may be a suitable *explanation* ***E*** for the observations: $[P \rightarrow O(R): P \rightarrow E]$. Conversely, if *observation* ***O*** follows ← from *explanation* ***E*** and domain *rule* ***R***, then *explanation* ***E*** is consistent with ∼ domain *rule* ***R***: $[E(R) \leftarrow O: E \sim R]$. The same can be expressed in the form of set theory or Venn diagrams: if a set of *hypotheses* H is known to have the set of functional *effects* e, and the *observation* set O is a subset of the *effects* of the *hypotheses* $e(H)$, then the hypotheses are consistent with the observations $[H \sim O]$. That is, abduction is performed by finding a set of *hypotheses* H, such that their set of *effects* $e(H)$ includes all the *observations* O. In artificial intelligence, logical abduction is particularly useful in diagnostic expert systems that perform complex problem solving in large domain-specific (expert) datasets by sorting through multiple variables via if–then rules (Kaufmann et al., 2023). Thus, the study of *conditionals* in grammar is a model for the formalisation of computer abduction, which is also used in (meta)grammatical inference when, instead of a set of explanatory hypotheses, an AI functional program finds a ruleset (metagrammar) for a dataset via statistical pattern matching and string-matching algorithms.

In sum, inferences are drawn by *analysis* in deductive reasoning or by *synthesis* in inductive and abductive reasoning. Metagrammatical reasoning additionally proceeds by functional pattern matching from natural grammar to our interaction with the world. It is concerned with critique more than with creation, at the intersection of critical thinking and problem solving. '[A] critical thinker must be skilled at translating normal human language into the premises and conclusion that make up a structured argument', but this is an 'art', a 'critical-thinking skill': '*logical translation cannot be done by algorithm*' (Haber, 2020, pp. 68–69, *my italics*). There is no recipe for critical thinking, no exhaustive metagrammar. The do's and don'ts of critical thinking are equally important. In this sense, critical thinking is best defined by negativity, by discarding its 'enemies': fallacies, metaphors, false analogies, biases, stereotypes, prejudices, propaganda, misinformation, disinformation, self-deception and points of view. Each of these 'enemies' has its metagrammar to be deciphered and deconstructed. For this reason, it is best to treat critical thinking as a *behaviour*, requiring discipline, habit formation and technique development through both study and practice.

The previous chapter already focused on the traps of figurative language and the distortion of truth by the constant use of mediating metaphors and false analogies. This chapter will now focus on fallacies and viewpoints. Subsequent chapters delve into biases, stereotypes, propaganda and crowd behaviour.

Fallacies

A fallacy is a faulty reasoning or invalid justification for an assertion, which is so often used that it usually passes unnoticed or unquestioned. Aristotle (2012 [c.347 BCE]) studied them systematically in his treatise *On Sophistical Refutations*, the last of the six books of his masterwork on logic, *The Organon*, compiled around 40 BCE. The treatise on refutations is divided into tactics for the questioner and tactics for the answerer. It identifies thirteen formal (logical) and informal (rhetorical) fallacies.

Equivocation is an informal fallacy based on false equivalence or calling two different things by the same name. It often takes advantage of multiple meanings or ambiguity of usage to confound the general and the particular (e.g., man = humans; man ≠ woman). This bait-and-switch or concept-swapping operation may also be used to conflate an extreme argument with a moderate one, also called the 'motte-and-bailey' fallacy. It works like this: if the extreme argument (e.g., 'There is an immigrant invasion') is challenged, the manipulator claims to really be making a modest argument (e.g., 'The border is not secure'). Since the challenger must agree with this commonly held view, he is seen as admitting the false extreme view as well.

Amphibology is a syntactic ambiguity created by word order as opposed to meaning. In the example, 'Our community mental health program', it is unclear if it is simply a community program or one about the community's mental health. Regardless, the meaning is tainted by the insinuation that mental health problems are prevalent in that community.

Composition fallacy is the false assumption that the whole will have the same characteristics of its component parts. Instead, it is well established in physics that subatomic particles behave differently from atoms and things made of atoms. Chemistry and materials engineering recognise that the same kind of atoms can form different structures (allotropes) resulting in materials with vastly different properties. Biology knows the different capabilities that *emerge* from a cell, an organ, an organism and an ecosystem. However, composition fallacies are much subtler. Everyone has a mind, but to extrapolate between the individual and the group, and assume that there is such a thing as a 'collective mind' is a composition fallacy. So is ascribing to society the psychological traits of individuals. One result is the insidious prejudice of blaming an entire group for the faults of a few. Similarly, in Keynesian economics, the same behaviour that benefits one individual (e.g., saving) can be ruinous to the whole of society: if everyone practices it, demand and economic output fall, and total income and savings decrease.

Division fallacy, conversely, is the incorrect assumption that if something is true or good for the whole, it must also be true or good for one or some of its parts. A related instance is the 'ecological' fallacy in interpreting data, when traits of an individual are deduced from the statistics of the group. This happens in Simpson's paradox of the median and the mean: one baseball player can have a higher batting average than another every year for several years and yet have a lower cumulative average for the same period. This is because the differences from year to year are not accounted for. By the same token, higher average does not mean higher probability and vice versa. The bell curve is determined by the median, not the average. For instance, the fact that group *x* has a lower average IQ than the general population does not mean that a random individual from that group is more likely to have a lower IQ than the general population as well, because the group's average may have been brought down by a few individuals, while the majority of the group has a higher-than-average IQ. It is the *median* or middle score, not the average or mean, that relates to probability. This recalls a humorous fallacy: a former governor of the State of Georgia was nagged by his counterpart to the south about all the people fleeing his state and moving down to Florida. 'Well, that is a great thing!'—exclaimed the Georgian. 'It is sure to raise the IQ of both our states!'.

Other Aristotelian fallacies include: figures of speech; stressing different words in a sentence to accent a different meaning; applying a general rule to an exceptional case; taking a proverb or rule of thumb as a universal law; putting forth an irrelevant conclusion that misses the point of the argument; circular reasoning ('The Bible is true because it says so in the Bible'); false cause or guilt-by-association; affirming the converse ('If it rained, the ground would be wet' / 'If the ground is wet, it is because it rained'—as opposed to hosing or irrigation); asking a loaded question that contains a controversial assumption ('When did you stop using drugs?').

Aristotelian logic has been immensely influential through the ages. Later thinkers have identified a host of other fallacies. Some are rather colourful, but beware: 'fallacious reasoning is far from benign' (Haber, 2020, p. 59). *Ad verecundiam* is the logical fallacy of affirming a conclusion based solely on the opinion of some 'infallible' authority. *Ad populum* is to respond to an argument or affirmation by appealing to the supposed opinion of 'many people'. *Ad ignorantiam* affirms that something is true or false because so far it has not been proven otherwise. *Ad antiquitatem* is asserting that if something has been done for a long time, it must be right. *Ad novitatem* is to claim that something is better because it is new or modern. The latter is a staple of advertising and the promotion of technology. *Ad consequentiam* is to argue that something is so, based on its supposed consequences ('The president is honest; otherwise, he would not have been elected'; 'He must be lazy because he doesn't have a lot of money'). *Ad crumenam* asserts that someone knows better because he is rich. The strawman's fallacy is to ridicule the opponent's argument by twisting and exaggerating it ('You don't want a border wall because you want open borders'). *Ad hominem* is attacking the person instead of the argument. One variant is the *tu quoque* (you too) fallacy, when someone answers an accusation by accusing the opponent of the same misdeed. *Ad baculum* is to affirm the validity of an argument based on force, threats or fear of alternative options. *Ad silentio* is to consider that those who keep quiet are ignorant of the matter; or conversely, that silence means agreement. The fallacy of the 'false dilemma' consists in presenting two options as the only possible ones ('If you are not with me, you are against me'). Ad nauseam is an attempt to convince by constantly repeating that something is true, like the scheme attributed to nazi chief propagandist Joseph Goebbels: 'Make a lie big enough, tell it a thousand times, and it becomes the truth –eventually even you will come to believe it'. *Ad misericordiam* is trying to gain sympathy for your point by presenting yourself as a victim.

Does any of this sound familiar?

Perspectivism and Point of View

A critical thinker is a neutral arbiter who must look at things from all relevant perspectives and accept that these may contradict each other. This means rejecting all absolutes and espousing *reasonable* relativism. We saw earlier that when we look at ourselves from the inside, as a grammatical subject, it is evident that we have free will, but when we look at ourselves from the outside, as a grammatical object, it is evident that we are determined by myriad circumstances. We saw a similar relativism in the ancient philosophical debate among idealism, materialism and dualism. I argued then that language is inseparably both physical and mental, the relative link between mind and matter. Physicist Niels Bohr famously observed that light behaves as both particle and wave, positing the *complementarity principle*, which has since been applied from quantum mechanics to bilingualism, psychology, law, economics and other fields. Werner Heisenberg discovered that if we determine the position of an electron, we cannot determine its speed and vice versa. His *indeterminacy principle* established that the observer's point of view affects the observation. Einstein's theory of relativity similarly established that matter and energy are constantly becoming each other. He also changed the perspective of Newton's gravity to one in which mass changes the fabric of space into a parabolic funnel or gravity well.

Perspectivism in philosophy is the principle of epistemology that all perception and knowledge are always partial and incomplete, as is the view of the observer. This incomplete view of reality differs from relativism's position that nothing is absolute, nor does it mean that all perspectives are equally valuable or true. The debate dates to the fifth and sixth centuries BCE in Heraclitus (reality is in endless flux) and Protagoras (change is a passing accident, true essence is unchanging). In the Renaissance, Michel de Montaigne argued for cultural perspectivism in his essay 'Of Cannibals' (1993 [1580]). There is a perspectivist tradition in German philosophy that runs from Leibniz to Nietzsche. Particularly in Book Three of *The Will to Power*, Nietzsche deploys his critique of knowledge arguing against positivism that there are no facts independent of the subject and that everything is interpretation, perspectivism.

> 'Everything is subjective', you say; but even this is interpretation. The 'subject' is not something given, it is something added and invented and projected Behind what there is. --Finally, is it necessary to posit an interpreter behind the interpretation? Even this is invention, hypothesis. [...] [The world] has no meaning behind it, but countless meanings. 'Perspectivism'. [...] Every drive is a kind of lust to rule; each one has its perspective that it would like to compel all other drives to accept as a norm. (1968, [1883, 1888], p. 267)

An heir to this tradition, José Ortega y Gasset expands this to an awareness of historical, social and political perspectivism, proclaiming the end of Eurocentrism and the emergence of a polycentric cultural world. In the anthropology of Franz Boas, this translates into the debunking of the racist interpretation of history based on a supposed evolutionary supremacy, which Nietzsche had forcefully refuted in 'Anti-Darwin' (1968 [1888], pp. 522–523). In 'Truth and Perspective' (1963, 1916]), Ortega reasons that different spectators see a different view according to their position and condition, and that truth can only be approached from multiple perspectives. He cites Leibniz's example of a village seen from multiple sides, its 'truth' being an infinite multitude of individual perspectives. Boris Uspensky (1983) observes that behind every point of view there is an ideology, a worldview or what C. S. Peirce (1877) considered a 'fixation of belief'. Jean Françoise Lyotard in *The Postmodern Condition: A Report on Knowledge* (1984) rejects all grand theories and master narratives, reflecting the intellectual stance of Postmodernism to disavow all universals and essentialisms. Perspectivism does portend a crisis of knowledge. The subjective perspective is untenable if it cannot be independently verified. The question of a single 'objective' and 'universal' truth has fallen into disrepute. And given the impossibility of attaining infinite perspectives, the standard that remains is the approximation of truth via *intersubjectivity* (intersubjective verification) and rational consensus in the public sphere, free from coercion, domination and manipulation (Habermas, 1990). There lies the danger in the easy propagation of misinformation and disinformation through the Internet. It manipulates perspective and gullible public opinion, undermining intersubjectivity as the last line of defence for critical thinking and truth.

Scepticism must apply to the things we consider, and more so to the things we are told, whether by word of mouth or social media. What is *believable*? This is a crucial question in the era of 'truthiness' and 'post-truth' (Cosentino, 2020). Narratives come to us in many shapes and from many directions, including advertising, political speeches and debates. The central question is what *authority* narrators have for knowing what they claim to know. Are they first-hand witnesses? Do they have a privileged perspective? This relates to the question of *verisimilitude* (semblance of truth) in narrative theory. Aside from the validity, cogency and empirical support of the contents, it is the rhetoric used in the telling what accounts for its persuasiveness, and within the rhetoric, it is the position, condition and perspective of the teller, in short, the narrative viewpoint. Here I turn to a classic study by narratologist Wayne Booth, 'Distance and Point-of-View' (1983, 1961]). The literary critic is possibly the best model of critical thinking outside the sciences, insofar as they approach the message dispassionately and without preconceptions, from a neutral, questioning and sceptical degree-zero standpoint.

Narrative Manipulation

Booth's typology is a masterful example of metagrammar based on functional diacritics. He first *differentiates* among the various types of narrators according to their *cases*—a grammatical operation based on the declension of nominals, as discussed in Chapter 6. He then *conjugates* the various types by their different positions or relations of *distance* to the characters and events in the story. How close to them is the narrator? The critic sets aside the old and simplistic classification of first- and third-person narration, observing that the following *functional distinctions* apply to both. (Propp's functional distinctions among character roles in his *Morphology of the Folktales* are here applied to narrator roles.)

First, there is the **implied author**, the persona or mask created for the purpose of the narrative, a 'second self' that is always wiser, more knowledgeable and engaging than the 'real man' and certainly more so than the audience. There is always an implied author to bolster the authority of the tale. Second, there is the **undramatised narrator**, supposed to be 'objective', who is not himself a character. Stories are usually presented as passing through the consciousness of a teller. When told in the first person ('I'), we are aware that there is an experiencing mind whose viewpoint *comes between us and the events*. But when there is no 'I', we may be fooled into thinking that the story comes to us directly, unmediated and unquestionable as though we ourselves were the eyewitnesses. When there is no explicit narrator, the teller's implied persona (who claims to have privileged knowledge) assumes the role of that authoritative undramatised narrator. We fall prey to a manipulation when we naively identify such all-knowing undramatised narrators with the limited 'real man' who creates them. Third, there is the **dramatised narrator**. Think, for example, of a news-anchor persona relating events from his privileged perspective as undramatised narrator; then, he goes to a reporter on the scene who interviews a witness. The latter, reporter and witness, are part of the story as dramatised narrators. In fact, narrators become dramatised (and limited) as soon as they refer to themselves as 'I'.

Booth's method is diacritical: definition and distinction by contrast or difference. Not all dramatised narrators are explicit, some are hidden, given that any speech and gesture of any character narrates. These are called **reflectors**. ('Oh, it's not just me who says it. These other people who are closer to the source say it too'.) Reflectors act as centres of consciousness through which the author filters his narrative. These third-person reflectors are one of three distinct types of dramatised narrators. The other two are: mere **observers**, who bolster the story as witnesses ('These other people saw it too'); as opposed to **narrator-agents**, who are themselves part of the action. Each one may have a different agenda. They all can relate the story to us primarily as *scene* (showing), as *summary* (telling) or as a combination of the two. They all vary in the amount and kind of *commentary* or editorialising they add to the narrative. Commentaries may be ornamental, rhetorical or integral to the story. Narrators may be aware or unaware of themselves as narrators. Some are fallible or **unreliable** to different degrees either because they are naïve or deceitful. Narrators may be **isolated** (unsupported or uncorrected by other narrators), or they may be **supported** or corrected. Some are **privileged** while some are **limited** in their access to information, there being different kinds and degrees of limitation. Their perspective may be **internal** or **external**. They may be ignorant of what is happening or not. Some may pretend to be omniscient and objective, while others may present multiple subjective perspectives. Finally, the inside view that they provide varies in depth (deep or shallow) and in the axis or angle of their plunge.

These different types—implied author, undramatised and dramatised narrators, and third-person reflectors—together with their different characteristics and *agendas* are conjugated with the different kinds and degrees of **distance** among them or with respect to the characters and the audience. There is distance in space and time (physical, temporal, age), social class (speech, dress), personal beliefs and qualities (moral, intellectual and emotional distance). Each type of narrator and relation of distance lends the narrative more or less authority and believability. We, the audience, detect the level of believability without much analysis, as a 'feeling'. Finally, there can be various levels of narration: 'I saw'; 'somebody told me' (hearsay); 'somebody told me that somebody told them'; etc. At each diegetic level, believability diminishes. These combinations of distance and points of view are manipulated as filters and prisms in *every* narrative.

Conclusion

This analysis applies to all narratives: personal stories by word of mouth or social media; testimonials; advertising; journalism; political discourse; legal, historical, ethnographic, technical and even scientific narratives. In the face of faulty reasoning, fallacies and unreliable perspectives, critical thinkers look for evidence, are sceptical and not easily persuaded. A final word may be said about self-deception. Neel Burton (2023) examines forty modes of self-deception, including Freud's defence mechanisms. They belong to five categories: abstraction, transformation, evasion through fraud or fantasy, evasion through people or the world and projection. Some interesting modes include denial, intellectualisation, rationalisation, scapegoating, dehumanisation, reconstruction of reality, grandiosity, humour, idealisation, devaluation and identification.

These are some of the fiercest enemies of critical thinking and personal problem solving.

References

Aristotle (2012 [347 BCE]). *On Sophistical Refutations*. R. B. Jones (Ed.) Translated by W. A. Pickard-Cambridge. *The Organon: The Works of Aristotle on Logic* (pp. 353–396). CreateSpace. Retrieved from https://www.rbjones.com/rbjpub/philos/classics/aristotl/obook_draft.pdf

Booth, W. C. (1983 [1961]). Distance and point-of-view: an essay in classification. *The Rhetoric of Fiction* (Chapter VI). The University of Chicago Press.

Burton, N. (2023). *Hide & Seek: The Psychology of Self-Deception*. Acheron Press.

Cosentino, G. (2020). *Social Media and the Post-Truth World Order: The Global Dynamics of Disinformation*. Palgrave Macmillan.

Haber, J. (2020). *Critical Thinking*. MIT Press.

Habermas, J. (1979). *Communication and the Evolution of Society*. Translated by T. McCarthy. Beacon Press.

Habermas, J. (1990). *The Philosophical Discourse of Modernity*. Translated by F. G. Lawrence. MIT Press.

Hurley, P. J. (2023). *A Concise Introduction to Logic* (14th ed.). Cengage.

Kaufmann, S., Over, D. E., & Sharma, G. (Eds.) (2023). *Conditionals: Logic, Linguistics and Psychology*. Palgrave Macmillan.

Lyotard, J.-F. (1984). *The Postmodern Condition: A Report on Knowledge*. Translated by G. Benington & B. Massumi. University of Minnesota Press.

Montaigne, M. (1993 [1580]). *The Complete Essays*. Translated by M. A. Screech. Penguin.

Nietzsche, F. (1968 [1883–1888]). *The Will to Power*. Translated by W. Kaufmann & R. J. Hollingdale. Random House.

Nietzsche, F. (1968 [1888]). *Twilight of the Idols*. Translated by W. Kaufmann. *The Portable Nietzsche*. Viking.

Ortega y Gasset, J. (1963 [1916]). Verdad y perspectiva [Truth and perspective]. *Obras Completas, 2* (6th ed.) 15–21. Revista de Occidente.

Paavola, S. (2004). Abduction through grammar, critic, and methodeutic. *Transactions of the Charles S. Peirce Society, 40*(2), 245–270.

Peirce, C. S. (1877). The fixation of belief. Popular Science Monthly, 12 (November) 1–15. Retreived from https://www.peirce.org/writings/p107.html

Peirce, C. S. (1935). *Collected Papers of Charles Sanders Peirce*. Scientific Metaphysics (vol. 6). C. Hartshorne & P. Weiss (Eds.). Harvard University Press.

Ryle, G. (1945). Knowing how and knowing that. *Proceedings of the Aristotelian Society, 46*, 1–16.

Uspensky, B. (1983). *A Poetics of Composition.* Translated by V. Zavarin & S. Wittig. University of California Press.

Vitello, M., & Salvi, C. (2023). Gestalt's perspective on insight: a recap based on recent behavioral and neuroscientific evidence. *Journal of Intelligence, 11*(224), 1–10. Retrieved from https://doi.org/10.3390/jintelligence11120224

11

Propaganda

Introduction

Let anyone free from bias cast the first stone! Since we all have personal and ideological interests that inform our very identity, we all have biases to one extent or another. As much as well-meaning people and the most rigorous scientists try to fight and neutralise their biases, these still creep up and distort our thinking in ways of which we are not even aware. For every assumption that we make there is a bias. Formulating a hypothesis is itself introducing a confirmation bias and acquiring a conflict of interest: the desire to succeed, to be right, to have our hypothesis verified. That is the reason why all serious academic studies must be peer reviewed. In statistical research, the way we frame the research question induces a bias; the way we sample the data induces additional biases; and, assuming that the statistical calculations are perfectly correct, the way we interpret the results inserts even more serious biases. This is why the study and critique of statistics, as part of a well-rounded education, are essential to the practice of critical thinking. In this era of artificial intelligence, mass and social media, insidious advertising, viral propaganda, polarising disinformation and weaponised discourses, biases are

E. Camayd-Freixas, *Metagrammar*, https://doi.org/10.1007/978-3-031-92337-1_11

intensified with the help of algorithmic amplification to the point of fanaticism.

Being conscious today is being constantly bombarded with information from all kinds of sources and increasingly from electronic media. What psychologists have identified as the imperious need to *simplify our cognitive life* so as not to be utterly overwhelmed and paralysed by excessive inputs has always been there but has quickly become more urgent than ever due to the omnimodal communications of the twenty-first century. We must be as selective as possible with our limited attention span and our valuable time. It also means that we must make generalisations and decisions with limited and often twisted information, rendering us extremely vulnerable to stereotypes, biases and all kinds of propaganda. *Cognitive simplification leads to cognitive bias* (Cherry, 2024; Schwenk, 1984).

Guarding against such natural vulnerabilities requires that we unlearn old habits of thought and learn a new way of critical thinking as a *behaviour* that requires some conscious discipline until it becomes our new habit. The answer is not to close our minds and follow a single one-size-fits-all conviction that we overgeneralise to every matter. We must allow our positions to be challenged by new knowledge, instead of looking for self-confirmation, if we are to continue learning. While we keep an open mind to all new things, we also need to start adopting, until it becomes automatic, the point of view of the critic and the devil's advocate, akin to Descartes' method of 'systematic doubt'.

I have opted in this chapter to approach critical thinking from its opposite: Propaganda. The idea is to deconstruct the metagrammar of propaganda and how it works on us to our detriment. This will give us a more concrete picture of our vulnerabilities to help us guard against them and do our best to counteract them.

From Populism to Extremism

The need to simplify our cognitive life effectually explains away the old elitist myth of the 'stupid masses' that need to be led by the 'intelligent few' (Bernays, 2004 [1928]). The individuals that make up the so-called masses are anything but stupid. The fact is that they are normal people concerned with work, family, plans and the personal interests of their daily lives. They cannot possibly give due consideration to every message and prompt that falls on their laps. We simplify our cognitive life in large part by adopting ideologies, beliefs, attitudes and stereotypes that we overgeneralise to broad areas of life as well as to filter and pigeonhole cognitive inputs. It is this that makes many people vulnerable to ideological propaganda, which does the thinking for them by feeding them *dogma*, ready-made conclusions without proof. We are all forced to take as 'true enough' many of the things we hear, yet we might dig deeper when the information appears vital or immediately relevant to our lives. When it pertains to important matters and decisions that require a serious commitment, prudent people engage in critical thinking, research and consultation as necessary to vet the information. 'We the people' and particularly voters are not all concerned with the same issues. Propaganda must then cast a wide net and compete for our attention with repeated pounding of self-serving half-truths, exaggerations and downright lies in the attempt to influence us. Statistically, masses of people are guaranteed to fall in its traps.

Amplified disinformation under media control is one of the greatest threats to modern society. It erodes the all-important *institution of trust*, the pillar upon which all civic societies are founded. Authoritarian regimes control and manipulate the information that reaches the people to repress and crush any dissent, and to plunder the national treasury. The atrocities of the Myanmar regime in the Rohingya genocide represent one of the gravest cases (Human Rights Watch, 2023). A closed society like North Korea, with totalitarian media and information control, has succeeded in creating a widespread religious myth about the divinity of their 'supreme leader' Kim Yong Un and his dynasty. Russia under Vladimir Putin has acquired totalitarian control of printed and electronic media through its Sovereign Internet Law (2019), which provides for Internet surveillance and partitioning from the World Wide Web, as well as spreading disinformation about their invasion of Ukraine. China's purchases of high technology and hardware from U.S. companies have allowed it increased Internet surveillance and censorship capabilities via the 'Great Firewall of China', effectually creating a separation known as *splinternet*. It blocks foreign websites and tools such as Google Search, Facebook, Twitter and Wikipedia, with plans to launch their own doctored version of the latter to rewrite history and reality. Iran has joined these powers and their proxies around the world to spread divisive disinformation designed to weaken democracies as well as to sponsor hacking and fraud. A repeat of the 2016 and 2020 U.S. presidential elections, during the 2024 election cycle, Russian operatives using their Storm 1516 pipeline flooded Internet media with fraudulent video clips which were then reposted and amplified throughout social media by conservative trolls and politicians.

Democracies are particularly vulnerable because they lack an appropriate metagrammar to regulate the Internet and electronic media or even to criminalise disinformation where due. They run into problems with civil liberties, freedom of speech, free market ideology and other dilemmas. This makes restrictions unpopular, and remedial legislation deadlock or too slow to keep up with technological changes. The unfettered access to the Internet and social media, which initially appeared as a democratising force, such as in the Arab Spring, now tears at the social fabric, while viral disinformation and propaganda weave a crisis of truth. Down this road, democracies appear doomed, destined to devolve into populist autocracies allied with oligarchies and corporatocracies.

The greatest threat in the United States comes from powerful domestic anti-government and antidemocratic consortiums associated with white male supremacy and Christian nationalism. Its roots reach back to the Ku Klux Klan, founded after the Civil War in the late 1860s by vanquished proslavery Confederate veterans. White nationalism has branched out over the decades into numerous interconnected far- and alt-right organisations well funded by an elite of business magnates and corporate interests.

The first strategic step in their metagrammar of propaganda was to found dozens of rightist 'think tanks': the ultraconservative John Birch Society (1958); Heritage Foundation (1973), publisher of the Christian nationalist *Project 2025* blueprint for a second Trump administration; ALEC: American Legislative Exchange Council (1973) which procures corporate sponsorship and drafts dual-purpose legislation for conservative politicians; Cato Institute (1977); FAIR: Federation for

American Immigration Reform (1979), the hate group founded by neo-Nazi John Tanton; Institute on Religion and Democracy (1981); Atlas Network (1981), promoter of right-wing international think tanks; CIS: Center for Immigration Studies (1986), an offshoot of FAIR; National Association of Scholars (1987); State Policy Network (1992), an umbrella of 64 rightist think tanks dealing at the state level; the white supremacist National Policy Institute (2005–2020) and numerous others. (See 'Counter Extremism Project' in References for a report on extremist groups in the United States, Europe and the Middle East.)

An example of their modus operandi is the Liberty Institute (1979), which sponsors conservative activists and recruits them for high posts in politics, government and the media. Its news website *Campus Reform* (2009) combats what it calls liberal bias on college campuses and feeds information to hate groups and trolls to threaten and intimidate scholars who support diversity, equity and inclusion (DEI). Many are 'nonprofit' entities which nevertheless lobby, recruit, finance and feed unsubstantiated studies, spurious statistics, conspiracy theories and tabloid antiliberal slander to their growing media network. This includes the 'nonprofit' America First Policy Institute (2021) devoted to promoting President Donald Trump's political agenda.

The second step was to branch out and segment the ideological market to broaden their membership by spinning and financing 'lite' organisations with a moderate veneer. A prime example is Roy Beck's anti-immigrant Numbers USA (1996), a third-generation descendant of white supremacist FAIR and CIS. Most importantly, white nationalism was euphemistically rebranded as *Christian nationalism* to cater to the large block of evangelical voters, megachurches, radio and tele ministries, many of which have a global reach.

The third step in their propaganda playbook was to expand their control of the media. This takes the form of discrediting mainstream news outlets as 'corporate media', 'enemies of the people' and providers of 'fake news', while parlaying their own media networks into the mainstream via Fox News and exploiting the federal equal-time rule (47 US Code sec. 315) to channel extreme minority views into mainstream media through controversial political candidates. Right-wing 'alternative' media exploded in the twenty-first century, starting with conservative talk radio (Rush Limbaugh and imitators like Sean Hannity and Glenn Beck). Hundreds of conservative and ultraconservative blogs, podcasts and websites leveraged by social media, like Daily Wire and the far-right Breitbart News Network, surged with the 2016 U.S. elections and the Trump White House.

Conservative talk radio and podcasts became a profitable industry. The more boisterous and extreme their affirmations, the greater their entertainment value, profitability and influence. A case in point is *Infowars*, a far-right conspiracy theory, hate speech, disinformation and fake news website owned by boisterous Trump supporter Alex Jones. During the 2016 presidential campaign, Russian government bots promoted his website while he made millions selling fraudulent health supplements online. Jones and his site were eventually banned from most social media platforms. In 2022, Texas and Connecticut juries ordered him to pay $1.4 billion in damages for his defamatory lies against the families affected by the Sandy Hook Elementary School massacre. He quickly filed for personal bankruptcy (Williamson, 2022).

The right-wing propaganda network was consolidated around Fox News as a national cable television channel. It was founded in 1996 by Australian-born media mogul Rupert Murdoch, under his U.S. umbrella company, News Corporation, later split into News Corp (2013) and Fox Corporation (2019) after numerous convictions for phone hacking, bribery and corruption ruined the reputation of several of its subsidiary brands. Significantly, Murdoch is recognised as the creator of the modern tabloid, starting with *The Sun* (UK 1969), *News of the World* (UK 1969), sex and scandal tabloid *The San Antonio News* (US 1973), supermarket tabloid *The Star* (US 1974), among others. Tabloid scandal sells, leading to Murdoch's financial and editorial success. He went on to found or buy numerous other tabloids and populist newspapers, owning over 800 media outlets in more than 50 countries, with political alliances and propagandistic influence, especially in Australia, the United Kingdom and the United States, where he has been the target of several investigations and lawsuits.

Tabloid metagrammar is illustrated by American Media, Inc. (AMI), renamed a360media, publisher of most major supermarket tabloids in the United States, including the *National Enquirer*, *Globe*, *Star* and

Examiner. They practised 'catch-and-kill' operations, buying exclusive rights to negative stories about Trump and not publishing them (Palazzolo et al., 2016). They also engaged in gossip mongering and even blackmail against Trump's opponents and detractors (Kim et al., 2019). Similarly, Fox News has been mired in controversy since inception due to its tabloid-style operations, slanted news and partisan political commentary. They have undermined journalistic integrity, truth and the institution of trust, contributing to the so-called culture wars and sowing deep divisions in American society (Jurkowitz et al., 2020). Their ratings and profits increased after 2015 with the propagandistic coverage of Donald Trump as a tabloid figure, becoming the most watched cable news network in the United States.

Another boost came after Mr. Trump's baseless claim (known as 'the big lie') that the 2020 elections had been stolen from him. Fox News deliberately spread lies in this regard and had to pay Dominion Voting Systems and others close to $800 million to settle defamation lawsuits involving the elections (Mangan et al., 2023). Trump became the first president to strategically exploit social media. His daily tabloid-style tweets were amplified by Fox News and repeated by mainstream media, which also profited from the scandalous rhetoric. This kept Trump constantly in the news and gave him the amplified voice to demonise immigrants, slander opponents and intimidate party moderates, leading to the radicalisation of the Republican Party and the legitimation of extremist groups linked to domestic terrorism.

The propagandistic network energises a militant movement that finally has a leader in President Trump. Their content pipeline circulates the same arguments and talking points over and over among the think tanks, which feed them to their media networks for constant repetition and exemplification by distorted or fabricated news. These are then spread to member databases and listservs to be amplified across social media by troll farms, activist groups, individual recipients, ultraconservative politicians and, lately, AI bots. In the process, the talking points are distilled into instant soundbites, memes and gaslighting that paint moderates and liberals as the 'radical left'. It is a highly organised, leveraged and entrenched twenty-first-century propaganda and disinformation machinery that fabricates its own reality and creates a splinter-media whose consumers reject all other information sources, thereby fostering a polarised and fractured society.

There is no such organised opposition movement. The bipartisan Center for Strategic and International Studies (CSIS, founded in 1962) states: 'The threat from Antifa [anti-fascist group] and other far-left networks is relatively small in the United States. The far left includes a decentralized mix of actors. [...] Twitter shut down several accounts that it said were operated by a white supremacist group called Identity Evropa, which was posing as Antifa' (Jones, 2020). This is part of a concerted effort to manufacture an imaginary enemy dubbed the 'radical left' that would pose an impending threat. The object is to create the illusion of a dysfunctional democracy that works against common people and threatens the nation, an illusion meant to propel a crusade to take over the government and replace liberal democracy with a populist autocracy. History provides numerous examples. The rhetoric and methods are not new. They are just amplified by unregulated media. This metagrammar of U.S. right-wing propaganda is replicated in other democracies, where globalisation and increased immigration have met a reactionary surge of populist nationalism. Its success or failure depends on the existence of similar elements and conditions versus the strength of civil society, democratic institutions and the legal framework to regulate deceptive practices in the media.

The disinformation pipeline is based not on rational arguments but on emotional manipulation. That is why it is so effective. Next to multi-channel repetition, there is a crescendo in the emotional tone of preachers and conservative talk show hosts, intensified further by extremist podcasters and violent hate group websites. This emotional crescendo fed the violent insurrection of 6 January 2021 against the U.S. Capitol, led by the Proud Boys and Oath Keepers militia groups on behalf of President Trump. The combination of talk radio, podcasts, social media and Fox News impacts everyday people with a recipe of lies, fear, outrage, anger and hate. Agitators and demagogues drive followers to become aggressive activists in schools, school boards, town halls, city and county commissions, healthcare agencies, local politics, the media, voting and other civic centres, where they threaten civil servants and yell insults, profanities and visceral opinions. Fanaticism is stoked by promoting the blinding emotion of *righteous anger*. The more extreme a person's views, the more susceptible to emotional manipulation. Heightened emotions of fear and anger are addictive as they release endorphins. 'There is also the psychological aspect of ego fragility and injury, often seen in narcissistic personalities; the rush behind anger can be triggered by underlying feelings of weakness or insecurity, a way to feel powerful in the moment and [...] briefly in control of things' (Kim, 2015). Normal people lured into daily consumption of outrageous propaganda find it difficult to break away from the cycle of anger, sublimated as a righteous pseudo-patriotic cult which they perceive as giving them meaning and purpose. Often their personalities are distorted to the point of becoming aggressive toward, distanced from and unrecognisable to their families and friends.

These, however, are still low-tech rudimentary methods. What looms in the horizon is the optimisation of emotions through artificial intelligence, aimed at financial gain, political control and social engineering. This evolving technology focuses on biometric extraction for emotional profiling, emotional-state measuring and automated empathy (Bakir & McStay, 2022). I will return to this *addiction triangle* in Chapter 15, 'The Parasitic Age'.

Public Opinion

There is much to unpack here, so let us start from the beginning. The classic study on the subject is *Propaganda* (2004 [1928]) by publicist Edward Bernays, with a must-read critical introduction to the 2004 edition by Mark Crispin Miller, who states: 'the investigative journalist is the propagandist's natural enemy' (p. 26). 'Propaganda --Bernays argues-- is the executive arm of the invisible government' (p. 48). In his view, the 'intelligent few' whom most people never see, acting behind the scenes, are the true administrators of democracy by 'regimenting' the opinion of the masses. His new profession of 'public relations counsel' is to be a consigliere to his powerful clients and a spin doctor for their agendas and products. We really must set aside his elitism, sexism, prejudices and positivist sales pitch to profit from his guile.

Propaganda is an old fact of history, but its modern version and systematic development began with World War I. President Woodrow Wilson was re-elected to a second term in 1916 based on a pacifist platform that promised to keep the United States out of the war in Europe. He was soon persuaded to promote the war as inevitable by publicists convinced that they could control public opinion. He named Denver journalist George Creel to establish the Committee on Public Information, later known as the Creel Commission, the first modern office of State propaganda. Edward Bernays was one of its early members. Within two years, the Creel propaganda machine had plastered posters and pamphlets in every corner, institution and newspaper in the country, canvased every school with 'volunteer' speakers hammering the same patriotic pro-war script and distributed short propaganda films to every organisation and theatre. Right or wrong, within two years the pacifist American electorate had been turned into a crowd of committed warmongers convinced of their patriotic calling to save America, democracy and the world by joining the war.

Bernays saw first-hand the practical power of propaganda, but he was not an original or innovative thinker. Instead, he exploited the prevailing theories of predecessors and contemporaries like Gustave Le Bon, Wilfred Trotter, Sigmund Freud and his closest source, opposition journalist Walter Lippmann, who became one of Creel's fiercest critics because of the Commission's systematic censorship and repression of anti-war voices. Lippmann, a liberal, went on to publish his classic *Public Opinion* (2004 [1922]) to warn against the vulnerabilities to propaganda that he saw as threatening modern democracy. Bernays followed a year later with his own *Crystallizing Public Opinion* (1923), the prequel to *Propaganda*, which he published five years later.

Walter Lippmann begins by examining the limitations of perception and cognition, the difference between the big wide world outside and the 'pictures in our head'. This 'inside truth' is nothing more than a man-made composite representation of the few things we experience directly, with the bulk being the images given to us by others (*Public Opinion*, pp. 3–21). Censorship and privacy intercept much of the information at the source. Opportunity for experience, contact, travel and education is unevenly distributed and favours the more affluent.

Other limitations include the time and quality of attention to mind public affairs, as well as the reporting of events being always incomplete, not always clear and never neutrally worded (pp. 23–51). Thus, the way propaganda works with communication media is by 'the insertion between man and his environment of a pseudo-environment [to which] his behaviour is a response. But [...] the consequences [...] operate not in the pseudo-environment where the behaviour is stimulated, but in the real environment where action eventuates. [...] The analysis of public opinion must begin then, by recognizing the *triangular relation* between the scene of action, the human picture of that scene and the human response to that picture working itself out upon the scene of action'. If the behavioural response involves concrete action on things or people, 'contradiction soon develops'; but if it involves thoughts and emotions, 'it may be a long time before there is any noticeable break in the texture of the fictitious world' (pp. 10–11, *my italics*).

In addition to personal tradition, the duration of the fiction allows for the formation and reinforcement of a stable system of stereotypes and biases that informs our beliefs, attitudes, opinions and our very identity. Lippmann's most significant contribution was in fact to give us the first redefinition and critique of *stereotypes* in the modern psychological sense and how they are exploited to 'manufacture consent'—the famous phrase he coined. Stereotypes are simplifications and generalisations about the world that compensate for cognitive limitations while serving a personal interest. We often hold to our stereotypes as a defence mechanism: 'The systems of stereotypes may be the core of our personal tradition, the defences of our position in society' (p. 63). Further, the 'pictures in our head' are not fixed. They change and develop, 'reworked by the poetic faculty into a personal expression of ourselves'. We personalise them, dramatise their relations and 'participate in the action [...] as some sort of allegory' (p. 101). Propaganda works through stereotypes to create the suggestion of a 'common will' out of the multitude of interests, opinions and images of the world. According to Lippmann, the 'mysterious power' of stereotypical *symbols*, from the totem pole to the national flag to a patriotic slogan, is essential for maintaining social unity and cohesion. 'Because of their transcendent practical importance, no successful leader has ever been too busy to cultivate the symbols that organise his following' (p. 150).

Noam Chomsky, in *Media Control: The Spectacular Achievements of Propaganda* (1997), issues an incisive critique of Lippmann and Bernays. In the process, Chomsky shows why the linguist's transfer of skills from natural language grammar to the metagrammar of social theory is so effective. He contends that such abstract symbols, ideals and slogans are so general and vague that no one can be against them and therefore they have no real practical meaning but are 'empty concepts like Americanism'.

> Who can be against that? Or, as in the Persian Gulf War, 'Support our troops'. Who can be against that? [...] In fact, what does it mean if somebody asks you: Do you support the people of Iowa? Can you say: Yes, I support them, or No, I don't support them? It's not even a question. It doesn't mean anything. That's the point. The point of public relations slogans like 'Support our troops' is that they don't mean anything. [...] The issue was: Do you support our policy? But you don't want people to think about that issue. That's the whole point of good propaganda. [...] Its crucial value is that it diverts your attention from a question that *does* mean something: Do you support our policy? (pp. 25–26)

Lippmann attempts to create a 'Democratic Theory of Public Opinion' that can deal with all the cognitive limitations of society by placing communications in the hands of responsible and ethical journalists, editors and policymakers, who have a duty to the public. Edward Bernays even had a strict code of ethics for news and public relations. They were of course writing before the rise of national tabloids, propagandistic news networks and unedited Internet and social media. In retrospect, Chomsky charges them with promoting a 'spectator democracy' where a specialised class 'deeply indoctrinated in the values and interests of private power and the state-corporate nexus that it represents' runs the corporate-monopoly media to create the 'necessary illusions' while the masses simply need to be distracted and *entertained* (1997, pp. 14–29).

In Lippmann's mind, he is promoting and defending responsible journalism from virulent accusations like the one he cites from Upton Sinclair's *The Brass Check: A Study of American Journalism*:

> The Brass Check is found in your pay envelope every week—you who write and print and distribute our newspapers and magazines. The Brass Check is the price of your shame—you who take the fair body of truth and sell it in the marketplace, who betray the virgin hopes of mankind into the loathsome brothel of Big Business. (quoted in Lippmann, p. 212)

Lippmann responds by pointing out the practical limitations of the press in terms of the difference between news and truth. The job of the press is to point out news events and to make them relatable to the readers. The job of digging out the truth behind those events belongs to the social scientists. He gives the example of 'the reporting of strikes'. The headlines call attention to the event, but in order to '*enlist* the interest' of the reader (notice the military draft terminology for 'engaging the attention') the strike must be described 'as the story of interference with the reader's life. [...] I think myself the crucial part, of what looks to the worker and the reformer as deliberate misrepresentation on the part of newspapers, is the direct outcome of a practical difficulty in uncovering the news and the emotional difficulty of making distant facts interesting' (p. 221).

It is a weak and naïve defence because the 'truth' of the social scientists is only accessible to an informed minority, whereas the public only receives the anti-labour spin of the press. The purpose of 'enlisting the interest' of the public is, after all, not only to sell newspapers but to sell advertising and serve powerful financial interests. Edward Bernays (1923) quotes Lippmann's exact same passage about reporting strikes, but his answer is straight forward: the public is 'malleable' and 'the counsel on public relations [...] simply utilises existing channels to obtain expression for the [corporate] point of view he represents' (pp. 45–46). Lippmann does not distinguish between harmless and harmful stereotypes; Bernays simply does not care. He advocates for whomever hires him. Bernays instrumentalises existing theories to develop systematic methods and techniques to refine Lippmann's views on 'manufacturing consent' into surgical procedures for *engineering* consent. In fact, the terms 'the herd' and 'the intelligent few' that Chomsky erroneously ascribes to Lippmann belong to Bernays instead.

The Masses

Bernays references Wilfred Trotter's *Instincts of the Herd in Peace and War* (1916) to portray the mindless masses (us) via the mediating metaphor of 'the herd', but Bernays' own spin is that the herd is to be driven (Bernays, 1923, pp. 35–40, 85; 2004 [1928], pp. 71–74). Trotter, a British neurosurgeon, took a rather biological approach to group psychology, adopting the concept of 'instinct' defended by William James to posit a gregarious predisposition common to all social animals. A product of evolution, Trotter's 'herd instinct' allows for sex, procreation, family-like affection and even altruism. The individual fulfils this profound need to be part of the herd by assimilating in response to the powerful 'unconscious' suggestions that the herd exerts, whose function is to maintain its cohesion and strength. Conflict and competition arise when individual experience clashes with the traditional 'voice of the herd' making for the modern dialectics between self and society. Individuals in the herd simply follow each other. Often, leaders will appear, but even the leader must heed the voice of the herd and not get too far ahead, or he will not be followed. Trotter insists that intercommunication is essential to herd cohesion and that as population grows so must the reach and sophistication of communication media.

Of course, the obscure notions of 'instinct' and 'unconscious'—like a black box with a hidden and mysterious mechanism that cannot be further analysed—have been superseded in modern social psychology by the rational concept of *conformity*. This shift to an analysable concept has made it abundantly clear that conformity is a damper to innovation and discovery, because it involves a stagnating abdication of critical thinking. There are two roads to leadership: critical thinking, innovation and discovery is the way of the scientist and the statesman; the other way is that of the *gambler*, hit or miss, make it big or crash and burn. The former may individually fail. The latter can bring their entire herd over the cliff. Bernays understood that only capital can do both, hire critical thinkers and gamble with their surplus investment assets. Let the reader judge who among today's leaders are true innovators, gamblers or diversified investors.

Following his uncle Sigmund Freud's *Group Psychology and the Analysis of the Ego* (1949 [1921]), Bernays exploited the process by which the 'herd' is organised into 'groups' susceptible to influence. Freud and Trotter met and drew from each other's work. Bewildered by droves of information and thus impossible to steer, the raw 'herd' is composed of individuals who blindly follow the haphazard mass judgements to which they are exposed. 'It is axiomatic that men who know little are often intolerant of a point of view that is contrary to their own. [...] How often this is true can be seen from the congressional records of controversies in which the personal attack supersedes logic'. Even scientists 'have lost their lives through refusing to see flaws in their theories'. We all have always been subject to 'what one psychologist has called "logic-proof compartments" [...] excellently summarised in the volume by Mr. Trotter' (Bernays 1923, pp. 36–39).

I prefer to designate this condition as being self-immune to argument, since it is normally accompanied by rationalisations and propagated talking points. Instead of 'compartments'—another black box—modern cognitive science sees *categorisation* as part of the need to simplify our cognitive life. Bernays understood that to mould public opinion, propaganda cannot be directed at the entire 'herd' of a highly diversified modern democracy. He then developed the notion of a target audience and proceeded to segment society into groups, of which he cited many institutions and associations, religious, governmental, civil, civic and professional, as well as special interest groups. 'The new salesmanship, [...] by understanding the group structure of society and principles of mass psychology, [...] has found it possible [...] to set up psychological and emotional currents which will work for him' (2004 [1928], pp. 76–77). His methods of social engineering have prevailed in propaganda, public relations and advertising, augmented by radio, television, the Internet, social media and video gaming; and are currently being exponentially refined by artificial intelligence and machine learning, through billions of iterations of the stimulus-reaction-modification *triangle* behind the growing addiction to electronic media.

The revealing source of these post-World War I bestsellers is Gustave Le Bon's *The Crowd: A Study of the Popular Mind* (2002 [1896]). We need to discount and indeed denounce Le Bon's prejudices even more so than those of Bernays, his intellectual heir. Le Bon was a racist pseudo-scientist, typical of the Positivist Era. His fallacies include the notions that psychological traits and the 'genius of a race' are inherited; that crowds act unconsciously by instinct and reflex; that crowds have a 'mind' as though they were a single individual; that crowds have an 'extreme mental inferiority' typically 'observed in beings belonging to inferior forms of evolution—in women, savages and children, for instance' (p. 18). Nevertheless, if we ignore his obsolete notions of psychological 'laws' and the causes that determine the 'mind' of the crowd, we will find that his descriptions of crowd *behaviour* are eerily accurate and consonant with modern theories of social psychology. His metagrammar of crowd behaviour gives critical thinkers these attitudes to guard against:

- Crowds acquire a collective unity that makes individuals feel, think and act quite differently from how they would in isolation. (pp. 6–13)
- Individuals in a crowd acquire by their sheer number an exhilarating sense of invincible power. Whether by imitation or peer pressure its sentiments and actions become contagious. They are much more suggestible than isolated individuals, resulting in a state of fascination resembling hypnosis. (p. 15)
- Crowds exhibit impulsiveness, mobility and irritability, so imperious as to annihilate the feeling of personal interest. (pp. 17–19)
- Crowds are credulous and readily influenced, showing obedience to suggestions and accepting as realities the images evoked in them. The unanimity of their numerous witnesses is one of the worst proofs that can be invoked to establish a fact. Exaggeration and ingenuousness lead them always to extremes, to not admit doubt or uncertainty and to excessive sentiments and actions. (pp. 20–26)

- Their servility to strong authority makes them intolerant, dictatorial, extremely conservative and hostile to changes and progress. The moralizing role of crowds is displayed in excessive, self-righteous devotion to lofty ideals such as glory, honour and patriotism, taken as absolutes to the point of blindly excusing violent, destructive, criminal and antisocial behaviour, which contrast with transitory displays of exaggerated prudishness and strict morality. The anonymity of individuals inside a crowd fosters diffusion of responsibility and abdication of personal morality, whereby the absorption in an irresponsible crowd assures impunity, lack of accountability, entire liberty and abandonment to follow the mob. (pp. 27–29)
- These factors facilitate a crowd's blind obedience to its leader together with the projection of exaggerated virtues onto their hero. The popular imagination has always been the basis of the power of statesmen. (p. 30)
- Contradictory ideas exist simultaneously because: (a) in modernity, the fundamental ideas of our forefathers, such as religion and democracy, are tottering, have lost all solidity and the institutions resting upon them are severely shaken; (b) every day there are formed a great many passing ideas created by the influences of the moment, such as infatuation for an individual or a doctrine, and some of these transitory ideas acquire vitality and preponderating influence; (c) some of these passing ideas are superposed on the old fundamental ideas, and the lack of mass critical thinking allows them to coexist without perceiving, or downright ignoring, their contradictions. The social influence of ideas is independent of the truth they may contain. (p. 31)
- Crowds are not influenced by reasoning, but instead they think in images that succeed each other without any logical or connecting link. Ideas influence crowds only if they assume a very absolute, uncompromising and simple shape, in the guise of images (today's *memes*) and are only accessible to the masses under this form. The convictions of crowds, whether moral, political or social, assume a religious form, accompanied by doctrinal fervour, fundamentalism, intolerance and fanaticism. (p. 31)
- The power of words, formulas and slogans is bound up with the images they evoke, independent of their real meaning. Baptising old

things with new names has great political utility. Crowds always prefer illusions to truths. Only costly experience can shake the convictions and illusions of a crowd. (p. 52)

- The crowd leader is often nothing more than an agitator. A crowd is a servile flock that is incapable of ever doing without a master. The leader is more frequently a man of action than a thinker. He is not gifted with keen foresight, as this quality frequently conduces to doubt and inactivity. He is especially recruited from the ranks of those morbidly nervous, excitable, half-deranged persons who are bordering on madness. His convictions are so strongly held that all reasoning is lost upon them. (p. 61)
- Affirmation pure and simple, free of all reasoning and proof, is one of the surest means of making an idea enter the mind of crowds. The more concise an affirmation is, the more destitute of every appearance of proof and demonstration, the more weight it carries. Affirmation, however, has no real influence unless it be constantly repeated and, so far as possible, in the same terms. Affirmation, followed by constant repetition, quickly spreads through the crowds by the powerful tendency to imitation and contagion of sentiment. The opinions and beliefs of crowds are especially propagated by contagion, but never by reasoning (pp. 64–66).
- In the case of electoral crowds, it is of primary importance that the candidate should possess prestige. Personal prestige can only be replaced by that resulting from wealth. Talent and even genius are not elements of serious importance. The capital importance of prestige is being able to force himself upon the electorate without discussion. The electorate, mostly composed of common working men, rarely choose a man from their own ranks because such a person typically enjoys no prestige among them. Prestige does not suffice, however. The elector stickles for the flattery of the candidate's greed and vanity, who should not hesitate in making the most fantastic promises. As for the rival candidate, an effort must be made to destroy his chance by establishing by dint of affirmation, repetition and contagion that he is an arrant scoundrel and that it is a matter of common knowledge that he has been guilty of several crimes. It is, of course, useless to trouble about any semblance of proof. Should the adversary be ill-acquainted

> with the psychology of crowds he will try to justify himself by arguments instead of replying to one set of affirmations by another; and he will have no chance whatever to succeed. But the candidate who hits on a new formula as devoid as possible of precise meaning and apt in consequence to flatter the most varied aspirations, infallibly obtains success. (pp. 91–92)

Le Bon's metagrammar of crowd behaviour, dating to 1896, retains an astounding currency in view of new populist demagoguery. Le Bon's currency shows that the projection of metagrammar has predictive and even prophetic value.

The Leader

In the 2016 U.S. presidential campaign, real estate developer Donald Trump attacked his rival, Secretary of State Hilary Clinton, with repeated accusations of crimes, the constant nickname of 'crooked Hilary', memes of her behind bars and conspiracy theories about the 'deep state' and the press as 'the enemy of the people'. Meanwhile, Hillary Clinton quoted First Lady Michelle Obama saying, 'When they go low, we go high'. It failed. Democrats responded with arguments that were no match for the insidious soundbites and memes. To seal his surprise victory, Trump hit on a slogan copied from former president Ronald Reagan and devoid of evidence or meaning (cf. Chomsky above), yet flattering the most varied aspirations, which—Le Bon assured—'infallibly obtains success': Make America Great Again! The 2024 Trump campaign repeated and even doubled down on the same old formula. This time the opposition, Vice-President Kamala Harris, was demonised as a 'radical-left lunatic'. Le Bon's insistence on repetition following affirmation without proof has been confirmed time and again by cognitive and social psychology studies under the *mere exposure effect*, which has become a pillar of advertising and propaganda to induce cognitive bias. In addition to desensitisation, repeated exposure leads to liking and persuasion, subsumed in the tenet 'familiarity breeds content'. By the same token, a lie, repeated, acquires the colour of truth.

Le Bon reminds us that contradictory ideas exist simultaneously in the crowd. Regarding the behaviour of populist leaders, from Fascism to McCarthyism, Mark Crispin Miller brings the matter into focus in his Introduction to Bernays's *Propaganda*, calling them '*fanatical and cynical at once*' (italics in the original): 'Such agitators work within a certain mental borderland, when one can never clearly see conviction as distinct from calculation. Indeed, that inner murkiness appears itself to be the very source or basis of the mass manipulator's enigmatic power and so we cannot comprehend it through schematic dualistic formulas. (Orwell's elusive concept of "doublethink" is highly pertinent here.)' (p. 22). Trotter, in turn, observes that the belief in affirmations 'sanctioned by the herd' goes on however opposed by evidence and reason. 'Totally false opinions may appear to the holder of them to possess all the characters of rationally verifiable truth and may be justified by secondary processes of rationalization which it may be impossible directly to combat by argument'. He notes, however, that 'verifiable truths may acquire the potency of herd suggestion', this being a way of counteracting false public opinions (p. 39). The 'herd'—he further argues—is inclined to a leader who presents 'the appearance and manners of authority and power rather than to one who possesses the substance of capacity', a leader who, 'by his gesticulations and his shouts, leaves his flock in no doubt […] It is touching […] to remember how often a great statesman in his country's need has had to contend not merely with her foreign enemies, but with those at home whose vociferous malignity has declared his magnanimous composure to be sluggishness, his cautious scepticism to be feebleness and his unostentatious resolution to be stupidity' (1916, pp. 118–119).

Freud's group psychology, Weber's patrimonialism and Festinger's theory of cognitive dissonance provide further explanation of the mechanisms by which we become subject to cognitive biases that threaten to atrophy our critical thinking. By 'atrophy' I mean that to the degree in which we fail to exercise critical thinking in one area, we will tend to do so in other areas, becoming rigid, dogmatic and suggestible. Confirmation bias and resistance to the new and different interfere with learning and problem solving. The habit of not thinking by ourselves makes us highly susceptible to manipulation by strong authorities and charismatic groups. In extreme cases, we can fall prey to a cult.

Freud (1949 [1921]) paid particular attention to the leader and replaced the notions of 'crowd' and 'herd' with the concept of different kinds of 'groups'—an idea picked up by Bernays. Trotter's 'contagion' became Freud's 'suggestibility' of individuals by the perceived unanimity of the group. This is akin to conformity and peer pressure in social psychology. Freud defines suggestion as unexplained 'influence without adequate logical foundation' and explains it as an unconscious drive to fulfil a primal desire, based on his concept of 'libido' (pp. 22–23). At its core, libido is an 'instinct' towards sexual union, but it is sublimated into all forms of affection, love, solidarity and loyalty. It gives cohesion to the group and builds the authoritarian leader into a surrogate father figure.

Freud's theory is consistent with Max Weber's concept of patrimonialism, in *Economy and Society* (1968 [1921]). Patrimonialism is a form of autocratic government where all power flows from the ruler. Its metagrammar models the monarchical governance of the family household or the family business, where the patriarchy is all powerful. The patrimonial ruler makes no distinction between the public and the private spheres and treats matters of state as his private business. He mimics a monarchy by bringing his family into the seat of government, surrounding himself with personal loyalists who act as hired mercenaries parallel to legitimate government officials and expects the army and police to be loyal to him rather than to the nation. Patrimonialism clashes with the functioning of the modern state as a rational-legal bureaucracy, where authority is grounded on legal rationality and legitimacy. Trump's presidency embodied every single one of these traits.

Strong explanation for his continuing support may be found in Leon Festinger's *A Theory of Cognitive Dissonance* (1962 [1957]). The theory is simple, but its ramifications are extensive. It states that people need inner harmony and consistency among their beliefs, values, attitudes, opinions and their new cognitions or information. When something contradicts our beliefs, we suffer a psychological discomfort called cognitive dissonance, which urges us to reduce the dissonance and achieve consonance. We look to confirm our beliefs and minimise, deny or avoid dissonant cognitions. If you do something for someone or put up with their misdeeds, cognitive dissonance confronts you with two propositions: 'I am a fool', which threatens your ego, or 'He is such a great, deserving guy'. Mr. Trump's increasingly outrageous comments and inappropriate actions not only desensitised the public but also placed most Republicans in the same predicament. To reduce dissonance, they exaggerated his value and diminished the seriousness of his misdeeds, which they saw as insignificant compared to 'making America great again'. Trump felt emboldened, and as the magnitude of his misdeeds increased, his followers dug in further, many to the point of fanatically excusing criminal and even treasonous behaviour. Festinger establishes that the magnitude of the dissonance is 'a function of the importance of the opinions involved' and of the magnitude of the expected results (p. 97). This also determines the magnitude of the public reaction to reduce the dissonance. The magnitude of importance involved here corresponds with deep-seated values, ingrained ideology, party loyalty and the Presidency of the United States.

Equally important is the strength of discomfort caused by what Festinger calls *post-decision dissonance* as well as the mechanisms employed to reduce it. Post-decision dissonance can be so strong that very committed people routinely 'misperceive' (misrepresent to themselves and others) or 'avoid cognising' (block out) new information. They swiftly dismiss and forget it as they 'set up quick defensive processes which prevent the new cognition from ever becoming firmly established' (p. 137). Some grow so committed that they deny reality and incontrovertible proof. A large group of people may maintain an opinion or belief for an extended time even when confronted with continual proof to the contrary. At times this rises to the level of mass delusions (p. 198).

There are several synergistic mechanisms to reduce dissonance. One of the most effective is to find social support among groups of like-minded people. Individuals in a group of followers reinforce each other's beliefs and opinions, such that groupthink substitutes for critical thinking. When challenged, they react with increased proselytising to add new converts to their ranks for further reinforcement. Groups produce, manufacture, seek and share new consonant cognitions. They spread and magnify party lines and spin doctors' talking points. Festinger's theory of cognitive dissonance lends rational explanation for the old black-box notions of 'herd instinct' and 'libido'. Committed individuals and groups who base their following on conformity and emotion, rather than evidence and logic, avoid discussions with people of the opposing viewpoint and can get aggressive when challenged. The group works to increase consonant cognitions and avoid dissonant ones. The avoidance includes not only interacting within the group to the exclusion of others, but also avoiding opposing sources of news and information and tuning in exclusively to friendly propaganda sources.

In personality theory, 'Dark Triad' refers to three offensive yet non-pathological *personality types* with overlapping traits: Machiavellianism, subclinical narcissism and subclinical psychopathy (Paulhus & Williams, 2002). 'Dark' means that they 'entail a socially malevolent character with behaviour tendencies toward self-promotion, emotional coldness, duplicity and aggressiveness' (p. 557). Machiavellianism refers to divisive, manipulative and exploitative treatment of others, vengefulness, ruthlessness, calculating self-interest and disregard for morality. Narcissism is characterised by hubris, egotism, attention seeking, dominance, lack of empathy, diminishing others, feelings of grandiosity, entitlement and superiority, self-enhancement and over-claiming bias, together with insecurity and ego fragility. Psychopathy has subsidiary traits of antisocial behaviour, bullying, impulsivity, selfishness, callousness, sadism and lack of remorse. These traits correlate with authoritarianism, populism, demagoguery, nationalism, anti-immigrant sentiments, extreme ideologies, supremacy and racism. A study comparing the personality traits and campaign styles of Donald Trump and twenty-one other populist politicians worldwide found Trump to rank highest or close to highest in all dark personality traits, and his campaign style highest in negative tone, personal attacks and appeals to fear (Nai et al., 2019).

The Coup

The decline of newspapers in the 1950s with the rise of television and in the 1980s with the spread of cable TV was nothing compared to its displacement by the Internet after the late 1990s. Classified advertising revenue succumbed to free online services like Craigslist. Internet sites were not only free to users but also had the powerful allure of being interactive (Fogg, 2003). Newspaper revenue plummeted after 2005, followed by a wave of closures after 2009. In the following decade, more than 2,000 venerable papers closed and the number of investigative reporters—whom Lipmann called the natural enemies of the propagandist—was cut in half. Profit-trained algorithms took the place of responsible human editors, and the peer-reviewed system of news based on independent verification collapsed. The strongest newspapers survived by expanding online. Tech giants like Google and Microsoft trained the industry on maximising advertising metrics, based on *reach*, *engagement* and *conversion*; that is, measuring screentime, clicks and purchases. Online newspapers were forced to follow suit by allowing interactive and *anonymous* commentaries from readers, a space quickly crowded by troll farms posting the same far-right talking points on every article, while investigative reporters received hundreds of hate emails and personal threats. Sensationalised fear and anger proved the most effective emotional triggers to induce or suppress behaviour. Demonising immigrants checked both boxes while stroking the ego of tribal racism, reframed as patriotic with twisted arguments about defending national sovereignty against a supposed invasion to be violently repealed. Then came software bots to exponentially increase automatic posts. Any semblance of editorial ethics that remained was counteracted and neutralised. The door was open to massive disinformation and fake news.

The next turn of the screw was the advent of *narrowcasting*, the opposite of broadcasting. The proliferation of cable channels targeting different interest groups was accompanied by a myriad of web platforms and tendentious blogs preaching to their own choir. News and information media splintered, feeding users what they want to hear; namely, targeted news and confirmation bias, intensified and optimised for emotional impact to monopolise their attention and screentime to the point of addiction. Hooked users check these outlets daily and even several times a day. Disinformation, conspiracy theories and extreme voices circulating in 'fringe sites like 4chan, 8chan, and Reddit, jump to Twitter to engage the press, and then migrate to Facebook for maximum effect. The slavish tracking of Twitter by journalists [willing to] report on things that trend there, has made news organizations complicit in the degradation of civil discourse' (McNamee, 2020, p. 102).

Social media has become the most powerful of venues, and Facebook the undisputed king with over three billion monthly users worldwide as of 2024, more than two billion of whom are daily active users. Of these, 194 million are in the United States, comprising 57% of the population. Facebook quickly adopted Bernays' formula by creating member groups with preference and filter bubbles which tailor News Feeds to user biases. 'Extreme views attract more attention, so platforms recommend them. People in a filter bubble become increasingly tribal, isolated, and extreme'. By enabling anonymity and group networks, social media 'has enabled personal views that had previously been kept in check by social pressure—white nationalism is an example'. The platforms enable 'like-minded people, including extremists, to find one another' creating 'the illusion of legitimacy' (McNamee, pp. 91–92). Bubbles configure and normalise a logic-proof alternate reality, shared by a fictitious majority, where the loudest voices dominate and seek to outdo each other. Fed by bad actors foreign and domestic, the result is the obfuscation of truth and the radical polarisation of politics and public opinion, creating the *online* impression of a difunctional democracy, falsely projected as street anarchy by social media, posing as the public square. The manufactured chaos can supposedly be fixed only by a strongman's coup. The Trump campaign, run by public relations tech firms, tapped into these trends from the moment he entered presidential politics on 16 June 2015.

The last nail in the coffin is the enormous collection and exploitation of user *metadata*, classified and conjugated by algorithms optimised through artificial intelligence for mass behaviour prediction and modification. Facebook has an estimated 29,000 datapoints per user profile, covering the most detailed determinants of behaviour. If you 'like' or 'share' one piece of disinformation, the algorithms will feed more to you and to those like you, targeting emotional triggers. The platform will also sell or grant third-party access to profiles and datapoints.

This practice led to the Facebook scandal involving Cambridge Analytica, the U.S. subsidiary of SCL Group, a psychographics datamining and public relations company with ties to the British Conservative Party. It started as a subcontractor for the British and American militaries, providing weaponised propaganda campaigns to turn the people against the enemy in theatres of war. It then moved to selling its services to far-right politicians, manipulating elections in dozens of developing countries by infiltrating social media to instigate anti-voting movements in some sectors of society while running voter recruitment campaigns in others. They finally hired experts to maximise their metadata and leverage it to manipulate elections in the United Kingdom and the United States. SCL did exactly that working for Leave. EU to slant the 2016 Brexit vote for Britain to leave the European Union. They weaponised social media to sow divisions and instigate an anti-immigrant movement, while painting Brexit and white nationalism as a patriotic defence of British freedom, sovereignty and independence. Interviews after the politically and economically disastrous vote showed that large numbers of Brexit voters had no clarity on what they had voted for. Cambridge Analytica was organised in the United States to avoid the illegality of SCL, a foreign company, meddling in U.S. elections.

Founded in 2013 and funded by Trump supporter, billionaire Robert Mercer, Cambridge Analytica (CA) used audience segmentation and psychographic profiling in 44 state and congressional races for the 2014 midterm elections on behalf of the Republican Party. It claimed to 'collect up to 5,000 data points on over 220 million Americans (the entire adult voting population) and use more than 100 data variables to model target audience groups and predict the behavior of like-minded people' (web.archive.org, 2015). CA worked for Ted Cruz in the primaries and Donald Trump in the 2016 presidential campaign. The operation was headed by CA vice president and Trump's chief advisor Steve Bannon with the advice of Trump legal counsel Rudy Guiliani. They ultimately secured a narrow victory for Trump.

Here is how they did it. Not only did CA roll over its data to Trump, but they augmented Project Alamo, a voter database created for his campaign by a Texas firm that focused on fundraising through political advertising on social media. In addition, CA acquired a custom app running on Facebook, which presented an innocent-looking and fun personality questionnaire that not only captured the profiles of 270,000 participants but infiltrated those of their friends of friends, harvesting 87 million American user profiles from Facebook and matching most of them to individual voters for personalised behavioural microtargeting. Then they used Facebook's own AI targeting tools and surfacing algorithms meant for advertisers, such as lookalike-audience ad targeting, to find people and social networks with specific datapoints shared by known Trump supporters. These tools allow demographic, geographic and psychographic microtargeting down to the neighbourhood level and narrow personal interests. They A/B-tested thousands of ad versions for maximum impact and delivered them via Facebook News Feed, the primary targeting tool through which users are exposed to content posted on the platform. A fear-and-anger political ad campaign then took a life of its own as it was shared and reposted across vast social networks and media outlets. For instance, CA created the soundbite and meme 'Crooked Hilary' (with handcuffs for the double-o) and instigated the chant 'Lock her up!' at numerous Trump rallies. Finally, CA identified first-time and possibly undecided voters called 'persuadables' and bombarded them with every kind of posting, doctored news and video clips, soundbites, memes, ads, blogs and websites designed to galvanise Trump voters and suppress turn-out for the opposition. They concentrated on a few swing states, to secure enough electoral votes, and initiated 5.9 million 'dark posts' (which cannot be traced back to them). CA strategist turned whistle-blower Brittany Kaiser called it 'weapon-grade' psychometric microtargeting (Noujaim & Amer, 2019).

Hilary Clinton won the popular vote by almost three million votes, but Trump won the presidency with more electoral votes from three CA-targeted swing states that he carried by fewer than 80,000 votes. The Facebook-CA election interference scandal erupted in 2018. CA and SCL quickly filed for insolvency to thwart further investigations, but their executives opened various 'election management' companies the following year.

The voter databases and propaganda networks remained in place, and the surgical methods continued to be refined by improvements in AI, machine learning and bots. In addition, with platforms like GPT-4, the ads and posts can now be AI generated, tested, optimised and deployed by the millions. Aside from Facebook, billionaire Trump supporter Elon Musk acquired Twitter, which had blocked Trump for spreading election lies, reinstated his account, fired most content moderators and rebranded

Twitter as *X*, an unbridled propaganda machine under the aegis of 'freedom of speech'. Russian government hackers and bots increased their operations for the 2024 elections, bolstering disinformation to sow divisions, conflicts and chaos in an effort to destabilise Western democracies. The same social engineering that produced Brexit and the Trump presidency is practised around the world, bringing about a rise in far-right autocratic governments. Just like the platforms with their filter-and-preference bubbles create the illusion of choice, so do the virtual realities they forge in cyberspace create the illusion of democracy.

Conclusion

The power of augmented propaganda and its ongoing optimisation in the age of social media and artificial intelligence—technologies that are now weaponised—was confirmed on 5 November 2024, when Trump was re-elected to a second, non-consecutive term despite his divisive hate speech, two impeachments, 34 felony convictions and 91 federal indictments. He squashed all criminal cases against him, making a mockery of the American justice system, to the international disrepute of democracy as a system of government. During his first term, he packed the Supreme Court with a 6–3 supermajority of conservative loyalists who, months before his second term, granted him immunity for potentially illegal presidential actions. In his first weeks in office, he started an illegal campaign of deportations without due process; appointed a loyalist cabinet of dubious qualifications and scant government experience, including Elon Musk as director of the new 'Department of Government Efficiency' (DOGE); and proceeded with his help to purge the federal government, firing thousands of employees, gutting the Agency for International Development, the Consumer Financial Protection Bureau, the Department of Education and the U.S. Office of Government Ethics. The firings included scores of inspectors general and heads of independent watchdog agencies that guarded against government and presidential abuses (Pelley et al., 2025). The breakdown of checks and balances signals the establishment of a patrimonial state.

There was a satirical bestseller, published in 32 languages, whose influence lingers, *The Peter Principle* (Peter & Hull, 2020 [1969]). It puts forth the ironic statistical argument that people in management tend to be promoted based on success in the functions of a previous job, until they reach and remain in a level of incompetence on a terminal job that requires different skills. The implication is that this happens through the application of the wrong metagrammar where it does belong. In Musk's case, the industrial efficiency model applied to labour and human agency resulted first in the firing of content moderators from Twitter, and then in the massive, indiscriminate layoff of federal employees by DOGE, disrupting research and the higher metafunctions of government. The loss of talent, experience and tacit knowledge is incalculable, fruit of a grossly rudimentary approach to efficiency. Fixated on the successful metagrammar of Tesla, Musk proves inept and self-serving in social media and communications, let alone in the proper metagrammar of government.

In Trump's case, his background is in real estate development within the patrimonial structure of a private family business where father is king. Real estate development is a world of vicious competition, low-balling negotiation, land grabbing and hostile acquisition through strongarm tactics, foreclosure and gentrification. The resort owner is paranoid about fencing out intruders and being 'stolen from' or taken advantage of by employees, contractors and all others. This has translated into the imposition of protectionist tariffs on neighbouring countries, allies and competitors, unleashing a global trade war (Boak et al., 2025).

Trump's tariffs have sewn chaos in equities markets and international trade, stoking fears of stagflation and global recession. On top of withholding and blocking foreign aid, tariffs have 'raised the rent' on depressed countries and become a political weapon for outlandish land grabbing ends. This includes pressuring Canada to become the 51st state, Panama to give back the canal, Denmark to sell him Greenland, Ukraine to give up half of its mineral resources in exchange for existential defence against Russia, Egypt and Jordan to receive Palestinians evicted from Gaza, in order to own it free and clear under foreclosure and develop it into a gentrified 'riviera'. This expansionism through economic pressure bears the mark of neo-imperialism. In the wake of undermining the

NATO alliance and the European Union, these aggressive policies signal that the United States is nobody's friend. The old practice of raining chaos at home and abroad to then pick up the pieces bears the mark of the Nero complex, after the emperor who famously fiddled while Rome burned.

References

Bakir, V., & McStay, A. (2022). *Optimising Emotions, Incubating Falsehoods: How to Protect the Global Civic Body from Disinformation and Misinformation*. Palgrave Macmillan Open Source.

Bernays, E. (1923). *Crystallizing Public Opinion*. Liveright.

Bernays, E. (2004 [1928]). *Propaganda*. IG Publishing.

Boak, J., Weisman, P., & Gillies, R. (2025, March 6). Trump's trade war draws swift retaliation with new tariffs from Mexico, Canada and China. *Associated Press*. Retrieved from https://apnews.com/article/trump-tariffs-canada-mexico-china-643086a6dc7ff716d876b3c83e3255b0

Cherry, K. (2024, May 7). How cognitive biases influence the way you think and act. *Verywell Mind*. Retrieved from https://www.verywellmind.com/what-is-a-cognitive-bias-2794963

Counter Extremism Project (2024). *Far-Right Extremist Groups*; *White Supremacy Groups in the United States*; and *Tech and Extremism Online*. Berlin. Retrieved from https://www.counterextremism.com/topics/far-right-extremist-groups

Festinger, L. (1962 [1957]). *A Theory of Cognitive Dissonance*. Stanford University Press.

Fogg, B. J. (2003). *Persuasive Technology: Using Computers to Change What We Think and Do*. Elsevier.

Freud, S. (1949 [1921]). *Group Psychology and the Analysis of the Ego*. Translated by J. Strachey. Hogarth.

Human Rights Watch (2023). *World Report 2023: Myanmar*. New York. Retrieved from https://www.hrw.org/world-report/2023/country-chapters/myanmar

Jones, S. G. (2020, June 4). Who are Antifa, and are they a threat? *Center for Strategic & International Studies*. Retrieved from https://www.csis.org/analysis/who-are-antifa-and-are-they-threat

Jurkowitz, M., et al. (2020, January 24). U.S. media polarization and the 2020 election: a nation divided. *Pew Research Center*.
Kim, E., et al. (2019, February 7). Jeff Bezos accuses *National Enquirer* publisher of blackmail, extortion. *CNBC.com*.
Kim, J. (2015, August 25). Anger's allure: are you addicted to anger? *Psychology Today*. Retrieved from https://www.psychologytoday.com/us/blog/culture-shrink/201508/angers-allure-are-you-addicted-anger
Le Bon, G. (2002 [1896]). *The Crowd: A Study of the Popular Mind*. Dover.
Lippmann, W. (1997 [1922]). *Public Opinion*. Free Press.
Mangan, D., et al. (2023, April 18). Fox to pay Dominion Voting Systems $787.5 million to settle election defamation suit. *CNBC.com*.
McNamee, R. (2020). *Zucked: Waking Up to the Facebook Catastrophe*. Penguin.
Nai, A., Martínez i Coma, F., & Maier, J. (2019). Donald Trump, populism, and the age of extremes: comparing the personality traits and campaigning styles of Trump and other leaders worldwide. *Presidential Studies Quarterly, 49*(3), 609–643. Retrieved from https://doi.org/10.1111/psq.12511
Noujaim, J., & Amer, K. (2019). *The Great Hack*. Netflix documentary.
Palazzolo, J., et al. (2016, November 4). *National Enquirer* shielded Donald Trump from *Playboy* model's affair allegation. *The Wall Street Journal*.
Paulhus, D. L., & Williams, K. M. (2002). The dark triad of personality: narcissism, Machiavellianism, and psychopathy. *Journal of Research in Personality, 36*(6), 556–563. Retrieved from https://doi.org/10.1016/S0092-6566(02)00505-6
Pelley, S., Chasan, A., Gavrilovic, M., & Ortiz, A. (2025, March 9). Watchdogs fired by Trump raise alarms over future of independent government oversight. *CBS News*. Retrieved from https://www.cbsnews.com/news/trump-firings-watchdogs-inspectors-general-60-minutes
Peter, L. J., & Hull, R. (2020 [1969]). *The Peter Principle: Why Things Always Go Wrong*. Profile Books.
Schwenk, C. L. (1984). Cognitive simplification processes in strategic decision-making. *Strategic Management Journal, 5*, 111–128.
Trotter, W. (1916). *Instincts of the Herd in Peace and War*. T. Fisher Unwin.
web.archive.org (2015). *Cambridge Analytica: About Us*. Retrieved from https://web.archive.org/web/20160216023554/https://cambridgeanalytica.org/about
Webber, M. (1968 [1921]). *Economy and Society*. Translated by G. Roth & C. Wittich. Bedminster Press.

Williamson, E. (2022). With new ruling, Sandy Hook families win over $1.4 billion from Alex Jones. *The New York Times* (November 10). Alex Jones files for bankruptcy. *The New York Times* (December 2).

12

Techno-Mythology

Introduction

One commonplace fallacy is that myths belong to indigenous societies, whereas 'modern man' is guided by science and technology. Early sociologists and anthropologists, from August Comte to Emil Durkheim, assumed that mankind had gone through stages of mental evolution: magic, religion and science. Nothing can be further from the truth. Claude Lévi-Strauss in *The Savage Mind* (1962) countered the racist concept of a 'pre-logical primitive mentality' of non-Western pre-industrial cultures. He argued that myths are simply each culture's natural way of explaining empirical phenomena in a way that makes sense to them, using the prevailing signs, vocabulary and belief system. Myths are based on experience and reasoning not unlike modern science, which also has its myths, now called *theories*.

Postmodernity considers a myth any theory that proposes an absolute essence or universal truth. Freud's psychoanalysis comes to mind as a mythology that articulates a metagrammar based on the mediating metaphor of bodily organs likened to mythemes like the ego, the id, the superego, the unconscious and other supposed universals, not to mention his appeal to Greek myths: Oedipus, Elektra, Ouranus,

E. Camayd-Freixas, *Metagrammar*, https://doi.org/10.1007/978-3-031-92337-1_12

Hermes, Aphrodite, Narcissus, Eros, as well as concepts like catharsis and anagnorisis borrowed from ancient Greek tragedy. In contrast, his 'defence mechanisms' do make up a verifiable metagrammar that explains how rationalisation and self-deception work. Narrative genius Jorge Luis Borges famously held that psychology, philosophy, theology and ultimately science are all genres of fantastic literature; and that man is and always will be a mythmaker.

Myths of Science and Technology

The myth of Progress is closely associated with science, industry and technology, under the (unscientific) *mechanistic ideology*. Progress is only one of three philosophies of history. Its opposite is the myth of the Golden Age, the belief that the simple life of old offered mankind greater happiness, fulfilment and moral value; and that History is a process of decline and corruption despite periods of advancement. Curiously, the myth of Progress is often conceived as the attainment of a Technological Utopia that would ultimately recuperate the values of the mythical Golden Age. Thomas More's *Utopia* (1516), which techno-mythology has appropriated for the distant future, literally means 'no such place' (*u-topos*) and was set in a primitive New World Island uncorrupted by the vices of 'modern' European society. Third is the myth of the Pendulum, the theory of rise-and-fall, the alternation of periods of progress, decline and homeostasis, with no net gain. A variation is History as a Spiral with moments of change and recurrence.

The *mechanistic ideology* is rather based on a narcissistic metaphysics, the myth of the *homo faber*: man as a machine, creator of machines in his image and likeness. Behind it is the *faith* in human progress through man-made technology, the hubris that the artificial is always an improvement over Nature, of which man is no longer a part but the master. Not without roots in Pythagoras and classical antiquity, this unscientific ideology was nevertheless stoked by the Scientific Revolution of early modern Europe, starting with Copernicus (1543), passing through Galileo, Kepler, Descartes, Hobbes and culminating with Newton's *Mathematical Principles of Natural Philosophy* (1687). Curiously, much of Newton's other writings dealt with the Apocalypse, alchemy and the occult, suggesting a *mystical* Pythagorean conception of mathematics, the 'laws' of motion and universal gravity, including his perplexing 'three-body problem'.

The mystical conception of universal mechanics or the 'clockwork universe', fruit of the Enlightenment and rationalism, was later overshadowed, if only temporarily, by the pragmatic ideology of the Industrial Revolution (circa 1760–1840) from the steam engine to the Potato Famine. I call it an *ideology* because the mechanistic metaphor is associated with a cluster of related ideas such as empirical rationalism, materialism, reductionism, atomism, determinism and behaviourism, among others. The metaphysics of universal science temporarily gave way to the practical, instrumental reason of Industry, in which actual machines replaced human labour for the benefit of factories, not people. Control of the means of production obeyed the political economy of Capitalism. The image of the machine chewing up men prevailed well into the twentieth century. It took just as long for a meaningful improvement in the standard of living to reach the average person. Meanwhile, empires of industry and commerce subjected vast sectors of the population and entire peripheral countries to neocolonialism.

The Technological Revolution, from the telegraph in the 1840s to the computer age, accelerated social improvement and led to a new faith. A heraldic figure was August Comte (1798–1857), considered the father of sociology. His doctrine of Positivism was formulated as a blind faith in the inexorable perfectibility of society through technology, a faith that culminated in his 'Religion of Humanity'. Darwin's mechanistic evolution brought the faith in perfectibility from society to the human species. Both ideologies led to pseudoscientific racism. The human was devalued and rendered meaningless as a new metaphysics spread the belief not so much in a clockwork universe but in a *mechanical mind*, a concept that is still debated (Putnam, 'Mind and Machine', 1960; Edelman, *Neural Darwinism*, 1987). Incidentally, every mechanism has a metagrammar independent of meaning, whereas human thought, behaviour and social processes have a more complex non-mechanical, meaning-based metagrammar whose source is natural language grammar. Chapter 14 next expands this discussion and traces artificial intelligence back to the telegraph. For now, note that all mechanisms are ultimately based on two myths: the construct of reversible or repetitive time and the existence of elemental units of space—atoms or discrete parts that the machine sets in motion. There can be no effective machine without constituent parts that reliably move in repetitive time.

Blaise Pascale (1623–1662) casted doubt on the existence of time, reasoning that the past no longer exists, the future does not yet exist, and the present has no span. Time is in fact a construct. There is no such substance. What exists is *change* in space. Time is simply a measurement of the rate of change in relation to a constant, the Earth's rotation in space (day) or its orbit (year). Time and space are indeed relative. Space makes sense only when we delimit it within some boundaries, otherwise it is a blur; and yet all such boundaries are arbitrary and based on abstract geometrical constructs: the point, the line and the curve.

As a construct of space often represented by the sphere, the *atom* or fundamental mechanical unit is a myth of Greek philosophy dating to the fifth-century BCE, hypothetically the smallest solid particle of matter, indivisible and unchanging but believed to come in different sizes and shapes to make for different materials. In Democritus even the soul was made up of the finest atoms. This remained the prevailing wisdom until the discovery of the electron in the late nineteenth century, paving the way for quantum mechanics. The solid conception of the atom collapsed under the knowledge that it is mostly empty space, composed of less than stable subatomic 'units' of matter-energy: a nucleus made of neutrons and positively charged protons with negatively charged electrons orbiting in layers. The electron's ability to simultaneously switch layers is described as the 'quantum leap'. Protons and neutrons also turned out to be divisible, made up of smaller 'units' of matter-energy: quarks, neutrinos, muons, accompanied by antimatter positrons and radiation of mesons, hyperons, photons and gluons—theoretical particle-wave 'units' detected only by spectroscopy based on the wavelength (colour) of the radiation they emit or absorb. In the end, all we have are instrument measurements, which we hypothesise as 'particles' and give them mythological Greek names according to their statistical behaviour and spin (colour change). Quantum mechanics is a highly coherent mythology. Beyond relative measurements, the ultimate nature of reality reverts to metaphysical belief.

Yet, the 'particle' myth remains. The electron is considered but one of the (so far) 61 elementary particles accepted by the Standard Model of theoretical particle physics. But are they really particles or simply visualization aids? Idealized 'particles' are hypothesized as necessary for laboratory measurements to fit into an equation relative to a constant. Similarly, in astrophysics, 'dark matter' is a mysterious hypothetical substance posited to explain gravitational effects not accounted for by the filed equation of general relativity. Rather than a particle, an electron is defined as a mathematical wave *function*; a particle only for the instant it is observed or measured, artificially frozen in time like a snapshot. Upon measurement, the wave function paradoxically collapses, according to the Copenhagen Interpretation of quantum mechanics. A more cogent alternative, the Schrödinger equation predicts how the quantum state of the universe evolves over time and the probability of a particle being at a certain location and time. Instead of a wave function collapse, the equation suggests that every observation splits the universe into parallel branches for each possible measurement. This is known as the 'Many-Worlds Interpretation' of quantum mechanics—a reminder that not everything that is mathematically possible is physically or biologically feasible. Is particle physics then a mechanics or a metagrammar? In common human experience, a particle is a solid. No one would speak grammatically of a particle of air or water, despite the knowledge that they are made of molecules. Here comes another problem of definition and linguistic categorisation, the question of the different states of matter. How many are there, 3, 4, 7, 18, 35, 50? It depends on the criteria.

On 19 February 2025 Microsoft introduced its Majorana 1 quantum chip, claiming they had produced a 'topoconductor' or topological superconductor—'a special category of material that can create an entirely new state of matter—not a solid, liquid or gas but a topological state' (Bolgar, 2025). Not so fast. There can only be seven proper states of matter dependent on temperature and pressure. At a human scale, solids have a melting point where they become liquid and a higher boiling point where they become gas. At extreme temperatures or in the presence of a strong magnetic field, there is an ionisation point where electrons break away forming a 'soup' of positive ions and free electrons called plasma. At super temperatures there is a critical point at which quarks and gluons break away from nuclear protons and neutrons to produce quark-gluon plasma (QGP). At this point the definition of 'matter' or 'particle' becomes extremely stretched as an abstract concept of theoretical physics. Evidence of the existence of QGP has been detected for a nanosecond by colliding heavy gold ions in the most powerful accelerators near the speed of light at 4 trillion degrees Celsius. This detection has served to theorise that QGP existed for a flash of time after the Big Bang before actual matter was formed through nucleosynthesis. QGP is not thought to exist anywhere else in the universe, save by conjecture, at the core of massive stars. It is a ceiling state beyond which unimaginable forces would have to break down elementary particles upending quantum mechanics. Below solids, at temperatures near absolute zero, there are Bose–Einstein and Fermionic condensates, the last two known states since all particles in the universe belong to only two types, bosons or fermions. The possibility of a dark matter condensate would be the stuff of science fiction. Any claim to the existence of other states of matter would manipulate the definition by counting transitional states like liquid crystals, emergent properties like superconductivity or different criteria such as electromagnetic fields.

Microsoft's new claim invokes the genius of physicist Ettore Majorana, who worked on atomic spectroscopy under Enrico Fermi, and developed an equation hypothesising the existence of Majorana fermions in 1937, the year before his mysterious disappearance at age 32 after buying a steamboat ticket from Naples to Palermo. The fact that its existence has never been confirmed adds to the controversy surrounding Microsoft's claim. The research, including Microsoft's, has produced several false alarms and embarrassing retractions (Frolov, 2021). The 2025 announcement suggesting that Microsoft has been able to not only observe but to 'control' Majorana fermions has been slammed as false advertising on Reddit. The concern about unconfirmed or premature claims is that they can lead to a loss of faith in quantum computing. Majorana fermions are theorised to produce more coherent qubits, resulting in a major breakthrough.

Fermions are a class of elementary particles including electrons. Theoretically there are two types, Dirac's and Majorana's. The Majorana relativistic wave equation describes the behaviour of hypothetical fermions that are their own antiparticles and can thus annihilate themselves. Hence their elusive detection in the lab and the near impossibility that they should exist in the universe beyond the Big Bang. Fermions are distinguished from bosons by two other properties: they spin at half integers of Planck's constant (1/2, 3/2, 5/2) and obey the Pauli Exclusion Principle, meaning that two cannot occupy the same quantum energy state. This last quality makes fermions resistant to condensation. Yet, half-spin electrons can pair up in Cooper pairs to form an integer spin and, when they spin in opposite directions, can occupy the same quantum state just like bosons. The latter tend to join and flow together in unison, whereas fermions are loners. However, a collection of paired fermions can interact to acquire the coherence of a boson and behave as a single particle, forming what is called a *quasiparticle* which, despite its name, is not a thing (matter) but an emergent phenomenon. The search for Majorana fermions has become a search for fermionic quasiparticles, of which Majorana's are theoretically the most controllable.

Bose–Einstein condensates (BECs) are obtained by freezing a gas of bosons (lithium, rubidium or sodium atoms) to near absolute zero, so they occupy the lowest energy state, rendering the emergent properties of superfluidity and superconductivity, the ability to flow with no friction or electrical resistance and thus operate with minimum energy at maximum speed. They were first obtained in 2001 and have since been explored for quantum computing by encoding information via two-component BECs serving as qubits. Fermionic condensates were first obtained in 2003 by freezing a gas of fermions, in this case potassium, and applying a magnetic field causing the fermions to form Cooper pairs, to condensate and behave like bosons at the lowest energy state. 'The strength of pairing in our fermionic condensate' made researchers dream of a revolutionary 'room temperature superconductor' which has never been achieved (Jin et al., 2004). Since 2008 numerous experiments have detected signature effects of the Majorana state but have failed to distinguish it from other trivial explanations. The experiments typically involve semiconductor nanowires proximate to superconductors and 'topological' insulators, which simply means that the particles flow on their surface and sides (topologically) as opposed to through the middle. Majorana's so-called Angel Particle could enhance quantum error correcting codes (to reduce decoherence by inducing unpaired electrons) with the goal of one day reaching FTQC or fault-tolerant quantum computing. Microsoft and others once again promise it in years, not decades.

It is important to remember that the scientific process begins with observation, from which inferences are drawn by *induction*. Once inferences are verified, related and measured, they form the premises of a theorem, from which further inferences can be drawn by logical or mathematical *deduction*. Given enough inferences, a relational pattern begins to appear in the form of a system, a mechanics comprised of Subject-Verb-Object propositions; that is, a *metagrammar*, such as the 'laws' of quantum mechanics. However, the concept of 'laws' for a set of relative principles is also a myth. The relative stability of atoms occurs only under moderate conditions beyond which they break down. The behaviour of particles is not exact but probabilistic, explainable only in terms of statistics and margins of error.

Together with noise and wave interference, decoherence and probabilistic error, motion and temperature affect the qubits making quantum computing experimental and error prone—one error per 100 operations at this writing. Qubits (quantum superposed binary-base vector digits that replaced transistors that replaced relays) must be kept in laboratory-like conditions, isolated from the smallest vibrations and cooled to near absolute zero. Operable quantum computing will thus be limited to large organisations, government, data and research centres. The immediate payout of quantum mechanics, however, is best seen in biochemistry. It explains the process by which atoms link to form molecules, lending chemistry added power of mathematical deduction, which can already be formalised into computer simulations to develop new materials, proteins, medications and indeed lethal poisons. Google DeepMind founder Demis Hassabis led the AI team who received the 2024 Nobel

Prize in Chemistry for developing AlphaFold3, the first machine-learning algorithm to solve the Protein Folding Problem (https://deepmind.google/science/alphafold). AlphaFold is a prime example of an expert AI system. It was developed for the specific task of predicting the natural 3D structure of proteins, the building blocks of life, from any sequence of amino acids, in minutes and with more than 90 percent accuracy. It has worked out millions of complex protein structures, which in turn determine their function and interaction with a broad spectrum of biomolecules. This paves the way for synthesizing new proteins, producing new medications and treatments, increasing global food supplies, as well as breaking down plastics and other environmental pollutants. If quantum computing reaches sufficient error reduction, the speed and complexity of accurate simulations will increase exponentially, as the on–off transistors are replaced by qubits capable of running many simulations and problem-solving operations in parallel sequences. The behaviour of proteins and enzymes will be seen in real time, as will the simulation of complex social problems. New challenges will arise; for instance, no encryption would be safe and deepfakes could run non-stop in real time. New scientific myths are beginning to appear. 'Michio Kaku: The language of the universe is the language of the quantum. […] Reverse engineering nature's computer could be a window on creation itself' (Pelley, 2024).

Myths of Artificial Intelligence

Anthropomorphism is the common tendency to attribute a human metagrammar to non-human entities, in this case, computers. It is a misleading metaphor akin to the personification trope, a form of magical thinking not far from animism, unbecoming scientists and those who pride themselves in their logical and objective reasoning. It is however an effective form of marketing and propagandistic deception. An axiom of advertising, consumers are more accepting and prone to buy inanimate products that are given human traits. They become less threatening, more trusted, even endearing, as humans identify with them and make them part of their home.

Computer techno-mythology developed by appropriating human language to describe machines. We saw in Chapter 4 the wholesale adoption of linguistic terms to describe the Boolean algebra of computer notation. That was just the beginning. Merchandising magician Steve Jobs baptised a whole line of products as humanoid: iPod, iPad, iPhone, iWatch. The *i* stood for intelligent, but also implied that the gadgets had a self, an extension of the buyer's *I*, as well as the ergonomic pitch that *you too* are intelligent if you buy them but dumb if you don't. The personification intent is confirmed by Apple's email domain: @me.com. Since these were proprietary Apple trademarks, the generic synonym 'smartphone' came to be, with 'Android' as the iPhone's main competitor. Smartphone meant that both the gadget and the buyer are smart. The effectiveness (and silliness) of the animistic deception became clear with the marketing success of the label SmartWater, meaning 'you are smart if you buy it', but also that the water itself is 'smart' simply because it contains electrolytes, chemically 'programmed' to replenish the body. There followed smart mops, smart flashlights, smart everything. It reminds me of a silly friend who exclaimed, 'What a dumb hammer!' if you smashed your thumb or 'That stupid pen!' if you stained your shirt.

I shall henceforth call 'The Demigod Complex' the tendency of inventors to aggrandise their accomplishments and themselves as 'creators'. In other languages and in earlier English usage, 'to create' is a verb reserved to God, to create something out of nothing. Artists compose and scientists devise, rather than create. Matter and energy, according to Einstein, can neither be created nor destroyed; they can only change form. Man, then, cannot truly create but only manipulate existing things and word-concepts. Yet, technologists in the computer age claim that they create rather than devise or invent. Hence the return of the Prometheus myth that man can steal the fire of the gods and create a machine that can itself create. 'The skilled creator makes things of all varieties. And things that are capable of creating for themselves are any creator's crowning achievement' (Husain, *The Sentient Machine*, 2017, p. 46).

Mathematician Alan Turing, inventor of the first electronic computer model, who achieved legendary status for his Enigma codebreaking machine, started dropping the hint with his paper, 'Computing Machinery and Intelligence' (1950). He predicted that 'machines' would eventually be able to 'think' (but only by falsifying the definitions of both terms). His Turing Test for AI, dubbed 'The Imitation Game', placed a person in one room and a computer in another, typing questions and answers back and forth for three judges to determine which was which. Artificial intelligence would be achieved when two of the three judges were fooled into believing that the machine was the person. However, the feat of fooling all the people all the time has never been achieved by AI nor will it ever, because two different metagrammars, one human and the other mechanical, can never yield the same exact result. 'Turing tests succeeded in fooling human questioners only with tricks and bluffing—not real understanding of language—a problem that still bedevils natural language efforts in AI today' (Larson, 2021, p. 48).

John Searle (1980) illustrated this with his own 'Chinese Room' argument: an Englishman is locked inside a room with a computer manual, while people outside pass him pieces of paper under the door containing enigmatic Chinese characters. Unbeknown to him, they are questions. He mechanically follows the computer operations in the manual and passes back pieces of paper under the door with equally enigmatic Chinese characters he doesn't even know are answers. The people outside are fooled into thinking that the man understood Chinese, when in fact he understood nothing. The moral of the story is that *machines can never understand meaning*, because abstract numbers, symbols and syntax by themselves cannot convey it. Only words and grammar can, whose meaning is ultimately supplied by humans. In fact, machines or large language models (LLMs) like ChatGPT can sound human only because they are fed human scripts which they manipulate statistically without regard to meaning.

The other side of the false coin is the notion that the human brain is like a machine and vice versa. Presumably, then, if we think of brains in terms of machines and make machines more like brains, eventually the difference will be virtually erased. On the one hand, cognitive science has been complicit for decades in this deception, by assimilating the brain to a machine that 'processes information' rather than an organ that produces and understands meaning through language. On the other hand, Geoffrey Hinton et al. (1986) popularised the brain-inspired processing model of multilayer recurrent artificial neural networks (RANN). This led to the so-called cognitive computer, an example of which is IBM's Watson with TrueNorth chip architecture (2014). Machine learning and AI algorithms were integrated into the microcircuitry of a 'neuromorphic' silicon chip modelled after the brain's neural networks. This increases the amount of data and the processing speed. After much improvement, IBM's NorthPole chip (2023) showed greater success in image recognition than in language. Programmed pattern matching in RANN takes place by backpropagating data through layers of interconnected artificial 'neurons' and feedforwarding it to measure the output against the input. The process recurs, with statistical weight corrections at each step, until the resulting digital pattern is deemed close enough to the analogue original by reaching an arbitrary statistical threshold. Obviously, the process is totally numerical and mechanical, nothing like the linguo-cognitive processes of the human brain. The artificial 'neurons' amount to a faster, more efficient and detailed method of statistical calculation. Whereas the earlier method of machine 'learning' worked by a recurring input-adjustment-output *triangle* (parlayed as an organic feedback 'loop'), RANN is capable of many more calculations per second, processing a greater number of factors and resulting in more detailed differentiation. This would now be called 'deep learning' in techno-parlance as the basis for advanced AI.

Metagrammatical analysis, however, reveals the critical discrepancy. RANNs are based on the myth that man thinks with the brain alone. This is an absurd reductionism. Humans think, in the context of the circumstances of their lives and environment, with their entire body, including the spinal cord and entire nervous system, but also all other systems: skin, muscular, circulatory, endocrine and particularly gastric—medically referred to as the brain-gut axis. They all affect the way we think. Bodily sensations are particularly involved in emotions: fear, attraction, sadness, happiness, compassion, empathy. They play a crucial role in ethical reasoning and the development of higher ideals like love. Metagrammatical reasoning dictates that two systems that have different internal functions or modes of operation can never yield the same exact result. At best, one will be a degraded imitation of the other. Intelligence, thinking and learning require the figuration of meaning. There is no intelligence without *understanding*, the very act of grasping meaning.

Perhaps the clearest demonstration that computers will never be able to think is that their output is utterly meaningless until it is interpreted as language by a thinking human person. Anthropomorphism defeats reason as soon as we *project* our own understanding onto the machine.

As the sales pitch goes, machines are far from being able to do this today, but in 50, 100, 200 years they will (Husain, 2017). Therefore, we should pump as much money as possible into their research and development, for the unfathomable dividends it will pay, and hail the new techno-prophets as gurus and demigods. Let's call this the 'Infinity Now' myth. I'll explain. Squaring the circle is one of the most ancient problems in geometry. No matter how many squares we put inside a circle, the edge will never be curved. It will always be serrated, unless of course we add an infinite number of squares, which requires the impossible: eternity. Infinity now equals eternity now. Transpose this problem to the megapixels in a digital image or screen. At one point they fool the naked eye, but when we look closer, we see the pixelation: analogue curves are rendered as digital squares forming serrated contours. The geometrical relationship between analogue and digital, man and machine, is asymptotic. They can only meet theoretically at a fictional infinity. This is also the problem with the Turing Test. If the machine fools us 70% of the time, it is supposedly, not that *we* are playing dumb, but that *it* is being 'smart'. If it fools us 100% of the time, it is simply that we are not looking close enough. And if it puts out nonsense, as ChatGPT is wont to do, the 'creators', in keeping with the anthropomorphic myth, claim that *it* (and not them) is 'hallucinating'!

The Apocalyptic Myth

The myth of the 'Sentient Machine' involves not only sensing stimuli but also feeling emotions, reasoning, volition, setting goals, making autonomous plans and decisions, becoming conscious, developing a sense of self to be preserved, being synthetically 'alive', exceeding and replacing humans. Techno-prophets are sounding the alarm of human margination and extinction: Kurzweil (2000, 2006, 2024), Barrat (2013), Bostrom (2014), Domingos (2015), Husain (2017), Viggiano, et al. (2023). Some at the same time try to dispel the Apocalyptic Myth and instead point the way to Technological Utopia. Generically, techno-prophets are called *futurists*. Their educated guesses and predictions are in dialogue with science fiction. To follow Jorge Luis Borges, this makes artificial intelligence a genre of fantastic literature.

The myth of the sentient machine runs into the philosophical problem of *other minds*. We can only observe behaviour and guess what is in someone else's mind, but we can never be sure. Say we build an AI robot with special sensors on its skin. We prickle it with a pin, and the robot recoils and says 'Ouch!' Did it really *feel* pain? We can never know but we can infer that it was just mimicking us. Let's say that we build an AI robot so human-like that its behaviour and speech are consistent in every way with feeling and thinking indistinguishable from ours. Is it truly intelligent or is it a fraud? Intelligence can never be proven due to the problem of other minds, but fraud can be inferred by metagrammatical reasoning. Here's how. I can never know if what you and I call 'blue' is actually the same colour. For all I know, what I call blue, in the sky, the sea and everywhere else, you consistently see in the colour I call red. We can never be sure, but I can infer that you do have a mind like mine and see the same colour because our bodies are nearly the same inside and function almost exactly alike. That is, we recognise the same metagrammar. The robot's AI system, however, is made of rigid microswitches (transistors) that trigger other microswitches electronically in discrete micro-steps, whereas my brain is fluid and changing, made mostly of water, with vastly more complex networks of electrochemical reactions, modulated by poorly understood hormones secreted in other parts of my body and stimulated by neurotransmitters and substances yet undiscovered in response my environment. Our metagrammars are as different as a square is to a circle. I can safely conclude that the perfect robot is an impostor.

Futurists' predictions sound plausible in theory because they project their detailed knowledge of computer metagrammar in a vacuum, without hindrances, obstacles or limits. Such is the myth of Kurzweil's 'law of accelerating returns' which posits an exponential and limitless advancement of technology. If there are no obstacles, they figure, all these things will be possible. They stimulate the imagination, and some of their ideas and applications may pave the way for future implementation, while others will not. This is because they do not consider interference by other metagrammars, such as commercial considerations; limited financial, material and energy resources; acceptance by people and society; laws, regulation and ethical limitations; among others. They also fail to consider that science does not advance continuously but in stages by the discovery of new revolutionary metagrammars or 'paradigm shifts' followed by a plateau (Kuhn, 1962). Further, certain plateaus in fact constitute a ceiling.

If live thinking machines cannot be invented, how about interfacing them with humans, from external devices to neural implants, and baptise them with mythical names? Virtual 'reality' (VR) is not reality. On the contrary, it is in many ways an alienation from reality. Its generalisation was given the grandiose name of Metaverse, an aspirational parallel fake universe that grew out of videogame graphics. Like most technologies, it has valid and important uses, but as an industry it is a push for addictive captive-audience entertainment to be monetised. Videogame communities like *Minecraft* and *Roblox* have hundreds of millions of monthly users, many of them children, and have become parallel marketplaces where billions of dollars are generated through advertising and exchanged through product sales (Ball, 2022). Videogames led to social media platforms that segmented the user market, Bernays-style, by interest groups and demographic sectors. The convenience of online interaction has a trade-off in the collection of personally identifiable information sold to third parties. Virtual cities and landscapes were created. People paid exorbitant prices in 'virtual' real estate to be the neighbours of and interact with celebrities like Snoop Dogg. Of course, the rapper was not going to spend his time piddling in the Metaverse. Instead, his rich neighbours would be interacting with surrogate programmers and chatbots after buying themselves an expensive conversation piece and dubious bragging rights. In 2021, Facebook ramped up expenses on its futuristic Reality Labs and changed its name to Meta in preparation for a chimerical Metaverse revolution. It was a fiasco. Company shares plummeted and only recovered when VR and AI expenditures were cut back, and the focus returned to its core business as a rudimentary social media company.

'Augmented' reality (AR) is a similar fallacy. Reality is what it is: it cannot be augmented. AR glasses project additional information onto the visual field, and AR devices capture 3D simulations on the computer screen, which can then be adjusted, rotated, manipulated and projected onto real surfaces. Some can be great precision measuring tools that save much time and work. Others are novelty gimmicks and kitsch. The point is that everything AR does can be done on paper, by hand, laboriously as it may be. Using a compass, binoculars, a microscope, a telescope or other instrument could more appropriately be called augmented reality, but they do not need the marketing hype. Da Vinci with his drawings and the great mapmakers of old were honest enough not to call their masterpieces 'augmented' reality in some parallel 'metaverse' but the opposite, schematic simulacra limited to specific ideas and partial aspects of concrete reality.

The final frontier is the brain-computer interface (BCI). Its connections vary in invasiveness, from gadgets we can handle and operations on a computer screen, to wearables like glasses, goggles, headsets, helmets and sensors, to implantation of microchip electrodes in the brain. First generation implantations include pacemakers and cochlear implants to restore hearing. In 2013, Second Sight introduced a retinal implant that sent electrical impulses to the optic nerve. Dark glasses with a small integrated camera and side-mounted processor sent ultralow resolution 60-pixel 2D images wirelessly to the retinal implant. This promising start was not financially feasible, the company dissolved in 2020, and the implanted patients lost all support for troubleshooting and side effects. Moreover, a retinal implant is no good when the optic nerve itself is compromised. Then, after decades of research, 2022 saw the first successful wireless Visual Prosthesis Brain Implant that bypassed the retina and optic nerve, connecting directly to the visual cortex (Hutton, 2022).

The road to BCI started with the field of neuroprosthetics, pioneered by John Donoghue in 1979, connecting the brain, not to a computer, but to a device that restores specific sensory-motor functions. The movement of prosthetic limbs through biofeedback training went from hardwired to wireless, but the myth that we can operate devices 'only with our thoughts' retarded research on how such process is *language mediated*. Patients initially said 'open' and 'close' to actuate a prosthetic hand. Going from outward speech to internal subvocalization should not obscure the language mediation, for as we saw in Chapter 2, language is the enactment and concretion of thought. Language-based research can lead to simpler and less invasive solutions: e.g., operating external gadgets and prostheses through *voice activation* and *eye tracking technology* instead of brain implants.

Launched in 2017 by Benjamin Rapoport, Elon Musk and a group of scientists and engineers, Neuralink focuses on BCI development. As opposed to Blackrock Neurotech's hardwired 2004 Utah Array (a subdural wire loom chip with a rigid nailbed of microelectrodes piercing the cerebral cortex), Neuralink developed a wireless chip the size of a coin that is inserted flush with the cranium with only a series of flexible microfilaments precision implanted into the brain by robotic surgery. Neuralink's 'bionic' vision BCI uses an eyeglass-mounted camera transmitting by Bluetooth to a smartphone with an app transmitting to the cranial chip and the electrodes stimulating the visual cortex. The system is not noticeable to others, but the image remains a rudimentary low definition black-and-white 2D pixel map limited by the number of filaments implanted. In January 2024, a quadriplegic was the first patient approved to receive a Neuralink BCI implant with 1024 microfilaments, expected to reduce the scarring, inflammation and rejection associated with the nailbed implant. The patient was able to control a smartphone, tablet, laptop and video games in real time (much faster than voice activation alone) purportedly using only his 'thoughts' as the chip 'translated' neural activity into action. Here is the myth: the magical claim that the machine can interpret thoughts directly from the brain, hiding the fact that the commands, intention and thought themselves are always mediated by language. Any claim to the contrary is pure quackery. Within four months 85% of the filaments had retracted due to normal brain movement, resulting in diminished transmission and accuracy. The company opted to modify the chip's recording algorithm rather than subject the patient to another brain surgery (Paul, 2024). It turns out that Neuralink appears to have known this flaw for years from monkey trials and yet failed to inform the patient (Levy, 2024). The solution to be tried on the next volunteers is to implant fewer filaments deeper into the brain (Winkler, 2024). This increases the potential for injury.

Meanwhile, Benjamin Rapoport, the real brain behind Neuralink, left the company within a year in 2018, due to ethical concerns about patient safety. He went on to found Precision Neuroscience, which has now started trials of its Layer 7 Cortical Interface and expects it to hit the market in 2025 (Mole, 2024). It is a thin film microelectrode array that conforms to the cortex surface without damaging tissue. It is a bidirectional record/stimulate modular-scalable system with speech, sight and movement capabilities, inserted via minimally invasive and reversible surgery through a tiny slit in the skull and dura, with a thin chip resting under the scalp. High-definition micron scale signals are transmitted back and forth to a smartphone via Bluetooth and relayed to a machine learning software that translates speech neural signals into computer code. Again, the neural signals are generated by subvocal language. The system can be used not only for restoring function but also for neuroscience research: subjects can be instructed to perform different tasks as the corresponding brain activity is observed and recorded in real time via fMRI.

Neurotech firm Synchron has integrated OpenAI's ChatGPT into its BCI to help patients with severe paralysis text, email, shop and bank, thus regaining more independence and social connection (Mitchelhill, 2024). The system inserts a retracted endovascular tube that laces a sensor mesh like a stent inside the central blood vessel next to the motor cortex, avoiding intracranial surgery. Wire leads come out to a skin-mounted telemetry port on the upper chest to which a module is connected to interface with a computer running a ChatGPT-based platform. The patient can click as well as receive and send ChatGPT-assisted messages at conversational speed 'directly' from brain (speech) signals, without eye trackers or external voice commands. Again, what they don't tell you is that 'brain signals' embody language-based intentions from inner speech or subvocalised mentalese. The ability to disconnect from the telemetry port has the advantage that the external hardware and software can be upgraded without bothering the implanted connection.

On August 14, 2024, researchers reported extraordinary success with a neural speech implant on an ALS patient who had lost the ability for intelligible speech. An example of intricate metagrammar, they implanted four stable nailbed type NeuroPort arrays by Blackrock Neurotech, carrying more microelectrodes than their original Utah Array. The system was hardwired via two HDMI pedestals screwed to the patient's skull and connected to a decoder and computer system operating three language models in series. The aesthetics need much improvement including wireless connections, but the trial was an effective proof of concept. After 15 training sessions, the patient was able to speak clearly through the system in his own voice (cloned from pre-disease recordings) drawing from a dictionary of 125,000 English words (roughly the active vocabulary of an educated person) with 97.5% accuracy, at a slow 32 words per minute (for comparison, optimal speech rate is 170 wpm). The patient's performance had been maintained and improved for more than eight months at the time of the report (Card et al., 2024; Chang, 2024; Mueller, 2024). Blackrock Neurotech has now unveiled Neuralace, the next generation neural implant consisting of an ultrathin brain-conforming scalable mesh with 10,000+ channels. This exponentially increases BCI capabilities, with the company's lofty goal of 'whole-brain data capture' (read futurist myth). The need and surgical implantation procedures are not clear, but why not shoot for the stars, right?

These systems threaten to render Musk's Neuralink obsolete as a failed gamble. Yet, in keeping with his tendency to overpromise and under-deliver, Musk envisions bestowing 'cybernetic superpowers' to people, who will be capable of controlling robots with their mind, 'offering a futuristic and unrealistic forecast for the opaque company's next steps' (Hart, 2024). Such claims cross over into science fiction, positing a future when humans will merge with AI through an intricate 'neural lace' (overcoming immense legal, financial, technical, practical, ethical and human limitations). This implies a jump from the legitimate metagrammar of specific problem solving to the dream of creating a new human race. We pass from feasible 'artificial narrow intelligence' (ANI) to the futile quest for 'artificial general intelligence' (AGI). 'AI-based perception and control algorithms, however, can endow mere humans with far more "superhuman" strengths'—including 'Prompting: *AI is always in your head suggesting ideas* [...] We will only achieve AGI [...]

when computer science and engineering innovations can master two things: intention—or the ability to do grander goal-setting; and self-awareness or "sentience"' (Husain, pp. 32–33; italics in the original). Dreaming is not free when you deceive people for industry gains. The imperious need to *simplify our cognitive life* (cognitive simplification), discussed in Chapter 11, makes me envision a poor human, plugged to an AI brainstorming ideas in his head, twitching uncontrollably, overwhelmed by stimuli, and ready to pull the plug! It also makes me wonder who in their right mind would allow some tech company with dubious ethics and aims be privy to and control their every thought.

The Apocalyptic Myth breaks down as soon as you consider AI the grammatical subject and humans the grammatical object, passively watching with arms crossed as machines take over their lives. The revolt, in the form of strikes and lawsuits, has already started. Soon after the launch of ChatGPT in March 2023, AI-driven labour strikes sought protections against parasitic appropriation and replacement by generative AI machines, robotics and computer-generated imaging (CGI) developed from videogames: Writers Guild (May–September), Actors Guild (July–November) and, indirectly, United Auto Workers union (September–October). In July, authors began suing Open AI and Meta for 'ingesting' their work. In December, *The New York Times* launched a lawsuit against OpenAI and Microsoft for copyright infringement. In May 2024, actress Scarlett Johansson sued OpenAI for cloning her voice from the iconic 2013 futuristic movie *Her* and using it as the new voice of ChatGPT. These are important legal precedents in the ongoing struggle to tame artificial intelligence.

Conclusion

At the very foundation of science there are elemental concepts that must be posited and accepted on faith, requiring what Coleridge (1817) called a willing 'suspension of disbelief' amounting to a 'poetic faith'. This is required for emotional involvement in any narrative, mythification, anthropomorphism and all forms of entertainment. At the other extreme, futuristic projection, the work of the speculative visionary stimulates the imagination but must be viewed with the scepticism of critical thinking as it resolves into science fiction. Science is the realm of the relative. It begins and ends in a myth, an unfathomable and unknowable absolute. But in that middle ground, which is its expansive territory, science accounts for some of the greatest achievements and hopes of humanity. Let's keep it there.

Some futurists believe that we are inevitably headed for a 'posthuman' era of genetic engineering, neuroprosthetics and artificial general intelligence in which human-centred semiotics and metagrammar may no longer apply. This is a topic of critical debate (Herbrechter, 2013). Such an apocalyptic future is not inevitable if we take stock of the fact that control of technology and artificial intelligence will always be a matter of human design—and responsibility.

References

Ball, M. (2022). *The Metaverse: And How It Will Revolutionize Everything*. Norton.

Barrat, J. (2013). *Our Final Invention: Artificial Intelligence and the End of the Human Era*. St. Martin's Press.

Bolgar, C. (2025, February 19). Microsoft's Majorana 1 chip carves new path for quantum computing. *Microsoft News*. Retrieved from https://news.microsoft.com/source/features/innovation/microsofts-majorana-1-chip-carves-new-path-for-quantum-computing

Bostrom, N. (2014). *Superintelligence: Paths, Dangers, Strategies*. Oxford University Press.

Card, N. S., et al. (2024). An accurate and rapidly calibrating speech neuroprosthesis. *New England Journal of Medicine, 391*(7), 609–618. Retrieved from https://doi.org/10.1056/NEJMoa2314132

Chang, E. F. (2024). Brain-computer interfaces for restoring communication. *New England Journal of Medicine, 391*(7), 654–657. Retrieved from https://doi.org/10.1056/NEJMe2407363

Coleridge, S. T. (1817). *Biographia Literaria*. Rest Fenner.

Domingos, P. (2015). *The Master Algorithm*. Basic Books.

Edelman, G. M. (1987). *Neural Darwinism: The Theory of Neuronal Group Selection*. Basic Books.
Frolov, S. (2021, April 12). Quantum computing's reproducibility crisis: Majorana fermions. *Nature*. Retrieved from https://www.nature.com/articles/d41586-021-00954-8
Hart, R. (2024, July 11). Elon Musk's Neuralink prepares to implant second human patient. *Forbes*. Retrieved from https://www.forbes.com/sites/roberthart/2024/07/11/elon-musks-neuralink-prepares-to-implant-second-human-patient/
Herbrechter, S. (2013). *Posthumanism: A Critical Analysis*. Bloomsbury.
Hutton, D. (2022, February 21). Surgeon completes first successful implantation of wireless visual prosthesis brain implant. *Ophthalmology Times*. Retrieved from https://www.ophthalmologytimes.com/view/surgeon-completes-first-successful-implantation-of-wireless-visual-prosthesis-brain-implant
Jin, D., Greiner, M., & Regal, C. (2004, January 28). NIST/University of Colorado scientists create new form of matter: a fermionic condensate. *National Institute of Standards and Technology*.
Kuhn, T. S. (1962). *The Structure of Scientific Revolutions*. University of Chicago Press.
Kurzweil, R. (2000). *The Age of Spiritual Machines: When Computers Exceed Human Intelligence*. Penguin.
Kurzweil, R. (2006). *The Singularity Is Near: When Humans Transcend Biology*. Penguin.
Kurzweil, R. (2024). *The Singularity Is Nearer: When We Merge with AI*. Viking.
Larson, E. J. (2021). *The Myth of Artificial Intelligence*. Harvard University Press.
Levy, R. (2024, May 15). Exclusive: Musk's Neuralink has faced issues with its tiny wires for years, sources say. *Reuters*. Retrieved from https://www.reuters.com/technology/musks-neuralink-has-faced-issues-with-its-tiny-wires-years-sources-say-2024-05-15/
Mitchelhill, T. (2024, July 16). Synchron, ChatGPT to help paralyzed patients text and chat again. *Coin Telegraph*. Retrieved from https://cointelegraph.com/news/synchron-chatgpt-help-paralyzed-patients-chat-and-text-again
Mole, B. (2024, May 28). Neuralink rival sets brain-chip record with 4,096 electrodes in human brain. *Ars Technica*. Retrieved from https://arstechnica.com/science/2024/05/neuralink-rival-sets-brain-chip-record-with-4096-electrodes-on-human-brain/
Mueller, B. (2024, August 14). A.L.S. stole his voice. A.I. retrieved it. *The New York Times*.

Paul, A. (2024, May 21). 85% of Neuralink implant wires are already detached, says patient. *Popular Science*. Retrieved from https://www.popsci.com/health/neuralink-wire-detachment/

Pelley, S. (2024, July 7). Google, IBM make strides toward quantum computers that may revolutionize problem solving. *CBS News*. Retrieved from https://www.cbsnews.com/news/quantum-computing-google-ibm-advances-60-minutes-transcript

Precision Neuroscience. Layer 7 Cortical Interface. Retrieved from https://precisionneuro.io

Putnam, H. (1960). Minds and machines. In S. Hook (Ed.), *Dimensions of Mind: A Symposium* (pp. 148–179). New York University Press.

Hinton, G., Rumelhart, D., & Williams, R. (1986). Learning representations by back-propagating errors. *Nature, 323*, 533–536. Retrieved from https://doi.org/10.1038/323533a0

Turing, A. (1950). Computing machinery and intelligence. *Mind, 59*, 433–460.

Viggiano, G. (Ed.) (2023). *Convergence: Artificial Intelligence and Quantum Computing*. Wiley.

Winkler, R. (2024, May 20). Elon Musk's Neuralink gets FDA green light for second patient. *The Wall Street Journal*. Retrieved from https://www.wsj.com/tech/neuralink-gets-fda-green-light-for-second-patient-as-first-describes-his-emotional-journey-a2707584

Part III

Metagrammar and Problem Solving

13

The Digital Metagrammar of Artificial Intelligence

Introduction

There are two major genres of metagrammar, digital and analogue, each with numerous subgenres. *Digital metagrammar* is quantitative, mechanistic, consistent, mathematical, rule-based, fully programmable and independent of meaning. *Analogue metagrammar* is qualitative, humanistic, inconsistent, linguistic, option-based, not fully programmable and centred on meaning. Other contrasts may apply.

This is a crucial aspect of problem solving because these different genres of metagrammar involve different strategies, methods, value judgements and goals. Digital metagrammar is profit driven in terms of metrics and return on investment. It favours structures of power, government, industry, companies, universities and institutions in general. Analogue metagrammar is driven by quality of life. It is human-centred favouring individuals, employees, families, students, teachers and neighbours. Many problems require the application of both, in conjunction, but they must be kept separate in the analytical process. Digital metagrammar by itself cannot make any claims to meaning or quality without incurring in (sometimes monstruous) errors. Analogue metagrammar usually depends on some (programmable) quantitative or

E. Camayd-Freixas, *Metagrammar*, https://doi.org/10.1007/978-3-031-92337-1_13

logical reasoning for support, without which it can devolve into ideological preaching and disinformation. Even when used in conjunction, they are fundamentally different modes of reasoning. To substitute for Caesar and God in Mark 12:17, 'Render to Machines what is due to Machines, and to Humans what is due to Humans'.

This chapter focuses on digital while the next, Chapter 14, centres on analogue. To illustrate complex problem solving through digital metagrammar, the following narrative traces the historical process that goes, in an unbroken chain, from writing and the telegraph to applied artificial intelligence.

Writing and Encryption

Digital metagrammar always depends on some form of meaning-free code that can be programmed through mathematical logic. Human senders and receivers share the key to decode the (digital) message into a meaningful (analogue) natural language narrative. Machines can do the math, but only humans can supply the meaning. Computers encrypt writing into a programmer's code and decrypt it back into writing, which is itself a code shared by all literate speakers of a language. That is, *writing* is an encryption of *speech*, which is an encryption of *meaning*. Ultimately a computer is nothing more than an encryption-decryption *internal communication machine*. The code itself has no meaning other than its functionality. But let us start slowly from the beginning.

It is significant that Claude Shannon, one of the developers, together with Alan Turing, of the computer and artificial intelligence, in 'A Mathematical Theory of Communication' (1948), delegates an entire portion of his theory to a fascinating book he cites, Fletcher Pratt's *Secret and Urgent: The Story of Codes and Cyphers* (1939) about the history and logic (metagrammar) of encryption. Pratt begins by defining writing as an encryption: 'Archaeologists believe written languages began as a series of pictures representing actions. [...] [T]hese pictures speedily lost their direct significance, and today all written language is cypher. Its symbols have no intrinsic meaning; they convey an idea only when interpreted according to a system whose secret is shared by the writer and reader'

(p. 11). To break this down into steps, alphabetic writing is an encryption of speech into consonants and vowels that form sequences: phonemes, syllables, words, phrases, sentences and discourse. The shared system that allows speech to encode and represent meaning is precisely natural language grammar. That is, writing is a digital encryption of grammatical speech which is an encryption of analogue human meaning. This will be central to understanding large language models (LLMs) and artificial intelligence.

Grammatology (the study of writing systems) explains the development of writing in greater details. Pictographic writing systems, like Mayan pictograms, were *analogic* representations of people, things, ideas, actions and dates as *mnemonic devices* to jog the memory of ancestral narratives passed on generation after generation by oral tradition. These narratives, together with the ability to read and write, were in the custody of a priestly class (the ancestors of today's programmers!) whose word was trusted on faith by the power of their black-box authority as *keepers of the secret*. By force of repetition, the pictograms of some languages slowly became conventionalised, needing fewer traits and details to be understood. They were stylised over time much like our handwritten signatures are. Through stylisation some languages may have become *ideographic* like Chinese—initially the monopoly of an imperial ruling class. Both pictographic and ideographic languages quickly developed differential (diacritic) syllabic strokes representing speech sounds, making them logo-syllabic.

However, the great invention of *alphabetic writing* is a paradigm shift that went from analogue to cypher in a quantum leap. Early semitic slaves in the Sinai Peninsula simplified Egyptian hieroglyphs (c. 1850 BCE) to represent logo-syllabic sounds of their own language (old Canaanite). This phonetic proto-alphabet and other hieroglyphs were further developed and stylised into Phoenician script (c. 1100 BCE), which was further synthesised and standardised for commerce (c. 900 BCE) into the world's oldest abjad or (guttural) consonantal 'alphabet' of 22 characters, leaving the vowels implicit, to be inferred (deciphered) by the reader. Abjad spread from the eastern to the central and southwestern Mediterranean as far as Carthage (c. 480–200 BCE) and branched out by land into Arabic, Hebrew, Persian Imperial Aramaic, the Turkic of the Ottoman Empire and all the hybrid abjad-alphabets of near Asia.

On a different branch, the Greeks (c. 750 BCE) adapted the Phoenician abjad and later (402 BCE) adopted the standard Ionic version, which completed the encryption of the five Greek vowels, becoming the world's first true alphabet. It was a momentous achievement in human history. Instead of hundreds of analogue symbols that took years of professional training for the few to master, the 26-character phonetic alphabet became democratically available to anyone who could afford to learn it. Literacy and the meeting of minds through writing grew exponentially. Given its unmatched capacity for fully recording grammatical speech, it became the precision vehicle for Greek philosophy and science; and, as the basis for the Romanic (Latin), Germanic and Cyrillic alphabets, it became the foundational instrument of Western Civilisation.

Notice, however, the problems that occur when extrapolating between digital alphabetic code and representational analogue writing systems. Generations of scholars had failed miserably at decoding analogic writing, particularly hieroglyphs, by falsely reducing them to what they knew: an alphabet. 'The general conclusion was that the problem was insoluble' (Pratt, p. 26). Then the Rosetta Stone was discovered by a Napoleonic expedition, and Champollion took a crack at it. He figured, against other experts, that the three texts on it, Greek, hieroglyphic and Egyptian Demotic, were translations of the same narrative. He then counted the number of symbols in the Greek alphabet and in the hieroglyphic text. The Egyptian script had three times as many. Therefore, there could not be an alphabetic correspondence. The Greek *rex* (king) was a tall man with a sword in hieroglyphic, and so the true deciphering began. On the other side of the world, the sixteenth-century missionary Fray Diego de Landa falsely reduced Mayan glyphs to an alphabet, while his religious zeal led him to burn countless artefacts and pictographic codices as the work of the devil. Again, the *false alphabet principle* (which confused digital encryption with analogic meaning—as does the notion of computer 'languages') retarded the decoding (problem solving) of Mayan script by 400 years, until the end of the twentieth century. Most significantly, with the imposition of the alphabet, the ability to read and write pictograms was lost, together with Mayan philosophy and science, as Amerindian civilisations were severed. In the end, the alphabet became the Trojan Horse of the cultural colonisation of America (Mignolo, 2003).

My earlier deduction that 'if writing is an encryption of speech, then speech is an encryption of meaning' needs to be reconciled with Saussurean semiotics. The Swiss linguist established that the link between sound and meaning is arbitrary. Different languages use different sounds to represent the same ideas. The meaning we attach to words is a convention, the product of an implicit 'social contract' tacitly agreed upon by the speakers of each language. This arbitrariness makes word sounds an encryption of meaning. However, Saussure split the concept of 'word' replacing it with that of 'linguistic sign', a binary but indivisible sound-image unit that results in referential meaning. He explained this unity with the analogy of two texts written on either side of the same page, which cannot be separated. However, to consider speech sounds an encryption of meaning is to split Saussure's atom, the unity of the linguistic sign. This suggests a Solomonic reconciliation: word sounds instantly trigger memory images (meaning) much faster than flipping Saussure's page to see the other side, which amounts to the same view but in slow motion.

Cryptology and Math

Fletcher Pratt clearly defines the digital metagrammar of encryption. The Greeks invented the *transposition cipher*, sliding the alphabet several places as a way of encrypting secret messages in war and diplomacy. The Romans invented the other great method: the *substitution cipher*, whereby letters of the 'clear' original are replaced by arbitrary ones, based on a secret *translation key*. All methods of encryption derive from these two, or their combination. Omissions of characters and addition of gibberish (noise) are accessory methods of adding confusion.

No matter the combinations and permutations, ultimately a *cipher* is an *algorithm* for converting plaintext into ciphertext. Conversely, an algorithm is the digital metagrammar of encryption. A receiver who knows the key can reverse engineer the ciphertext and convert it back to plaintext. An interceptor who does not have the key uses cryptanalysis or codebreaking methods and techniques to mathematically recompose the plaintext via a decryption algorithm. *Transposition* has a simpler arithmetical solution found by sliding the alphabet a different number of places to find the length of the key. The letters of the alphabet are counted, as well as the number of spaces between one letter and another, known as *mathematical coordinates*. In short, the letters are converted into number pairs according to their differential positions in the alphabet. *Substitution* is more difficult to decrypt requiring frequency tables that record how often letters, digrams, trigrams, full words and bigrams or word sequences occur in each natural language. It then becomes a matter of statistics and probability. Both mathematical methods for transposition and substitution are used in conjunction to resolve cryptograms. Various aspects of encryption will later become part of both Alan Turing's computing machine and Claude Shannon's information theorems.

There are various ways of complicating transposition and substitution. In simple substitution the letters of the clear are always replaced by the same letters of the code. This can be complicated by suppression of frequencies, when very common letters, like E, are omitted or replaced by different characters each time, but are recognised from context later in the reading (like the missing vowels in abjad). Double substitution replaces letters of the clear following a keyword. A transposition cipher may be simple, sliding the alphabet the same number of places as in the Julius Caesar cipher, or more complex: shuffling the letters of words in a prearranged pattern. A primer in simple transposition is a keyword placed at the beginning of the regular alphabet, sliding it to the right. A decoder knowing the primer (or the number of letters in it) can slide the alphabet back and recompose the clear. However, in the British Playfair cipher, the keyword substitutes the first letters of the alphabet, which are then skipped in the rest of the message. The result is a two-step cipher or double encryption but also a combination cypher that mixes complex transposition and simple substitution. The Playfair cipher includes a third step. After eliminating the J from the 26-letter alphabet to make a 5 × 5 letter matrix, if any two letters of the clear appear together, the second letter is replaced by the one next or below. This third step is called a syllable cipher, which transposes or substitutes syllables, letter pairs (digrams) or triplets (trigrams). Nulls (random letters or words thrown in as *noise* to confuse the decoder) can be added to any cipher. This can be further complicated when the clear is a jargon instead of normal speech, although this increases the chances of misinterpretation. Another limitation is that a cipher of more than three steps makes the message too difficult to decipher and prone to error while encoding or decoding.

Classical cryptology was lost to the Dark Ages but reappeared during the Italian Renaissance to serve the intrigues within and among competing city-states. From there the art spread to the rest of Europe. No significant advances in cryptology occurred until the invention of the *polyalphabetic* substitution cipher, first described by Leon Battista Alberti in 1467 and implemented as a metal disc with a clear alphabet engraved on the fixed outer rim and a spinning inner disc with a jumbled alphabet for single substitution. Cryptologist Giovan Battista Bellaso published his more elaborate double substitution method in 1553, while occultist scientist and mathematician Giambattista della Porta published his own in 1563, designed to defeat frequency tables, which work well for simple but not for double substitution. Both used a 13-shift Caesar transposition. The Porta cipher used a 13 × 13 matrix chart with half the alphabet, A-M, on the first line and N-Z on the second line. The left column contained key letter pairs, A-B, C-D, E-F, all the way to Y-Z. The second line (N-Z) was repeated with one shift to the left on each line below. By knowing the key letter pair on the left column, the receiver would use the 13 letters on that line as the cipher. Each letter of the clear on the first two lines was then matched with the corresponding letter on the cipher line. This offered 13 possible alphabets, while a single letter of the cryptogram could represent any one of 11 letters of the clear, throwing frequencies out the window. But here is where the digital solution met an analogue problem. The Porta cipher was impractical. Not only was it error prone, but also the sender and receiver were forced into the dangerous practice of carrying the key-charts and ciphertexts around with them.

French diplomat in Italy Count Blais de Vigenère, educated in Greek, Hebrew and Kabbala, figured there had to be a better way. His 'automatic' cipher, devised in 1586, incorporated a primer key at the beginning of the ciphertext, such that each message began with its own unique key. His 'Vigenère tableau' could be reconstructed onsite each time without carrying key-charts around. It was a 26 × 26 matrix or *tabula recta* that wrote out the entire alphabet from A to Z on the first line as well as on the first column to the left, such that the second line began with B, the third with C and so on. That is, each line had one shift to the left, forming diagonal 'stripes' of repeating letters. To encipher, the cryptographer would write down the clear, and above it, the primer, letter matching letter, and repeat the primer as necessary to cover the length of the clear. Next, he would run along the alphabet on the top line to find the first letter of the primer; then drop down the left column to find the first letter of the clear. The coordinate letter at the junction of the line and column is the first letter of the ciphertext. This is repeated for every letter. To decipher the encrypted message, the receiver would follow the process backward using the primer at the beginning of the message. The Vigenère tableau had some analogue disadvantages: its simplicity was distrusted compared to the elaborate frequency-suppression system then in use; and its operation, suitable perhaps for diplomats, was considered too slow and lengthy for the battlefield, having to write down the 26-alphabet tabula recta each time and then destroy it, since its possession gave away the method.

In response, German officer Graf von Gronsfeld devised a faster variant in 1665. He combined the simplicity of the quick Caesar transposition cipher with Vigenère's slow polyalphabetic method. Instead of letters, the Gronsfeld cipher used as a key a few digits easy to memorise, such as 1984, which equalled the letter spaces between the *mathematical coordinates* of ciphertext and plaintext. For example, if the clear was HOLD FIRE, the key 1984 was repeated (in this case twice to cover the length of the message) such that the H would right shift 1 place to become I, the O would shift 9 places to X and so on. The resulting ciphertext would then be: IXTH GRZI. Notice that *this converts alphabetic substitution into numerical transposition.* Each digit transposes the alphabet a number of spaces for each letter, such that shifts 0-1-9-8-4 equal ABJIE in the Vigenère cipher. In effect, the ciphers were basically the same, except that Gronsfeld digitised the alphabet for mathematical calculation. The Gronsfeld cipher was quick and easy to use without the need for a letter matrix, but it had the digital disadvantage that it could use only the digits 0 to 9, that is, 10 combinations instead of 26 alphabets. This made it easier to decode than Vigenère's. If the message was intercepted, it would serve only to gain operational time before it was deciphered.

Vigenère had called his own system 'the indecipherable cipher', and it remained so for three centuries, but it had weaknesses. Gronsfeld had shown that it could be digitised, and it had the programmable idiosyncrasy that, due to the coordinate junction of line and column, the three corresponding letters for clear, keyword and message *always formed a right triangle*. And so, in 1863, Friedrich Kasiski devised a decryption method to defeat keyword polyalphabetic substitution ciphers like Vigenère's and Gronsfeld's. The Kasiski test looks for strings of three or more characters repeated in the ciphertext. The *greatest common divisor* of the distances between consecutive strings reveals the length of the key, given that those distances are always a multiple of the key length. Kasiski then wrote the ciphertext repeatedly in lines below each other, forming a matrix. On each line the alphabet shifted by the length of the key. Finally, he treated each column as a single substitution ciphertext and applied frequency analysis to decode each letter of the message. Claude Shannon (1948) would use the *greatest common divisor* in circuit design.

Meanwhile, the old Alberti cipher disc from 1467 became popular in the nineteenth century due to its practicality and ease of use, which required no calculation. Pinwheel cipher discs were used in the American Civil War, the Franco-Prussian War and other conflicts. Imagine a slide ruler (also used for encryption) bent into a circle. The disc had a clear alphabet engraved on its stationary outer rim. In the centre, it had a rotating disc with letters jumbled at random making an *irrational alphabet*. The starting point was secretly determined by a code letter, say N, to align with the A of the clear alphabet. There are 13 shifts from A to N. Therefore, the disc would be shifted counterclockwise 13 places to align the clear and jumbled alphabets for simple substitution. If the receiver was given the code letter along with the ciphertext, the distance

(13 spaces) between the A-N mathematical coordinates is the length of the key. This would make it breakable with the Kasiski method, but unlike the fixed Vigenère tableau, the disc cipher key could be changed quickly and often.

After Kasiski the number of military manuals and openly published books on cryptology multiplied, proposing new variants and decryption methods. This development of encryption literature would play an important strategic role in codebreaking the Nazi Enigma machines during World War II.

Enigma

The Nazis used Enigma encryption machines, considered undecipherable, for their strategic communications across command posts, battlefields, air and sea. Their Kriegsmarine was able to send U-boat wolf packs undetected to sink hundreds of Ally supply vessels and warships across the Atlantic and the English Channel. From 1939 to 1943 they had the upper hand in World War II. To break Enigma the British established a major operation at their cryptology centre in Bletchley Park, gathering top cryptanalysts and mathematicians, like Alan Turing, Jack Good, Gordon Welchman and Claude Shannon. They cracked the Enigma and turned the tide of the war by applying decryption methods and mechanising the process by adapting existing business machines.

To understand the relationship between writing, encryption, computers and artificial intelligence, let us contemplate the fundamental principle they share. Aside from noise by adding or omitting random characters, true encryption has two and only two operations: *transposition* and *substitution*. Transposition slides a sequence by a number of places: it works by *contiguity*, whereas substitution creates a *similarity*. According to Hume (1748), thought works by association of ideas according to *contiguity* or *similarity*. Graphically, this is represented by the Cartesian plane, forming a two-dimensional matrix, of which the Vigenère tableau is an example. Further, linguists Saussure and Jakobson establish that contiguity (diachrony, metonymy) and similarity (synchrony, metaphor) are properties of language (see Chapter 7).

Language is sequential, letter after letter, word after word, but the functions and meanings of words establish nonsequential paradigmatic relations of similarity between distant words, thereby weaving a text (see Chapter 6). Earlier I ventured to say that writing is an encryption of speech which is an encryption of meaning, which in turn is a partial *sampling* of thought. This suggests that Hume may be wrong, that contiguity and similarity are not properties of thought but of language. Many operations of thought (intuition, imagination, emotion, will) exceed those of language but are reduced to Hume's binarism only when organised into meaning and encrypted into speech (parole), which is a small personal sample of the entire language system (langue). This means that language, much less speech, can only partially capture thought. Speech is a static snapshot of the stream of consciousness.

Transposition, like contiguity, is purely empirical, mechanical, *digital*; whereas substitution is *analogue*, meaning-based and assigned by shared human determination. We will see ahead that substitution can be mechanically reduced to transposition, but only when it is detached from meaning, abstracted into a formula. Similarly, cipher discs can be converted into tables and back to discs. This correspondence is possible because when letters are stripped of meaning, they can be enumerated according to their place in the alphabet, such that encryptions can be produced and solved mathematically.

Now imagine cipher discs stacked vertically side by side to become a series of interacting wheels or *rotors*, of which Enigma had three or more. Their set of operations is an algorithm, which creates a cipher. If instead of letters, the rotors had numbers and their algorithm was addition, we would have the old adding machines and cash registers with a 10 × 10 table array of buttons 0 to 9. The top row indicates the *contiguous* place in the decimal system (1000, 100, 10, 1, 0.00, from right to left). The columns indicate the value to be *substituted* for each decimal place (e.g., $1,984.98). From the *initial state* 0.00, the operator would encipher a quantity by punching-in a different value to substitute for each digit and crank the manual lever on the side to rotate the wheels to *interim state 1* (1984.98) displayed on a *rotating counter* (like an odometer). Each time this was repeated with a new number, the lever would advance the digits, adding up to a new *interim state 2* and so forth. The total or *end state* is a *measure of change* from the initial state 0.00. All interim states, however, are *discarded* as rough notes. Only the *end state* total matters, which could be obtained by different sets of additions. This end-state total in fact represents and substitutes for the entire addition algorithm (all the possible operations that add up to the end state). This concept of a single symbol summarising an entire algorithm will be central to Turing's computer design.

Next, a mechanical operation could be selected for the subtraction algorithm, which reversed (decrypted) addition. Multiplication was achieved by repeating the same addition. Division (which decrypted multiplication) was achieved by repeating the same subtraction. The calculator was born. The manual lever was replaced by an electric motor with position gears for faster operation, resulting in electromechanical machines. If instead of numbers, the rotors had letters, moved by a transposition and substitution algorithm, the result was the Enigma encryption machine. If many algorithmic machines for different purposes could be plugged into a master selector machine that could activate any of the different algorithmic programs (now called *software* applications) by pressing or clicking on the symbol that summarises it, the result would be a general-purpose calculator. Alan Turing (1936) called it a 'universal computer' (pp. 241–243)—the prelude to the myth of artificial general intelligence (AGI), obtained by pretending that meaning had not been stripped off the letters; that math could somehow become language.

The history of cryptology is full of cypher discs converted into tables such as Vigenère's, and back into discs. Further, analogue substitution could be turned into digital (key-length) transposition such as in the Gronsfeld cypher. This is the same conversion we saw in the old adding machines with their substitution table *array* of numbered buttons actuating (translating into) transposition rotors. Such is the fundamental correspondence between transposition discs and substitution tables. Discs, however, were ideal for mechanisation and business machines. Let us now look at the role of table arrays.

In the Vigenère tableau, like in the Cartesian plane, the junction or interception between row and column is a coordinate, a *binary digit* or 'bit'—the same information unit used by communication systems and computers. The linguistic *portmanteau* or word-blend 'bit' was first published by Claude Shannon (1948) quoting his Bell Laboratories colleague John W. Tukey who coined it in a company memo. The bit is the logical state of a switch, relay or transistor, with two possible values or initial states, 1 or 0, on or off, A or B, true or false or other binarism. A schematic of electrical switches or relays performing on–off operations were called 'flip or flop' circuits; hence the 'floppy' discs of 1980s computers. Switches, buttons and keyboards are manually operated, whereas relays are electrical switches automatically operated by the flow of an electrical charge. In 1947, the year before Shannon's relay-based communication circuits, transistors were invented to replace relays. They were made ever smaller and faster, requiring minimal current, allowing for the microcircuit arrays or 'chips' of modern computers. The 2024 Nvidia Blackwell superchip has 200 billion transistors requiring minimal energy. Bit switches or transistors are arranged by 'relay logic' into integrated circuits that electronically perform the same sets of operations (algorithms) of the old mechanical calculator or any analogue mechanical machine they digitise. Said algorithms can in fact direct a physical machine, as in the computer numerical control (CNC) of robotic arms, which can act with digital precision on a 2D table (the Cartesian plane) or in 3D space (two perpendicular Cartesian planes). The bit state is determined by the presence or absence of current, light, a pressed button or lever, even the holes or blanks on the table array of a *punched card*, the ancestor of the computer chip and the dot matrix printer.

The punched card was invented by weaver Basile Bouchon in 1725 to store information in table form. He attached the cards together forming a continuous tape to control the steps (algorithm) for making intricate designs on a fabric loom. This ancestor of the CNC precision machine was perfected in 1804 by Jacquard to automatically control the loom's operation. Jacquard inspired mechanical engineer Charles Babbage who used punched cards to perfect his 1820 Difference Engine (a single-purpose mechanical calculator for tabulating polynomials) converting it into his 1837 Analytical Engine, the first digital multi-purpose mechanical computer tabulator, the direct precursor of the Turing Machine and ancestor of today's search engines. In 1886, inspired by the Jacquard loom and the Babbage engine, Herman Hollerith invented the electromechanical Tabulating Machine to sort out and compile data stored in punched cards. It was used successfully for the 1890 U.S. census as well as general accounting and inventory control. Various companies began manufacturing tabulation machines capable of processing up to 150 punched cards per minute. In 1911, Hollerith's and three other companies merged to form CTR, the Computing-Tabulating-Recording Co. (the three main functions of a computer). In 1924, the company was renamed International Business Machines (IBM), which manufactured new CTR models with added capabilities, until going fully electronic in 1952 with their first commercial computer, IBM 701, followed in 1953 by IBM 650 Magnetic Drum Data Processing Machine, the world's first mass produced computer, and eventually the first personal microcomputer in 1981, IBM PC model 5150. Not only did tabulation pave the way for the modern computer following Turing's design, but the Hollerith tabulator was used by Alan Turing and his team to design the Enigma analogue emulator that broke the Nazi code at Bletchley Park.

The early twentieth century marked the rise of the business machine. Each customer's bank account was identified by unique perforations on a 'master card'—now the trade name of a major credit card. The telegraph had enabled communications, but the manual Morse Code (1844) was too lengthy and slow for business applications. In the 1870s, Émile Baudot invented the much faster 5-bit Baudot Code in which the punched card became the machine-punched paper tape. His 5-bit and 7-bit codes crammed more data than ever before. The 'baud' became a measure of symbol-transmission rate, and the data compression race was on. Punched tape was used for stock market ticker machines and early teleprinters. The typewriter's keyboard array was attached to a teletype transmitter–receiver and a perforator printer. In 1923, Germany bought the patent for a Dutch bank-to-bank encryption teleprinter, which became the prototype for the Enigma.

The Enigma's typewriter array actuated three 26-character transposition rotors via a plugboard interface. (See the Enigma at the links for the Imperial War Museum and the CIA Legacy Museum provided under References at the end of this chapter.) The plugboard connected letter pairs (digrams) for reciprocal substitution, such that no letter could encrypt itself or be the same in the ciphertext as in the plaintext. The 26-letter alphabet was thus reduced to 13 substitution pairs in the first step of decryption. This eliminated half of the possible 159 quintillion (18 zeros) combinations. Large scale eliminations were also possible through various decryption techniques. German frequency tables were used to eliminate non-occurring digrams and trigrams, and to compute the *sequential conditional probability* of each letter following the previous ones, known as a Markov sequence—the same basic process of AI for predicting the next token. Frequency analysis helped reconstruct digram tables for the plugboard connections. This complemented the expectation of military jargon, pat phrases and previously deciphered fragments. Letter sequences were discovered by comparing several of the ciphertexts intercepted by radio each morning. Early Enigma broadcasts were in Morse Code but soon changed to 0–1 binary code. To facilitate message comparison, punched 'Banbury' sheets were created for each message at Bletchley. They consisted of typed A-Z columns constantly repeated with digits 0 to 9 across the top as in the Gronsfeld cipher. The letters of each message were punched-in on one Banbury sheet. By superposing the punched sheets, the holes of different messages would align, letting light through and revealing the letters repeated in different ciphertexts. This manual process which Turing called 'Banburismus' was too slow. It needed to be mechanised.

Turing and Gordon Welchman designed a sorting and tabulating machine based on the Hollerith tabulator. It was called the Turing-Welchman Bombe in recognition of its prototype, the Polish Bomba built before the war as an Enigma emulator. The rotors of the Enigma were emulated by forward-facing dials. (See the Bombe at The National Museum of Computing link provided under References at the end of this chapter.) The Bombe had three arrays of 3 × 12 dials each, one array for each rotor of the Enigma. It emulated the probable settings of 36 Enigma machines at a time. In addition to the plugboard configuration, cracking the Enigma code meant deciphering the rotor order and settings. The Polish Cipher Bureau's 'clock' method was a shortcut for determining rotor order, initial position and turnover point by using the *index of coincidence* (letter sequences repeated in different messages). Crucially,

Gordon Welchman gave the back panel of the Bombe a diagonal configuration like that of the Vigenère tableau. This minimised false positives, dramatically increasing the accuracy of the machine, and making the Bombe a success.

Fittingly, the engineering and construction of the Bombe design was awarded to the British Tabulating Machine Company, while the contract for the U.S. Navy version of the Bombe went to the National Cash Register Corporation.

The Universal Turing Machine

German mathematician David Hilbert presented his colleagues with 23 problems at a Paris congress in 1900. Some have been solved, others not, but they set a research agenda for the rest of the century. At the base was Hilbert's commitment to formalism against the intuitionist school. He held that all of mathematics consistently follows a system of incontrovertible axioms from which all solutions can be proven without contradiction; that is, the system of mathematics has *completeness* and *consistency*. Further, he held that math is a conceptual system endowed with internal necessity whose operations can only be so and not otherwise; that is, it has *decidability*. This means that everything can be described and proven through math alone; that everything, even human intelligence, can be artificially mechanised.

His positivist project ultimately failed. It was not based on mathematical logic but on belief. It was a philosophy, an ideology, a metaphysics. In 1931, Kurt Gödel's *incompleteness theorems* disposed of the claims to *completeness* and *consistency*. Gödel showed that no formal system can demonstrate its completeness, without contradiction, based on its own axioms alone. This left Hilbert's *entscheidungsproblem* or decidability problem, which Turing tackled in his 1936 paper 'On Computable Numbers'. Turing used for his demonstration a *hypothetical computation machine* and ultimately showed that Hilbert's decidability problem can have no solution. In so doing, he laid the groundwork for computer design.

The magnetic tape had been developed pre-computers in 1928 for sound recording and reproduction. It came to replace the punched card and paper tape as a more compressed storage medium. A single roll held the data of 10,000 cards. The ability to record and erase on magnetic tape gave Turing the clue for his 'computing machines': 'The machine is supplied with a "tape" (the analogue of paper) running through it and divided into sections (called "squares") each capable of bearing a "symbol"' (Turing, 1936, p. 231). The squares with symbols in the memory tape are 'scanned' by a magnetic head and become part of the machine's 'configuration' (programming software). 'The possible behaviour of the machine at any moment is determined by the *m*-configuration and the scanned symbol'.

> In some of the configurations in which the scanned square is blank (i.e. bears no symbol) the machine writes down a new symbol on the scanned square: in other configurations it erases the scanned symbol. The machine may also change the square which is being scanned, but only by shifting it one square to right or left. In addition to any of these operations the *m*-configuration may be changed. Some of the symbols written down will form the sequence of figures which is the decimal of the real number being computed. The others are just rough notes to 'assist the memory'. It will only be these rough notes which will be liable to erasure. (p. 231)

Contrary to the holes in a punched card, the 'squares' on the magnetic tape could be erased, written on and transposed one step to the right or left. This flexibility was a paradigm shift. Like the intermediate states of the old calculator, the 'rough notes' are liable to erasure. Further, the *a*-machine is *automatic* if its movements are completely determined by the configuration. Sometimes *c*-machines may be *chosen* for specific purposes which are only partially determined by the configuration.

In the era of business machines, Turing does not distinguish among hardware, software and data. They are all part of 'the machine'. This is understandable from the physical model that was built. The hardware was limited to the small machinery that controlled the electromagnetic recording head and the reel-to-reel that moved the tape forward and backward. The tape contained both the program and the data. Symbol manipulation followed a *table of rules* based on the binary possibilities, 1,

0, Any and None (p. 234). The true abstract Turing machine would have unlimited, infinite tape on both reels. Despite its limitations, the linear tape was adequate for the sequential mathematical operations that Turing theoretically needed to address Hilbert's decidability problem. Later the Multi-tape Turing Machine was designed with tape 1 having the configuration (software) and the other tapes starting out blank for receiving data. Each tape had its own magnetic head for reading, writing and erasing. The first commercial computer, UNIVAC 1, released in 1951, used magnetic tape to supplement its small internal memory. However, sequential memory tape made search and retrieval slow. In 1956, IBM introduced the first hard disk drive enabling Random Access Memory (RAM). This meant a return to the cypher disc for the rest of the century, in hard drives, soft PC floppy discs and rigid optical CD-ROMs. Then back to the table with transistor arrays and memory chips. The introduction in 2010 of the Linear Tape File System (LTFS), which separates metadata from the objects it records, was a welcome answer to Big Data, network computing and the Internet. LTFS metadata, stored on solid-state drives, provides faster retrieval than a hard drive alone. LTFS is open standard, allowing for multivendor use and system migration. LTFS-based architecture is referred to as FLAPE, a portmanteau of flash and tape memory. It is all a problem-solving process, a transposition and substitution metagrammar seeking greater storage and processing efficiency with every generation.

In the end, Turing proves that Hilbert's decidability problem is unsolvable; that mathematical yes-or-no questions cannot always be decided by computation. Turing developed his theorem around his concept of a 'universal machine'. 'It is possible to invent a single machine which can be used to compute any computable sequence. If this machine *U* is supplied with a tape on the beginning of which is written the S.D. [Standard Description, i.e. program algorithm] of some computing machine *M*, then *U* will compute the same sequence as *M*' (pp. 241–242). Turing's most interesting proof addresses the undecidability of the *halting problem*: whether the algorithm of universal machine *U*, supplied with the S.D. of machine *M* and a problem input, can determine or 'decide' if the machine will halt the problem's computation or continue running forever. Simply put, each program will refer to its own rules, and this can lead to an endless and contradictory halt-and-run loop. This raises the question of self-referentiality (a machine fed to itself or to another machine)—and runs against any claim of artificial general intelligence (AGI) as the mechanisation of human thought. For one, machines cannot doubt or accept a contradiction—a smart privilege of critical thinking.

Shannon's Theorem

Claude Shannon worked at Bell Laboratories and published 'A Mathematical Theory of Communication' (1948) in the company's technical journal, a premier forum for electronics and communication research. Marconi, in competition with Nikola Tesla, invented the first working wireless telegraph in 1895. Radiotelegraphy improved and became transoceanic, transmitting radio wave pulses of two different lengths, received as the binary dots and dashes of Morse Code. This worked by simply using a clicker to turn the transmission on and off, regardless how noisy. Then came modulation: the method of encoding information on radio waves by varying the amplitude, frequency, phase and other factors. Noise now became a problem. Shannon writes: 'The recent development of various methods of modulation such as PCM and PPM which exchange bandwidth for signal-to-noise ratio has intensified the interest in a general theory of communication' (p. 1). It is this general theory that Shannon is after. The crux of his theorems is *quantising* continuous analogue signals by mathematically encrypting PPM (pulse position modulation), an analogue modulation of *continuous* waves, into PCM (pulse code modulation) a digital method of sampling the wave at equal intervals to break it down into *discrete* coordinates—that is, reducing representation to communication, analogue to digital. Once digitised, the signal can be more accurately manipulated to cancel noise and maximise channel capacity by sending several tracks per channel and compressing information through more efficient coding. Shannon begins by doing the math for the simplest binary signal, that of the telegraph, and applying it to systems of higher complexity. Indeed, the rest of this chapter shows that artificial intelligence is scarcely more than a glorified telegraph. Here is 'how'—the metagrammar of digital conversion.

An oscilloscope shows radio waves streaming on a screen over the 2D grid of a Cartesian plane, with its vertical *y*-axis and horizontal *x*-axis. The wave is a time-modified circle: if you put a pencil somewhere on *y* and trace it around the centre, you will have a perfect circle, but if you do it on a left-moving paper, the circle comes out as a sine wave. If you do the same thing on *x*, you will draw a cosine wave. The higher the *y* the bigger the circle, the taller the wave and the broader the amplitude or bandwidth, which requires more electric power. The higher the value of *x* the longer the wave and the lower the frequency. The best way to mathematically describe a wave is by a logarithmic function. Just like addition-subtraction and multiplication-division revert or decode each other, logarithm is the reversion of an exponent (2^x = N; $\log_2 N$ = *x*). The 'natural logarithm' $\log_e$ (Euler's number *e* is a constant close to 2.71828…) owes its name to the fact that it naturally appears in the analysis of *continuous* functions (curves), like π (3.14159…) appears as the fundamental constant of the circle, the ratio of diameter to circumference. Both *e* and π are irrational (cannot be expressed as a fraction or the ratio of two integers) and transcendental (their decimals go on forever to infinity). As such, they are not 'computable numbers' in Turing's terms. Shannon approximates Euler's $\log_e$ (2.71828…) to the 'binary logarithm' $\log_2$ by applying the standard base conversion formula: $\log_b a = (\log_c a)/(\log_c b)$. Radio dials express frequencies in decimal numbers using the 'decimal logarithm' $\log_{10}$, but Shannon sticks to $\log_2$ noting that their ratio is 3.32, almost 3 1/3, an easy conversion. The binary logarithm allows him to compute coordinates and reduce logarithmic functions to simple trigonometric additions using sines and cosines. This is owed to the fact that drawing a radius from the centre to any value of *y* and going straight down to the *x*-axis to find the *x* coordinated *always draws a right triangle*—this being a property of coordinates, as we saw earlier on the Vigenère tableau. Thus, the digital sampling of continuous analogue waves to yield measurable right triangles is another attempt at squaring the circle. The waves are no longer smooth and continuous but discrete and serrated like a dotted line.

Shannon applies this, from the 2D telegraph signal to 2D modulated radio and 3D television signals, suggesting a digital computational model expandable to *n* dimensions. The next step is eliminating *noise*, that is, everything outside the wave pattern that does not fit the formula beyond the statistical margin of error. Noise causes distortion, reducing fidelity and wasting channel capacity. A *limiter* is applied to the signal amplitude, frequency and phase. This is the same process of elimination used by Turing at Bletchley Park. Next is adding a *correcting device* (Fig. 13.1).

The monitoring-measuring-correcting function is *recursive*. It increases *redundancy* (the opposite of choice, uncertainty and entropy) by measuring and reinputting the difference between the initial state and the target state. Adding the corrective function changed the machine's *m*-configuration. It is, in short, the basic principle behind machine 'learning'. Each 'neuron' in an AI neural network performs this same error-reduction operation, receiving, correcting and transmitting data.

Now let us perform a metagrammatical analysis. If a substantive part of speech (noun or verb) is omitted (e.g., 'I…books' omitting *read*), the construction is ungrammatical, but if an accessory adjective or adverb is omitted, the construction may be grammatical but incongruent. The same thing happens when a machine does not work well, the diagnosis being a missing factor which makes for a discontinuous sequence. For

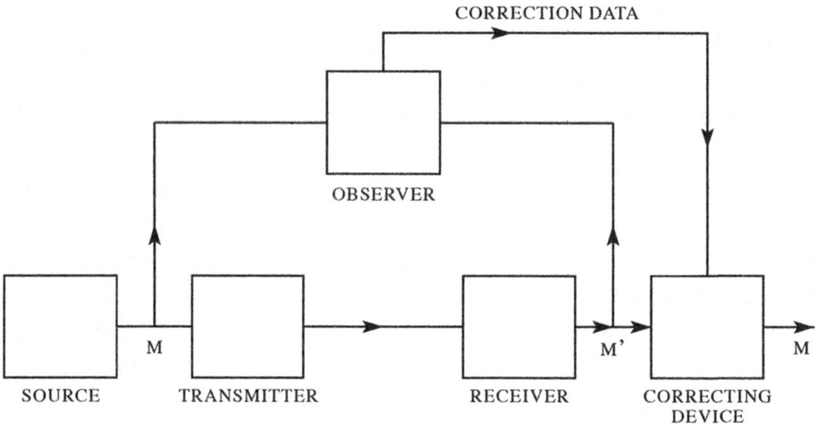

Fig. 13.1 Schematic diagram of a correction system (Shannon, 1948, p. 21)

example, early automatic transmissions in cars shifted gears suddenly with a jerk. A missing modulator, actuated by oil pressure, was added to the sequence to smoothen the gear shifts. When a coil was too hot and burned the spark plugs and points, a resistor was added to tone it down. In Shannon's case a correcting system was added to reduce the noise.

But where it gets truly interesting is when Shannon combines these methods with Turing's approach to Enigma and his cryptology experience from working together at Bletchley Park, in order to mathematically devise a machine approximation to the English language, as described below. This laid the groundwork for Natural Language Processing (NLP) and large language models (LLMs) like ChatGPT.

The Cradle of 'Artificial Intelligence'

Shannon, who was very impressed with Turing's 1936 paper 'On Computable Numbers', approaches language in terms of information theory: 'One minus the relative entropy is the *redundancy*. The redundancy of ordinary English [as verified by various methods] is roughly 50%. This means that when we write English half of what we write is determined by the structure of the language [grammar rules] and half is chosen freely [functional options]' (1948, p. 14). The free part (uncertain word choice) is the relative entropy which, following Turing, can be computed by means of statistics and probability. The key to Turing's success was using a conditional probability model known as a Markov sequence or chain: based on frequency tables, the probability of occurrence of each new letter or word depends on the ones before it. A continuous-time Markov chain leads to a probability distribution, such as the bell curve. A discrete-time Markov chain leads to a square Markov matrix, also known as a stochastic or substitution matrix. It contains the transition probabilities for each pair of coordinates. In a 1906 paper studying the occurrence of the first 20,000 words of Pushkin's novel in verse, *Eugene Onegin*, Russian mathematician Andrey Markov developed this method of describing the limited randomness of stochastic processes for use in linguistic analysis, wherefrom it spread to the statistics of all fields of science and technology.

Shannon's 'general theory of communication' would not be complete if he had not attempted to apply his work on information channels to the simulation of natural language. He writes:

> [A] sequence of symbols governed by a set of probabilities [is the source of] a stochastic process [i.e., a Markov sequence]. [….] [A] discrete sequence of symbols chosen from a finite set may be considered a discrete source. This will include such cases as:

1. Natural written languages such as English, German, Chinese.
2. Continuous information sources that have been rendered discrete by some quantizing process. For example, the quantized speech from a PCM [pulse code modulation] transmitter. (p. 5, passim)

This suggests that thought is a continuous process, grammatical speech is an organised sampling of thought and writing is an encryption of speech. Next, as he did with the telegraph, Shannon begins with the simplest case: a three-letter alphabet (A, B, C) with each letter having the same 1/3 probability. 'The next increase in complexity would involve trigram frequencies but no more'—where the probability of each letter depends on the ones before (Markov chain). Next, he cites Fletcher Pratt regarding letter, digram and trigram frequencies, as well as Dewey's 1923 *Relative Frequency of English Speech Sounds* which 'tabulated' word frequencies (p. 6, n. 5). He then draws a table of choices with the associated probabilities for the different combinations of consonants and vowels that make up the possible 'words' of this very limited language.

'These artificial languages are useful in constructing simple problems and examples to illustrate various possibilities. We can also approximate to a natural language by means of a series of simple artificial languages [...] each letter having the same probability that it has in the natural language'. He assumes 'a 27-symbol "alphabet", the 26 letters and a space' (p. 6). The probability of each new letter is $x/27$. Finally, he embarks on 'the series of approximations to English':

> 1. Zero-order approximation (symbols independent and equiprobable).
> 2. First-order approximation (symbols independent but with frequencies of English text).
> 3. Second-order approximation (digram structure as in English).
> 4. Third-order approximation (trigram structure as in English).
> 5. First-order word approximation [based on] *n*-gram structure.
> 6. Second-order word approximation [with] word transition probabilities.
>
> The resemblance to ordinary English text increases quite noticeably at each of the above steps. (p. 7)

Shannon's best result, however, is an ungrammatical jumble of English words. He hopes that with enough '*n*-gram' approximations, the circle will be squared enough to the naked eye, so to speak, and the simulation of natural English will fool most of the people most of the time, as in the Turing Test.

In the following decades, computers became increasingly able to perform successive approximations, giving rise to computational linguistics and statistical Markov word-sequence language models for bigrams, trigrams and *n*-grams. The word-sequence *n*-gram language model based on approximate frequency tables was greatly improved by the multi-pass process of recurrent neural networks, which were in turn superseded by large language models. LLMs can compute highly accurate *n*-gram frequencies from vast corpora of texts through pattern- and string-matching algorithms and statistical operations still based on Markov-Good-Turing frequency estimation.

How close is close enough? Here is where the Turing Test, dubbed 'The Imitation Game' comes into play. In his 1936 paper Turing had exploited the original meaning of 'computer' as a person who does calculations on paper: 'We may compare a man in the process of computing a real number to a machine' (1936, p. 231). Turing uses 'he' to refer to the hypothetical machine designed to emulate a human computer. This same anthropomorphism carries over to his 1950 paper, 'Computer Machinery and Intelligence'. First, human intelligence was *reduced* to computing numbers, nothing having to do with meaning: 'The human computer is supposed to be following fixed rules; he has no authority to deviate from them in any detail' (1950, p. 436). In his latter paper the potential abilities of computing machinery are *exaggerated*. It begins with the question, 'Can machines think? .... [T]he present interest in "thinking machines" has been aroused by a particular kind of machine, usually called an "electronic computer" or "digital computer"' (pp. 433–436). Before going further Turing shows his little regard for meaning by manipulating those of 'machine' and 'think'. He does so through a series of tortuous counterarguments to the possible objections of his critics (since he has no proof of his own). This is to eliminate all other options except the practical application of his Turing Test (described in Chapter 13) where a computer programmed to imitate a man can fool a judge 70% of the time—close enough to be called intelligent. Turing admits that no existing machine can do this; so, he replaces the question of whether machines can think, with 'Are there imaginable digital computers which would do well in the imitation game?' (p. 442). He predicts there might by the end of the century, based on the faith that with successive approximations and error elimination (as in the process of decryption) the circle will eventually be squared enough.

The stage was set for coining the term 'artificial intelligence'. It happened in the proposal for the 1956 Dartmouth summer workshop on 'artificial intelligence' (McCarthy et al., 1955) inspired by Turing's 1950 paper on 'Computing Machinery and Intelligence'. Turing himself could not participate. The war hero at Bletchley Park who shortened the war by several years and saved some 14 million lives was not only deprived of recognition, as the Enigma project remained a secret until the 1970s, but also suffered government persecution for homosexuality. Convicted for 'indecency', he suffered the grotesque British justice of the time, forced to accept chemical castration over prison. This led to his suicide by cyanide in 1954 at age 41.

The Dartmouth workshop was a two-month brainstorming session by a small group of experts on 'artificial intelligence'. The provocative term helped them secure a grant from the Rockefeller Foundation. All the main terms of art still used in AI can be found in their proposal, as well as the doctrine of machine anthropomorphism. Machine operations were now called 'behaviour', and, conversely, human behaviour would be thought of in terms of the 'serial order' of its 'cerebral mechanism'.

Among the organisers, McCarthy was interested in the relation between language and intelligence but reducing language to a universal Turing machine with rules of conjecture and reasoning. Minsky, a junior fellow in mathematics and neurology, held that it was 'not difficult to design a machine' that can be 'trained' to exhibit 'learning' and 'goal-seeking' behaviour. The machine would 'build up within itself an abstract model of the environment' and, given a problem, 'it could first explore solutions [internally] and then attempt external experiments [which] would appear to be rather clever, and the behaviour would have to be regarded as rather "imaginative"' (p. 6). Shannon proposed to work on the application of 'information theory' to 'computer machines and brain models' (p. 5). Rochester sought to induce originality and creativity in machine performance by programming 'randomness' together with prediction or 'foresight'. Studies of the 'serial order' in the behaviour of 'neuron nets'—he claimed—suggest 'that mental action consists basically of constructing little engines inside the brain which can stimulate and thus predict abstractions relating to environment' (pp. 7–9). The proposal promised to tackle problems such as: automation; natural language programming; neuron nets to form 'concepts'; machine learning and self-improvement; abstractions from sensory data; building internal models of its environment; randomness and creativity.

Among the speculation, conjectures and mechanistic science fiction, there is a general agreement that the true measure of intelligence is understanding natural language. The following year, Noam Chomsky gained fame with *Syntactic Structures* (1957)—his Turing-like hypothetical language machine for transformational-generative grammar. Machine translation became the next frontier. Vast government resources poured into it, yielding poor results until 2017. That year Google Translate converted from statistical machine translation (SMT) to neural machine translation (NMT). SMT used Markov chain predictive algorithms for word search, but it was deficient in grammar. NMT uses an artificial neural network to predict Markov word sequences based on grammar rules. The gain in accuracy was enough to make human proofreading and correction less laborious than translating from scratch. However, both systems ultimately depend on Google's search engine and

Big Data to draw from vast corpora of bilingual web documents previously translated by humans. This is also true of large language models (LLMs), which use these methods together with linguistic classification (parts of speech, cases, etc.) and domain parsing to facilitate searches that are essentially parasitic on human content creation.

Conclusion

After no significant advances in AI for the rest of the twentieth century, Big Data, search engine optimisation and computational linguistics brought new possibilities for exploiting human content and perpetuating the fraud of the 'thinking machine'. The doctrine acquired the mystical status of a materialistic religion, a sterile, profit-driven struggle to maintain the illusion of transcending materiality. The new futurists adopted the persona of pop prophets. The cheap substitution of religion is evident in Ray Kurzweil's *The Age of Spiritual Machines: When Computers Exceed Human Intelligence* (2000) and *The Singularity is Near: When Humans Transcend Biology* (2006). The mystical merging of humans and machines is billed as a technological nirvana where the promise of symbiosis seeks to obscure the fact that Big Tech and their AI machines are parasitic on humans. Turing had made a parallel between biological evolution and the 'more expeditious' process of technological development via the 'training' of self-improving computers to impersonate humans (1950, p. 456). Kurzweil developed this into his 'Law' of Accelerating Returns (LOAR). It is the fallacy of the infinite projection of digital metagrammar, unchecked by analogue realities. As history shows, instead of an exponential or even linear advancement, the physical limitations of circuit architecture, bandwidth and data compression, among others, cause technological efficiencies to slow down and plateau. Turing's colleague, Jack Good, had issued his 'Speculations Concerning the First Ultraintelligent Machine' in 1965. This history of prophesy has been the fictional backdrop for a branching myth, leading to works like Nick Bostrom's *Superintelligence* (2017). The rest has been left to greedy tech industries, Hollywood movies and fanciful blogs.

It is significant that among Turing's counterarguments about the possible *objections* to his 'thinking machine' (theological, mathematical, consciousness-based and others) no consideration whatever is given to the objection that I have been raising all along: *meaning*. In fact, Turing so disregards meaning that he does violence to it when he concludes that machines can 'think' but in a *different* way that human's do. This is not only to change the meaning of 'think' but to decree an entirely different meaning tailored to machines. 'Why, for instance, do we even use the term artificial intelligence, rather than, perhaps, speaking of "human-task-simulation"?' (Larson, 2021, p. 30). Meaning is an imitation game spoiler to be avoided at all costs. Shannon confesses from the start that 'These semantic aspects of communication are irrelevant to the engineering problem' (1948, p. 1). Chomsky (1957) reduces language to a notation: 'the set of "sentences" of some formalized system of mathematics can be considered a language' (p. 13); and makes his transformational-generative grammar 'independent of meaning' (p. 17). Machines will never break the barrier of *meaning*, the perpetual Achilles heel of artificial 'intelligence'.

References

Bostrom, N. (2014). *Superintelligence: Paths, Dangers, Strategies*. Oxford University Press.

Central Intelligence Agency Legacy Museum. *Artifacts—Enigma Machine*. At https://www.cia.gov/legacy/museum/artifact/enigma-machine

Chomsky, N. (1957). *Syntactic Structures*. Mouton.

Good, I. J. (1965). Speculations concerning the first ultraintelligent machine. *Advances in Computers, 6*(6), 31–88.

Imperial War Museums. *How Turing Cracked the Enigma Code*. At https://www.iwm.org.uk/history/how-alan-turing-cracked-the-enigma-code

Kurzweil, R. (2000). *The Age of Spiritual Machines: When Computers Exceed Human Intelligence*. Penguin.

Kurzweil, R. (2006). *The Singularity Is Near: When Humans Transcend Biology*. Penguin.

Larson, E. (2021). *The Myth of Artificial Intelligence: Why Computers Can't Think the Way We Do*. Harvard University Press.
McCarthy, J., Minsky, M. L., Rochester, N., & Shannon, C. (1955). *A Proposal for the Dartmouth Summer Research Project on Artificial Intelligence*. Retrieved from http://jmc.stanford.edu/articles/dartmouth/dartmouth.pdf
Mignolo, W. D. (2003). *The Darker Side of the Renaissance: Literacy, Territoriality & Colonization* (2nd ed.). University of Michigan Press.
Pratt, F. (1939). *Secret and Urgent: The Story of Codes and Cyphers*. Robert Hale Ltd.
Shannon, C. E. (1948). A mathematical theory of communication. *The Bell System Technical Journal, 27*, 379–423, 623–656. Retrieved from https://people.math.harvard.edu/~ctm/home/text/others/shannon/entropy/entropy.pdf
The National Museum of Computing (UK). *The Turing-Welchman Bombe*. At https://www.tnmoc.org/bombe
Turing, A. M. (1936). On computable numbers, with an application to the Entscheidungsproblem. *Journal of Mathematics, 58*(345–363), 230–265. Retrieved from https://www.cs.virginia.edu/~robins/Turing_Paper_1936.pdf
Turing, A. M. (1950). Computing machinery and intelligence. *Mind: A Quarterly Review of Psychology and Philosophy, 59*(236), 433–460.

14

The Analogue Metagrammar of Human Intelligence

Introduction

Meaning is the motivation and purpose of all natural languages, and what artificial or 'formalised languages' are incapable of conjuring. The magic of meaning lies in the fact that understanding is a sudden, irreducible moment. An *axiom* in philosophy is a truth so obvious and self-evident that it requires no proof or explanation. Grasped suddenly and intuitively, the axiom is the 'atom' of logic, theorems and arguments. Mathematical or logical *intuition* is likewise the unitary understanding of the most elementary ideas upon which rests the entire edifice of inference and deduction. Plato considered intuition the immediate perception of ideas and knowledge, and Aristotle, the act of direct cognition used to formulate the first principles of science and define the goals of activity. Theoretical intuition 'grasps immutable and primary concepts. In reasoning, practical intuition grasps ultimate concepts' (Piętka, 2015, pp. 23–33). The grasping of meaning is accompanied by rewarding feelings of satisfaction and accomplishment, in a scale that goes from a micro to a full 'Aha!' experience.

A term coined by Karl Bühler and developed by Gestalt psychologists Wolfgang Köhler (1917) and Max Wertheimer (1945), the *'Aha!'*

E. Camayd-Freixas, *Metagrammar*, https://doi.org/10.1007/978-3-031-92337-1_14

moment has been variously referred to as the 'eureka effect', epiphany or, in current cognitive psychology, *insight*. The Gestalt theory of *insight problem solving* posits 'a direct [analogue] parallelism between perceptual experience and higher-order forms of cognition [...] restructuring of one's initial representation of the problem's elements, leading to a sudden leap of understanding' (Vitello & Salvi, 2023, p. 1). Before Gestalt, problem solving was considered a process of (costly) trial and error, requiring no creativity or innovation, something that can be digitised and mechanised. Instead, this *representational restructuring* is what Thomas Kuhn (1962) calls a *paradigm shift*. I call it a translation from a new, reconfigured grammar gestalt into an analogue metagrammar gestalt. 'Thinking outside the box' is an analogue process. Analogue metagrammar is human centred and fundamentally based on *meaning*, which is the product of the multidimensionality of language: denotation, connotation and evocation. Meaning is polysemic, contextual, situational, historical and communal, involving the entirety of a culture.

Analogue Problem Solving

Digital or mathematical problem solving is of utmost importance for measuring, testing hypotheses, analysing data, developing quantitative evidence and similar tasks. Computers can keep track of many more variables than humans ever could and almost instantly submit them to multiple statistical operations. Nevertheless, computation is only the second half of the problem-solving equation. The first half is analogue, based on the human factor.

The first AI programs arising in the 1980s were 'expert systems', which simulated the decision making of human experts in a particular field. They are closed rule-based programs with two main components: domain-specific 'knowledge' in the form of *rule tables*; and an 'inference' engine (not unlike a transposition and substitution disc) which mechanically applies the logical rules of deduction and induction to the 'knowledge' base. Expert systems come in two types: production systems consisting of if–then rules about 'behaviour' applied to *conditions* (if) for triggering *actions* (then); and logic systems, programming that represents a 'knowledge' base as a set of sentences in logical notation organised into theorems to solve domain-specific problems by deriving *conclusions* from *conditions*. Expert systems are basically *answer search programs* than run through binary trees and computational linguistics. They may use forward chaining, an elimination process based on repeated modus ponens syllogisms (if P implies Q, and P is true: Q is true); or *backward induction*—reverse engineering a series of optimal choices starting from the goal, much like reverse game theory where the goal is given, but the mechanism is unknown. Mathematical optimisation can be computed by a series of quadratic equations in multivariate calculus following the theory of global maxima and minima. The meaningful *values* of the different alternatives, however, are supplied by humans according to analogue principles. Similarly, AI expert systems formalise and mechanise *discrete* snapshots of *continuous*, analogue human expertise (see Shannon's Theorem in Chapter 13).

These essentially linear systems must abide by their ruleset and therefore cannot enable a paradigm shift. A partial remedy has been the programming of expert systems using artificial neural networks by backpropagating inputs and feedforwarding outputs typically through three or more layers of neural networks that adjust the weight of initial-state variables to approximate a target state in multiple recurring steps. The resulting machine 'learning' adds flexibility to the expert system and can shift only among preprogrammed paradigms. They assist with trial-and-error simulations as well as testing of hypotheses and theorems, which may support but not replace human intuition, innovation and creativity. In conjunction with analogue problem solving, these systems can be extremely helpful for medical differential diagnosis, technical troubleshooting and multivariate problems in specific domains. The state of the art can be judged from the performance of chatbots for customer service, medical, legal or psychological assistance (reminiscent of the Turing Test for impersonating humans). Chatbot savings come at a price. Customers prefer to 'speak to a human' while chatbot automation runs contrary to customer retention. Medical, legal and psychological bots come with the caveat and disclaimer that they are not substitutes for professional services. Psychological chatbots, for example, may not intervene appropriately with users (not to be called 'patients'). Their justification is predicated upon the number of people who do not have access to or will not seek professional services, a number incentivised in turn by the availability of chatbots. Machine learning systems are justifiable tools for tackling specific problems. Their ruleset has an inherent bias for 'learning' specific things. They are designed for *narrow* problem-solving applications. The more successful they are at a specific task, the less successful they are at others (Larson, 2021, pp. 28–30). System specialisation, utility and reliability run contrary to the pointless pursuit of 'human-level' artificial general intelligence (AGI) inspired by the chimerical Turing Universal Machine.

Problem-solving strategies may be classified as linear, matrix, backchain or gestalt and may be applied in combination. Linear strategies include if–then contingency decision trees and algorithmic binary trees. However, before an algorithm can be designed, humans must assign meanings, values and goals, based on an analogue understanding of the problem. One such problem which can be computer-assisted but not fully digitised is Enterprise Resource Planning (ERP) which cycles through procurement, production, distribution, accounting, human resources, corporate performance, customer service and sales. An analogue linear strategy is the '5W2H analysis' (what, who, when, where, why, how, how much). It is the metagrammar of investigative journalism, while 'how' (in what way) is the metagrammar of the problem itself. *What* is the full description of the situation and the gap to reach the desired outcome. *Who* are the dramatis personae, agents, players, moving pieces or stakeholders. *When* and *how often* does the problem arise. *Where* are the areas affected. *Why* does the problem arise, its causes, drivers, level of urgency or importance. *How* does it develop, its structure and mechanisms, the functions of its agents and processes, and how can countermeasures, alternatives, organisational strategies, planning and project management be implemented. *How much* is the impact, the quantification of damage, costs, people or units affected, time and resources to aid in efficient planning and prioritising.

Another linear method is the 'SCQA framework' (situation, complication, questions, answers) for structuring problem-solving. *Situation* is the recognisable context and precise problem statement. *Complication* is the thickening of the plot, the reasons, dangers, opportunities and obstacles that make up the gap between the situation and the desired outcome. *Questions* arise from S and C above and break down the problem into smaller bites by asking what can be done about said reasons, dangers, opportunities and obstacles. *Answers* are proposals of possible alternatives to be tried out for addressing the Qs, that is, hypotheses to be tested, once they are accurately formulated to predict the best course of action.

'Tree structure' is a linear but hierarchical representation that branches out from a main category. It is commonly used in organisational charts and genealogical trees. Binary trees are used as a computational data structure navigated through algorithmic paths. It is also useful for breaking down categories into components at each level. An example is a business model in which the central category [Profit] branches down into [Revenue – Costs] and [Costs] into [Fixed + Variable] and so forth. On the left side of the tree, [Revenue] branchers down into [Price x Units Sold] which branches down into [Locations × Order Size × Number of Customers]. [Order Size] breaks down into [Order Frequency × Items per Order], which further break down into [Quantity per Use × Frequency of Use]. Metagrammatical analysis consists here in locating weaknesses and identifying the functions of the different agents at each level to discover efficiencies.

Matrix strategies include the 'MECE principle' (Mutually Exclusive, Collectively Exhaustive) which is used in conjunction with other strategies to ensure that the problem is broken down into elements that do not overlap and that together cover all the angles. It is usually represented graphically as a square or rectangle filled by blocks that do not overlap and that can be labelled with the different aspects of the problem. 'SWOC analysis' (strengths, weaknesses, opportunities and challenges) is similarly represented as a 2 × 2 matrix. 'Priority quadrants' include the 'Eisenhauer Matrix', 2 × 2 quadrants that plot Importance (low/high) against Urgency (low/high). Variations can plot Effort vs. Impact, Risk vs. Reward, etc., or in a 3 × 3 matrix, Impact (low, mid, high) vs. Probability (low, mid, high). 'Decision matrices' can be simple (a list of Pros and Cons with + or – scores) or extensive (a column of *n* alternatives vs. a row of *n* criteria, each of them weighted or scored). (For illustrative examples, see Neuronswaves Lab, 2024).

Backchain strategies work backward in linear fashion from a goal or desired outcome to the initial situation. In an analogue process, however, they tend to work recursively and dialectically from the goal down and from the starting situation up, adjusting and providing for contingencies along the way. Dialectic strategies work by bridging the gap bidirectionally between problem and solution. Stepped problem-solving strategies require *progress monitoring* to verify that they are going in the right direction in closing that gap, which can usually be quantified and measured. A paradigm shift, however, involves a qualitative insight that results in a *representational change*.

Gestalt strategies see a unitary pattern or new path forward towards a solution as a sudden insight, sometimes mediated by spatial figuration together with radical metagrammatical restructuring that amounts to a paradigm shift. They are fully analogue and non-computable. Insight can be spontaneous or induced (learned). With the right approach and understanding its stages, insight can be induced by self, a teacher or coach, or by talking and conferring with peers. *Insight learning* has five stages: (1) Preparation—fully defining and analysing the problem, engaging in some trial and error, gauging the gap between the initial state and the desired outcome; (2) Incubation—letting ideas mature and the problem sit and simmer, talking it over with peers, then coming back to it with fresh eyes; (3) Insight—the Aha! moment when the different elements of the problem come together into a gestalt pattern, into a syntax that shows a promising path to a solution; (4) Verification—testing the solution to see if it closes the gap between situation and goal, analysing and understanding its syntax (metagrammar) by breaking it down into steps; (5) Generalisation—transferring the same pattern learned to other similar problems. This is precisely the role of comparative grammar (see Chapter 2) in expanding our repertoire of solution patterns as they vary from language to language. On the one hand, grammar corresponds with our experience of the world and organises it into patterns. On the other, grammar gestalts (syntactic contours) are internalised in memory as a template that guides our higher order thought processes and are then transferred back onto the world in the form of metagrammar for conceptualising phenomena and structuring our actions and designs, thereby expanding our problem-solving toolbox.

The Human Factor

Conscious psychology is a neglected area of science. Psychology as a field has developed around a mystifying concept of a 'subconscious' black box. This not only applies to Freudian psychoanalysis and less reputable variants like Dianetics and the Church of Scientology, with its conscious 'analytical' mind and its subconscious 'reactive' mind, the therapist assuming the aura of a shaman, the only one who knows what is inside the magic hat. It also applies to behaviourism, which reduces our intellect to an unconscious 'conditioned response' to seek pleasure and avoid pain—a convenient binarism for reducing human intelligence to a controllable size. Not too far is cognitive psychology, which measures micro-reactions in milliseconds or automatic mechanisms of the parasympathetic nervous system, and cognitive neuroscience, which maps brain activity under fMRI observation. Social psychology as well tells us about unnoticed factors that affect social facilitation or the attribution of emotional meaning to physiological states in response to environmental cues. By conscious psychology I do not mean the explanation of consciousness, which boggles the philosophy of mind. Rather, there are many things that are not subconscious but to which we simply pay no attention because they are negligible for our conscious purposes, for enacting our intentionality. Precisely, what I am concerned with here is *the psychology of purposeful behaviour*: decision making, the pursuit of goals, tactics and strategies, interpersonal relations, negotiations and so forth.

We have already considered numerous examples of purposeful behaviour. Let us now consider the ever-present problem of *dilemma*, which ethics and theology attempt to resolve via the *doctrine of double effect*. It applies to the doctor who can save either the mother or the baby but not both. The doctor asks the next of kin to make the terrible choice and executes their wishes. The doctor may justifiably *intend* to save one, while the loss of the other is ethically excused as an unintended consequence, double effect or byproduct. This is a perfectly conscious decision. Yet this is an idealised case: the doctrine implies that both effects have similar weight. Nevertheless, the doctor may not agree to save the one who has lesser chances of healthy survival. Similarly, if there is any reasonable way to avoid or minimise the loss, the doctor will attempt it. There is an ethical responsibility to do so.

In technology the dilemma of double effect is called *dual use*. Technologies can be used for doing good as well as wrong, but the impact and probability of good must far outweigh the wrongful use, and every effort must be made to avoid or minimise the latter. Intentions are not enough: there must be concrete and convincing evidence of the balance for good and the effectiveness of loss mitigation. Otherwise, development must cease, and the technology must be withheld or withdrawn from the market, something to be enforced by governmental regulatory and consumer protection agencies. This departs from the mother and baby dilemma, because it affects many more people. In war and police raids the dilemma is framed as expedient *collateral damage*, which suggests a dehumanising disregard for someone else's life and property. It recalls Israel's Gaza war in retaliation for the Hamas terrorist attack of 7 October 2023, in which 1,200 innocent Israelis were massacred and 251 taken hostage. A year later, Israel's disproportionate bombing raids had killed 40,000 Palestinians, most of them innocent men, women and children, and destroyed Gaza's infrastructure leaving a secular sequel of trauma, famine and disease. Given no cessation or meaningful mitigation, the International Criminal Court charged both Hamas leaders and Israeli Prime Minister Netanyahu with war crimes (Federman, 2024).

In psychology, many instances of double effect are termed *secondary gains*. The typical example is the case of children and some adults who engage in antisocial or self-defeating behaviour because they crave attention. Secondary gains are usually emotional and contrary to any rational goal. Emotional drive can be extreme, leading some people to pursue illness or engage in self-destructive or aggressive behaviour to relieve feelings of frustration, depression or social isolation. Certainly, psychological secondary effects are not as evident as palpable dual use or collateral damage, but this does not mean that they are unconscious. Rather, they may be unavowed, disguised, ignored or supressed out of feelings of shame. They are recognised when pointed out, which may lead to adamant denial.

Double effects are an integral part of analogue metagrammar. They apply to decision making, planning, goal setting, problem solving, conflict resolution and negotiation. Every decision has a cost in the form of renouncing other alternatives. In such cases we can talk about *secondary losses.* Contrary to digital metagrammar, perfect solutions are rare in human affairs. They run into analogue dilemmas that require compromise, giving rise to the proverbial '80% solution'. Every intention has a counterpart, a built-in devil's advocate. When we give to the poor or do someone a favour, the double effect is that we feel good about ourselves. They call it 'the pleasure of giving'. We also empathise and therefore lend help to relieve our own vicarious pain. This does not mean that there is no such thing as true altruism, as behaviourists proclaim. There is perhaps 80% or so. Neither absolute is true. Most importantly, the secondary effect is conscious because we *feel* it. We don't want to dwell on it or give it the importance of the primary goal because that would bring feelings of shame, hypocrisy and egotism. But the secondary effect is there, making humans contradictory. The key for effective critical thinking and human (analogue) problem solving is not to brush it under the rug but to fully make it part of the equation.

Recognising double effects is the first step in developing goal-oriented strategies. When I experience interpersonal conflict, especially an argument with a loved one, my first instinct is to give free rein to my emotions, to discharge my anger and frustration, to 'get even', get my way, win the argument, whatever it may be. But then I ask myself: What is the *outcome* you really want? The question alone may be enough to reconsider. The legitimate aim is of course for things to be good again, for everyone to be happy, for there to be no hard feelings. Instead of ignoring, I recognise and own up to my secondary motives, and ask myself, what is the right metagrammar, the 'how', the rational and constructive path forward? And only when I *compromise,* have I taken the first step towards true problem solving. Obviously, the answer is to prioritise a lasting solution, instead of a temporary quick fix or a passing emotional impulse. If I can conquer my emotions, I defuse the situation and start working things out right then and there. ('Deal with problems while they are still small'—Lao Tzu.) If not, I take the shortest break possible, enough to calm down and return with a constructive attitude. ('I'm going out to clean the pasture spring; I'll only stop to rake the leaves away and wait to watch the water clear'—Robert Frost.)

Conflict resolution is always a form of negotiation, not too different from buying a car. Buyer and seller know that there are numerous points of negotiation or propositions of value, not only the sales price. Here, double effects are in fact multiple. Some values are expressed, others kept inside like secondary gains or emotional motives behind a poker face. A good negotiator, like a good problem solver, puts herself in everyone else's place, considers all the elements of the problem, all propositions of value for each of the parties and stakeholders. Car buyers are interested in price, terms, resale value, warranty, service, mileage, safety, reliability, features, practicality, aesthetics, prestige and other factors. They discuss priorities and values with their partner and other stakeholders. The dealer is interested in price, terms, paperwork, time invested, form of payment, same day closing, monthly quotas, referrals, extended warranty, premium, options and accessories, buyer preferences and other points of negotiation. The principle of double effect is why negotiations are never a zero-sum game but a win–win proposition. A fair deal is one in which everyone gets something of value, plus an intangible—*good will*—is created and maximised. Zero-sum thinking leads to ill will, bad reputation, getting even next time, recalls and complaints, poor subsequent service, no repeat business, no referrals and a gradual sociopathic distortion of the purported winner's self-image and personality.

Computational-Representational Theory of Mind

It must be emphasised that the Turing machine was never a physical device but an abstract or idealised mathematical model. So is Chomsky's transformational grammar device a hypothetical machine inspired in Turing. However, *grammar is a system for generating meaning*, whereas Chomsky deals only with transformation of *syntax*, *independent of meaning*, hence the title of his book, *Syntactic Structures* (1957). But once inside the book, he slides 'grammar' in substitution for syntax, thus feeding the myth of artificial intelligence. Computer science borrows the term 'syntax' from natural language and takes it *beyond the sentence*, to mean the rule-based (i.e., computable) ordering of symbols regardless their meaning. This ordering is not a grammar but an algorithmic *meta*-syntax.

In this same regard we can establish that digital metagrammar is in fact meaning-free meta-syntax, whereas analogue metagrammar (or simply 'metagrammar' for short) includes (meta)syntax but is also bound to human *meaning*, like grammar itself. To see that these are not mere labels, consider that Halliday's Systemic Functional Grammar (discussed at length in Chapter 6) establishes that every sentence, every utterance, has three inseparable levels of meaning he calls *metafunctions*: ideational, interpersonal and textual. They work together to produce meaning. If we artificially isolate the textual metafunction (syntax) which provides ordering, cohesion and continuity to the other two, we no longer have a language but a notation divorced from meaning. Only in this limited sense can we say that function is the first iteration of meaning (e.g., we see a chair and we give it the *operational definition* 'meant for sitting'). We cannot go beyond that because syntax alone lacks the ideational and interpersonal metafunctions, the representational and referential aspects of natural language meaning.

Hilary Putnam (1967) followed up with machine-state functionalism: 'anything capable of going through a succession of states in time can be a Turing machine' (p. 183). Putnam's Computational Theory of Mind (CTM) hinged on multiple realisability, the idea that the same mental state can be produced by different physical events, such as biological brain events as well as machine processes. This is contrary to metagrammar, which holds that different underlying mechanisms cannot possibly produce the same exact result. For example, the Model T Ford had mechanical brakes operated by cables, while Chrysler introduced hydraulic brakes. They both worked but not the same. Cables applied more pressure to one side causing the Ford to fishtail. Hydraulics applied even pressure for straight braking. Moreover, Putnam's'succession of states' is a discontinuous linear function, a sequence of dashes and dots rather than an unbroken line. The snapshot of one state leads to the next in a causal chain governed by a set of rules of transformation as in a software program. This is of course an *idealised* system that organises static-state snapshots into a single string of meta-syntax, theoretically abstracted out of the complex uninterrupted flow of multisensorial mental images and processes.

Putnam (1975) saw an even deeper problem which led to his 'conversion' and repudiation of CTM. All such approaches were limited by their internalist perspective, sometimes called Chomsky's nativism, the belief in innate cognitive functions independent of outside-world experience. Mental states and transitions purportedly could be conceptualised from within the thinker's mind alone, independent from experience, as a form of computation. Putnam called it 'methodological solipsism': 'grotesquely mistaken views of language which [...] treat cognition as a purely *individual* matter [...] ignore [...] other people and the world; a better science of language must encompass both' (p. 193). Syntactic internalism is defeated by semantic externalism. Putnam realised that the missing element, *meaning*, depends on *representation* and intentional *reference* to things outside the mind. 'The most serious drawback of all this analysis [...] is that it does not concern the meaning of words. [...] [T]he dimension of language associated with the word "meaning" is, in spite of the usual spate of heroic if misguided attempts, as much in the dark as it ever was' (p. 131). Absent meaning, all language models boil down to syntactic play.

Putnam's PhD student, philosopher Jerry Fodor (1977) continued to develop CTM for its practicality but incorporating some form of representation: 'Computation presupposes a medium of computation: a representational system' (p. 27). CTM would depend on a Representational Theory of Mind (RTM): 'The agent finds himself in a certain situation (S) [the initial state] [and] believes that a certain set of behavioural options (B_1, B_2, ... B_n) are available to him in S; [...] The probable consequences of performing each of B_1 through B_n are predicted; [...] A preference ordering is assigned to the consequences. The organism's choice of behaviour is determined as a function of the preferences and the probabilities assigned' (pp. 28–29). Computation, in this utilitarian tradition, reduces thought to a linear calculation of advantage among various options, but at least RTM considers other people and the *environment*, even if meaning is operationally reduced to weighted preferences, probabilities and consequences.

This limited definition of representation was still not meaningful to Putnam: 'operational definitions' are insufficient because meanings are not in the mind, 'meanings are public property' (1975, p. 134). Putnam draws on 'thought experiments' to prove his point. Twin Earth was the first one, a planet in identical state as Our Earth, except that here what we call 'water' refers to H_2O, while there it refers to XYZ (pp. 139–149). Both worlds call 'water' a liquid that looks the same but is not. Something similar could be said about different minds, languages and cultures. Words that have the same denotation or conceptual content (ideational metafunction) can have different connotations and evoke different experiential memories in different people (interpersonal metafunction). 'Every linguistic community exemplifies the sort of division of linguistic labour just described, that is, possesses at least some terms whose associated "criteria" are known only to a subset of the speakers' (p. 146). Meaning is multiple. Contrary to computational equations and logical symbols, it has no one-to-one correspondence.

'An ant is crawling on a patch of sand. As it crawls, it traces a line in the sand. By pure chance [...] it ends up looking like a recognizable caricature of Winston Churchill' (Putnam, 1981, p. 1). Is it a representation? Putnam says no. Representation requires intentional reference to the world outside. *Reference*, an intentional act, is the ultimate key to meaning. Machines cannot generate their own intentions. They must come from outside, generated by human minds. 'The argument is simple; what we said about the ant's curve applies to any physical object [including computers]. No physical object can, in itself, refer to one thing rather than to another [...] Thoughts have the characteristic of intentionality they can refer to something else; nothing physical has "intentionality", save as that intentionality is derivative from some employment of that physical thing by a mind' (p. 2). Putnam doubles down with 'Brains in a vat', a thought experiment that strangely resembles current AI concepts like the brain-computer interface, virtual reality and the metaverse. A perfectly functioning brain has always been immersed in a tub of nourishing fluid and fully wired to a supercomputer that furnishes it with all the sensations of the world identical to those perceived by a normal human being. Putnam argues that it cannot refer to a real 'tree' as we can, but only to a computer-generated image. And when it correctly answers through the computer which is more bitter, an orange or an apple, is there true meaning behind the answer? Referential meaning requires prior knowledge of that which is the subject of reference.

Script Theory and Case-Based Reasoning

Script theory is a further approximation to artificial intelligence based not on the meaning of words but of sentences and stories (scripts). The theory originates with the work on affects (emotional responses) by psychologist Sylvan Tomkins (1979). It suggests that human behaviour follows *patterns* as though scripts that guide our actions to maximise positive affect and minimise negative affect. Tomkins employs the theatre as a mediating metaphor wherein actions follow scripts within a *scene*, understood as a series of events whose experience triggers new affects followed by awareness and response in the form of scripted actions. Affects and response patterns or scripts are classified according to personality criteria and intensity. The theory is used in psychotherapy as well as in personality profiling.

Roger Schanck (1972) adapts scripts to his Conceptual Dependency Theory (CDT) of *natural language understanding*, the true test of artificial intelligence. CDT simplifies sentences, an approach influential in early machine translation, which required the use of Standard Business English to eliminate ambiguities and reduce machine translation errors. In CDT: 'Any information in a sentence that is implicit must be made explicit [...] The meaning propositions underlying language are called conceptualizations [which] can be active [Actor Action Object Direction (instrument)] or stative [Object (is in) State (with Value)]' (Schanck & Abelson, 1977, pp. 11–12). Verbs like 'give, take, go, put' are reduced to their 'primitive element' [**transfer**] which could be physical [**ptrans**], abstract (like possession) [**atrans**] or mental (ideas) [**mtrans**]; the same for other primary verbs like **propel**, **grasp**, **ingest**, **expel**, **build**, **speak**, **attend**, etc. Verbs and nouns are reduced to their simplest *operational definition* within a semi-formalised language. Schanck's scripts are 'causal chains' forming 'ordered memory packets' based on humans having episodic memory, such as 'going to a restaurant'. The memory packet is unpacked into a theatre scene: 'Script: RESTAURANT; Track: Coffee Shop; Props: Tables, Menu, F-Food, Check, Money; Roles: S-Customer, W-Waiter, C-Cook, M-Cashier, O-Owner' (pp. 42–43). The various steps are represented by a notation of *tokens* and arranged in a binary decision tree for computation.

Script theory had limited success in computer applications, although the concept played a role, for example, in customer service chatbots. Its significance lies in providing a line of approach to the interplay between digital and analogue metagrammar as well as an alternative approximation to natural language. Roger Schanck moved beyond it in *Explanation Patterns* (1986), backchaining the script from goal to retroactive explanation as an operant definition of understanding. He converts the Turing Test into an'explanation game' in which the machine must convince the examiner. 'For COGNITIVE UNDERSTANDING, the program must be able to explain why it came to the conclusions it did, what hypotheses it rejected and why, how previous experiences influenced it' (p. 15). Humans, in contrast to computer scripts, project an internalised grammar gestalt, experienced as the insight of understanding; that is, you first have to understand in order to explain, and this is where script theory falls apart. Undeterred, Schanck develops the AI theory that the machine's misapplication of explanation patterns to anomalies and unusual situations may lead to creativity, innovation and problem solving (1986, pp. 140–177). In *The Creative Attitude* (1988), however, he falls in line with C. S. Peirce's abduction and applies this error-correction theory of machine 'creativity' back to the analogue process of human creativity, based on the model: 'Anomaly + Explanation = Creative Thought' (pp. 127–168). He now calls attention to 'the perils of script-based thinking' (p. 71). For all their usefulness in daily life, scripts are rather rigid and can prevent us from finding new solutions to emerging problems.

Schanck's work, modelling human processes to make them computable and then reflecting back to explain human processes, shifted later in his career from machine learning to human learning in the classroom. His best approach to AI and human cognition is Case-Based Reasoning (CBR) (Schanck & Reisbeck, 1989). CBR entails applying past solution patterns to new problems. It works through a '4R' process: **Research** similar problems and their solutions in a memory base of cases and domain knowledge; **Reuse** previous solutions; **Revise** or adapt previous solutions to new cases via simulations; **Retain** the learned validated solution as a new case in memory. 4R as a method applies to analogue human problem solving as much as to machine learning. The relationship between solution patterns in CBR and metagrammar cannot be overstated. The difference is no less edifying. Machine CBR tends to search within a particular expert domain or knowledge base. Human CBR is not so limited as it can search across domains. Biomimetics or the search for human solutions by imitating natural forms is a common practice and example. Machine CBR is an idealisation (or formalisation) of human CBR. The difference is the subject of Putnam's caveat: 'It is only when we mistake operational definition for more than convenient idealisation that it becomes harmful' (1975, p. 171).

While Putnam raises the objections of *meaning* and *referentiality*, John Searle (1980) focuses on *intentionality*: 'Any attempt literally to create intentionality artificially (strong AI) could not succeed just by designing programs but would have to duplicate the causal powers of the human brain'. As to the claims that machines can literally understand the story and explain how humans understand it, Searle retorts: 'Both claims seem to me to be totally unsupported by Schanck's work' (p. 417). Searle uses his notorious Chinese Room thought experiment to demonstrate it. To recall, a man in a closed room receives pieces of paper under the door with enigmatic characters that unbeknown to him happen to be questions in Chinese, a language he does not understand. However, by following a manual blindly step by step, he is able to trace characters on a piece of paper and pass it back under the door. The people outside see that these are answers to their questions and mistakenly believe that the man inside understands Chinese. There is no more intentionality than in the ant's sketch of Winston Churchill.

Conclusion

Analogue (grammar-based) problem solving and its digital or mechanical (math-based) counterpart are different but complementary methods. Digital metagrammar is used for the formalisation and validation of theory. Analogue metagrammar comes to bear on its application, wherein the principle of double effect, as in all human affairs, is, so to speak, part of the 'equation'. This principle suggests that meaning, motives and goals are not singular but a fluid network of continually negotiated relative values imparted via natural language. Metagrammar holds that human cognition of natural and social patterns is grammatically encrypted in language, and so are the solutions we devise and apply in the world outside, projections of internalised grammatical patterns. As such, grammatical mediation facilitates human pattern recognition and transfer across domains. The insight of a grammatical pattern or procedural gestalt may be transposed from previous experience and generalised as a pattern for future solutions.

References

Federman, J. (2024, May 20). War crimes prosecutor seeks arrest of Israeli and Hamas leaders, including Netanyahu. *Associated Press World News*. Retrieved from https://apnews.com/article/icc-khan-netanyahu-070941d21ccd1f2b9611032b88527575

Fodor, J. (2001). *The Mind Doesn't Work That Way: The Scope and Limits of Computational Psychology*. MIT Press. Retrieved from https://archive.org/details/minddoesntworkth00camb/page/n3/mode/2up?view=theater

Köhler, W. (1917). *Intelligenzprüfungen an Anthropoiden.* Royal Prussian Society of Sciences. *The Mentality of Apes*. Translated by E. Winter. Routledge, 2019.

Kuhn, T. S. (1962). *The Structure of Scientific Revolutions*. University of Chicago Press.

Larson, E. (2021). *The Myth of Artificial Intelligence: Why Computers Can't Think the Way We Do*. Harvard University Press.

Neuronswaves Lab (2024). *Critical Thinking, Logic & Problem Solving*. Neuronswaves.
Piętka, D. (2015). The concept of intuition and its role in Plato and Aristotle. *Organon, 47*, 23–40.
Putnam, H. (1967). The mental life of some machines. In H.-N. Castañeda (Ed.), *Intentionality, Minds, and Perception* (pp. 177–200). Wayne State University Press.
Putnam, H. (1975). The meaning of 'meaning'. *Minnesota Studies in the Philosophy of Science, 7*, 131–193.
Putnam, H. (1981). Brains in a vat. *Reason, Truth and History* (pp. 1–21). Cambridge University Press.
Schanck, R. C. (1972). Conceptual dependency: a theory of natural language understanding. *Cognitive Psychology, 3*(4), 552–631.
Schanck, R. C. (1986). *Explanation Patterns: Understanding Mechanically and Creatively*. Lawrence Erlbaum Associates.
Schanck, R. C., & Abelson, R. (1977). *Scripts, Plans, Goals and Understanding: An Inquiry into Human Knowledge Structures*. Lawrence Erlbaum Associates.
Schanck, R., & Childers, P. (1988). *The Creative Attitude: Learning to Ask and Answer the Right Questions*. Macmillan.
Schanck, R. C., & Riesbeck, C. K. (1989). *Inside Case-Based Reasoning*. Lawrence Erlbaum Associates.
Searle, J. R. (1980). Minds, brains and programs. *Behavioral and Brain Sciences, 3*(3), 417–457.
Tomkins, S. (1979). Script theory: differential magnification of affects. In R. A. Deinstbier (Ed.), *Nebraska Symposium on Motivation 1978* (pp. 201–236). University of Nebraska Press.
Vitello, M., & Salvi, C. (2023). Gestalt's perspective on insight: a recap based on recent behavioral and neuroscientific evidence. *Journal of Intelligence, 11*(224), 1–10. Retrieved from https://doi.org/10.3390/jintelligence11120224
Wertheimer, M. (1945). *Productive Thinking*. Harper.

15

The Parasitic Age

Introduction

Machines have always been parasitic on humans, and computers increasingly so. Historically, artisans made tools and products by hand after developing *mastery* through years of apprenticeship and experience in traditional trades. Crafted tools and machines facilitated physical labour more than replaced it. Master trades then came together in organised manufacturing. Gradually, the craftsman's skill was 'built into the machine' and replaced 'to produce uniform and interchangeable parts' through *standardisation* (Stevens, 1995, pp. 10–29). Mass production marked the end of mastery, turning the artisan into a replaceable worker, another interchangeable part of the machine.

In 1765, James Watt improved the lever steam engine by having it rotate a shaft. Its multiple applications ignited the Industrial Revolution (c. 1760–1840). There followed steel foundries, the internal combustion engine and the electric motor, powering the entire era of analogue invention that lasted until the computer age. The Age of Invention (c. 1840–1950) was marked, especially in the United States, by an explosion of patents for the application of traditional mechanics and

E. Camayd-Freixas, *Metagrammar*, https://doi.org/10.1007/978-3-031-92337-1_15

new core inventions to suit the widest range of human needs: locomotion (railroads, ships, bicycles, cars, trucks, airplanes), work and home (manual and power tools, lighting, refrigeration, appliances), communication (telegraph, telephone, radio, television) and many others. This unprecedented period of innovation and problem solving called 'The Golden Age of Invention' coincided with an era of high literacy, in which classics and comparative grammar were a central part of education. The resulting grammatical proficiency correlates with achievement, pattern and skills transfer, innovative metagrammar and general intelligence (see Chapter 5).

The present Information Age may be divided into overlapping phases: the Digital Revolution (c. 1950–1990), the rise of the World Wide Web (c. 1989–2005), the rise of gaming and social media (c. 2005–2020) and the Age of Generative AI (c. 2020–). The Digital Revolution is marked by the parasitic translation (rather than innovation) of earlier mechanical and analogue solutions. In this sense, digital metagrammar is parasitic on analogue metagrammar, whose mechanical devices still mimicked and replaced human labour, although to a much lesser extent. Digitalisation allowed for mathematical manipulation, increased storage capacity, searchable databases and fast data transmission. Analogue technical drawing had always made use of geometry and mathematical measurement, which were later digitised. Manual machining was replaced by mechanical machining, then by punched tape programmed automation, computer numerical control (CNC), precision robotics, software integration, Internet of Things (IoT) and machine learning—all parasitic on the master craftsmen they replaced. Analogue standardisation became digital interoperability, enabling Application Programming Interface (API). Data centres are outgrowing the power grid and building their own nuclear power plants.

The World Wide Web led to Big Data, extracted from human hosts now called *users* (much like drug addicts). Gaming, social media, search engines and other Internet platforms exploit this raw material via obscure algorithms, crowdsourcing and machine learning, augmented by artificial intelligence, while analogue machines appropriated manual skills, and expert computer systems appropriated technical knowledge, generative AI appropriates and mechanises intellectual abilities via the ultimate parasitism: *automated human datamining and decision making*. A fundamental relationship has been reversed. Throughout history, humans have used machines as tools. Now humans are the tools of the machines.

Human Datamining

Zuboff (2019) defined *Surveillance Capitalism* as 'a parasitic economic logic' based on the free extraction of human data for behaviour modification, prediction and sales, leading to an unprecedented concentration of wealth. According to Metcalf's law, the commercial value of a communications network is proportional to the square of the number of users. The hooks are 'free to users' and *convenience* in exchange for privacy and free behavioural data. The economic model is a virtual mega factory that prompts users to render interactive behaviour, their reaction being run through data analytics for the stated purpose of returning service improvements. In the dark background, however, they extract much more. The millions of A/B-tested adaptations to improve 'user experience' refine psychological tactics of persuasion and addiction designed to keep the audience captive, extract more data and maximise *reach*, *engagement* and *conversion* (purchasing) to boost sales and advertising revenues. Vast amounts of 'surplus' behavioural data are deep processed for behaviour modification and prediction products, which drive the value of the processed data. The platform sells advertisements and prediction products, while surplus behavioural data is sold or licensed to third parties. Most of the surveillance revenue is pure profit. A smaller part covers operation costs to keep the virtual machinery going (pp. 63–97). The combination of high output and low cost is due to free data, automation, inexpensive reproduction, viral propagation and the lack of friction in data transmission compared to physical materials handling. In a few short years, global tech players like Amazon, Apple, Facebook, Google and Microsoft became the world's most profitable companies and the most valuable in terms of market capitalisation.

Analogue automation replaced repetitive physical labour. Digital automation replaced repetitive office labour. Artificial intelligence replaces higher intellectual labour, culminating in *automated decision making*. As expected, all kinds of social biases, stereotypes and prejudices are reflected in the data, codified, perpetuated and *hidden* by algorithmic masking. This has a devastating effect on minorities and the less privileged by curtailing housing, education and employment opportunities while slashing public benefits (Eubanks, 2019). Crime prediction software is but a minute instance of current grand-scale profiling. Automated datamining, prediction and decision making are the functions of AI algorithms. They run Bayesian statistics on Big Data to rank variables according to their impact on target outcomes; they decide who gets filtered out and who gets hired, monitored, promoted and fired (Schellmann, 2024). This unnatural selection governs access to rentals, mortgages, credit, insurance and higher education. The more vulnerable are subjected to high-interest predatory loans and ominous credit card debt. The 'striving (and more easily cheated) underclass' is targeted by dubious yet highly profitable online 'universities' (the modern version of degrees-by-mail) which mass produce diplomas of 'scant value in the workplace' (O'Neil, 2016, p. 69). The more desperate fall prey to all kinds of online scams.

Nevertheless, surveillance capitalism; impersonal profiling; the advertising avalanche; the propaganda machinery; the message overload; the barrage of robocalls, spam, phishing, pings and notifications; and above all the *false socialisation* and the distorted *artificial reality* created online affect us all and tears at the fabric of society. *Numerical technology has taken over the fundamental metafunctions of natural language grammar*, which we saw in Chapter 6: to *construe reality*, *structure our actions* and *enact our social interactions*. Now its algorithms control perception, behaviour and interaction, based on a non-human, *unnatural metagrammar*.

Employees on the job can expect to be monitored, more than by cameras, by performance metrics dictated by technology in terms of those variables that can be captured and quantised as data, regardless their relevance to the quality of our work. Broad sectors of service and knowledge jobs, even at universities, are turned into stressful metrics-driven sweatshops. This stress, together with data-entry and message overload (reporting apps, work emails, voicemail, videocalls, instant messaging, texts, chatrooms) have decimated productivity, job satisfaction and quality of life. *Technology, mechanisation and automation all benefit institutions at the expense of individuals*. Instead of bringing people together, false socialisation, work at home and artificial reality immersion have created an epidemic of loneliness and alienation, aggravated at work by algorithmic opacity (Vrendenburgh, 2022). Teenage depression and suicide have exploded. Screentime has increased, while personal engagement and real-world activities have declined. Smartphone addiction causes countless texting-and-driving accidents and deaths. Technology erodes family life, sleep, health and happiness (Wadhwa & Salkever, 2018).

The extent of human datamining cannot be overstated. 'Essentially every action we take in public and online leaves a trail of data for someone to capture. Most of that data eventually gets bought, sold, or traded. The result is that data voodoo dolls exist for each of us, even if we never use internet platforms' (McNamee, 2020, p. 303). *Digital voodoo dolls* are complex, high-fidelity AI-generated person-specific models that contain anything from shoe size to personality traits, estimated propensities and vulnerabilities including emotional stability (Slavkovik et al., 2021). They are created from the screen inputs of a multitude of people, categorised and assembled into a training dataset fed to a prediction model that generates voodoo doll *types*. Then a repeating triangulation ensues, whereby tailored voodoo-doll prompts are presented to you; your subsequent screen inputs are fed back into the prediction model, which perfects your voodoo doll, making it increasingly accurate over thousands of iterations.

Self-identification from activities and affiliations increases with your social network. Stop by the ATM, use a credit card, carry a smartphone, travel by air, road or foot, go online and your activities and affiliations are being tracked. Talk about a blender, and the next time your friend takes his phone out of his pocket an ad pops up. Be in the neighbourhood at dinner time, and a notification might ping for a recommended restaurant. Companies like Google, Yahoo! and Microsoft scan your emails and attachments. WhatsApp and LinkedIn tap your phonebook and contacts. Facebook taps your friends and tracks you on and off the site. It even tracks non-members through third-party inputs. Go to any of the million partner websites that provide sign-in using your Facebook or Google account, and you will be double-tracked. Social media platforms are by far the biggest data blackholes, and they frequently share data. Facebook (now Meta) acquired WhatsApp, Instagram and close to one hundred other platforms, consolidating its monopoly position and combining user data. Google acquired YouTube, Motorola Mobile with Android, DoubleClick, Waze, Fitbit and over 250 other platforms. Microsoft produced Xbox and acquired Skype, Nokia, LinkedIn, Activision Blizzard and over 270 other companies. Apple abstains from tracking and remains the most ethical of the Big Tech companies, although its devices and wearables are enormous data ports.

The Emotional AI Lab, directed by Andrew McStay, studies the social impact of AI-read emotional biometrics of human-state changes in response to automated empathy. Emotional AI refers to technologies that sense, analyse and interact with human emotional states. They 'aim to read and react to emotions through text, voice, computer vision, biometric sensing and, potentially, information about a person's context'. The technology is expected to interface with a person's datapoint profile, enhancing their digital voodoo doll with emotional content. The Lab acts as a watchdog that scrutinises technology development and roll out, from social, cultural, legal and ethical perspectives. Identified human datamining methods include mood and *sentiment analysis* of online language, text, emojis, images and video, processed by *large language models* to deepen human-system interaction; *facial coding of expressions* (including pupil dilation) through face recognition of live camera feed, photo, video recording and streaming; *voice analytics*; *eye tracking*; camera tracking of body language; *gesture, behaviour and internal physiology* tracking, such as remote heart rate sensing. *Wearables* transmit skin responses, muscle, breathing, heart and brain activity. *Virtual Reality* (VR) allows remote viewing and tracking of the wearer's experience and reactions. Headwear may contain EEG and face muscle sensors. *Augmented Reality* (AR) allows remote tracking of attention, reactions and interaction with digital objects (Emotional AI Lab, 2024; italics in the original). Bias and error in machine reading may be even more damaging than accuracy.

The Addiction Triangle

Automated empathy is not a good thing. It is used to manipulate your emotions and behaviour for profit or political gain and hold you hostage to a program, agenda or ideology. I call 'addiction triangle' the simple but powerful metagrammar behind automated empathy. Triangular trade is a mark of imperial domination and colonial exploitation. The Molasses Triangle is a classic example. Colonial New England traded rum to West Africa for slaves destined for sugarcane plantations in the Caribbean, while the 'Sugar Islands' sent molasses back to Boston to be distilled into rum. Southern American colonies sent cotton and tobacco to England, which sent textiles to West Africa for slaves destined for Virginia. With American supply, the British East India Company converted Indian plantations from cotton to opium, mixed it with tobacco, which boosted consumption and addiction, and sent it to China in exchange for tea, silk and other commodities. In dependency theory, colonial relationships of dependent domination, marked by Hegel's master/slave dialectics, also exist within countries (factory/worker), communities (landlord/tenant), households (lord/servant) and indeed families. What about technology/user? Can our minds be dominated and colonised? Can we become tech addicted? Of course. These are rhetorical questions. Here is how.

A lab mouse had electrodes inserted in the pleasure centre of the brain, stimulated by a lever, inside an operant conditioning chamber or 'Skinner Box'—in honour of the Father of Behaviourism. The white mouse discovered that pressing the lever several times would stimulate its pleasure centre. Gradually, the mouse lost interest in the other lever which delivered food pellets, as well as in the watering pipe, with the impactful result that the poor rodent pressed the addictive lever to death. This happens to humans too. Operant conditioning does not entail substance abuse, but rather behavioural addiction, inability to stop despite harmful consequences. Granted, humans are more complicated than mice, more aware of what they are doing, so conditioning must be more refined. In this case, the 'lever' is a stimulus or prompt that hits the drive for survival, an evolutionary adaptation deeply ingrained in our cerebellum or primitive brain. When the mouse was rewarded every time (continuous reinforcement schedule), and the rewards suddenly stopped, it was not long before the mouse stopped pressing the lever (the behaviour was extinguished). When a reward was given for pressing the lever a fixed number of times (fixed-ratio schedule), the behaviour lasted longer, but when the number of times was unpredictable (variable-ratio schedule), the behaviour lasted the longest. Variable reward schedules are highly addictive. Casino slot machines are based on this model. Now, suppose there is a delay (interval) between pressing the lever and getting the reward. This multiplies the addictive effect even if it is a fixed interval, but a variable-ratio variable-interval reinforcement schedule is so powerful as to be morbidly addictive. The gambling addict not only finds it difficult to tear away from the slot machine, card or roulette table due to variable-ratio wins, but winning some nights (at variable intervals) keeps him coming back until his life is ruined. Technology works the same way, and when combined with AI automated empathy, repeated A/B testing optimising every pixel and the use of machine learning in RLHF (Reinforcement Learning from Human Feedback) to align AI agents with human preferences, the result is a weapon-grade persuasion technology for behaviour modification.

I insist on the addiction triangle model to debunk the false representation of a 'feedback loop' fabricated by technologists. Loops and curves are analogue figures, digitised only by discontinuous sampling of discrete coordinates. The term 'feedback' comes to us from electronics, when an output signal returns as an input. If the input signal is in phase with the output, it is positive feedback; if it is out of phase, it is negative feedback. So far so good, but when the concept is metaphorically extended to any self-regulating mechanism, it proves to be triangular feedback. In persuasive technology, it starts with (i) a prompt or *stimulus*, followed by (ii) an impact *measurement* (the distance between the user's response and the desired behaviour), leading to (iii) an *adjustment* of the stimulus sent again to the user to reduce the distance to the target state. The same triangle applies to biological evolution: mutation, adaptation, procreation—the survival imperative.

In conjunction with the addiction triangle, let us consider the *survival tree*, which has three primal branches or drives: *food*, *reproduction* and *preservation.* Studies show that smartphones are associated with food and sex (Hayes, 2017). Social media addiction is further associated with *reproduction* as self-propagation. Disclosing our thoughts and feelings on social media 'engages neural and cognitive mechanisms associated with reward. Five studies provided support for this hypothesis. Self-disclosure was strongly associated with increased activation in brain regions that form the mesolimbic dopamine system' (Tamir & Mitchell, 2017). When it comes to *food*, humans are primally hunter-gatherers and labourers. Online shopping, bargain hunting, surfing the web, making money, all satisfy this drive and reward us with dopamine. So does *preservation*, which branches out into the flight (fear) or fight (anger) response. *Fear* inclines individuals to flee to safety-in-numbers and join a group, where fighting an 'enemy' or scapegoat becomes a common cause that facilitates the spread of *anger* in a crowd, while anonymity and mutual encouragement facilitate aggressive or *violent rhetoric and action*. This is especially easy online, where aggressors do not see their enemies or the real-life impact of their posts. Anonymity further compounds the online *disinhibition effect*. Cyberspace creates a buffering bubble, a fish-bowl illusion that dissociates the abstract online environment from its concrete consequences. Social media platforms exploit this by providing viral propagation through member groups, networks and nodes designed to increase the userbase, keep users returning and engaged to maximise their screentime. In sum, the key triggers of propaganda are sex, food, violence, fear and anger.

In 'How Technology is Hijacking Your Mind' (2016), former Google design ethicist and founder of the Center for Humane Technology (https://www.humanetech.com) Tristan Harris enumerates some of the tactics by which platform designers exploit our perceptual and psychological vulnerabilities. (1) They control our choices by **limiting menu options** to those which take us down rabbit holes optimised for them. (2) They design phones, apps and platforms following **slot machines**, with addictive variable rewards to stimulate dopamine secretion. This gets the average person to check their phone 150 times a day. I would add what I call the *tabloid effect*, the sensationalism of propaganda built into the arousing sights, sounds and pyrotechnics of slot machines, videogames, thumbnails, apps and devices. (3) They manipulate FOMO, the **fear of missing out** on a potential reward or on something related to our survival tree. (4) They exploit our need for **social approval** by controlling *likes, shares, tags, views, comments* and *follows.* Platforms like Facebook, Instagram and Snapchat promote this by automatically suggesting what posts and people to reward via 1-click buttons. (5) They capitalise on our sense of obligation and need for **social reciprocity**, to follow our followers and return their approvals. '*Email, texting and messaging apps are social reciprocity factories*'—says Harris. LinkedIn is designed to create social obligations like 'accepting a connection, responding to a message, or endorsing someone back for a skill'. They exploit our impulse to add a person or accept a connection by prompting us with an endless list of contacts shared by others in our network and showing their affiliation and competitive number of contacts as a sign of popularity or importance. This creates the illusion and allure of online social climbing. Companies cash in by ensnaring millions of people into a click-obligation-reciprocity triangle. (6) YouTube, Netflix, Instagram, TikTok, Spotify, even online news sites use **infinite feeds** and **autoplay** to keep us scrolling or watching. (7) **Instant interruptions** are more persuasive at getting people to respond and dispose of the urgency than asynchronous or delayed deliveries via email or inbox. Facebook Messenger, WhatsApp, Snapchat and others are designed to interrupt users with notifications, pop-ups and chat boxes. (8) Platforms **bundle our reasons with theirs**: '*Facebook wants to convert every reason you have for using Facebook, into their reason which is to maximize the time you spend consuming things*'. (9) Platforms present us with **inconvenient choices** that make it difficult to unsubscribe, cancel or uninstall, but make the choices they want easy. The pursuit of engagement and screentime has changed business aims from delivering goods and services to *engineering experiences* (Schüll, 2014, p. 53).

Internet and Technology Addicts Anonymous (ITAA, 2024) offers resources and virtual meetings worldwide in several languages, as well as local in-person meetings to help with tech addiction. Internet Addiction Disorder has long been identified as akin to Pathological Gambling (Young, 1998, p. 237). The American Psychiatric Association and the World Health Organization have included Internet Gaming Disorder in their diagnostic manuals, DSM-5-TR and ICD-11. The signs are the same as those of other Internet addictions: preoccupation with gaming, withdrawal symptoms (sadness, anxiety, irritability, sense of isolation, emotional absence), building tolerance, inability to reduce or quit, loss of interest in other activities, continuing despite problems, hiding or deceiving others about screentime, recurrent use to relieve negative moods (guilt, hopelessness) and risk or loss of a job or relationship. Dopamine triggered by Internet and technology addiction has been shown to cause structural changes in the brain like those produced by substance abuse, leading to impairments in decision making, reasoning, cognitive and executive function, short-term memory, reward expectation, emotional processing and impulse control. Tech addition is associated with attention deficit hyperactivity disorder (ADHD), anxiety, increased substance abuse, depression and suicidal ideation or actions (Solly et al., 2021). ITAA identifies addictions to streaming, phone, videogames, porn and information consumption or compulsive online research. Generative AI addiction is newly recognised (Eliot, 2024; Mahari & Pataranutaporn, 2024).

The collective impact is profound even for moderate users. The loss of productivity from idle screentime is massive. Millions waste their efforts chasing unrealistic expectations and vying for attention in the crowded online space, lured by the success of a few influencers and YouTubers, into a posting frenzy, a lottery-like addiction. Online platforms suck the economic blood of individuals, families, communities, countries and the globe. Data is the new oil, and users the new merchandise. The global addiction triangle fuels hyper-consumption (Stacey, 2024). Cheap labour from poor countries and communities churns out excess production to feed the hyperbolic consumption of the Internet Age. Products are disposable, single use, non-repairable and short lasting, following the manufacturing principle of calculated *planned obsolescence*. It is more profitable to push new products than to store and discount the old ones. This results in industrial, merchandising and individual dumping at a grand scale, meaning millions of tonnes of trash to be buried or burned every year, including toxic waste that sips into the ground, water and air. Thousands of shiploads of discarded electronics, unusable clothing, home goods and non-recyclable plastics are dumped back to cash-strapped countries in Asia, Africa and Latin America, completing the triangle of cheap labour, hyper-consumption and cheap dumping.

Digital Forgery

It all started innocently when the artful craft of film photography and retouching was replaced by digital imaging, and Adobe Photoshop fixed our pictures and removed red eye. Goodbye Kodachrome. With a digital camera, later integrated into the iPhone, we all became photographers taking hundreds of bad pictures to choose a few good ones without wasting any film. Once again, mastery was built into the machine. Digital images filled the Internet, downloadable for free or by subscription to databases like Getty or Shutterstock. They could also be shared online. That is how Facebook started from a Harvard dorm room, posting pairs of headshots downloaded from the school's online directories and letting users choose who was the 'hotter' person. Yet a new craft sprung from digital imaging and word processing, enabling a professional class of desktop publishers, graphic artists, designers and publicists. That was until *their* mastery was built into computer-generated imaging (CGI) and Gen AI, which now replace them.

The analogue original was replaced by the digital copy, and the copy was massively reproduced for profit, both in print and more so by online distribution. This brings back Walter Benjamin's *The Work of Art in the Age of Mechanical Reproduction* (1935). At the time, mechanical reproduction meant photography, film, printing or mould casting. Benjamin holds that the 'aura' of a work of art, its authenticity and cultural power are lost in reproduction. Such is the difference between the Mona Lisa and a forgery, poster or digital image. There is a value-annulling disconnect between the artefact and the hand of the original artist. Mastery gets lost in reproduction. Digital copying recalls Plato's argument about the copy of a copy being twice removed from the truth. CGI and Gen AI further blur the distinction among digital reproduction, forgery and fraud.

AI voice cloning, now widely available, is increasingly used for scams and extorsion. A scammer captures a few seconds of your voice from social media, voicemail or by calling and recording you. Your voice sample is run through a voice cloning app and within seconds, everything the scammer types or says comes out in your voice. He calls a loved one, fakes an emergency with your voice and asks for money to be wired via Zelle or payment app to a temporary account that will be closed once the money is withdrawn. Worse, they can claim you have been kidnapped and ask for a sizable ransom. Starling Bank says millions could be targeted and encourages loved ones to agree on a 'safe phrase' for identification (Cooban, 2024). The Federal Trade Commission reports that scams involving business imposters have risen to almost $1 billion USD per year (Saeidi, 2024).

Easily available AI nude-generator websites and CGI phone apps that enable pasting faces from social media onto naked bodies are used for sextortion and even child pornography. In some versions, they threat with public humiliation, demanding explicit photos, sexual favours or money. Automated sextortion emails have caught the attention of authorities (New York State Police, 2024). Scammers buy emails and personal information on the dark web to contact victims with claims that they have installed cyberstalking spyware like Pegasus on their phone or computer and have compromising images, often attaching a photo of the victim's home pulled from Google Maps. They demand payment in Bitcoin to avoid detection. The FBI encourages victims to report incidents to its Internet Crime Complaint Center via www.ic3.gov or 1-800-CALL-FBI. The dark web is an international marketplace for fraud and money laundering, accessible through special software. There, criminals sell personal and financial information as well as illicit services like sex trafficking or murder-for-hire which may also be scams. They send phishing emails en masse and clone official websites where victims enter personal and financial information. Visiting an unsafe website or downloading an infected file allows them to install malware to steal data from a computer and track the user when filling online forms. Cybercrime continuously morphs with technology. Thousands of unsuspecting people are lured by computer job offers and paid trips only to be trafficked by organised crime and enslaved in labour camps, forced to conduct phone and online scamming (Bernard, 2024; Qian, 2023).

Catfishing is a form of trolling scam that involves the creation of a fake identity on Facebook and other social media platforms that have lax account verification. It may start through phishing on social media or sometimes on dating sites where perpetrators (catfish) post fake photos and lie about themselves to start an online relationship that extends to social media, email and dozens of instant messaging apps, from WhatsApp to Snapchat or the cross-platform Telegram. Catfish may enhance their own identity, create a new one or impersonate someone else. The fictitious persona appears deceptively attractive, exciting, wealthy, professional, well connected and trustworthy to ensnare the victim. Motivations include stringing the mark along into a romantic (love bombing), social or financial relationship, stealing personal information and identities, evading legal or criminal exposure, sexual predation, influence and social engineering, malicious trolling for power and abusive control, as well as personal satisfaction and amusement. Often lives are ruined, and victims feel violated. Catfishing has been linked to several suicides and has been used to lure victims to dangerous meetings leading to robbery, rape and murder. Whether damaging or benign, the practice has become so common as to inspire several movies, TV shows and documentaries.

'*Seeing is no longer believing*' is one tech company's tagline. CGI, a product of the videogame industry, combined with face recognition, voice cloning and generative AI, has given us deepfakes which can hardly be discerned from reality. Deepfake videos can make any politician or public figure appear to say or do anything. We have reached the age of AI disinformation. Generations have been addicted to videogames, developed tolerance (demanding ever more realistic imaging) and have been exploited through parasitic crowdsourcing to bring us deepfakes. We can now see it as a *parasitic addiction triangle*. All addiction is in fact parasitic. Online videogames also capture user metrics to make gaming more engaging and addictive. Visual and sound effects, fast action, gory combat violence, sexualised content and optimised empathy have moved onto the TV screen's repeated plots of violence, injury and vengeance, normalised also in real life and made part of the culture through desensitisation, tolerance building and craving. On the softer side, AI-CGI technology can make famous actors look young again and can even create virtual actors, commercials and entire movies via *digital puppetry* and AI text-to-image world-generator models, while ChatGPT writes empathy-optimised scripts. The aura, mastery, authenticity, heart and soul of the human actor will be lost in reproduction.

Memes and Disinformation

Disinformation started as and remains, among other things, a form of entertainment. In Japan, *manga* illustration and animation inspired the *anime* boom. Enthusiasts were drawn to *otaku* subculture, obsessed with comics, anime, videogames, computers and sci-fi. In 1999, Hiroyuki Nichimura launched 2channel, an online imageboard dedicated to anime. In the highly regimented Japanese society, otaku found in 2channel a liberating outlet for their countercultural eccentricities, satire, mockery, fanciful stories and speaking their mind without fear of judgement. Their posts became filled with anime images and video-clips competing for attention and comments based on their subversive humour and shocking entertainment value. These cartoonish, composite pop images with captions were the precursors of Internet memes.

The tone of revenge of the nerds, rejects and misfits, fostered an outcast identity. As users became socially withdrawn, immersed and addicted, posts turned more outrageous, depicting anime violence and sex. They developed tolerance which required greater excitement. Not satisfied with their online pranks, they started pushing members to enact them as extreme behaviour and vandalism in the real world, attacking buses and people. Soon 2channel became politicised. The long economic downturn after the 1991 bubble burst had brought hardship to many people who felt left out and disenchanted with Japanese democracy, as well as resentful of the foreign influence of South Korean K-pop. They formed the ultranationalist Net Right which virtually overran 2channel, turning otaku into *neto-uyo*, far-right netizens (Internet citizens) emboldened by interacting only among themselves, cut off from the rest of society. Net Right shares nationalist views with Western far-right populism and the alt-right, such as imperial and authoritarian nostalgia, historical revisionism, rejection of immigrants and minorities, distrust of mainstream media, anti-elitism, anti-Establishment and anti-Chinese sentiment. They became allies of Trumpism and attempted to influence the 2020 elections with disinformation posts like 'former President Obama arrested' (Kurayama, 2020).

The key is that 2channel was the first totally *anonymous* website, a fertile ground for radicalisation and hate speech without repercussions.

The Japanese experience was repeated in the West. In 2003, a 15-year-old Christopher Poole aka 'Moot' downloaded the 2channel code and relaunched it in English as 4chan, which grew quickly due to the accessibility of English and the international cult of anime and Pokémon. Users created their own online world communicating with peers worldwide. Those with social anxiety, avoiding problems at home, unpopular in school, eventually jobless, disconnected or feeling outcast from society built an uncensored Internet persona complete with an anonymous codename and avatar, often the opposite of their real-life selves. Most others simply did so for fun. Kids who grew up with the Internet soon became voting adults, primed for influencing.

The 4chan format (image, captions, comment and discussion threads) developed into *the precursor of social media* as we know it. The site added more bandwidth, crazy GIFs and videoclips and became known for its creation of *internet memes*. 4chan videos of kids pulling stunts became staple memes on YouTube. Their posts turned viral when they jumped to corporate social media like Facebook, Twitter and Reddit. Founded by college roommates in 2005, Reddit, a news aggregator social network, where channers and others post news on their boards and rate them for popularity, was bought in October 2006 by Condé Nast as a subsidiary of Advance Publications. Sites like 4chan remained grassroot resource-starved operations, but the Reddit user-generated news platform skyrocketed to become publicly traded in 2024 at a $10 billion valuation. Powered by corporate platforms, Internet memes became the main vehicle for spearheading disinformation.

Further, 4channers developed hacking and trolling techniques that became standard. One of those is the bait-and-switch tactic of 'rickrolling', disguising a hyperlink behind another. They applied it to high traffic weblinks, which when clicked redirected to a 1987 MTV video of a manicured Rick Astley singing 'Never Gonna Give You Up', uploaded to YouTube in 2009. It was a quirky video with a silly dance move, but it was the lyrics 'Never gonna stop' that fit the bill. Once rickrolled, the video repeated incessantly, and the only way to get out was by restarting your computer. Rickrolling turned that video into a meme and bumped it to 1.5 billion views. The prank became a hacking technique, but also confirmed the power of collective online action. YouTubers discovered that using sexy or outrageous bait-and-switch thumbnails pushed the views of their unrelated videos. In early January 2021, rickrolling jumped out onto the real world when it morphed into *meme stocks* promoted on social media. A Reddit group, heirs of 4chan culture, inflated the battered stocks of iconic GameStop and AMC movie theatres, creating a short squeeze where short sellers and brokerage firms had to keep buying at higher and higher prices. In less than a month, by 28 January, GameStop shares had skyrocketed to 30 times their value, before plummeting again. Fortunes were made and lost, and the meme-stock saga continued.

Memes are symbolic cultural packets that spread through imitation. The term comes from the same Greek root as mimetic and mimicry combined with the suffix *eme* to indicate the smallest linguistic constituent, as in phoneme, morpheme, grapheme, lexeme and tagmeme. It is a linguomental unit packed with cultural meaning. The term was coined by biologist Richard Dawkins in *The Selfish Gene* (1976). Since then, it has been conceptualised via the mediating metaphor of biologic evolution as *self-replicating*, like a virus or a gene. They propagate, mutate and are subject to natural selection. Their survival depends on their continued propagation, itself dependent on their ability to morph and adapt. The Darwinian principle continues to apply to Internet platforms. 4chan posts were ephemeral, short lasting, to reduce storage space, a model adopted by Instagram and TikTok. Those which received more comments were bumped to the top; others would fall and die out. The same criterion influences the ranking of Google search results. Despite their short life, 4chan posts cascaded so quickly that they created a constant flow of new content and rolling images that hooked viewers into *endless scrolling*, the basis of all social media.

The Antisocial Network (Jones & Angelini, 2024) documents the historical metagrammar that goes from 4chan to the present disinformation crisis. Historical metagrammar identifies those landmark moments, inflections and turning points which form a causal chain of articulated events that explains how things came to be. Initially 4chan had a single board for anime and videogames. Several boards were later created for different interests, including politics, thus segmenting their userbase into groups and allowing users to find their tribe. Boards had a permissive moderator who only blocked illegal content, like child pornography.

Everything else was uncensored and anonymous. The site had no user registration or verification, and anyone could post anything at any time. Inevitably it took a life of its own and devolved along the same path as 2channel but magnified by their sheer growth. Jokes turned into pranks, then into trolling. When channers tapped into the immense networks and engagement tactics of corporate social media, their memes and style acquired enormous influence, changing social media itself, followed by mainstream media, pop culture, public discourse and even fashion.

Otaku culture first moved into the real world by holding conventions where people came dressed as anime and comics characters and later as 4chan memes. At the first Otakon anime convention held in Baltimore in 2005, 4chan held its first panel where Moot appeared in person for the first time and reported that the site was receiving three million pages a day. This innocent stage changed as users started trolling people and organising collective pranks called Raids. Rumours spread that online game Habbo Hotel was somehow blocking Blacks. In late 2005, a group of 4chan *griefers* (bad-faith gamers) raided the site crowding it with avatars of Black men in black suits and big afros. They were arranged forming a swastika, to disparage the site, and blocked the hotel's virtual pool posting 'closed due to AIDS'. Then they graduated to trolling in real life dressed as the Black avatar, hanging offensive signs on swimming pools and organising flashmobs that reenacted the swastika formation in public. There were numerous complaints, leading Moot to ban raids.

The ban was not well received. Hacktivists would not be censored and started signing their posts 'Sincerely, Anonymous'. Kirtaner (Aubrey Cottle), a professional programmer from Toronto, and his group of 'hackers on steroids' consolidated the hacktivist collective 'Anonymous' to combat authoritarians and Internet censorship. They rose to notoriety when they adopted the Guy Fawkes mask from the 2006 cult movie *V for Vendetta* about a shady hero, mixture of Zorro and Batman, who came to dispense justice for government corruption and blow up the British Parliament. As Kirt said, they set out to exact retribution for fun and chaos. They trolled neo-Nazi radio host Hal Turner with incessant prank calls and account hacks to the point of driving him out of business. In 2008, Anonymous called for a worldwide raid on Scientology

Churches to 'shut down a cult of misinformation and greed'. Ten thousand protestors with Guy Fawkes masks descended on churches across Australia, North America and Europe, garnering international media coverage. 'Chanology' showed that they could organise online and have a powerful real-world effect. In 2011, they supported 'Occupy Wall Street' and the first Arab Spring.

After Chanology, Anonymous turned into what Kirtaner calls 'a formless beast'. A pivotal year was 2008. At a 4chan conference, people started throwing Nazi Sieg Heil salutes, which had plenty of mindless imitators. With the Habbo Hotel raids, the swastika had become somewhat of a meme, and so did the Nazi salute once imitated in public and posted to social media. While many did not take this seriously, it became a magnet for infiltration by neo-Nazis and White nationalists. Moot had lost control of 4chan, and Kirt of Anonymous. Some users devolved into grotesque Internet predators. One hacked Oprah's website claiming to be a member of a paedophile network. This morphed into the #pizzagate conspiracy theory during the 2016 U.S. presidential elections, claiming that Democrats were running a child trafficking ring from the basement of a pizzeria.

A paradigmatic sedimentation process of *crowd radicalisation* ensued as moderates started leaving, while the hardcore remained. By 2010, Anonymous had become a decentralised anti-establishment collective seeking vigilante justice online, intent on 'raining chaos on what existed to destroy it and start anew' (Jones & Angelini, 2024). The 2011 Occupy Wall Street demonstration was brutally dispersed by New York police. Kirtaner and his colleagues responded with a series of retribution hacks against Rupert Murdoch newspapers and police websites around the country. Some disrupted FBI, CIA, U.S. Senate and Pentagon websites and were labelled cyberterrorists. The FBI outed many 'Anons', conducted searches and arrests and broke up the collective. Anonymous collapsed.

Many left 4chan. The most despairing and angry remained. They felt powerless, turned dark and nihilistic, and took to playing Depression Quest, an interactive game launched by Zoë Quinn in 2013. The group migrated to 8chan, created that same year by software developer Fredrick Brennan, then a 19-year-old afflicted with brittle bone disease. It was a site created for venting, complaining and competing to see who was more miserable. But 8chan had a major vulnerability. It invited users to create their own boards without admin intervention. Some boards turned dark and extreme as a result. One of them was Gamergate, which started as an ex-boyfriend attack on Zoë Quinn and women in gaming but turned into a vicious campaign of harassment and threats against women, feminism and diversity. Moot fought to ban it from 4chan in 2014 and sold the domain within a year, in defeat and disgust. Gamergate trolls created their own 8chan board and continued coordinating their attacks. As moderates left, White nationalists flocked to Gamergate and made 8chan their home, exploiting all the negativity and turning the site into a hate group.

Followers brought Gamergate to the attention of supremacist Breitbart News, which promoted it from 2014 to 2022. Owner Steve Bannon, who became Trump's first Chief of Staff, called for conservative media to embrace Gamergate and 8chan, to strategically 'activate' that 'army' of discontent and angry 'rootless white males' and turn them onto politics and Trump. This call on 'conservative media' meant that the vicious *tone, content and methods* incubated by 4 and 8channers would be rickrolled across the conservative propaganda machinery described in Chapter 11 and officialised by Republican politicians. Gamergate's false accusations and misogynism turned against presidential opponents Hillary Clinton in 2016 and Kamala Harris in 2024. As the public became desensitised, violent rhetoric, divisive lies, outrageous claims and actions, insults and cartoonish name calling became normalised. For conservative followers, it did not have to be true, only to feel right. Suddenly Democrats were the 'radical left'; opponents were 'crooked' and extreme; and mainstream media, not the trolls, concocted 'fake news'. The attack on traditional news outlets as the 'enemy of the people' went hand in hand with conspiracy theories. If the news could not be trusted, they were part of the conspiracy, or so the circular reasoning went. Social media feeds took over the news, letting users weave outlandish stories, which repetition built into memes.

Founder Fredrick Brennan repudiated 8chan and cut ties in 2016, when it was seized by pornographer and QAnon conspiracy theorist Jim Watkins. After Trump was elected, 8channers felt empowered. The

Watkins posse posted as 'Q', pretending to be a high-ranking government official with security clearance and a direct connection to the president. Q started posting language that appeared to anticipate Trump's tweets by a few minutes. Their predictions gained traction. 'Q is real!' and 'The Great Awakening' circulated across social media, together with calls to 'spread the info'. Q started dropping clues and breadcrumbs of secret conspiracies, as well as loosely connected pictures with the caption 'Do you believe in coincidences?' lifted from the movie *V for Vendetta.* Republican politicians claimed that Q's predictions were becoming true and called him a patriot for exposing the opposition's crimes. In reality, QAnon, the supposed anonymous followers of Q, were doctoring the timestamps of their posts to falsely appear to anticipate Trump's pronouncements. The old #pizzagate fiasco morphed into the main QAnon conspiracy theory that Democrats were 'a cabal of satanic paedophiles', leading to the meme 'Save the Children'. Who can be against that?

Q signs and banners appeared in Trump rallies and, after losing the 2020 elections, in the Capitol insurrection of 6 January 2021, fuelled by Trump's false claim that a 'deep state' conspiracy had rigged the elections against him, inspiring a new battle cry: 'Stop the Steal'. After several of Q's predictions missed the mark, QAnon lost steam. Their response: 'It doesn't matter if it's not real. It is the most *entertaining* thing on the web'. Kirtaner recalls being furious when he heard his grandmother talking about 'Save the Children' and QAnon. 'All of us who had built the culture started seeing our work being used by people we utterly despised. And because we all left the chan culture, there was no one there pushing back' (Jones & Angelini, 2024). Kirt got back into the game with his old Anonymous gang. They hacked Epik, the webhost of the hate speech sites: Gab (Patriots.win, AR15.com), Parler (The Daily Stormer, The Proud Boys), 8chan (InfoWars, The Oath Keepers). Anonymous published the hacked customer data and photos to match the footage of the Capitol insurrectionists, helping the FBI identify and arrest more than 1,500 attackers, resulting in 1,100 convictions and 600 prison sentences ranging from a few days to 22 years (Reilly, 2024).

Meme Wars (Donovan et al., 2022) explains the history and process by which propaganda turned Trump himself into a meme. They outline what they call 'the four Rs of media manipulation'. *Repetition* is widely reposting, retweeting, liking and sharing. *Redundancy* is sharing the content across multiple platforms. *Responsiveness* refers to the comments and discussions that a post generates, which create more content and sharing while building tribal community. *Reinforcement* is the platforms' algorithmic empathy and promotion of outrageous content through clicking or scrolling recommendations and search results designed to keep users interacting (p. 19). This is the prime method for spreading disinformation and influencing public opinion on a grand scale. It can easily sway an election. Trump won in 2024 by carrying three swing states with a difference of only 74,000 total votes.

Disinformation is often used as a military weapon for destabilising groups and societies. Its use for social, business and political purposes has reached crisis proportions, simply because it is so easy to implement. AI text-to-image meme generators and text-to-voice podcast generators are the latest tools, free and widely available, since the platforms profit from more user content creation. A single troll with a handful of bots and sock-puppet accounts can infiltrate various groups and platforms, inject them with memes that press the right buttons and watch them snowball into a social engineering machine.

Human-Competitive AI

Large language models embody the ultimate parasitism. They seek to approach general intelligence and replace higher human functions and indeed jobs, by feeding on troves of human data, billed as LLM 'training'—another anthropomorphic delusion. They seek to fake innovation, originality and creativity—properties of human intelligence—by throwing in some random variables. Twentieth-century AI theorists knew that any human connection between the machine and the real world was due to 'the perceptual experience and knowledge of the [human] designers' (Putnam, 1981, p. 11). They could not foresee, however, the vast amounts of third-party human data soon to be fed into the machine via text corpora—a searchable database of millions of pages covering the gamut of human experience. Two main ingredients had been missing:

Application Programming Interface (API) and cloud computing. The mechanistic theory that the mind is 'modular' guided the API integration of task-specific and expert programs and machines. As opposed to bidirectional computer-user interface, an API is a set of rules that interconnects multiple programs from a software library as well as several computer servers or CPUs housed in a global network of data centres (see Amazon, Cisco, IBM and Microsoft in References). Any personal computer, laptop, tablet or smartphone is now a gateway that can access the vast computing power of a public cloud service provider. Shannon and Turing would be overjoyed with this API level of information flow and functionality which more than ever approaches their dream of a 'universal computer'.

Before May 2023, few foresaw the game-changing success of OpenAI's ChatGPT, and the paradigm shift that Generative AI represents. It was followed in 2024 by GPT-4o, which transforms not only text but also audiovisual content. Within a few months, numerous AI assistants, linked to many popular applications, were launched. Again, two other ingredients had been missing: artificial neural networks (ANNs) and large language models (LLMs)—new forms of software architecture supported by advances in computer hardware, memory and processing speed.

Neural networks are a case of biomimetics, modelled after the structure of neurons, each branching out into several axons that network with other neurons. Any number of layers of artificial 'neurons' are stacked together with distributive interconnections to perform several integrated functions almost as if they were different API-linked computers exchanging data. Apologists will claim that they are non-linear, but they are in fact multilinear, performing the same old arithmetic operations (addition, subtraction, multiplication, division) and logical operations (if–then, and, or, not). The same applies to quantum computing.

LLMs are a type of ANN, which grew out of advances in machine translation. GPTs (generative pre-trained transformers) are a type of LLM. They are in part multi autoregressive (AR) models, like the reverse or backchaining Markov model used to compute the probable sequence of values in a time series. The output thereby depends on its own previous chain of values computed by a stochastic recurrence equation. In particular, the vector autoregressive model (VAR) handles multiple interacting random variables and stochastic equations, used to predict word sequences (bigrams, trigrams, *n*-grams) through quantitative discourse analysis of word co-occurrence, proximity and collocation (placement) in large text corpora and Big Data.

The Yarowsky (1995) unsupervised learning algorithm for word sense disambiguation was a significant breakthrough. It exploits the redundancy of 'two powerful properties of human language: 1. One sense per collocation: Nearby words provide strong and consistent clues to the sense of a target word, conditional on relative distance, order and syntactic relationship. 2. One sense per discourse: The sense of a target word is highly consistent within any given document' (Yarowsky, p. 189). Given a small number of *training examples*, the algorithm disambiguates thousands of instances of polysemous words like *plant* (living/factory), with a consistency of 99.8% (p. 190). This made it possible for LLMs to replace the less reliable statistical word-frequency model of machine translation. LLMs are in fact sets of API-integrated machines working in parallel: word parser, domain classifier, tokeniser, embedder, search engine, inference engine, etc. The key is that text, image and sound are all made LLM-computable by substituting their meaningful elements with searchable *meaning-free* alphanumeric *tokens* apt for mathematical (not linguistic) computation. Research in monosemanticity may help tech companies understand their own LLMs, how to reduce semantic errors and make their answers more trustworthy—a work that is still in its infancy (Anthropic, 2024).

One would hope that tokenisation would finally bring the myth of the 'thinking' machine to an end. Instead, generative AI has renewed futuristic visions of human-like artificial general intelligence (AGI) that will bring either a new Golden Age or the utter demise of human civilisation. Even authors who seek to 'fix' AI see the thinking machine as a future possibility, based on alternate definitions of intelligence, notions of 'accelerated evolution' in biology and technology, game theory or the growing understanding of brain function. 'Yet every step towards an explanation of how the mind works is also a step towards the creation of the mind's capabilities in an artifact –that is, a step towards artificial intelligence' (Russell, 2020, p. 14). Others point out the failed promises of AI, which despite all the hype has only reached a level of *narrow* intelligence for specific applications in closed systems, such as self-driving cars, whose unreliability attests to the rudimentary state of the art. A tech-hopeful solution is to 'reboot' AI by steering away from narrow intelligence and towards general, open-ended and adaptable systems tailored to 'partnering' with humans (Marcus & Davis, 2019). The opposite is true: task-specific or 'narrow' expert systems work; general systems do not. I find serious problems with technology-based fixes that envision some future panacea dependent on technology itself. To begin with, they want to apply digital metagrammar to an analogue problem, for instance, the rampant *misuse* of technology by humans.

AI agents 'trained' on human data are increasingly replacing areas of human agency. They work in different kinds of environments encompassing all types of AI technologies. Virtual agents like LLMs, GPTs and chatbots are in a passive language-observation space within a linguo-mental human environment. Most are trained with massive, Internet-scale human data. Physical agents (robots) operate in an action space within a specific tokenised physical environment whose objects and parameters are preprogrammed into the machine. Hybrid agents write code and adaptive software bridging the gap between language space and action space. AI agents have different degrees of autonomy. Autopilots and cruise control are an early case of narrow autonomy, acting by itself to complete a narrow task or goal. They require a fairly simple set of rules or instructions. Self-driving cars accomplish a broader set of tasks requiring somewhat broader autonomy and a more complex ruleset with many more instructions. They are improved by experimenting with robotic agents that measure the parameters of an environment, detect shapes and colours, 'learn' and change or manipulate the environment, acting autonomously within its boundaries without any instruction other than its original internal program. Big tasks are broken down into simple mechanical tasks. Gradually, multiple simulated environments are introduced, building an agent 'who' theoretically goes out into the world, explores and learns new things by itself without additional training. The combination of training and machine learning would lead in theory to a highly autonomous adaptive Artificial General Agent (AGA) that pursues artificial general intelligence (AGI). Google is working on developing a SIMA (Scalable Instructible Multi-world Agent) trained with large amounts of instructions formulated and imparted in natural language which the agent tokenises (Besse, 2024).

Game theory provides the logic for the design and training of AI agents. This is in the first place because games are based on a set of rules or instructions that control behaviour, strategy and decision making, which are problem-solving activities (Carpenter & Robbett, 2022). Algorithmic game theory is the field of interception between analogue game theory and computer science (Nisan et al., 2007). Game rulesets are easily tokenised, and their solutions are based on probabilities and mathematical calculation. Videogames provide a crowdsourcing opportunity and a simulated training environment for AI agents to collect experience and decision-making data. Games like Tetris in which players earn points as a reward serve as training agents for machine learning. *Reinforcement learning*—aimed at maximising a score—is programmed into the machine, such that the AI agent self-rewards on the way to achieving a goal, where maximum efficiency results in maximum points. Google DeepMind developed the Deep Q-learning Network (DQN) in which the reinforcement learning algorithm teaches AI agents to assign values to their actions and make optimal decisions in complex model-free environments. Such autonomous learning systems require, on the surface, little training on human data. Other games like Minecraft, which allow exploring and crafting the environment without any points or reward, are no-goal training agents that require human datamining and imitation learning to mimic and predict what a human would say or do next. Like in LLM predictive text, the objective is to predict what is the next token. In partnership with game developers, AI agents are trained in many different game environments, looking for *generality* and *transfer*. 'Same as games, we train LLMs by prompting them to do all sorts of things: to write a poem, code, role play' (Besse, 2024). In every case, games are safe sandboxes for AI training and development. The problem comes when they are deployed in real life.

Conclusion

All machine learning, and therefore all AI systems, including LLMs, GPTs and autonomous learning agents, require a foundation of human input in the form of *data labelling* and annotating. 'In machine learning, data labelling is the [human] process of identifying raw data (images, text files, videos, etc.) and adding informative labels. For example, labels might indicate whether a photo contains a bird or car, which words were uttered in an audio recording, or if an x-ray contains a tumour. Data labelling is required for a variety of use cases including computer vision, natural language processing, and speech recognition' (Amazon Web Services, 2024a, 2024b). Annotations, tags and labels are tokenised by the machines, classified and processed to make them searchable and produce a model that can make predictions on new data. The model requires thousands of similar tagged items, be they birds, cars or humans by age, gender and race, to generate pattern-matching parameters used to identify and classify new items. This is what they call 'learning'. An annotated data set is hugely more valuable than unusable raw data. Machine learning models for different purposes require their own dataset annotated according to their specifications and criteria. Further, the models are proprietary, so they are not usually open-source or shared by different companies. This means that the AI industry will continue to need a global army of millions of human annotators, even as unsupervised machine learning does some of its own labelling.

This leads to what is probably the vilest form of parasitic exploitation, under the deceitful rubric of 'humans-in-the-loop' as though technology was suddenly turning humane. OpenAI, Google, Meta, Amazon, Microsoft and other AI companies become insulated by hiring dozens of intermediary labour-recruiting firms that tap refugees displaced from conflict zones and high unemployment regions of developing countries for cheap annotating labour. They lure them offering 'AI jobs' and a chance to be part of the 'AI Revolution'. One key region goes by another deceitful euphemism, the 'Silicon Savannah', an impoverished version of Silicon Valley used by foreign tech companies for offshore business process outsourcing (BPO). It is centred in high unemployment Kenya and is spreading throughout Africa, as well as countries like India, the

Philippines and Venezuela where they find well educated but unemployed populations. Annotators 'spent eight hours a day in front of a screen studying photos and videos, drawing boxes around objects and labelling them, teaching the AI algorithms to recognize them'. They work for measly wages in a sweatshop environment where they are pressed to meet standards, production quotas and unrealistic, punitive deadlines 'with often just seconds to complete complicated labelling tasks' (Stahl, 2024). Some call it 'modern day slavery' rendered akin to debt bondage or indentured servitude by chronic unemployment and desperate financial need. Workers are hired for specific projects, under contracts lasting a few months, weeks or days, and are usually fired if they complain. The less fortunate—hundreds in Kenya alone—are forced for days on end to sifts through images which AI companies want to filter out, involving pornography, aberrant sex and graphic atrocities that lead to permanent trauma and psychiatric damage.

Meanwhile, 'humanistic intelligence' is another deception that purports a false humanisation of technology. Some versions of humanistic AI claim a perspective from which machines 'collaborate' rather than compete with or replace humans. It is as though machines had volition and the benevolence to stoop down and 'collaborate' with us mere mortals. No, true humanistic technology restores the reality that there is no such thing as AI 'agents', that machines are *nothing but our tools*, which like AI can be used for good or ill, for our benefit or to our harm. As such, humanistic AI is just another alibi for ambitious futurists who preach salvation by wearable or implanted computing, feeding like AI parasites on the human host. In a discourse full of childish techno myths, three old men proclaim from their towering visionary labs:

> Humanistic Intelligence is intelligence that arises because of a human being in the feedback loop of a computational process, where the human and computer are inextricably intertwined. When a wearable computer embodies HI and becomes so technologically advanced that its intelligence matches our own biological brain, something much more powerful emerges from this synergy that gives rise to superhuman intelligence within the single 'cyborg' being. (Minsky, Kurzweil & Mann, 2013, p. 16)

Submitting to the super parasite—they would have us believe—is our only chance not to be rendered obsolete and irrelevant by the superintelligent machines. This unholy trinity dreams of the glory of the gods in creating a new master race, in a sterile attempt to rise above the human condition, from their AI tower built over the anthill of countless 'humans-in-the-loop' annotators. Behind every dream of glory toils an army of slaves.

References

Amazon Web Services. (2024). *What Is a CPU (Central Processing Unit)?* Retrieved from https://aws.amazon.com/what-is/cpu/

Amazon Web Services. (2024). *What Is Data Labeling?* Retrieved from https://aws.amazon.com/what-is/data-labeling

Anthropic (2024, May 21). *Mapping the Mind of a Large Language Model.* Retrieved from https://www.anthropic.com/research/mapping-mind-language-model

Benjamin, W. (2008 [1935]). *The Work of Art in the Age of Mechanical Reproduction* Translated by J. A. Underwood. Penguin.

Bernard, S. S. (2024, September 10). Lured by a Promising Job, He Was Forced to Scam People. *The New York Times.* Retrieved from https://www.nytimes.com/2024/09/10/business/scammers-trafficking-cybercrime.html

Besse, F. (2024, September 25). *Google DeepMind: The Podcast. 'Gaming, Goats & General Intelligence'.* At https://www.youtube.com/watch?v=64pndvbbokA&list=PLqYmG7hTraZBiUr6_Qf8YTS2Oqy3OGZEj

Carpenter, J., & Robbett, A. (2022). *Game Theory and Behavior*. MIT Press.

Cisco (2025). *What Is a Data Center?* Retrieved from https://www.cisco.com/c/en/us/solutions/data-center-virtualization/what-is-a-data-center.html

Cooban, A. (2024, September 18). This Bank Says "Millions" of People Could Be Targeted by AI Voice-Cloning Scams. *CNN*. Retrieved from https://www.cnn.com/2024/09/18/tech/ai-voice-cloning-scam-warning/index.html

Dawkins, R. (1976). *The Selfish Gene*. Oxford University Press.

Donovan, J., Dreyfuss, E., & Friedberg, B. (2022). *Meme Wars: The Untold Story of the Online Battles Upending Democracy in America*. Bloomsbury.

Eliot, L. B. (2024, August 24). Being Addicted to Generative AI. *Forbes*. Retrieved from https://www.forbes.com/sites/lanceeliot/2024/08/24/being-addicted-to-generative-ai
Emotional AI Lab. (2024). *What Is Emotional AI?* Retrieved from https://emotionalai.org/so-what-is-emotional-ai
Eubanks, V. (2019). *Automating Inequality: How High-Tech Tools Profile, Police, and Punish the Poor*. Picador.
Harris, T. (2016, May 18). How Technology Is Hijacking Your Mind—From a Magician and Google Design Ethicist. *Thrive Global*. Retrieved from https://medium.com/thrive-global/how-technology-hijacks-peoples-minds-from-a-magician-and-google-s-design-ethicist-56d62ef5edf3
Hayes, H. M. (2017, April 12). Food, Sex & Smartphones. Can you be addicted to a behavior? *Binghamton University News*. Retrieved from https://www.binghamton.edu/news/story/505/food-sex-smartphones
IBM (2024, April 9). *What Is an API (Application Processing Unit)?* Retrieved from https://www.ibm.com/topics/api
Jones, A., & Angelini, G. (2024). *The Antisocial Network: Memes to Mayhem*. Netflix Documentary.
Kurayama, M. (2020, December 14). Both *netoyo* Entertainers and Abe Believers Will Only Disappear from Society. *SPA!* Google translated from the Japanese at https://web.archive.org/web/20201214035332/https://news.yahoo.co.jp/articles/b0ed4202a9e415f966879cbaeb9bbef1c207ff63?page=1
Mahari, R., & Pataranutaporn, P. (2024, August 5). We Need to Prepare for Addictive Intelligence. *MIT Technology Review*. Retrieved from https://www.technologyreview.com/2024/08/05/1095600/we-need-to-prepare-for-addictive-intelligence
Marcus, G., & Davies, E. (2019). *Rebooting AI: Building Artificial Intelligence We Can Trust*. Pantheon.
McNamee, R. (2020). *Zucked: Waking Up to the Facebook Catastrophe*. Penguin
Microsoft. *What Is the Cloud?* Retrieved from https://azure.microsoft.com/en-us/resources/cloud-computing-dictionary/what-is-the-cloud
Minsky, M., Kurzweil, R., & Mann, S. (2013, 27–29 June). The Society of Intelligent Veillance. *IEEE International Symposium on Technology and Society (ISTAS): Social Implications of Wearable Computing and Augmediated Reality in Everyday Life*, Toronto (pp. 13–17). Retrieved from https://doi.org/10.1109/ISTAS.2013.6613095
New York State Police. (2024, September 19). *New York State Police Warns of Nationwide Automated Sextortion Scams*. Press release. Retrieved

from https://troopers.ny.gov/news/new-york-state-police-warns-nationwide-automated-sextortion-scams
Nisan, N., Roughgarden, T., Tardos, É., & Vasirani, V. V. (Eds.). (2007). *Algorithmic Game Theory*. Cambridge University Press.
O'Neil, C. (2016). *Weapons of Math Destruction: How Big Data Increases Inequality and Threatens Democracy*. Crown/Random House.
Putnam, H. (1981). Brains in a Vat. In *Reason, Truth and History* (pp. 1–21). Cambridge University Press.
Qian, I. (2023, December 17). 7 Months Inside an Online Scam Labor Camp. *The New York Times*. Retrieved from https://www.nytimes.com/interactive/2023/12/17/world/asia/myanmar-cyber-scam.html
Reilly, R. J. (2024, November 3). Days Before the Election, DOJ Continues to Prosecute New Jan. 6 Cases. *CBS News*. Retrieved from https://www.nbcnews.com/politics/justice-department/new-jan-6-arrests-sentences-ahead-2024-election-rcna178505
Russell, S. (2020). *Human Compatible: Artificial Intelligence and the Problem of Control*. Penguin.
Saeidi, M. (2024, May 17). Voice Cloning Scams Are a Growing Threat. Here's How You Can Protect Yourself. New York. *CBS News*. Retrieved from https://www.cbsnews.com/newyork/news/ai-voice-clone-scam
Schellmann, H. (2024). *The Algorithm: How AI Decides Who Gets Hired, Monitored, Promoted, and Fired and Why We Need to Fight Back Now*. Hachette.
Schüll, N. D. (2014). *Addiction by Design: Machine Gambling in Las Vegas*. Princeton University Press.
Slavkovik, M., Stachl, C., Pitman, C., & Askonas, J. (2021, July 30). Digital Voodoo Dolls. In *Proceedings of the 2021 AAAI/ACM Conference on AI, Ethics, and Society* (pp. 967–977). Retrieved from https://doi.org/10.1145/3461702.3462626
Solly, J. E., Hook, R. W., Grant, J. E., Cortese, S., & Chamberlain, S. R. (2021). Structural Gray Matter Differences in Problematic Usage of the Internet: A Systematic Review and Meta-Analysis. *Molecular Psychiatry, 27*, 1000–1009. Retrieved from https://doi.org/10.1038/s41380-021-01315-7
Stacey, N. (2024). *Buy Now! The Shopping Conspiracy*. Netflix documentary.
Stahl, L. (2024, November 24). Labelers Training AI Say They're Overworked, Underpaid and Exploited by Big American Tech Companies. *CBS News 60 Minutes*. Retrieved from https://www.cbsnews.com/news/labelers-training-ai-say-theyre-overworked-underpaid-and-exploited-60-minutes-transcript

Stevens, Jr., E. W. (1995). *The Grammar of the Machine: Technical Literacy and Early Industrial Expansion in the United States*. Yale University Press.

Tamir, D., & Mitchell, J. (2017). Disclosing Information About the Self Is Intrinsically Rewarding. *Proceedings of the National Academy of Science, 109*(21), 8038. Retrieved from https://www.pnas.org/doi/10.1073/pnas.1202129109

Vrendenburgh, K. (2022, February 9). Freedom at work: understanding, alienation, and the AI-driven workplace. *Canadian Journal of Philosophy 52* (1), 78–92. Retrieved from https://doi.org/10.1017/can.2021.39

Wadhwa, V., & Salkever, A. (2018). *Your Happiness Was Hacked: Why Tech Is Winning the Battle to Control Your Brain, and How to Fight Back*. Berrett-Koehler Publishers.

Yarowsky, D. (1995, June). Unsupervised Word Sense Disambiguation Rivaling Supervised Methods. In *33rd Annual Meeting of the Association for Computational Linguistics*. Association for Computational Linguistics (pp. 189–196). Retrieved from https://aclanthology.org/P95-1026.pdf

Young, K. S. (1998). Internet Addiction: The Emergence of a New Clinical Disorder. *CyberPsychology & Behavior, 1*(3), 237–244. Retrieved from https://doi.org/10.1089/cpb.1998.1.237

Zuboff, S. (2019). *The Age of Surveillance Capitalism: The Fight for a Human Future at the New Frontier of Power*. Hachette.

16
Translational Science

Introduction

Translational science developed in the medical and public health fields with the aim of translating research data into concrete applications and interventions that directly benefit humans. A paradigmatic field is ergonomics, defined as the science of fitting the workplace to the user's needs, with the aim of increasing efficiency and productivity while reducing discomfort, health hazards and harmful long-term effects. The approach is extensive to science and technology, psychology, economics, social sciences and public policy, systems theory, mechanism design and all aspects of applied research. The translation of fundamental research into practice aims at identifying and tackling *specific problems*. In this sense, translational science generally involves a translation from digital to analogue metagrammar, focusing on the human factor. The U.S. National Institute of Health proposes a strategic approach that cycles through creativity and innovation; focus on unmet needs; generalisable solutions; cross-disciplinary team science; boundary-crossing partnerships; diversity, equity, inclusion and accessibility; bold, yet rigorous approaches; optimising for efficiency and speed through, once again,

E. Camayd-Freixas, *Metagrammar*, https://doi.org/10.1007/978-3-031-92337-1_16

creativity and innovation. The use of any similar approach to serve institutional clients in business, industry, education or government is not humanistic translational science. Its legitimate metagrammar is not only 'human-centric' but centred on *individual wellbeing*, not on institutional control of individuals or any abstract concept of humanity, society or other collective. The aim is to restore an equilibrium in the dynamics of power and control too heavily stacked on institutions and against people and individual rights.

In the case of artificial intelligence, some futurists engage in the vain pursuit of AGI, envisioning a utopian fate, while others warn of a dystopian or catastrophic result. AI ethicists on the other hand argue that futuristic predictions serve only to distract from present-day harms and to shift priorities away from concrete solutions. The mid-range argument focuses on the international AI race, especially between the United States and China (Lee, 2018); but also, among the Big Tech companies (Webb, 2019). The race came to a tipping point on 10 January 2025, when Chinese LLM developer DeepSeek launched its low-cost open-source R1 chatbot, which rivalled those of OpenAI and Google, surpassing them in number of free downloads (Metz & Tobin, 2025). DeepSeek adopted the free-to-users model of data capture, raising security concerns and prompting U.S. legislative attempts to ban its use and criminalise its download. The policy to ban the export of advanced Nvidia chips to China backfired when DeepSeek used eight times fewer GPUs with earlier H800 Nvidia chips and trained its model faster at one tenth the cost of U.S. rivals. This was made possible by metagrammatical improvements in DeepSeek-V3 Mixture-of-Experts (MoE) and Multi-head Latent Attention (MLA) architectures, as well as multi-stage pre and post training (DeepSeek-AI, 2024). The danger in the race is that unbridled development may take precedence over ethics and collateral damage. Given the difference in political systems, it is a two-body problem: first, Big Tech needs regulation; second, the superpowers need a treaty of cooperation based on mutual responsibility.

I am concerned here with the first part, in the context of constitutional democracy. Can Big Tech police itself? That has never happened when powerful financial interests are involved. In the steel and auto industries, for example, checks and balances were necessary in the form of such things as labour law and trade unions. Can AI companies at least self-regulate? Can more technology alone tackle the problems that AI is creating? Translational science in AI focuses instead on the human factor and defines the problem as one of *safety* and *alignment* with human needs.

If machines interacted only with machines, the result would be perfectly predictable, not when they interact with humans. 'Agent action affects human response that affects agent action. This back-and-forth conversation is still missing in AI agents' (Dragan, 2024). AI is an adaptive technology that asks what the human user wants. But who is that human user? Individuals have competing and conflicting values and preferences. Is it an 'average' human? From what group? What about minorities? Can you average out qualitative values? Is what people want the same as what they need, what is good for them or for society? Ask a tech addict. Recommendation systems have a single reward function to optimise user engagement. Is this for the benefit of the person or the company? A preference ranking algorithm serves people's confirmation bias. Social media and news feeds give people empathic political content which makes them like their faction more and be angrier at the opposition. Opinions do not necessarily change; they just become more extreme due to algorithm-driven *affective polarization*. 'That is not good for society even if that is what people want' (Dragan, 2024). This elusive alignment is not a problem but a paradox. Tech problems cannot be solved by tech alone. They are analogue, requiring human intervention at a scale and level of authority that can only be provided by what Big Tech dreads most, *government regulation.*

Systemic Solutions

The problems we have considered along the past several chapters are so varied, complex and dynamic that they require a dedicated government entity along the lines of a Technology Regulatory Agency (TRA). Tech companies resist regulation, work around impediments and resort to litigation. Solutions that require protracted litigation or concerted public pressure for legislative action, such as those proposed by McNamee

(2020, pp. 291–315), are unlikely to succeed because the public derives extensive benefits from technology and are subject to its powerful promotion. A TRA, as an agency of the executive branch of government, cuts through the chase by issuing orders based on administrative law and promoting evidence-based legislation.

The European Union has taken significant steps through the General Data Protection Regulation (GDPR). It requires data processing to be lawful, fair and transparent. Personal data can only be processed if there is a legal basis for doing so. GDPR includes provisions for purpose limitation, data minimisation, accuracy, storage limitation, integrity and confidentiality. Each member state has its own independent European Data Protection Board (EDPB), a supervisory authority to hear and investigate complaints and impose administrative sanctions. The different countries' EDPBs are autonomous yet fully integrated for cooperation, data sharing, mutual assistance and joint operations. The 'right to be forgotten' was adopted by the GDPR as the right to erasure of unfair and incorrect personal data in conjunction with the right to compensation. Further, personal data must be encrypted for anonymisation, and data subjects can object to automated decision making. The non-profit European Centre for Digital Rights focuses on strategic litigation based on GDPR regulations, suing platforms like Facebook, WhatsApp, Instagram and Google for 'forced consent'—employing user agreements that require consent to unlimited data processing without opt-in choices for non-essential data. The United Kingdom adopted the European model after Brexit, and several countries around the world are implementing similar regulations. Through the 'Brussels effect', the Court of Justice of the European Union globalises GDPR regulations by compelling transnational and certain foreign companies with access to European subjects to abide by its data protection principles (Ryngaert & Tailor, 2020). In August 2024, the European Union implemented the Artificial Intelligence Act, which bans applications with unacceptable risks, imposes compliance assessments on high-risk applications and transparency requirements on limited risk applications (European Commission, 2024). Anonymous websites pose an unacceptable risk as incubators of disinformation and conspiracy theories and must be universally banned. Jurisdictions collaborate internationally to block and infiltrate the dark web marketplace for cybercrime.

A landmark 2018 case against Facebook brought forth the question of whether a social media platform is a publisher liable for the content it allows, including disinformation. Facebook has traditionally adopted the comfortable position that it is just a neutral tech platform with no editing role or publishing responsibility other than to weed out illegal content. On the other hand, making people's content public *is* publishing. Journalism professor Kathleen Culver has called attention to the fact that the terms 'platform' and 'publisher' are inadequate. 'What we're navigating is a space where the language we have to date does not match the technology that has now been developed' (Levin, 2018). It is a complex problem beyond that of changing legal definitions. Certainly, the scope of 'illegal content' can be broadened for platforms by outlawing such difficult things to define and litigate as instances of disinformation. This faces the practical problem that no amount of human content moderators could screen such amount of traffic. AI can help by adding trained LLMs to factcheck, detect and block disinformation following the Open-Source Intelligence (OSINT) framework. Moreover, there is a threshold where social media platforms become publishers, and that is when they add News Feeds, which should be held to the same editorial standards as any reputable news outlet.

However, on 7 January 2025 Mark Zuckerberg announced that Meta is lifting restrictions on 'free speech' and stopping most content moderation and all fact checking on Facebook, Instagram and Threads. Following Elon Musk's *X*, which has become a disinformation pipeline, this will save these companies billions of dollars and make them billions more from increased posting, sharing and the new 'community notes' designed to debate the posts. Further, they are colluding with Trump to lift government restrictions and press other countries to stop protecting their citizens and give free rein to social media (Megerian, 2025; Nix et al., 2025). To be clear, the problem is not free speech but increased human data mining, emotional microtargeting and algorithmic amplification of lies, anger and hate for profit.

On the economics side, mechanisation and digitalisation create a ballooning surplus value effect whereby the manual processes they replace are rendered geometrically inexpensive to produce, whereas limited savings are passed on to the consumer. Mass (re)production in the Industrial Age and more so in the Digital Age (due to frictionless transmission) results in an enormous accumulation of wealth and political power by Big Tech and other technology-intensive firms, coupled with increasing economic inequality affecting the larger part of the population. Monopolistic practices, licensing agreements and vertical integration unfairly stave off competition. Antitrust regulations have been lax and mostly ineffective in the face of free market forces. Longtime talks of breaking up Google, Amazon and Meta have stalled because of legal complications. Moreover, Zuboff (2019) warns that such breakups without prior regulation will only multiply the number of surveillance capitalist firms. The bulk of election campaign advertising funds (59% in the United States) goes to Facebook, now used throughout the world as a political weapon.

Nobel Laureate economist Paul Romer (2019) asserts that 'the digital advertising model pioneered by Google and Facebook poses a growing threat to democracy' and argues for an excise 'ad tax' applied to revenue from sales of targeted digital ads. In response to objections regarding the difficulty in defining 'targeted' advertising and the ability of platforms to work around such definitions, Romer (2021) appears to broaden the scope to all digital advertising. He proposes an ad tax on revenue instead of income, because companies can offset income and move it to lower tax jurisdictions, something they cannot do with revenue. The mechanics is an incremental tax schedule with zero tax for the first $5 billion in revenue, 5% for $5—$10 billion and brackets up to 72.5% for revenues above $60B. By Romer's, 2021 estimates, Microsoft would have paid $100 M, Amazon $2B, Facebook/Meta $14.7B and Google $18.6B. However, an 'ad tax' has serious limitations. It requires unpopular legislation and applies only to the United States. It is not a global solution. Platforms already pass much of the cost to consumers through paid subscription models and premium services. A higher service cost would reduce the number of users in detriment of smaller advertisers. Increasing advertising price would hurt millions of individuals and small businesses who depend on digital marketing, thus reducing competition for corporate marketers who can afford the hike.

My proposal is for a 'data tax' as a property tax on data inventory. Many countries, states and municipalities tax business inventory as tangible personal property. There are established inventory tax accounting rules. The basis for data inventory tax is clear: the number of *users* in a platform plus the number of *datapoints* per user, each multiplied by a specific *rate* ($T = ur_1 + dr_2$). The rate should be applicable only to data inventory as a special non-tangible class, so as not to impact economic growth for businesses with tangible inventory and property, whose tax may even decrease, especially for local small businesses. Startups and smaller platforms with fewer than five million users should be exempt. This is a global solution applicable to *any* jurisdiction based on the users' place of residence, regardless of where their data is processed or marketed.

Taxation metagrammar does not depend on litigation like challenging user agreements and forced consent, but instead regulates incentives, benefits and disincentives. In this case, a higher tax on datapoints (dr_2) creates a disincentive for platforms to use the massive amounts required for microtargeting, behaviour modification and digital voodoo dolls. Together with ur_1 it penalises limitless storage of user data and the practice of inflating the number of users to compete for advertisers and charge higher rates. Conversely, data tax incentivises the deletion of inactive users and obsolete data with a prescribed limited shelf life. The reduced load will increase the efficiency of energy-hungry, noise-polluting and environment-degrading data centres.

And let us not forget that this data stockpile comes from the appropriation of users' digital assets via free human datamining. In systems theory, every system begins with a stock of inventory or raw materials which must be replenished by purchasing or leasing sustainable resources (Meadows, 2008). Free unlimited data leads to unfair enrichment at the expense of common people, who are entitled to fair compensation. Notwithstanding self-serving tax-deductible corporate philanthropy, the many billions levied in data tax should revert to the community, reducing income and services inequalities by raising the minimum wage, lowering retirement age and investing in schools, communities, public health and social services. As AI automation becomes ubiquitous, increasing production while reducing jobs, a 4-day workweek coupled with 'guaranteed minimum income' or 'universal basic income' will become necessary tools for social stability (Lee, 2018, pp. 206–208).

A Technology Regulatory Agency (TRA) should function in similar fashion to the U.S. Consumer Protection Agency (CPA) and the Food and Drug Administration (FDA). The CPA protects consumers from deceptive adverting and unfair market practices through the Federal Trade Commission. The Consumer Product Safety Commission is a separate regulatory agency that protects the public from unreasonable risks of serious injury or death from consumer products that pose fire, electrical, chemical, mechanical hazards or can injure children. They develop safety standards, investigate hazards and mandate recalls. The FDA regulates the safety of consumable and radiation emitting products and medical devices, investigates hazards and mandates recalls. Crucially, the FDA grants approval for every step in the development of new medications, from initial research to clinical trials, before they can be released to the public, and mandates recalls of products that are no longer safe, pure or potent. *Permission is dependent of their intended purpose.* Similarly, a TRA should review and approve research and development of new technologies based on their specific use and the translational human benefit they aim to fulfil. Piracy of unauthorised digital products must be persecuted and penalised for developers, distributors and users. This is the opposite of the status quo, in which specific technologies like spectrographic speech recognition, biometric face recognition and CGI are combined to produce voice cloning and deepfakes. A TRA should approve development, testing and release to the public, as well as mandate recalls of digital products that are proven harmful. It should also regulate age appropriateness and registered licensing for entities that have a legitimate use for such products and services.

Consumer safety technologies are entering the market every year due to popular demand. Safe phones for kids and teens like Gabb or Bark Phone provide GPS location, content monitoring and limits on screentime, browsing, gaming, social media, downloads, contacts, picture messages and group texts, through tamper-proof parental controls. The Children's Online Privacy Protection Act (COPPA) provides some safeguards against online data harvesting for children under 13. Smartphone apps like Focus, Freedom, Moment and Unglue limit use to a specified maximum. However, some apps that aim to reduce tech addiction, like Space by the 2017 startup Dopamine Labs, have been blocked by the Apple app store. Space has become unavailable, and the name Dopamine Labs has been taken over by a series on companies that boost addiction and online gambling.

Wadhwa and Salkever (2018, pp. 141–157) and McNamee (2020, pp. 317–330) discuss personal strategies for reducing tech dependency, including limiting screentime, avoiding social media and going to reputable news outlets. Aided by defensive technologies and user awareness, personal strategies can become systematic. Smart routers like Torch and router attachments like Circle enable parental controls, Internet filtering and family-safe device management. Virtual Private Networks such as NordVPN create an encrypted tunnel for your Internet connection to protect your data, route your connection through a remote server and hide your IP address and location to protect your privacy even in public Wi-Fi hotspots. Safer browsers like Apple's Safari block trackers. DuckDuckGo offers a variety of safety and privacy products such as a secure search engine; a browser extension that changes your searches to DuckDuckGo, blocks trackers, encrypts website connections and grades the privacy of each site. They also offer email protection, VPN subscription with personal information removal and identity theft restoration, and a tool that automatically tells websites not to sell or share your personal information.

At work, Inbox When Ready protects your focus, manages email time for your deep work routine, allows you to batch-process your inbox at the best time of day and monitors your adherence to your budgeted time. SafeNet is an identity and access management (IAM) organisational solution that provides a VPN and services such as multi-factor authentication and one-time passwords, tracking and auditing of users and their privileges, as well as authorisation policies. Global cybersecurity companies such as CrowdStrike and Palo Alto Network further secure company and institutional data. However, their *centralisation presents a weakness*, revealed by the massive 2024 computer outage related to a faulty CrowdStrike update that caused some 8.5 million Microsoft operating systems to crash worldwide, affecting finance, healthcare, government, transport, media, retail and other sectors (Browne, 2024).

Decentralisation is key for controlling technology and arriving at systemic solutions. It affords local control, limits error propagation and allows for collaboration among independent entities. As we saw above, the European Data Protection Board is decentralised by country, and the implementation of the European GDPR is distributed among administrative, judicial and law enforcement authorities. The U.S. Consumer Protection Agency is an umbrella of specialised functions carried out by different federal agencies and state counterparts. Beware of central control, which kills flexibility, diversity and innovation and pushes for a single agenda based on an overarching narrative.

In a colourful example of centralisation, doomsday futurists Amy Webb envisions a catastrophic conspiratorial scenario brought about by 'G-MAFIA BAT' (Google, Microsoft, Amazon, Facebook, IBM, Apple; Baidu, Alibaba and Tencent on the Chinese side). Salvation would come about by the creation of the 'Global Alliance on Intelligence Augmentation' (GAIA—to appropriate the name of the mythical earth goddess) in a saga inspired by Isaac Asimov's science fiction. GAIA would 'join forces with the G-MAFIA and the world's most advanced economies' (developing countries excluded) to form an international body of 'AI researchers, sociologists, economists, game theorists, futurists, and political scientists from all member countries' who would guide ignorant governments and direct the orderly 'transition from ANI to AGI', ensuring that 'robots must not injure a human being' on the road to the promised land of artificial general intelligence (Webb, 2019, pp. 235–258). Back to Earth, a serious analysis of global dynamics should take stock of the fact that the modern world-system is not monolithic, but a complex braid composed of a capitalist world-economy, a states-system (nation-states, colonies and the interstate system) and a geoculture of ideologies, social movements and trends (Wallerstein, 2007).

Risk assessment has become central to decision making in modern society, especially since the advent of the World Wide Web and Generative AI. Harms that are not contained locally can propagate globally in a butterfly effect. Whereas errors can be fixed, harms that become permanent and widespread may come rather from successful solutions that benefit a particular system whose mission is given absolute precedence by a group. What appears as an immediate reward can result in long-term escalating damage to other systems and groups. If the originating group is powerful, selfish and unregulated, it will continue to press its agenda despite expansive collateral damage. Social systems theorist Niklas Luhmann (2012, 2017, 2018) describes societies as divided into specialised functional subsystems and considers systemic risks to emanate not from individual behaviour but from (centralised) optimistic institutional groupthink. There is a disconnect between scientific statistical risk analysis and the observer-dependent *perception* of risk, whereby risk-related behaviour deviates systematically from objective evidence. Risk management faces questions of risk tolerance: What is an acceptable level of risk? What is the threshold beyond which risk entails a catastrophic result? These dilemmas are at the centre of the blind pursuit of AGI, the regulation of Gen AI and the public release of technologies that facilitate widespread fraud and disinformation. The risk of regulation is far lower than those of voice cloning, deepfakes and other technologies that should not have been approved for release and which may still be recalled as a measure of damage control. Entities that have a legitimate and constructive use for such technologies may always be granted permits pursuant to registration, certification and licensing.

Watermarking provides a systematic solution to many types of digital forgery. All products derived from digital reproduction and manipulation, CGI, Gen AI, chatbots and similar technologies, which are not evidently so, constitute a form of public deception and potential fraud, unless they are subject to digital watermarking. Legislative efforts to demand digital watermarking have been met with misinformation from tech sources alleging that it is a fairly new technology and that watermarks are easily lifted, stolen and affixed to fraudulent documents (Heikkilä, 2023, 2024). OpenAI has withheld its ChatGPT watermarking tool pending additional security but also recognising the impact on their bottom line as 30% of users might then be deterred from using their platform (Seetharaman & Barnum, 2024). The pressure has concentrated on Big Tech under the assumption that smaller companies would not have access to the technology. In fact, the technology has been around for a long time, including watermarking devices available to smaller companies. The watermark may be visible or not, and its encrypted metadata is not easily removed, certainly not by most users. The risk resides in not employing it.

Building on steganographic work begun in 1993, mathematicians Moreno de Ayala and Tirkel (2010) developed theorems and patents for digital watermarking and fingerprinting devices. A multidimensional set of watermarking arrays is generated by algebraic sequencing using exponential, logarithmic, index or polynomial functions, with each array being constructed by convolving a multi-periodic shift array, while multiple columns of the arrays are additionally substituted with pseudo-noise sequences. Defeating the mark without the original template would require breaking a strong multidimensional encryption. 'Digital fingerprinting is a technique for tracing the distribution of multimedia content and protecting it from unauthorized manipulation' (Moreno de Ayala & Tirkel, 2013, p. 4). The technique traces the originator and recipients of the digital signal. Traditional watermarks and fingerprints produced by random number generators are vulnerable to collusion attacks, in which an adversarial clique of malicious users collate their copies to detect and eliminate the random variations, reverting to the clean original. The defence is a synchronisation watermark, which conceals the secret data in a pattern of polarity reversals of the pseudo-random noise array. Recipients are issued the same synchronisation watermarks, rendering collusion attacks ineffective. Fingerprinted copies are distributed to recipients, while the reference and raw files are kept by the distributor (p. 14).

The Coalition for Content Provenance and Authenticity, through its C2PA standard, binds cryptographic metadata with provenance information to AI and digital media, certifying its source and recipient history (C2PA, 2022). It joins the Adobe-led Content Authenticity Initiative (CAI) with Project Origin launched by Microsoft and the BBC to tackle disinformation in digital news, through an alliance of Adobe, Arm, Intel, Microsoft and Truepic. C2PA and CAI are open-source and can be integrated by companies and developers into any platform, product or tool. Google's SynthID uses a different watermarking protocol to fingerprint text, audio, image and video in their AI-generated content. In May 2024 Google added it to its Gemini AI model, and in October the company offered it as a free open-source toolkit (Orland, 2024). In addition, fingerprinting data can be stored on distributed ledger technology (DLT) commonly known as blockchain, a decentralised database in which encrypted data blocks are distributed across an exclusive peer-to-peer (P2P) network. The view that blockchain cryptocurrencies are private and untraceable has enabled illegal darknet transactions involving drugs, weapons, money laundering, human trafficking, terrorism and cybercrime (Eisermann, 2020). Several countries and international organisations are developing blockchain standards. Some tech companies are providing tracking solutions for businesses, banks and governments to protect consumers, while more transparent public blockchain cryptocurrencies like XRP are built with support from the business community. In response, cybercrime is moving to new private cryptos in a game of cat and mouse, until they, together with anonymous networks, are outlawed and dismantled.

The means of technology control do exist and are rapidly developing in response to public pressure. The central factor of government regulation requires political will to take precedence over vested interests. The Biden Administration issued an Executive Order directing 'the most sweeping actions ever taken to protect Americans from the potential risks of AI systems', including 'content authentication and watermarking' as well as 'rigorous standards for extensive red-team testing to ensure safety before public release' (The White House, 2023). A dedicated regulatory agency is still missing. In contrast, the Trump Administration is anti-regulation. The donations and support from the likes of Elon Musk and Mark Zuckerberg, based on shared interests, signals the typical mutualism which obtains among oligarchs and autocrats. Musk was named director of the new Department of Government Efficiency (DOGE), which has illegally attempted to dismantle the Consumer Financial Protection Bureau (CFPB) in a move fraught with conflicts of interest and corrupt practices (Allyn, 2025).

Translational Technologies

AI and other technologies are indeed used for many applications that directly benefit humans. The mark of translational technologies is that they are developed for specific purposes in response to concrete needs and are prioritised in terms of their timely beneficial impact as opposed to their marketability. Following translational science, technologies should be guided by the three metafunctions of language: conceptualise phenomena, organise strategic actions and optimise social interaction.

In Japan, a 2016 government initiative proposed Society 5.0, a plan to integrate the digital and physical spaces to address real-world living challenges guided by the outlook of a human-centric society. The concept divides social development into five stages: Society 1.0 (hunting-gathering), 2.0 (agricultural), 3.0 (industrial), 4.0 (informational) and Society 5.0, which could be called translational—from analogue to digital to analogue. The concept was a response to 'the fourth industrial revolution' or Industry 4.0 proposed in Germany, which centres on AI-driven industrial production and cyber-physical systems (CPS). The latter proceeds along five levels of increasing integration: I—smart connection via sensor network, II—data-to-information processing via analytics and multidimensional data correlation, III—memory modelling detecting variation and similarity for developing digital twin models for components and machines, IV—integrated simulation for collaborative diagnostics and decision making, V—machine self-configuration, adjustment and optimisation. In line with Japan, Germany came back with the now internationalised concept of Industry 5.0 adopted by the European Commission in 2023. It is an update of Industry 4.0 aimed at the transition to a human-centric economy that prioritises worker wellbeing and training in evolving skills over profits, as well as resource-efficient, sustainable and resilient industries that respect the planet's production limits in the transition to a fully circular economy. Its metafunctions focus on preservation of resources, climate change and social stability. See also Nousala et al. (2024).

Before ChatGPT, AI was merely a reception rather than a production technology (search engines, pattern matching, voice and face recognition, machine learning, etc.). Advances in machine translation, especially at Google, made use of neural networks leading to large language models (LLMs) such that AI was able to produce translations as an intermediate step to Gen AI. ChatGPT was a proof of concept that Gen AI was able not only to receive and process data but also, for the first time, to generate new tokens, new synthetic data. Generative adversarial networks (GANs) could then be used to generate ever more realistic models. GANs are a type of AI algorithm that uses multilayer neural networks (deep learning) to generate new synthetic data that reconfigures and resembles its real-world training dataset. It works with two competing neural networks: a Generator produces a model based on an input data sample, while its output becomes the input of a Discriminator, which compares it to its own real data, determines the differences and feeds back to the Generator the corrective weight changes it needs to make to approximate reality after several iterations. A Generator can also cycle through a chain of Discriminators. GANs work particularly well for images and models. It improves 3D modelling, printing and machining in digital fabrication; it can help detect digital forgery, image fraud and disinformation; and it generates accurate digital twins for realistic simulations. An ambitious project is Digital Twin Earth, which can simulate and predict weather globally as well as model the future effects of climate change (Nvidia, 2024).

Computer simulation (CS) for dynamic systems modelling is among the most useful applications of these emerging technologies. Optimisation theory requires *qualitative*, *quantitative* and *simulative* approaches. CS produces a numerical model of the functional relationships within a real system in the form of a computer program whose weighted values can be changed to test for different results. It works like a sandbox in which an algorithm calculates the state of a system and evaluates the results in terms of their fit with the parameters of target outcomes and goals. Hypotheses can be tested, and results visualised as animated computer graphics. Simulations allow for extensive virtual experimentation which would be impractical or unsafe in the lab or the physical world. Its endless uses include architectural rendering, engineering design and prediction, macroeconomic analysis, wargame simulation, social dynamics, weather forecasting, manufacturing and logistics optimisation, chemical reaction modelling and materials development, biomedical research and general systems emulation. Simulation results are compared to both, physical conditions to improve the model and theoretical predictions to refine the theory. The analogue metagrammar of a physical system is thereby digitised and its functions *approximated* by mathematical equations.

What is lost in the translation from analogue to digital? The answer is the human factor: implicit or *tacit knowledge*. Michael Polanyi (1966) theorised that implicit human knowledge of how the world functions and how to best function in it (i.e., metagrammar) is much broader and nuanced than our ability to pinpoint and explain it, let alone formalise, codify, automate or program it. Ask an expert 'How do you know?' and the answer might be 'I just know' or 'How do you do it?—I don't know, I just do it'. It is a holistic experiential knowledge that cannot simply be broken down into parts. How do you ride a bicycle? I can give you some basic instructions, but you must do it for a long time to really understand it. Riding a bicycle involves the entire body in unison: muscle memory, vestibular balance, complex sensory-motor coordination, vision, sound, touch, environmental cognition, reflexes, negotiating the road, anticipation and pre-emption. In short, don't think it, just do it. Malcolm Gladwell (2008) popularised the idea that it takes 10,000 hours of methodical practice to attain mastery. Tacit knowledge is the difference between a chef and a recipe, between a maestro and the sheet music. It is the part of mastery that cannot be built into the machine: the knack, tricks of the trade, sixth sense, judgement calls, maternal instinct, artistic sensibility, adept improvisation and troubleshooting of the master bricklayer, carpenter, mechanic, surgeon, poet and scientist. Polanyi considered tacit knowledge to be much broader than explicit knowledge. Economist David Autor (2014) called this phenomenon the Polanyi's paradox, which has come to be understood as a limit to the power and impact of automation and AI.

As we saw in Chapter 13, mathematician and cryptologist Alan Turing, the inventor of the computer, proved in his paper 'On Computable Numbers' (1936) that some things are not computable, namely those which are so complex that they can only be described by uncountable numbers, whose calculation would require infinite steps, and therefore can never be reduced to an algorithm. I would define tacit knowledge as one of those things. Moreover, Zeno's paradox of infinite fractional measurement shows that we can never get to the bottom of things, that every measurement must halt at an approximation and that true precision requires an incomputable number. Children discover the qualitative equivalent of this at an early age, when they keep asking 'Why?' after every answer: 'Why do you step on the brakes? Because I drive defensively. Why? Because drivers do stupid things. Why? Because they are distracted. Why? Because their children keep asking why. Why? You tell me'. Adults run out of answers when it gets to tacit, unexplainable knowledge. They lose their patience and think that kids do this to annoy them, when in fact children are just fascinated by the discovery.

The limits of computation can best be discerned when considering closed versus open systems. Computers can beat chess masters and Chinese Go champions, because board games have finite rulesets that govern every move. They are closed systems. An AI flight simulator consistently beats an ace fighter pilot, not only because it can compute many more possibilities and sensor readings with faster reaction time, to correct course several times per second and execute more accurate manoeuvres, but ultimately because airplane sensors and controls are part of a closed digital system with finite parameters. Any system governed by a ruleset is a closed and finite system. However, put AI on a World War I fighter plane with few analogue gauges and controls, and I'll put my money on the Red Baron, the ace-of-aces credited with 80 combat kills across the World War I skies. A mixed case is that of self-driving cars. They do okay within the speed limit and the rules of the road and may even be safer than most drivers, but the presence of unpredictable pedestrians and human drivers makes the road an open system which automatons can never fully master. Most systems outside the laboratory or the parameters of computer simulation are indeed open systems subject to Polanyi's paradox.

Computer simulation, however, is a powerful *tool*, not as a replacement but as an aid to tacit human knowledge and mastery. Of particular interest for the advancement of knowledge is its application to the *discovery of mechanisms* (i.e., metagrammars) through pattern recognition and (meta)grammar induction enabled by machine learning. In translational science, mechanism discovery begins in biology, biochemistry and genetics, expands to industrial design through biomimetics and yields models applicable to social and behavioural sciences. Tacit knowledge is involved from beginning to end.

An *analogue* precursor of mechanism discovery (after DaVinci and Dürer) is classics scholar and biomathematician D'Arcy Wentworth Thompson, *On Growth and Form* (1917), which led to the field of *morphogenesis* or the generation of forms in nature. He is a brilliant example of classical comparative grammar's application to the conceptualisation of natural phenomena. Thompson emphasised the role of physical mechanisms in the growth and transformation of biological forms over Darwin's reliance on genetic mutations as drivers of evolution. He placed plant and animal forms on the Cartesian coordinate plane to measure their transformations, pioneering mathematical biology. He used geometric formulas to develop models of biomechanical structures reproduced in architectural design; and dwelled on the logarithmic spiral of shells which grow by geometric progression, the phyllotactic spirals of pinecones and leaves or the crisscross spirals of sunflowers which follow the Fibonacci sequence based on the golden ratio, as well as the irregular spirals of animal horns affected by torsion. These physical models and their partial differential equations reappear in the vortices of fluid mechanics, the spirals of cyclones, spiral galaxies and the double helix of DNA, as it has for centuries in the spiral dynamics of history proposed by such thinkers as Vico and Herder.

The first *digital* model of dynamic biological formations (growth) comes from none other than Alan Turing, in his lesser-known paper, 'The Chemical Basis of Morphogenesis' (1952). In addition to Thompson's use of classical mechanics, Turing uses chemical reactions as physical determinants of non-directed (automatic) growth. In his 1936 seminal paper 'On Computable Numbers', Turing had arrived at the 'halting problem' of determining whether a computer program set in motion by an input leading to a non-computable number would halt or run forever. Any algorithm designed to halt the program would send the machine into an endless loop of halt-run commands. This *binary* arrangement of opposing forces has become the computable action-inhibition model behind the conceptualisation of mechanisms in the physical, cognitive and behavioural sciences. In this case, Turing sets out to 'discuss a possible mechanism by which the genes of a zygote may determine the anatomical structure of the resulting organism' (p.37). He considers genes to be catalysts for the chemical reactions that produce active substances he calls *morphogens* or 'form producers' which diffuse through tissues. Genes themselves may be considered morphogens of a special non-diffusible class. 'It would be more accurate to regard them as radicals of the giant molecules known as chromosomes' (p. 38).

Turing advanced the science by applying these binary forces to, not one, but two systems: chemical reactions (describable by quantum mechanics) and molecular diffusion (describable by classical mechanics and thermodynamics). For this he developed new two-component reaction–diffusion equations. Chemical reactions are fuelled by the availability of adjacent substances and are halted by their depletion as the system returns to equilibrium. He gives the example of a bacteria culture that grows until the food supply runs out. Parenthetically, in systems theory this equates to the depletion of inventory stock, and in human data mining it results in the inequity of what Turing calls 'infinite free fuel'. Concurrent with reaction, diffusion provides a time factor, a rate of movement from areas of high concentration to areas of low concentration until an equilibrium (entropy) is reached. The rate of diffusion accelerates as adjacent spread-opportunities increase and decelerates as opportunities decrease towards equilibrium, describing a computable sinewave on the Cartesian plane. Diffusion works both, in the spread of chemical reactions and in the spread of the resulting morphogens through tissue.

Exactly like a computer program, Turing posits a 'state of the system' consisting of two parts: the mechanical and the chemical. Changes in the state proceed digitally step-by-step. The initial state is dormant equilibrium without growth, but it may 'develop a pattern or structure (growth) due to an instability of the homogeneous equilibrium, which is triggered off by random disturbances' (p. 37). However, Turing's genius recognises that diffusion itself will cause a stable system to become unstable, generating growth patterns. All this can be approximated by reaction–diffusion equations, which are a composite of well-established equations and formulas of the past. Thompson and Turing both note the reiteration of growth forms within single organisms following the principle of self-similarity as evidence of a repeating mechanism or equation. This would later be developed in *The Fractal Geometry of Nature* (1982) as the Mandelbrot set. Turing's concept of 'random disturbances' producing orderly patterns in nature would be central to Mandelbrot and form part of Chaos Theory (Lorenz, 1963). From Turing to Chaos Theory, a small random disturbance at the initial condition can have huge consequences magnified by the 'butterfly effect' which can be modelled by algorithmic amplification. By the same token, disinformation memes in social media can spread virally and snowball into conspiracy theories.

Crucial to computer modelling is Turing's use of geometry to complete his morphogenetic model which describes growth patterns such as the formation and distribution of spots on the skin of certain fish and other animals and plants. These are fittingly called Turing patterns, which paved the way for many reaction–diffusion models now visualised through animated computer graphics. Turing posits the geometric form of a 'circle of cells', which can be expanded to the tubular formation of bones, limbs, tentacles, plant stems and so forth. Now, if you trace a circle along a time span, the result is a spiral, which on the two-dimensional Cartesian plane describes a sinewave whose equation is well known from the study of radio signals, sound waves and oscillation. Further, following the Fourier series for periodic signals or the Fourier transform for non-periodic signals, the sinusoidal oscillation can be analysed into harmonics and expanded from ring to spherical harmonics with several azimuthal lines, approximating various natural forms. Each cell and the ring of cells itself are subject to reaction–diffusion oscillation, which can make growth depart from a perfect circle, with the ring developing into quasi regular spirals like those described by Thompson's spiral dynamics.

Setting other equations aside, Turing begins his paper with the following admission: 'This model will be a simplification and an idealization, and consequently a falsification [...] cells are idealized into geometrical points [and] the matter of the organism is imagined as continuously distributed' (pp. 37–38). This is exactly the case with all scientific theories and representational models (including LLMs). They leave out 'extraneous' variables and consider ideal situations resembling perfect geometrical figures that do not occur in nature. Underlying such idealisation is the assumption that natural variations have a normal bell-curve distribution, in which the ideal model would be at the probabilistic top-centre of the normal distribution. Turing further simplifies the model by using linear equations. For their still complex calculations, however, Turing enlists the help of the 1951 Manchester University digital computer.

Edward Lorenz as well used a conventional computer without artificial intelligence (the 1956 LGP-30)—together with his tacit expertise—to model weather patterns by computing 12 variables such as temperature, pressure, moisture and wind. AI now makes computation much more powerful while still using earlier expert principles. For example, probabilistic systems apply the Gaussian distribution or 'bell curve' to each random variable, analysed by the mean, median, mode and variance of a sample population. The curve may be skewed by different factors or deviate in amplitude, length and phase, but it can be 'normalised' as per the central limit theorem and measures of central tendency. The normal distribution represents the *idealised* situation of highest probability which makes the symmetrical bell curve a perfect geometrical figure that serves as the index against which deviations are measured. The multivariate Gaussian distribution can model numerous variables and their bell curves in *n*-dimensional non-Euclidean space. We cannot visualise more than three dimensions, so we can just imagine all these bell curves floating in space, but the machine does not need to 'visualise'. It calculates the compounded bell curves of numerous variables through the Gaussian multiple approximation process that underlies machine learning and can plot several curves on the same plane or on successive planes for visualisation. The enhanced processing speed of modern CPUs that makes AI possible allows the effects of value changes to be visualised as animated graphics. The multilinear processing capacity of quantum computing promises to represent these changes in real time allowing for live visualisation of such processes as the synthesis, behaviour and effects of enzymes and proteins, with great value for medicine, pharmacology and the molecular design of biocompatible materials. Further, machine learning can automatically detect patterns in random datasets and identify statistically significant variables used to construct models for complex problem solving. It can, for example, identify the geographical distribution of disease factors from a body of raw data.

Nevertheless, everything from the formulation of hypotheses, theories, strategies and creative experimental designs to the interpretation of results requires tacit human expertise. Bayesian statistics incorporates tacit knowledge in its view of probability as a degree of belief (credence) based on previous results but also on prior knowledge and beliefs. In 'Strategies for Discovering Mechanisms', Darden (2002) emphasises that 'Discovery proceeds in stages of construction, evaluation and revision, each constrained by what is known or conjectured about what is being discovered' (p. 354). This case entails a protein synthesis mechanism that goes from DNA replication, its transcription to RNA and translation into a protein. The stages include characterising the phenomenon, constructing a schema, evaluating it and revising it. The strategies include schema instantiation, modular subassembly and forward/backward chaining. This shows that metagrammar is akin to the field of mechanical philosophy (Glennan & Allari, 2017).

Computer simulation aids in discovering new mechanisms for bioconjugation, consisting in binding synthetically modified biomolecules to track cellular behaviour, enzyme function, protein diffusion or biomarkers, as well as delivering medication to targeted cells, including antibody–drug conjugates (ADCs) that attack cancer tumours without hurting healthy cells. Bioconjugation is starting to be used to enhance CRISPR-Cas9 gene therapy by binding Cas9 proteins with markers, drugs or other molecules that improve DNA repair during gene editing. Cas9 follows a guide RNA to cut a faulty DNA strand and replace it with the proper one. CRISPR (clustered regularly interspaced short palindromic repeats) is derived from a language palindrome, that is, a word like kayak that is spelled the same backwards and forward. In the antiparallel double-stranded DNA or RNA molecule, it means a short sequence of nucleotides (like TCGA) in one strand, which appears 'backward' (AGCT) in the opposite strand. A DNA segment containing a set of morphogenic instructions for making different kinds of proteins is a gene. Each nucleus of a human cell has 23 pairs of homologous chromosomes, each pair containing the same genes from the mother or father. Each X-shaped chromosome has hundreds of genes making up an estimated 25,000 genes in the human genome. Despite great discoveries, genetics is still in its infancy. A deeper understanding is to be expected the more its constituents (proteins, enzymes, genes, DNA, RNA, chromosomes and cells) are'read' or conceptualised as a systemic functional grammar, like language, endowed with multifunctionality, multidimensionality and higher metafunctions.

Translational science applied to this gene-editing technology dictates that it be used for specific purposes answering specific human needs. CRISPR is used in cancer immunotherapy and to correct genetic variants for treating a growing number of genetic diseases like sickle cell anaemia as well as viral infections like HIV and COVID-19. Other uses include modifying mosquitoes to make them resistant to the malaria parasite, improving crops, developing new medicines and studying the function of genes by activating or inhibiting their expression. As with cloning and genetic engineering, gene editing presents serious ethical considerations. In many countries it is illegal to alter the human germline making the changes inheritable, as opposed to the somatic line which only alters individual bodies, but not the genes of embryos, eggs or sperm cells. There is also an ecological concern. The Cas enzyme is part of the antiviral immune system of several bacteria and can easily be harvested from bacteria cultures using low-tech methods. Kits are available for biohackers, who may use it to 'cure' or 'upgrade' themselves or release modified species into the wild, with unknown long-term effects.

The credence of computer simulation is not as high when dealing with people's non-mechanical behavioural processes in complex problem solving for social, economic and policy goals. The aim here is to optimise the decision making, behaviour and outcomes of people confronted with problems in dynamic social systems. Human empathy and tacit knowledge are required to define goals and break them up into subgoals. The mental representation of the system to be managed—required for model building—is challenging when its network of variables is unknown, necessitating data collection to formulate hypotheses. This can be aided by machine learning. However, broadening the knowledge base requires self-questioning using one's own culturally bound conceptual or linguo-mental structures. An LLM can help in designing a process of intention generation, selection and regulation. The effect of decisions and actions is monitored and evaluated, followed by self-reflection to adapt and improve it. Once built, a computer simulation model that can run different scenarios would be helpful as well. Significantly, the most efficient strategy for building and adapting a model is having it reconstruct past behaviour before it can be used for prediction. Bayesian decision theory uses conjugate distributions by calculating a model's outcome probability distribution before new evidence is added (conjugate prior) and comparing it to the conjugate posterior distribution. It then weighs the benefit of each outcome to guide the decision-maker.

The same simulation model may only be used for problems belonging to the same metagrammatical family or *genre*, which may be interdisciplinary. This requires different models to be designed with a narrow purpose for specific applications. The more general the program, the less accurate and effective. As the scope of a model broadens, the breadth and depth of tacit knowledge that remains beyond its grasp becomes insurmountable, leading to the diminishing credence and eventual collapse of general intelligence models.

AGI, artificial general intelligence, is dead. Translational science and tacit knowledge require LLMs to be trained as closed systems for specific purposes. This requires supervised training and a curated knowledge base, which is not scalable to general open systems. Semi-supervised training may be adequate for certain applications, and then unsupervised machine learning takes place within specific expert parameters. Unsupervised training open to the rubbish heap of the Internet cannot guarantee content quality for precision applications. The future is a return to AI expert systems for specific professional purposes. Many tech companies are moving in this direction. Nvidia Inference Microservices (NIMS) trains modular AI experts for specific applications in industry, which can be integrated via Application Programming Interfaces (APIs) to form AI expert teams that interface and learn from each other. An AI expert system for the professions, such as medical specialities, gathers the knowledge base of accredited subject-matter experts (SMEs) and is curated by expert users, while machine learning algorithms incorporate new expert decisions, evidence and mechanisms in an open-ended quest for *approximating* tacit knowledge in areas of high specialisation.

Developmental Education

Translational science equally applies to education, which should be developmental in the measure that it affords the individual a multidisciplinary basis for critical thinking and problem solving with which to approach and evaluate future experience in personal and professional life. This has been associated traditionally with a well-rounded liberal arts education, which has been periodically updated since the ancient trivium of grammar, logic and rhetoric (argumentation and composition), followed by the quadrivium of mathematical arts (arithmetic, geometry, music and astronomy). The seven liberal arts were the basic *thinking skills* as opposed to practical skills like theology, medicine or architecture. However, as society, knowledge and technology became more diversified, this educational scheme was repeatedly revised and today must include computer science and artificial intelligence. Moreover, thinking skills do not develop in the abstract but are inseparable from practical applications.

The concept of liberal arts has been superseded by that of the *core curriculum*, which combines theoretical and applied skills. However, higher education has been coopted by the wrongful application of business metagrammar to educational institutions, now run like businesses based on market competition and return on investment. A prime example is the emphasis placed by technocrat U.S. President Barack Obama on science, technology, engineering and math (STEM). The acronym falsely exploits the recent isolation of human embryonic stem cells (1998) and the derivation of induced pluripotent stem cells from differentiated somatic cells (2006–2007). Stem cells are embryonic cells that can differentiate into the multitude of body (somatic) cell types forming organs and tissue. This mediating metaphor purports that STEM disciplines are the new quadrivium, the new core of education from which everything else proceeds, even though it circumvents the foundational trivium of grammar, logic and rhetoric which are the very basis of reasoning. This misrepresentation dovetails with the flow of funds from government, business and industry for highly specialised (as opposed to core) sponsored research. The entire educational apparatus bends to these funds like a plant seeking sunlight. Companies and surrogate governments seek premature specialisation to pass along the cost and responsibility of on-the-job training to colleges and universities, which are made to pursue institutional benefit at the expense of individual students. The role of the core curriculum and undergraduate education is to impart foundational thinking life-skills to individual students and show that they are primed and trainable for a variety of opportunities after graduation. That is, students *are* the stem cells, empowered by *liberal* education to *freely* differentiate according to personal interests, aptitudes and opportunities.

A developmental core curriculum for the twenty-first century should recognise four basic forms of thinking: (a) comparative grammar, (b) mathematical and propositional logic, (c) statistics and probabilistic thinking, and (d) historicism. These should be conjugated with sets of applied fields: physics, chemistry, biology and computer science (enabled by logic and statistics); psychology, sociology and history (enabled by statistics and historicism); writing, rhetorical and narrative studies (enabled by comparative grammar and logic). A balance of science and humanities is the foundation of a translational approach to all specialised fields.

Schank and Cleary (1995) criticise standard school curricula and uniform reading lists supposed to make for an 'educated person' as a way of learning facts and memorising formulas. They proposed an opposite, single-goal approach, learning *how to reason* within different disciplines instead of mastering a multitude of facts, an approach they call 'cultural uniliteracy' (pp. 63–64). They point out that learning takes different forms: natural, incidental, practical, exploratory, and reflective through case-based and goal-directed learning on an open curriculum. They even specify the kind of software needed to create educational 'engines' (pp. 175–181). Bureaucracies and politicians had other ideas, and Roger Schank went on to criticise all the policies and failures of the K-12 educational system in years of sharp blog posts collected under the title, *Education Outrage* (2016).

The vehicles of instruction and the methods of delivery are now driven more by technology than by pedagogical principles. Distance learning has moved from courses by mail to those on audio tape, video,

CD-ROM or download and now to online courses. Online platforms dubbed Virtual Learning Environments (VLE) or most often Learning Management Systems (LMS) quickly appeared: Moodle (2002), Blackboard (beta 1997, stable 2014), Canvas (2011) and numerous others. Massive open online courses (MOOCs) began in 2008 and peaked in popularity towards 2012. They require discipline, motivation and unsupervised dedication, and thus many students fail to keep up and finish the courses. The modality was commercialised by companies like Coursera, offering global MOOC access to thousands of courses on a monthly or yearly subscription basis. Individual instructors could market their courses on the clearinghouse. The number of poorly paid unaffiliated 'gypsy' professors grew to the detriment of the profession, resulting in a lack of continuity for students and a lack of commitment to the institution and to peer-reviewed research. Fully online universities offering substandard degrees capitalised on the business model.

During the COVID-19 pandemic, most universities had to quickly migrate courses online, leading to lasting structural changes despite efforts to repopulate the campus. Professors hoping to develop a stable online course after intensive preparation were disappointed. Migrating from one LMS to another took major course redesign. Adobe Flash multimedia file format (SWF) stopped being supported. HTML5 (Hypertext Markup Language 5) is now retired and succeeded by HTML Living Standard, both dependent on JavaScript. New functionalities are continuously added to the chosen LMS, such that online courses remain a work in progress, defeating the purpose of automation. On the positive side, LMS platforms with expanded functionality allow for multimedia content, distribution of extensive course materials, as well as discussion boards, group projects and videoconferencing to compensate for the lack of in-person interaction. Direct student-instructor contact may even increase over in-person modalities through LMS messaging. There are advantages and disadvantages. The online convenience allows for global reach but reduces enrolment in local in-person courses. Videoconferencing and other synchronous activities, in which instructor and students log on at the same time, are difficult to schedule, and students who cannot attend resent it as unfair. Online students prefer asynchronous and even self-paced courses, which cut down on interaction with instructor and peers. Over time, online courses become 'canned', more uniform and less personalised, with such things as *scripted feedback*, commonly used in AI-assisted courses.

AI has become a secular educational disruptor since the release of ChatGPT on 30 November 2022. It began with the realisation that students were using *it* instead of their brain in widespread copying and plagiarism. The alarm increased when it was shown that ChatGPT could write essays and pass science tests and even the law bar exam. The first reaction was to police students by detecting cheating, plagiarism and AI-generated content, which is not easy to do in the absence of digital watermarking. Students who performed better than usual became immediate suspects. Teachers were required to run student work through a search engine as well as through ChatGPT and third-party apps to see which portions were lifted right out of the Internet. Methods were disseminated to try and identify tell-tale signs of AI-generated content. Commercial detection apps soon hit the market. None of it was quite successful. Soon educators and instructional designers realised that policing students does not work, and neither does resisting AI since it can help in many ways, students will always have access to it and employers will expect AI literacy.

The solution is to develop a metagrammar for teaching with AI. This entails redesigning assignments, projects and assessments. The first step is to *focus on process*, not product, letting students develop AI literacy by using it, discovering its strengths and weaknesses and above all critiquing its output. Improving Gen AI output is a function of improving the input by formulating better questions and prompts. 'Prompt engineering' requires experimentation, preferably following expert tips (Bowen & Watson, 2024, pp. 48–61). The second step is to turn the assignment into a multi-part project with strategic and achievable milestones. The focus on process is reinforced by requiring students to present transcripts or screenshot of their interaction with ChatGPT or other LLM for each part of the project. AI assignments become engaging when they show their value and relevance to students. Translational metagrammar helps by framing data, abstract concepts and theories in terms of their benefit for students and their goals. Assignments should support skills development in written, multimedia and oral expression, including reasoning and critical thinking skills. At advanced levels, students can suggest and design projects to suit their interests.

Linguist Bela Bathany (1996) introduced the concepts of divergent and convergent thinking in design metagrammar, which the British Design Council represented as the 'double diamond' innovative design process. The first diamond represents the problem and the second one the solution, each divided in half. The first half of the problem is to discover it by talking to a (divergent) variety of people affected by it. The second half is to clearly define it in a (convergent) organised way based on the issues discovered. In the design solution, the first phase is to develop different (divergent) answers by brainstorming, looking at several other designs and involving different people in the design team. The second phase is to try different solutions and incorporate the best ones into a (convergent) prototype to be tested and improved in various iterations.

Using this process, instructors can design a wide range of assignment types requiring critical thinking based on the capabilities of the platform and the requirements of the subject to be taught. LinkedIn Learning offers preliminary MOOC modules on critical thinking, leadership, career planning and other skills for higher education. AI assignments can move from simple text activities to complex multimedia. Basic activities include iterative writing feedback, collaborative text analysis using a social annotation tool like Perusall; critiquing AI responses to course related questions; student-driven discussions about specific topics on a behaviour incentive social media platform like YellowDig or Harmonise; AI-assisted presentations; learning-games with content creation platforms like H5P; ChatGPT financial planning asking about budgeting, investments, retirement, insurance and taxes; iterative problem solving and more. Multimedia AI projects involve creating complex scenarios and virtual environments. Examples include virtual science labs, measurable topography, astrolabe ocean course plotting, design solutions, social media campaigns, podcast creation, AI-generated fictional community for sociological and ethnographic exploration, modelling ecologies; problem solving in conflict zones, the environment and social justice; or conducting virtual genetic research in CRISPR-Cas9 technology. PlayPosit enables professors to embed interactions into video content for student engagement. Kritik offers an AI course creator that generates customisable assignments and rubrics, provides accountable collaboration and enables anonymous bias-free peer evaluations. At the level of primary and secondary school, the non-profit Khan Academy has set the standard for critical thinking in AI education with Khanmigo, an AI tool that contrary to ChatGPT or Bard does not give answers but guides students to find the answers themselves. Khanmigo is an AI teaching assistant that helps with curriculum and lesson planning, student groupings, essay review, quiz questions, rubrics, grading and feedback; as well as a learner assistant that acts as a study and debate partner, writing coach, tutor, code reviewer and homework helper—all linked to a content library that covers most academic subjects. As far as those annoying *Why?* questions of younger children, I suggest accompanying them to the very patient ChatGPT, starting with prompts like *Why is the sky blue?*—and turning annoyance into exploration learning.

Microsoft Copilot, a Gen AI chatbot based on the GPT-4 LLM platform, was launched in 2023. A recent television advertisement shows a young professional who has a major business presentation due the next day. He asks Copilot to take existing texts and images on file, and presto! The chatbot spits out a 150-page report and summary presentation. Where is the critical thinking? Writing, composing and designing are exploration processes in which new insights arise. This begs the question of *skills atrophy*, which we may provisionally dub the 'calculator effect'. It is not too much of an exaggeration to note that when calculators came out arithmetic skills declined, just like handwriting in the texting generation. I must confess that as a high-school student, when the Texas Instruments SR-50 scientific calculator came out, I stopped calculating square roots, sines and cosines, logarithms and factorials. When IBM's SPSS statistical software came out, I forgot the formulas for analysis of variance and multiple regression. Certainly, academics and specialists will continue to delve deeply into principles and formulas, but what about the general population? AI assistants will increasingly do the thinking for us. Mere mortals will abdicate critical thinking and problem solving, become tools, dependent on and directed by the machines. It is already happening. Combatting this is a central battle for developmental education.

Once the initial uproar surrounding ChatGPT calmed down, people started noticing its flaws and limitations beyond oversimplified answers and occasional 'hallucinations'. The systemic limitations of LLMs are much deeper. Contrary to AI expert systems, which are closed, that is, trained on curated human data, general-purpose LLMs are open to the polluted Internet. This is because updating and growing curated content is not a scalable or cost-effective corporate model. It is easier to feed on free data from the web, even though sifting through it requires ever greater and costlier computing power and energy consumption, both of which are limited. This is where Kurzweil's futurist 'law of accelerating returns' which imagines a limitless exponential growth of technology, collapses. That is not the only thing that collapses. A series of problems arise when AI feeds off the Internet, which receives hundreds of billions of words and millions of images per day from AI-generated *synthetic data* mixed with human-generated *real data*. 'Imagine a medical advice chatbot that lists fewer diseases that match your symptoms, because it was trained on a narrower spectrum of medical knowledge generated by previous chatbots. Or an AI history tutor that ingests AI-generated propaganda and can no longer separate fact from fiction' (Bhatia, 2024). When Gen AI is trained on its own output over and over, the results degenerate over time. This is because AI is a predictive system based on probabilities, and each pass is strongly biased to the centre of the bell curve. Eventually, the curve gets taller and narrower until it collapses, and the output drifts away from reality. When AI was trained thirty times with its own generated digits 0–9, their shape became an identical blur. The same thing happened when AI was trained with a series of human faces. They started looking more and more alike, until they became the same blurred face generated by a collapsing probabilistic model. In every case the result was a *loss of diversity*. This amplifies biases and erases minority data. AI companies can try to avoid their own output with patches and watermarking, but there are already vast amounts of undetectable synthetic data on the web.

There is, however, a collapse in diversity that is already underway. Users of ChatGPT and other LLMs immediately noticed that their output comes in the form of uncomplicated sentence constructions and common vocabulary with limited variation. This is our present *initial state*, due to the same central tendency of all probabilistic systems. Guo et al. (2024) tested for *linguistic diversity* along the lexical (vocabulary), syntactical and semantic dimensions when recursively training language models on synthetic text. The metrics show that semantic diversity remained relatively stable, but intersentence coherence dropped. The decline in lexical diversity was significant across three tasks with increasing degrees of freedom: news summarisation, scientific abstract generation and story generation. Compared to human performance, the language models initially dropped an average of 30% in lexical diversity and 53% by the sixth iteration. The researchers note, however, that *syntactic diversity* 'suffers remarkably' and 'manifests a decreasing trend, especially for creative tasks, comparable to the decline in lexical diversity'. They conclude: 'as language models increasingly rely on predecessor-generated text for training, there is a tangible risk of diminishing linguistic richness and variety in their outputs' (pp. 7–8).

When it comes to critical thinking and problem solving, syntax is the greater part of lexicogrammar. An impoverished syntactic repertoire and vocabulary means a more limited and less flexible metagrammar with which to conceptualise the world and organise goal-directed action. The effect increases when the simplified, analytic English grammar is translated into the world's synthetic languages. The loss of lexicogrammatical diversity is the opposite of the expansive flexibility obtained from comparative grammar which, as we saw in Chapter 5, correlates with general intelligence and higher cognitive function. AI cannibalism aside, I am now ready to replace the 'calculator effect' with a new paradox: as AI gets smarter, humans turn dumber!

Conclusion

This book has been an evidence-based exploration of the idea that the metagrammar of human conceptualisation and behaviour is an extension of our natural language grammar. Metagrammar is a critical tool and a way of articulating elements into meaningful structures, which are organised into genres by similarity and family resemblances. Its structures, like those of grammar, cut across many genres and disciplines and are applicable to everyday life. It is a language-bound system whose elements are multifunctional and whose ethos is to serve the higher order metafunctions of human understanding and expression, strategic action and social interaction through the exchange of meaning and ideas.

A small error or correction of metagrammar can have a snowballing, butterfly effect. In 2008, I used this critical method to deconstruct an abusive trial in U.S. federal court against some 400 defendants, most of whom were illiterate indigenous migrants slaving away at a meat-packing plant. They were accused of an ill-fitting crime, 'aggravated identity theft', an antiterrorist charge introduced in the wake of the 11 September 2001 attack on New York City. The evidence? They had been sold 'working papers' they could not read, including a made-up social security number they knew nothing about. The identity theft statute is U.S. Criminal Code section 1028A: 'Knowingly uses the form of identification of another person' in furtherance of a crime. The latter is the 'predicate offence', in this case 'social security fraud'. Never mind that both offences refer to one and the same act, resulting in circular reasoning. The dubious claim of the prosecution was that the adverb 'Knowingly' applied only as far as 'the form of identification' but not 'of another person'. They could convict without proving that the defendants knew of such other person. The scheme had led to hundreds of convictions upheld in three appeal courts. In plain English usage, however, the adverb 'Knowingly' unquestionably applies to the entire clause. How could so many educated lawyers and judges fail Grammar 101? The answer: bias. The snowball: this mass prosecution was a pilot project to be replicated on a grand scale across the country for deporting millions of undocumented workers as 'criminal aliens' to boost deportation statistics and secure increasing funding from Congress—another misapplication of business metagrammar, here to law enforcement, based on 'return on investment'. My report additionally reduced this scheme to the absurd calling it a 'lottery of justice': the lucky ones with a vacant social security number could not be prosecuted! Using Propp's narrative theory, I deconstructed the proceeding and the wrongful metagrammar of immigration policy. The counter-snowball: my report reached the U.S. Supreme Court, who echoed my points in a unanimous 9–0 ruling

(USSC 08–108, 4 March 2009) to disallow such prosecutorial scheme, thereby removing the threat of wrongful criminalisation for millions of workers and future generations (Camayd-Freixas, 2008, 2013).

Three endeavours I hope should follow from this book. First, the subject of metagrammar requires further intersubjective development in the form of analysis and critique from other voices, perspectives and fields. I have touched with my limited perspective upon different fields on which I am not a specialist but rather an informed layperson. In particular, psycholinguistic experimental studies are needed concerning internalised functional grammar gestalts. Second, the implementation of comparative grammar should go beyond simple second-language education to a team-taught college course design starting with an introduction to functional grammar and metagrammar, followed by class sessions taught by instructors of different languages covering the basics of the writing system, word formation and contrastive syntax of the nominal, verbal and prepositional systems. Each module should be capped by available resources and study-abroad opportunities. It would be a foundational course as well as a sampler of language programs for optional future studies. This one-semester course could be part of the core curriculum at many institutions where the traditional two- or four-semester language requirement is under pressure. The course should be followed by a longitudinal study of student achievement. Third, it is appropriate to envision an AI grammar-induction platform that could discover matching patterns between multilingual functional grammars and the metagrammars of different processes and designs, categorised into genres.

The overarching conclusion of this book is that the metaphysical dogma of mechanical philosophy (which underwrites computer science) that everything can be reduced to and explained by a mechanism is a gross distortion of reality. At the risk of oversimplifying, metagrammar can be divided into three kingdoms: the **mechanical**, which is physical, rigid and deterministic; the **organic**, which is more flexible, susceptible to random accidents and endowed with morphogenesis, the capacity for growth, healing and self-repair; and the **mental**, which is the most flexible and undetermined. They each follow radically different metagrammars. The mental kingdom, made up of sensory images attended by mentalese propositions and linguomental categories to form what we call reasoning, as well as its outward expressions and representations, are fundamentally structured by natural language grammar. Reasoning clones grammatical structures beyond the sentence to formulate the metagrammars by which it apprehends and represents all mechanical, organic and mental phenomena. Language is the window through which we frame reality.

References

Allyn, B. (2025, February 12). Elon Musk's DOGE takes aim at agency [Consumer Financial Protection Bureau] that had plans of regulating X. *NPR News*. Retrieved from https://www.npr.org/2025/02/12/nx-s1-5293382/x-elon-musk-doge-cfpb

Autor, D. (2014, September). Polanyi's paradox and the shape of employment growth. NBER Working Paper 20485. Cambridge, MA: National Bureau of Economic Research. Retrieved from http://www.nber.org/papers/w20485

Bathany, B. H. (1996). *Designing Social Systems in a Changing World*. Springer.

Bhatia, A. (2024, August 25). When A.I.'s output is a threat to A.I. itself. *The New York Times*. Retrieved from https://www.nytimes.com/interactive/2024/08/26/upshot/ai-synthetic-data.html

Bowen, J. A., & Watson, C. E. (2024). *Teaching with AI: A Practical Guide to a New Era of Human Learning*. Johns Hopkins University Press.

Browne, R. (2024, July 19). How a software update from cyber firm CrowdStrike caused one of the world's biggest IT blackouts. *CNBC*. Retrieved from https://www.cnbc.com/2024/07/19/what-is-crowdstrike-crwd-and-how-did-it-cause-global-it-outages.html

C2PA. (2022, January 26). Digital content provenance: possibilities & opportunities for the future of the Internet in the deepfake and disinformation era. Digital Content Provenance Event. Retrieved from https://c2pa.org/jan-2022_event

Camayd-Freixas, E. (2008, July 11). Interpreting after the largest I.C.E. raid in U.S. history: a personal account. *The New York Times*, p. 1. Retrieved from http://www.nytimes.com/2008/07/11/us/11immig.html. https://cdn1.nyt.com/images/2008/07/14/opinion/14ed-camayd.pdf

Camayd-Freixas, E. (2013). *U.S. Immigration Reform and Its Global Impact: Lessons from the Postville Raid*. Palgrave Macmillan.
Darden, L. (2002, September). Strategies for discovering mechanisms: schema instantiation, modular subassembly, forward/backward chaining. *Philosophy of Science, 69*(53), 5354–5365. Retrieved from https://doi.org/10.1086/341858
DeepSeek-AI. (2024, December 27). *DeepSeek-V3 Technical Report*. At https://web.archive.org/web/20250130173134/https://arxiv.org/html/2412.19437v1#S2
Dragan, A. (2024, September 3). AI safety…Ok doomer. *Google DeepMind: The Podcast*. At https://www.youtube.com/watch?v=ZXA2dmFxXmg&list=PLqYmG7hTraZBiUr6_Qf8YTS2Oqy3OGZEj&index=3.
Eisermann, D. (2020, April). *Cryptocurrencies as Threats to Public Security and Counter Terrorism: Risk Analysis and Regulatory Challenges*. Translated by H.-J. Schindler. *Berlin Risk*. Retrieved from https://www.counterextremism.com
European Commission. (2024, August 1). Press Release: AI Act enters into force. At https://commission.europa.eu/news/ai-act-enters-force-2024-08-01_en. Artificial Intelligence Act text: https://eur-lex.europa.eu/legal-content/EN/TXT/?qid=1623335154975&uri=CELEX%3A52021PC0206
Gladwell, M. (2008). *Outliers: The Story of Success*. Little, Brown & Co.
Glennan, S., & Allari, P. (Eds.) (2017). *The Routledge Handbook of Mechanisms and Mechanical Philosophy*. Routledge.
Guo, Y., Shang, G., Vazirgiannis, M., & Clavel, C. (2024, April 16). The curious decline of linguistic diversity: training language models on synthetic text. Annual Conference of the North American Chapter of the Association for Computational Linguistics (NAACL) (Findings paper). Retrieved from https://doi.org/10.48550/arXiv.2311.09807
Heikkilä, M. (2023, January 27). A watermark for chatbots can expose text written by an AI. *MIT Technology Review*. Retrieved from https://www.technologyreview.com/2023/01/27/1067338/a-watermark-for-chatbots-can-spot-text-written-by-an-ai
Heikkilä, M. (2024, March 29). It's easy to tamper with watermarks from AI-generated texts. *MIT Technology Review*. Retrieved from https://www.technologyreview.com/2024/03/29/1090310/its-easy-to-tamper-with-watermarks-from-ai-generated-text
Lee, K.-F. (2018). *AI Super-Powers: China, Silicone Valley, and the New World Order*. Houghton, Mifflin, Harcourt.

Levin, S. (2018, July 3). Is Facebook a publisher? In public it says no, but in court it says yes. *The Guardian*. Retrieved from https://www.theguardian.com/technology/2018/jul/02/facebook-mark-zuckerberg-platform-publisher-lawsuit

Lorenz, E. N. (1963). Deterministic nonperiodic flow. *Journal of the Atmospheric Sciences, 20*(2), 130–141. Retrieved from https://doi.org/10.1175/1520-0469(1963)020%3c0130:DNF%3e2.0.CO;2

Luhmann, N. (2012). *Introduction to Systems Theory*. Translated by P. Gilgen. Polity.

Luhmann, N. (2017). *Risk: A Sociological Theory*. Translated by R. Barrett. Routledge.

Luhmann, N. (2018). *Organization and Decision*. Translated by D. Baecker & R. Barrett. Cambridge University Press.

Mandelbrot, B. (1982). *The Fractal Geometry of Nature*. San Francisco: W.H. Freeman & Co. Retrieved from https://archive.org/details/fractalgeometryo00beno/page/n5/mode/2up

McNamee, R. (2020). *Zucked: Waking Up to the Facebook Catastrophe*. Penguin.

Meadows, D. H. (2008). *Thinking in Systems*. Chelsea Green Publishing.

Megerian, C. (2025, February 10). How the Trump Administration moved to shut down the Consumer Protection Agency's headquarters. *PBS News*. Retrieved from https://www.pbs.org/newshour/politics/how-the-trump-administration-moved-to-shut-down-the-consumer-protection-agencys-headquarters

Metz, C., & Tobin, M. (2025, January 27). How Chinese A.I. start-up DeepSeek is competing with Silicon Valley giants. *The New York Times*. Retrieved from https://www.nytimes.com/2025/01/23/technology/deepseek-china-ai-chips.html

Moreno de Ayala, O., & Tirkel, A. Z. (2010). *Digital Watermarking U.S. Patent 8934663*. Retrieved from https://patents.justia.com/patent/8934663; https://www.academia.edu/28079422/Digital_Watermarking_United_States_Patent_8934663

Moreno de Ayala, O., & Tirkel, A. Z. (2013). *Digital Communications WO 2013067589 Al*. Retrieved from https://www.academia.edu/28079748/DIGITAL_COMMUNICATIONS_WO_2013067589_Al_pdf?hb-g-sw=2471782

Nix, N., Oremus, W., & Gregg, A. (2025, January 7). Meta ends fact-checking, drawing praise from Trump. *The Washington Post*. Retrieved from https://www.washingtonpost.com/technology/2025/01/07/meta-factchecking-zuckerberg

Nousala, S., Metcalf, G., & Ing, D. (Eds.). (2024). *Industry 4.0 to Industry 5.0: Explorations in the Transition from a Techno-Economic to a Socio-Technical Future*. (Translational Systems Sciences, vol. 41). Springer Nature. https://doi.org/10.1007/978-981-99-9730-5

Nvidia. (2024, March 18). Press Release: NVIDIA Announces Earth Climate Digital Twin. *NVIDIA Newsroom*. Retrieved from https://nvidianews.nvidia.com/news/nvidia-announces-earth-climate-digital-twin

Orland, K. (2024, October 24). Google offers its AI watermarking tech as free open-source toolkit. *Ars Technica*. Retrieved from https://arstechnica.com/ai/2024/10/google-offers-its-ai-watermarking-tech-as-free-open-source-toolkit

Polanyi, M. (1966). *The Tacit Dimension*. Doubleday.

Romer, P. (2019, May 6). Opinion: A tax that could fix Big Tech. *The New York Times*. Retrieved from https://www.nytimes.com/2019/05/06/opinion/tax-facebook-google.html

Romer, P. (2021, May 17). *Taxing Digital Advertising*. At https://adtax.paulromer.net

Ryngaert, C., & Tailor, M. (2020). The GDPR as g*lobal* data protection regulation? *AJIL Unbound, 114*, 5–9. Retrieved from https://doi.org/10.1017/aju.2019.80

Schank, R. C. (2016). *Education Outrage*. Constructing Modern Knowledge Press.

Schank, R. C., & Cleary, C. (1995). *Engines for Education*. Lawrence Erlbaum Associates.

Seetharaman, D., & Barnum, M. (2024, August 4). There's a tool to catch students cheating with ChatGPT. OpenAI hasn't released it. *The Wall Street Journal*. Retrieved from https://www.wsj.com/tech/ai/openai-tool-chatgpt-cheating-writing-135b755a

The White House. (2023, October 30). Fact Sheet: President Biden issues executive order on safe, secure, and trustworthy artificial intelligence. Retrieved from https://www.whitehouse.gov/briefing-room/statements-releases/2023/10/30/fact-sheet-president-biden-issues-executive-order-on-safe-secure-and-trustworthy-artificial-intelligence

Thompson, D. W. (1992 [1917]). *On Growth and Form*. Cambridge University Press. Retrieved from https://www.gutenberg.org/files/55264/55264-h/55264-h.htm#p587

Turing, A. M. (1936). On computable numbers, with an application to the Entscheidungsproblem. *Journal of Mathematics, 58*(345–363), 230–265. Retrieved from https://www.cs.virginia.edu/~robins/Turing_Paper_1936.pdf

Turing, A. M. (1952). The chemical basis of morphogenesis. *Philosophical Transactions of the Royal Society of London, 237*(641), 37–72. Retrieved from https://royalsocietypublishing.org/doi/10.1098/rstb.1952.0012
Wadhwa, V., & Salkever, A. (2018). *Your Happiness Was Hacked: Why Tech Is Winning the Battle to Control Your Brain, and How to Fight Back*. Berrett-Koehler Publishers.
Wallerstein, I. (2007). *World-Systems Analysis: An Introduction.* Duke University Press.
Webb, A. (2019). *The Big Nine: How the Tech Titans & Their Thinking Machines Could Warp Humanity*. Hachette.
Zuboff, S. (2019). *The Age of Surveillance Capitalism: The Fight for a Human Future at the New Frontier of Power*. Hachette.

Index

E. Camayd-Freixas, *Metagrammar*, https://doi.org/10.1007/978-3-031-92337-1

F

G

The manufacturer's authorised representative in the EU is Springer
Nature Customer Service Centre GmbH, Europaplatz 3, 69115 Heidelberg,
Germany. If you have any concerns regarding our products, please
contact ProductSafety@springernature.com

Printed and bound by CPI Group (UK) Ltd, Croydon, CR0 4YY
30/09/2026
02225583-0014